The Early Heidegger's Philosophy of Life

John D. Caputo, *series editor*

PERSPECTIVES IN
CONTINENTAL
PHILOSOPHY

SCOTT M. CAMPBELL

The Early Heidegger's
Philosophy of Life
Facticity, Being, and Language

FORDHAM UNIVERSITY PRESS
New York ∎ 2012

Fordham University Press has no responsibility for the persistence or accuracy of URLs for external or third-party Internet websites referred to in this publication and does not guarantee that any content on such websites is, or will remain, accurate or appropriate.

Fordham University Press also publishes its books in a variety of electronic formats. Some content that appears in print may not be available in electronic books.

Library of Congress Cataloging-in-Publication Data

Campbell, Scott M.
    The early Heidegger's philosophy of life : facticity, being, and language /
Scott M. Campbell.
        p. cm. — (Perspectives in Continental philosophy)
    Includes bibliographical references (p.) and index.
    ISBN 978-0-8232-4219-1 (cloth : alk. paper) — ISBN 978-0-8232-4220-7
(pbk. : alk. paper)
    1. Heidegger, Martin, 1889–1976. 2. Life. I. Title.
                                                        B3279.H49C265 2012
193—dc23
2012002894

Printed in the United States of America

14 13 12   5 4 3 2 1

First edition

Contents

Abbreviations

Note: *G* refers to Martin Heidegger, *Gesamtausgabe* (Frankfurt am Main: Klostermann, 1976–). The number following is the volume number. In the parenthetic references in the text the number after the colon is the page number, and the number after the slash is the page number of the English translation. Full information for each title is in the bibliography.

BT	*Being and Time*. Originally published as *Sein und Zeit*.
G 9	*Wegmarken*. Translated as *Pathmarks*.
G 17	*Einführung in die phänomenologische Forschung*. Translated as *Introduction to Phenomenological Research*.
G 18	*Grundbegriffe der aristotelischen Philosophie*. Translated as *Basic Concepts of Aristotelian Philosophy*.
G 19	*Platon: Sophistes*. Translated as *Plato's Sophist*.
G 20	*Prolegomena zur Geschichte des Zeitbegriffs*. Translated as *History of the Concept of Time*.
G 21	*Logik: Die Frage nach der Wahrheit*. Translated as *Logic: The Question of Truth*.
G 56/57	*Zur Bestimmung der Philosophie*. Translated as *Towards the Definition of Philosophy*.
G 58	*Grundprobleme der Phänomenologie*.
G 59	*Phänomenologie der Anschauung und des Ausdrucks: Theorie der philosophischen Begriffsbildung*. Translated as *Phenomenology of*

Preface

The impetus for this book came from a set of observations that Dr. William Richardson, S.J., once made in a public forum. He said, and I paraphrase: What about the facticity of the situation?—the immediacy of life?—this is what Heidegger was trying to work out early on—especially in his analysis of Christianity—where life and death are right on your doorstep—this is the immediacy of factical life. This was gutsy stuff, and I was hooked. Not knowing anything about facticity, I decided to find out what, exactly, the factical immediacy of life meant for the young Martin Heidegger.

By that time, I already knew from P. Christopher Smith that Heidegger had delivered a lecture course on Aristotle's *Rhetoric* in the summer of 1924. I was now intrigued by the problem of facticity, and knowing that the course on rhetoric came from around the same period as the courses on facticity, I decided to pursue the possibility of developing a sense of authentic living and speaking from Heidegger's thinking. What I found was that factical life and factical language were critical concepts for the early Heidegger that figured prominently in his development of the Being-question. In the light of these relationships, the thesis of this book came to focus on how Heidegger's understanding of Being is germane to the life that human beings live and to the language that they speak.

The primary thesis that I advance in this book is that the early Heidegger makes the experience of Being relevant to human life. He does so by connecting his understanding of Being to the experience of history, religion, and language. My argument is allied with those who claim that Heidegger's philosophy is pertinent to human life. But I also present an approach different from that of my allies. In this preface, I briefly detail the argument of the book, its connections to other readers of the early Heidegger, and the advances I try to make both through and beyond those interpretations.

The methodology of the book is both chronological and thematic. I provide close readings of Heidegger's lecture courses spanning the years 1919–25, as well as manuscripts and letters he wrote from that time. Through these analyses I develop six main ideas related to current debates about the early Heidegger. These divide into points of scholarship (S1–S2) and points of philosophy (P1–P4).

S1. One of the main ideas I develop in the book, as my first point of scholarship, is that the early Heidegger was very much concerned with the question of Being. It may seem a moot point to argue that Heidegger was interested in this question, considering how much has been said both by and about Heidegger concerning the meaning of Being. Recently, however, some readers of Heidegger have maintained that not only was the question of Being not the main concern of the early Heidegger but that even in his later work, Heidegger was interested in something more than and different from Being itself. Through close readings of the early lecture courses, I show that Heidegger was attempting to bring together the question of Being with questions about human life.

S2. Through this analysis of the relationship in the early Heidegger between Being and life, I am able to make my second point of scholarship, which is that these issues crystallize in the concept of Dasein. It is remarkable that the primary subject matter of Heidegger's magnum opus, *Being and Time,* is neither Being nor time, but Dasein, which develops out of his early interpretations of factical life. In some ways, this book could be thought of as a biography of Dasein, a phrase I considered, along with some variations, as a title for this book. My focus, however, is more on the notion of life, which enables me to show how Heidegger's interest in ontology, especially in Greek thought (Plato and Aristotle), merges with his interest in life and history in the notion of Dasein. Indeed, Dasein is where life and Being come together.

More important, I think, than these issues of scholarship are the main philosophical ideas that I develop in this book.

P1. The first concerns Heidegger's understanding of what it means to be human. Interestingly, Heidegger accepts Aristotle's definition of the human being as a rational animal or ζῷον λόγον ἔχον. What Heidegger does, however, is provide a factical analysis of this definition by looking at it from within the historical context of Greek life. He concludes that for the Greeks, λόγος did not mean "rational"; it meant "speaking." Further, ζῷον did not mean "animal"; it meant "life." Thus, using Aristotle's definition, Heidegger asserts that the human being is a living, speaking being in the world with others.

P2. In my analyses, I show the development of this idea of human life up through Heidegger's reading of Aristotle and Plato in 1923–25, and I draw the conclusion that for Heidegger human life cannot be understood without recognizing the connection human beings have to various contexts of meaningful relationships. Thus, the second main philosophical idea that I develop in this book is that these contexts of meaningful relationships are essential to understanding Heidegger's analyses of factical life in the early lecture courses.

P3. In showing the importance of these contexts, I am able to clarify some of the confusion surrounding Heidegger's understanding of the world. When readers of Heidegger write about what he means by world, they do one of two things. Some claim that, for Heidegger, the world is deceptive, fallen, and inauthentic, a source of shallow conformity. Others say that for Heidegger the world is a rich texture of experience, and, especially with respect to the early Heidegger, they say that he was able to deconstruct the metaphysical theories of science, especially in Aristotle, Plato, and medieval scholasticism, back down into the primordial sphere of factical lived experience. I trace this confusion back to Heidegger's own descriptions of the ambiguity of factical life in the early lecture courses.

P4. Heidegger's reading of the ambiguity of factical life, as both a source of deception and a source of vitality, has led to the conclusion by some readers of Heidegger that he is presenting a dichotomy: either nonconformist or conformist, clear-sighted or muddled, resolute or indecisive, in short, authentic or inauthentic. According to this reading, Heidegger is saying that one's inauthentic life must be destroyed or deconstructed so that one might then live a life of clear-sighted resolve and determination.

I argue against this view to show that authentic life cannot be permanent. It is not a condition that one maintains. In reading these early lecture courses, I follow Heidegger's own lead when he says that Dasein is simultaneously both in the truth and in untruth. Accordingly, Heidegger's ambivalence about factical life and living in the world is, rather, a way of describing the ambiguity of the human condition. By showing the dark side of human life, Heidegger presents a realistic description of life, one that is prone to mistakes, and even perversity, but which is nonetheless open to meaning. Heidegger's notion of authenticity is not exemplary, nor is it an ideal. Rather, as William Richardson has astutely suggested, authenticity helps us see those elements of light and darkness in human life "like the shadows in a Rembrandt painting."

In each of the chapters of this book, I demonstrate how Heidegger was trying to draw out the positive elements of lived experience against the background of the various deceptions and distortions that are, nonetheless, built into factical experience. In Chapter 1, on science, I show how he wanted to overcome the predominance of theory through a return to lived experience. Chapter 2 is on religion, and it demonstrates Heidegger's interest in the temporal immediacy of the faith of the early Christians. Chapters 3 and 4 present the various masks and deceptions we encounter and try to overcome in human life as well as the temporal structure of life that can be retrieved from those distortions. Chapter 5 shows the breadth of Heidegger's analyses in his attempt to bring the entire histories of philosophy and theology back down to factical life. Chapter 6 shows his attempt to resuscitate the value of average, everyday experience in his development of the hermeneutics of facticity. Chapters 7–9 focus on language, but in each chapter we see Heidegger's interest in the facticity of speaking. Chapter 7 focuses on Heidegger's discussion of how the deceptions of language that emerge through a deconstruction of the proposition open up the richness of the world. Chapter 8, on Aristotle's analyses of rhetoric, presents the conceptuality of Aristotle's world and thus the various ways in which everyday speaking with others informs the development of philosophical concepts. Chapter 9 concludes the analysis of language with an explanation of the way that words and language open up the meaningfulness of the world.

All of these analyses enable me to draw conclusions about what Heidegger means by worlding. I believe that on one reading of destruction or deconstruction in Heidegger, the world is purely fallen. On that reading deconstruction is a retrieval of the authentic historical, philosophical, and theological sources of our ideas. But on this reading, there is no meaningful present into which one can legitimately bring these retrieved ideas. In other words, if we are faced with the dichotomy of an inauthentic present and an authentic past, then there is no sense to be made of Dasein as a worlding being. On such a reading, the world we live in currently does not have enough substance or meaningfulness, even with the retrieval of a more authentic past, to provide any positive sense of living in a world. Such a reading accepts Ricoeur's criticism of Heidegger as a purely vertical thinker, who saw value only in the past. My view of worlding presents Heidegger's horizontal thinking, concerned as it was with those meaningful contexts within which we live. On my reading, the world and human life are filled with prephilosophical meanings. Deconstruction or destruction is thus a fulfillment of that meaning and not a replacement of it. On my reading, the later Heidegger's attempts to deal with art, technology, and poetry as modes of worlding do not contradict his earlier understanding of factical life and the world, as some have claimed. Moreover, my analysis provides a background to the later Heidegger's interest in language, which seemed to come from nowhere, but which I show has a rich and provocative history in the early work.

There are currently three book-length analyses of the early Heidegger: *The Genesis of Heidegger's Being and Time* by Theodore Kisiel, *The Young Heidegger: Rumor of the Hidden King* by John van Buren, and *Heidegger's Religious Origins: Destruction and Authenticity* by Benjamin Crowe. Kisiel's book is chronological; van Buren's book presents a thematic approach, but it is, nonetheless, a historical overview. Both are outstanding resources for readers of the early Heidegger, but neither takes the focus on living and speaking that I take in this book. Both van Buren and Crowe place special emphasis on the influence of Luther on Heidegger. Crowe, in particular, focuses on destruction as necessary to Heidegger's development of the ideal of authenticity. My focus is not on religion, as Crowe's is. Moreover, I look at both religion and Heidegger's interest in the Greeks in my analysis of factical life.

for Marianne

Acknowledgments

Some of the work presented in this book has already appeared in academic journals. For material that is presented in Chapters 3, 4, 7, and 9, the author acknowledges its original publication in *Philosophy Today*, *Existentia*, and *Heidegger Studies*. The author thanks the editors of these journals for their permission to publish this work, as well as Duncker & Humblot GmbH, the publishing house for *Heidegger Studies*.

I am grateful to John Caputo, the series editor for Perspectives in Continental Philosophy at Fordham University Press, for publishing this book.

A project like this one requires assistance from many quarters. I give special thanks to my mother, Jeanne Campbell. For her love and support, I am profoundly grateful. I also thank my brother, Keith Campbell. In many ways, I owe my start in philosophy to him. During the process of writing this book, my brother's support, most notably his singular sense of humor, was a consistent and reliable source of inspiration for me. Allow me also to acknowledge my extended family: Karina Barany, Pat Campbell, Bill Randolph, Kate Randolph, Betsy Randolph, Katie Campbell, Charles Omell, Annie Dontzin, Mary Grossman, Paul Grossman, Nancy Dontzin, Jürgen Fleckenstein, Jochen Fleckenstein, Janin Fleckenstein, Evelyn Hörster, Thomas Hörster, Linda de Las Cuevas, Monica Lin, Tommy Lin, Cheli de Las Cuevas, and Karin Vogt. The people in my family are always there when I need them, and I am truly thankful for that.

I am lucky to have many good friends who have come to me from the world of philosophy. I thank Paul Bruno, Ann Bruno, Ed McGushin,

Serena Parekh, Max Latona, Roseanne Latona, Steve Findley, Pascale Perroudin, Richard Lynch, Jim Boettcher, Linda Riviere, Gary Gurtler, Marc Lucht, and Mark Goodman. Much of my understanding of what philosophy is and of what friendship is has come about through experiences I have had with these friends. I have had excellent teachers in my life. In particular, I acknowledge my gratitude to Richard Kearney, Jim Bernauer, Richard Cobb-Stevens, and Jacques Taminiaux.

Others whom I want to acknowledge here, although not philosophers as such, are all good friends who keep me honest, and if you are not honest, you cannot study philosophy: Mark McCloud, Andrea Allen, Horst Schreiber, Kevin Tringale, Brenda Pizzo, Andy Evans, Melissa Ludwig, Nathan Franus, Sara Cannon, Colleen McCallum, Kelly O'Leary, Loren DeVries, Joel Benzing, Veronica Benzing, Bob Holste, Suzanne Guiod, Theo Schnaufer, Ellis Cose, Jack Horner, Hal Shoup, Mayanne Shoup, and Andy Fenenbock. I am very grateful for their friendship.

I had a thorough grounding in the German language before I went to live in Germany, and for that I thank my professors at the Middlebury College Summer Language Program, especially Herr Christopher Wickham. My facility with speaking German improved dramatically during the year that I spent at the Ökumenisches Wohnheim in Heidelberg. For not only helping me learn German but also, and more important, for their friendship, I thank all the Öki's, especially Dorothea Münch, Susanne Rüge, Thomas Kiauka, Joachim Schauß, Marlinang Butar-Butar, Fernando Enns, and Renate Enns.

For the research fellowship that enabled me to live and study in Heidelberg while conducting research at the Marcuse Archive in Frankfurt, I express my gratitude to the German Academic Exchange Service (the DAAD, Deutscher Akademischer Austausch Dienst). I also thank the College of Arts and Sciences at Nazareth College and its dean, Dr. Deborah Dooley, for a subvention grant that generously supplied some of the permission costs for the artistic image on the book cover.

I am profoundly grateful to my colleagues in the philosophy department at Nazareth College. Indeed, they are not just colleagues; they are also friends. From them I have learned about the real value of "learning for the sake of knowledge, itself." John Edelman, Patricia Bowen-Moore, and Heidi Northwood, I thank you for showing me the true meaning of a liberal arts education. I also owe a debt of gratitude to other friends and colleagues whom I have come to know from teaching at Nazareth. In particular, I acknowledge Joe Pestino, Tom Lappas, Becky Pietropaoli, Joe Kelly, Pat Kelly, Jerry Denno, Beverly Brown, Nevan Fisher, Tim Thibodeau, Susan Thibodeau, Monica Weis, Sharon Murphy, Adrielle Mitchell, Olena

Prokopovych, Dave Tang, Ed Wiltse, Lisa Perks, Josh Perks, Ginny Skinner-Linenberg, Kathy Edelman, Johnny Bowen-Moore, Greg Foran, Trish Foran, Sara Varhus, David Hill, Deb Dooley, Paul Mittermeyer, George Eisen, Cynthia Eisen, Georgette Viteri, Pam Griffin, and Sandy Posato. I also thank my students at Nazareth College. Talking to them about philosophy is a great source of inspiration for me; I often stand in awe of their commitment to learning.

Two philosophical institutions have contributed significantly to my understanding both of Heidegger and of philosophy. I first attended the Collegium Phaenomenologicum in 1997, and I have returned twice. It is an excellent organization, as is the North American Heidegger Circle, which I try to attend every year. To the colleagues I have come to know from these institutions, I thank you for contributing so significantly to my understanding of this profound thinker. Some of you probably do not know what a lasting impression you have had on my philosophical formation. I especially acknowledge Ted Kisiel, Larry Hatab, Andrew Mitchell, Anne O'Byrne, Francois Raffoul, Jim Winchester, Graeme Nicholson, Benjamin Crowe, David Ciavatta, Kym Maclaren, Leslie MacAvoy, Bret Davis, Babette Babich, Walter Brogan, Brian Schroeder, Silvia Benso, Bernie Freydberg, David Pettigrew, John Rose, Dennis Schmidt, John Sallis, Charles Scott, Susan Schoenbohm, Richard Polt, Eric Nelson, and Richard Capobianco.

I owe a profound debt of gratitude to the reviewers of this manuscript. The reviewers provided critical insights and thoughtful suggestions, and I am truly grateful for their efforts. This is a much better book because of their knowledge and criticism.

My thanks go out, as well, to the editorial director at Fordham University Press, Helen Tartar, and her highly capable assistant editors, Josh Jones and Tom Lay. I am grateful, as well, to Eric Newman, the managing editor, and for close and careful editing work, I am grateful to Teresa Jesionowski.

I have dedicated this book to my wife, Marianne. For offering love, patience, kindness, and understanding, especially when I stayed at work instead of coming home at a reasonable hour, I am grateful in ways that I may never be able to show.

Finally, I thank two professors, without whom this book would not have been possible. P. Christopher Smith was everything a person could want in a critical reader of my work: thorough, challenging, and encouraging. He is a knowledgeable and excellent teacher from whom I have learned a great deal, and he has been a critical part of this effort from the beginning. In our many discussions he has always given me sound, honest criticism. I am very grateful for all of his help.

I am particularly grateful to Professor Smith for advising me to live and study in Heidelberg. He facilitated my research there by telling me where to find some of Heidegger's unpublished lecture courses. Also, the whole experience made it possible for me to meet, during office hours, with Professor Hans-Georg Gadamer, who deepened considerably my understanding of the living, factical presence of his teacher Martin Heidegger.

In the last place, I thank Father William Richardson, S.J. My understanding of Heidegger came about from being a student in his classes at Boston College. Working on this project, I met with Father Richardson often to talk to him about what I was doing. Throughout, he made available to me his vast knowledge of Heidegger, and he provided critical insights into my own developing understanding. At the same time, though, he allowed me the freedom to do my own research. He has been at all times an ideal teacher and adviser.

Dann herrscht heute, wie wir
hören, ein großer Streit unter den
Philosophen, ob die Philosophie
"Lebensphilosophie" sein soll. Von
der einen Seite wird behauptet, die
Philosophie kann nicht Lebensphilosophie sein, von der anderen, sie
muß es ja doch sein. "Lebensphilosophie" ist wie "Botanik der
Pflanzen"! Die emphatische
Behauptung, die Botanik habe es
mit Pflanzen zu tun, ist genauso
komisch und unsinnig wie das
Gegenteil.

What prevails today, then, as we
hear, is a great quarrel among the
philosophers, whether philosophy
should be "philosophy of life."
On one side, it is asserted that
philosophy cannot be life-
philosophy, and on the other side,
that it most certainly must be.
"Philosophy of life" is like "botany
of plants"! The emphatic assertion,
botany has to do with plants, is just
as strange and nonsensical as
the opposite.

—**Martin Heidegger,**
Basic Concepts of Aristotelian Philosophy

Introduction

> Rather, we need to see that experiencing in the fullest sense of its authentically factical context of enactment is to be seen in the historically existing self. And this self is in one way or another the ultimate question of philosophy.
>
> **—Martin Heidegger, *Pathways***

From the beginning of his philosophical career until the end, Martin Heidegger followed one path. He was interested in the question of Being. Much has been said about the path Heidegger traveled. Being, for Heidegger, is the original event or process that lets all beings be. It is that original source that, though not itself a being or thing, enables everything that is to be what it is. Heidegger's lifelong endeavor was to continue to probe this original source, the Being of beings. In the pages that follow, I engage Heidegger's question about Being once again by looking at two major concepts from the philosopher's early work, life and language. I believe that these concepts were critical to Heidegger's development and understanding of the Being-question. Accordingly, this book is an attempt to demonstrate that the early Heidegger's analyses of life and language played a pivotal role in his first attempts to work out the question of Being. It is furthermore an attempt to explain how these analyses subsequently open life and language to the meaning of Being. The basic argument that I present here is that the early Heidegger made the experience of Being pertinent to the life that human beings live and the language that they speak. In very general terms, then, this book is an explication of how the early Heidegger understood life and language, an investigation of how life and language figured into the Being-question, and an interpretation of what it means to live and to speak with, in, and through an experience of Being's relevance to and bearing on human existence.

For Heidegger, life and language were philosophically relevant only insofar as they were experienced. When philosophy is construed as theoretical detachment from experience—a looking on at how people live and speak from some exterior point—then it is no longer connected to life. It has removed itself from the very experience of life with which it is trying to come to terms. In contrast to philosophy's tendency toward theoretical detachment, Heidegger wanted to develop a kind of philosophizing that would try to understand life and language from the experience of being an active participant in life and language. This means that philosophical activity investigates the experience of life as it is lived and the experience of language as it is spoken. To catch life in the act of being lived and language in the act of being spoken was Heidegger's project from early on. Throughout this book, I show what consequences follow from Heidegger's demand that living and speaking become thematic for philosophical inquiry.

To distinguish the kind of philosophical activity that attends to the experiences of living and speaking from the kind that observes life and language from a theoretical distance, Heidegger employs the term "facticity." The facticity of life and language indicates those dimensions of human experience by which human beings are able to understand themselves as living and speaking beings: not looking on at life but participating in it, and so living; not looking on at language but participating in it, and so speaking. Living and speaking are for the early Heidegger the "stuff" of philosophy. My topic, accordingly, is the facticity of life and language.

In choosing the concept of facticity and its relations to life and language, I take account of Heidegger's initial experience of the Being-question as it presents itself to him at the very beginning of his way. Factical life and factical language were problems that Heidegger developed only in the beginning of his career. As such, I restrict my analysis to the years that extend from 1919, when the young philosopher first uses the term "factical life" in a lecture course, to the publication of *Being and Time* in 1927. During the eight years of this period, Heidegger goes from being Edmund Husserl's assistant and *Privatdozent* at the University of Freiburg (1919–23) to becoming professor *Extraordinarius* at the University of Marburg (1923–27). I look almost exclusively at lecture courses, where facticity was, from the start, a pivotal concept through which Heidegger first engaged the complex, yet intriguing, connections among living, speaking, and Being.

In making my argument, I am deviating from what some commentators on Heidegger's work have alleged, namely, that the question of Being was not the primary topic for the early Heidegger and, for that matter, that Being was never Heidegger's primary topic. In Benjamin Crowe's outstanding analysis of the concept of destruction in the early Heidegger, he makes it clear from the beginning of his book that he will not be discussing Being much at all.[1] For him and others, Being is not *die Sache selbst* for Martin

Heidegger. Crowe points out that according to John van Buren, since Heidegger eventually ceased using the term "Being," we ought to stop claiming that it was his primary interest. Theodore Kisiel asserts that from early on, Heidegger's focus was not so much on Being, but rather on that context of meaningful relations, the world and its dynamic activity, that makes things significant.[2] Perhaps most vehemently, Thomas Sheehan claims that the topic of Being has become so confused in the secondary literature on Heidegger, especially Big "B" Being, that the word itself ought to be abandoned.[3] For Sheehan, Being is often written about in such a way that it is taken to be a hypostatized thing, a metaphysical entity, which is precisely the opposite of what Heidegger was trying to say. Sheehan suggests that we relegate the term "Being" to metaphysics, asserting that *die Sache selbst* for Heidegger was human finitude, which opens up the world.[4]

But Heidegger insists on the difference between Being (*Sein*) and being (*Seiendes*). Even if this, the ontological difference, is not *die Sache selbst* for Heidegger, it is nonetheless essential for understanding his approach to philosophy as well as his critique of the history of ontology. This is the reason why I continue to capitalize the "B" in Being throughout this book, to emphasize that there is, for Heidegger, an ontological difference between the two; this difference becomes confused when the capitalization is lacking, as a difference between "being" and "being." This is particularly important when looking at the early Heidegger, where he will sometimes refer to *ein Sein* (see, for example, *Toward the Definition of Philosophy*, G 56/57:45/36, 46/37, 54/43). When *Sein* is translated with a lowercase "b" as in "being," it is impossible to know whether "a being" refers to *ein Sein* or *ein Seiendes*. Sheehan is correct when he says that that there is confusion about what Being means for Heidegger and that the term often takes on a metaphysical nuance that Heidegger did not intend. But perhaps this is an opportunity to grasp Heidegger's own philosophical experience in looking at the history of philosophy and recognizing similar, if not even deeper, confusions about the meaning of Being, confusions that had become embedded within philosophical inquiry over thousands of years. In *Being and Time*, instead of abandoning the term, Heidegger sought to restore its original meaning. Indeed, there is a fidelity to Heidegger's own approach to philosophy in attempting to rethink terms and concepts in their originality, instead of simply abandoning them.

After years of rigorous analysis into the question of the meaning of Being, Heidegger does eventually abandon the term "Being," as John van Buren points out, but I do not see how this is a reason for commentators on the early Heidegger to limit its use, as Crowe seems to be suggesting.

Moreover, Heidegger's abandonment of the term is motivated by an attempt to probe the meaning of Being even further, to discern that original event that gives both time and Being. In this sense, instead of saying that he abandoned the term, it might be more correct to say that he attempts to ground Being in something more primordial. Even if we were to say that Being is not *die Sache selbst* for Heidegger, it would be impossible to explore Heidegger's primary topic—whatever that may be—without it. Heidegger understood the exploration of Being as an essential experience through which to grasp what was for him *die Sache selbst*.

It is Kisiel who shows most clearly the way in which existential concerns from Heidegger's early period transform into ontological concerns in *Being and Time*, even if both of these concerns were operative for him all along. What I find most compelling about Heidegger in these early lecture courses and manuscripts is the reciprocity between Being and life. Sheehan alludes to this when he writes, "The most extraordinary thing about all of Heidegger's thought, both early and late, is his unwavering insistence that *human being* is that 'open' and thus *is* 'the thing itself.' From the beginning to the end of his career, he never got beyond that point."[5] Sheehan is suggesting here that the focus on Being can drain the sense of humanity from Heidegger's philosophical experience. I think this is correct. Nonetheless, Sheehan's focus on the human being and its finitude could mark something of a paradigm shift *back* to the way Heidegger was initially understood (or, as Richardson and many others have claimed, misunderstood), namely, as an existentialist. It was Heidegger's genius to bring together life with Being, existential concerns with ontology, openness with that which opens. In the early period, before *Being and Time*, it is facticity that names that reciprocity between Being and life.

One of the remarkable things about *Being and Time* is that the primary topic of that text is not Being; nor is it time. The topic, rather, is Dasein, a term that is often confusedly identified with the human being. According to Heidegger, Dasein is the human being *insofar as it is concerned about its own Being*. This is not the same as saying that Dasein is identical with the human being. Indeed, Heidegger is explicit that Dasein is not the human being. In *Being and Time*, he analyzes Dasein as preparation for grasping the meaning both of Being and of time as the horizon for the interpretation of Being. *Being and Time* tells us a great deal about who Dasein is, but there is more to the story of Dasein than what we find in *Being and Time*. I show in this book how Heidegger's analyses of facticity and factical life develop into his notion of Dasein. Within Dasein, Heidegger's existential concerns about the meaning of life and human existence come together with his ontological project, which, in many respects, is an exploration of the ontological origin of life. Factical life, one might say, is the *there* or openness of Being in a world. In making this analysis of factical life, therefore, I am trying to provide a biography of Dasein, drawn from the early lecture courses.

It is well known that when Heidegger began his university studies in Freiburg in 1911, neo-Kantianism dominated the German universities. It comes as no surprise, then, that facticity is a term that Heidegger adopts from the neo-Kantians, perhaps from Heinrich Rickert, who was a neo-Kantian philosopher of values in Freiburg during this time and whom Heidegger admired very much.[6] Whether this is where Heidegger first encountered facticity, it was a term from the neo-Kantian tradition: In the framework of neo-Kantian epistemology, facticity had a temporal-historical sense that was set against supratemporal logicity (*Logizität*). As such, it meant temporal, individual, concrete, unique, nonrepeatable. Surprisingly, Joachim Ritter's *Historisches Wörterbuch der Philosophie* (Darmstadt, 1972), 2:886, omits the word's prehistory by starting its entry on *Faktizität* with Heidegger.[7] For that matter, the word also has a pre-neo-Kantian meaning. According to W. T. Krug's *Allgemeines Handwörterbuch der philosophischen Wissenschaften*, the word *Faktum*, in contrast to *Tatsache*, had a historical meaning and not a strictly philosophical one. *Faktum* meant not givenness, *Gegebenheit*, but occurrence or event, *Begebenheit* or *Ereignis*. Not only is this provocative for Heidegger studies, it also suggests that the neo-Kantians' adaptation of the term suppressed some of its original meanings. Heidegger took it to indicate the historical particular, not in contrast to (and thus dependent on) the ahistorical, as in neo-Kantian epistemology—whereby facticity becomes the individual, historical moment of transcendental or logical determination—but, in its own right, as the full historical situation of the concrete individual *self*. In a text dating to 1919 or 1920, titled *Karl Jaspers's Psychology of Worldviews*, around the time when he first adopts the term, Heidegger makes some brief references to facticity. In stated contrast to Husserl's project in the *Logical Investigations* of partitioning off particular domains of theoretical experience (aesthetic, ethical, religious) Heidegger writes,

> Rather, we need to see that experiencing in its fullest sense is to be found in its authentically factical context of enactment in the historically existing self. And this self is in one way or another the ultimate question of philosophy. . . . *That our factical, historically enacted life is at work right within "how" we factically approach the problem of "how"*

*the self, in being anxiously concerned about itself, appropriates itself—
this is something that belongs originally to the very sense of the factical
"I am."* (G 9:35/30–31)

From the beginning, then, facticity indicates the full historical experience
of the self and "how" the self, in an "anxiously concerned" manner, appropriates its own history—even as its own history effects that appropriation.
This meaning of facticity, as the self's participation in its own historically
constituted existence, will continue, in one way or another, from 1919 to
Being and Time.

It is important to see here that the self's factical appropriation of its own
history is closely related to both factical life and factical language. If facticity is the self's experience of its own historical constitution, then factical
life and factical language indicate the different ways in which the historically constituted self lives and speaks. In taking account of life's facticity,
Heidegger shows how history influences human existence. Looking at life
and language, one can see that there are historical meanings and motivations operative in human existence that are constitutive of how we live and
speak. By recognizing their own facticity, human beings open themselves
to these historical motivations.

Of critical importance here is Heidegger's contention that at the same
time that these historical meanings play a constituting or motivating role
in how we live and speak, they can become hidden. With the passing of
time, life's original, historical motivations can get covered over. Indeed, the
very fact that life is temporal and historical can get covered over, or better
put, forgotten. Life construes itself in theoretical, objective terms and destroys (by covering over or forgetting) its own historicality. This concealment
of life's historicality is what Heidegger will call "ruinance" and, later, "fallenness." Originally developed through Aristotle's maxim that "vice is easy,
virtue is difficult," the terms "ruinance" and "fallenness" refer to the ways in
which life is inclined to forget itself and avoid itself by covering up its own
historical structure. They describe the ways in which human beings avoid
their own temporal-historical constitution: an avoidance of the fact that
they are historical and, therefore, an avoidance of how historical meanings
are operative in their lives.

In a sense, Heidegger's project in the early lecture courses can be described as an attempt first to take account of life's temporal-historical constitution and, with that, an endeavor to recover or retrieve temporal-
historical motivations. Facticity allows for the retrieval of the various ways
in which history affects human existence. The concept of retrieval will
come up again and again throughout this book. In every case, it refers to

the recovery of various temporal-historical dimensions of life and language that, through time, have been covered over or forgotten.

If facticity is what allows Heidegger to engage in the work of temporal-historical retrieval, as is my claim, then it is also an important element in his initial pursuit of the Being-question. This is because, inasmuch as facticity is a retrieval of history, it is also a retrieval of that within life's history which is the origin of its temporal-historical structure. That origin, as Heidegger comes to see, is Being. Facticity, then, is what allows the self to retrieve its own temporality and history as it retrieves its own Being. This is another way of saying that the self can appropriate its own historical existence.

An important aspect of grasping temporality, history, and Being through ruinant fallenness is what Heidegger variously calls distress, disquiet, urgency, and anxiety. Taken as a whole, these structures describe Heidegger's varied attempts to determine how temporality can be retrieved from objectivity. They indicate life's vigilance, born of temporality, in pursuit of Being; they work against the different modes of fallenness and the tendency of these modes to objectify life and life's historicality. As such, they are part of the process of historical retrieval, which Heidegger engages in again and again in the early lecture courses as he works through different thinkers such as Paul, Plato, and Aristotle, different disciplines such as science, philosophy, theology, and rhetoric, and different concepts, such as faith, dialectic, and λόγος. In all of these instances of retrieval, facticity names the full historical situation (along with its constituent distress) of whatever thinker, discipline, or concept is under review. Because human beings are factical, Heidegger claims that these historical situations can be retrieved.

What this means in the concrete is that Heidegger is interested in retrieving the conceptuality of concepts, that is, the *conceptuality* of Pauline faith, of Platonic dialectic, and of Aristotelian λόγος. This conceptuality names the factical situation of a thinker as the origin of his or her concepts. Facticity, factical life, and factical language are indications of the original historical experiences of these thinkers that informed the concepts they developed. This is not some crude form of subjectivism that says that the whole of Aristotle's philosophy, for example, can be explained by what happened in his life. Rather, it is a retrieval of the original (factical-historical) situation of a thinker in his world. World becomes thematic in this regard and the defining feature of life's facticity.

Indeed, in 1923 in a lecture course titled *Ontology: The Hermeneutics of Facticity*, factical life becomes Dasein as Being in a world. For Heidegger's students, if "Dasein" was a relatively new term making its way into their teacher's philosophical vocabulary, "world" certainly was not. At least as early as 1919, Heidegger had been discussing the relationship between factical life and the world, construed at first in terms of the different life-worlds (the self-, with-, and surrounding-worlds). In this course, though, factical life is identified with the Being in a world of Dasein. Moreover, inasmuch as factical life has become Dasein, the question of Being has become integral to the problem of historical retrieval. Prior to 1923, Heidegger spoke of factical life in terms of having an origin, which I interpret as a clear indication that Heidegger was, as early as 1919, moving toward the meaning of Being, construed initially as the origin of the factical life-world. I argue, then, that Dasein is the name for factical life insofar as it is construed as emerging from an origin: Factical life (*Da*) emerges from an origin (*Sein*).

If, then, factical life becomes Dasein as Being in a world in 1923, then facticity is clearly linked to Heidegger's working out of the Being-question in *Being and Time*. Moreover, insofar as facticity indicates the historical situation of a thinker, then the transformation of factical life into Dasein as Being in a world clearly has a historical dimension to it. Facticity enables Heidegger to retrieve history in such a way that Being is concomitantly being retrieved. This becomes clear once Heidegger travels to Marburg and interprets the Greeks in terms of Dasein. It is perhaps peculiar that Heidegger would use the term Dasein in relation to Plato and Aristotle. Insofar as factical life is Dasein's earlier self, however, then this is not so peculiar. Dasein indicates the historical retrieval of the conceptuality (the Being in a world) of Plato's and Aristotle's concepts. This is more fully developed in Heidegger's work on Aristotle than in his work on Plato. In both cases, though, he is interested in how Being in the world determines their concepts: for Plato, the Being-in-the-world of dialectic, and hence of λόγος, and for Aristotle, the Being-in-the-world of rhetoric, and hence of λόγος.

In trying to recover the factical-historical *origin*ality, the Dasein as Being in a world, of Platonic dialectic and Aristotelian rhetoric, Heidegger uncovers the cardinal importance of λόγος. The Greeks lived in the spoken language, so much so that Heidegger explains how originally λόγος did not mean reason, logic, or rationality. Λόγος meant speaking.[8] In this sense, speaking is the facticity of λόγος: a historical retrieval of the Platonic and Aristotelian situations of people speaking in the world with others. As a consequence, in the factical analysis of λόγος as speaking, Heidegger is interested not just in speaking but rather in the origin of speaking. Recovering the conceptuality of Plato's and Aristotle's concepts is, more originally, a historical retrieval of how they experienced the relation between Being and λόγος. Since, as I have claimed, what was origin in 1919 becomes Being, then the facticity of λόγος (speaking) is grounded in Being.

All of this develops slowly. It is clear, though, in Heidegger's course on Aristotle's *Rhetoric* (which I address in Chapter 8) that he is as interested in the problem of speaking as he is in the problem of the Being of beings, what, in that course, he often describes as the Being of the *there* of a being. As a historical retrieval of Aristotle's situation (the conceptuality of Aristotelian concepts), Heidegger's analysis in that course concludes that the Being of a being must be construed in terms of limit, finitude, and nothingness, which, he says, is how the Greeks and especially Aristotle understood the Being of a being. Speaking, therefore, originates in the anxiety (distress) of nothingness. The recovery of Aristotle's historical situation has revealed the importance of speaking as a way of gaining access, through anxiety, to Being construed as limit and the nothingness that is constitutive of limit. The kind of speaking that attends to the limit, finitude, and nothingness of Dasein's Being, I argue, is an authentic factical speaking. In Chapter 8, I argue on behalf of the possibility of this kind of speaking in Heidegger's early work.

The issue of nothingness (*das Nichts*) recurs throughout this book, and so what Heidegger means by nothingness should be clarified, to some extent at least, from the beginning. The issue of nothingness is made thematic for the first time in *Phenomenological Interpretations of Aristotle: Initiation into Phenomenological Research* (G 61), the lecture course in which Heidegger spends the most time explicitly studying factical life. In that course, he explains that factical life temporalizes as a crash (*Sturz*) through the nothingness. This means that the temporality of factical life is such that it is hidden within different modes of life's objectivity. By objectifying itself, life denies or says "no" to its temporality. As such, factical life's temporality is negated; it is hidden. It becomes clear from this analysis that nothingness is related to factical life. The nothingness is not absolute nothingness but rather always the nothingness *of* factical life. It refers to factical life's not being an object or thing, i.e., its no-thingness. In other courses that I investigate here, this sense of nothingness recurs. In the course on Paul, Heidegger explains nothingness in terms of the second coming. Even here, though, Heidegger does not take nothingness to mean complete annihilation. It is not the nothingness of the nihilist that is at work here but rather the no-thingness that dynamizes one's faith and hope. When Heidegger turns to the Greeks, this dynamic sense of nothingness as the no-thingness of factical life is sustained. He explores Greek words such as δύναμις (potentiality), στέρησις (absence), and διχῶς (doubling) in terms of the movement of beings in their Being and thus in terms of the very sense of no-thingness that dynamizes the temporality of factical life and thus the temporality of Dasein. Therefore, throughout this book, I show how Heidegger's use of nothingness does not refer to absolute nothingness, but rather to the no-thingness of factical life. As such it indicates the Being of factical life, that is, the Being of Dasein, in that Heidegger understands Being to be not a being or thing, but rather no-thing. No-thingness, in this sense, is, as the later Heidegger makes clear, the withdrawn illumination of Being within beings.

A final point of emphasis. If facticity allows Heidegger to engage in the work of historical retrieval and if the facticity of λόγος is the sense of speaking that is more original than the interpretations of λόγος that have fallen away from that originality (reason, rationality, and logic), then there must be something about the factical situation that admits of fallenness. Indeed, how did λόγος as speaking become reason, rationality, and logic? In this regard, the question of facticity is as much about retrieval as it is about that which necessitates retrieval. There must be something about factical life that allows it or even causes it to lose its original vitality and freshness and thus become something other than it is. Probing the fallenness of facticity, Heidegger determines that deception and distortion belong to factical-historical originality. Indeed, in trying to recover the original-factical-historical situation of Aristotle, Heidegger discovers that speaking is the original source of deception and distortion. Through numerous twists and turns, it becomes clear that this is the case because speaking is grounded in Dasein as Being-in-the-world and, hence, in Dasein's Being, which is its limitedness and finitude (its negativity) as much as its uncovering of the world. The Being of Dasein is its power to uncover and disclose the world— through speaking, perception, and understanding—but only insofar as this power is bound up with the deception and distortion that accompany its negativity and finitude. Throughout this book I show that distortion belongs to the negativity of Being and that this develops from the analysis of facticity. As Heidegger states clearly in *Being and Time*, because Dasein is factical, it is, at the same time, both in the truth and in the untruth (222/265).

If facticity shows us anything, it shows us that in living, a world has been disclosed to us already. Since factical Dasein is both in the truth and in the untruth, the distortions of truth accompany the disclosure of a world. With explicit reference to facticity, Heidegger writes in *Being and Time* that

> only in so far as entities within-the-world have been uncovered along with Dasein, have such entities, as possibly encounterable within-the-world, been covered up (hidden) or disguised. (*BT*, 222/265)

Entities, beings, within the world can be disguised only insofar as they have been disclosed. Our task, then, as human beings is to develop tools with which to discern distortions from within the finite situations that are disclosed to us within our world; this is what facticity makes possible. Heidegger recognized that the source of the distortions immanent in factical life and, therefore, in metaphysics—which builds systems out of factical life—is Being itself. As such, whatever ways we develop to make do with these distortions (practical wisdom, or φρόνησις, is one of these ways, as we will see; authentic factical speaking is another) will involve an experience of the power of Being's influence on how we live our lives. We need such tools to discern, as best we can, the distortions that Being brings to bear on factical life.

This book is a study of what Heidegger says about the factical living and speaking of human beings in the world. As such, I take account of the original vitality of life as well as the distortions that are necessarily a part of living and speaking in the world with others. The early Heidegger's analyses of facticity developed as a way of reading metaphysical systems down into the factical world of living and speaking human beings in order to remove their transcendental overlay. Heidegger wanted to restore the original freshness of factical life to science, theological dogma, medieval scholasticism's appropriation of Aristotle, and even Plato's dialectic. I believe that these retrievals of factical living and speaking open life to Being in a world. In other words, by showing that Aristotelian metaphysics, Platonic dialectic, Pauline faith, and even scientific objectivity can all be traced back to their advent in factical (temporal-historical) life, Heidegger makes it possible for us to retrieve the original experiences of these concepts. Accordingly, he makes it possible for us to discern the distortions that, because of the nature of Being itself, are built into metaphysics, dialectic, faith, and science as we continue to live, factically, with these concepts.

Heidegger, Dilthey, and the Being of Life

The aim of this book is to show the connections between Being and life in Heidegger's early work. Some commentators have claimed that in terms of method and of how one should approach philosophy, the early Heidegger was influenced more by Wilhelm Dilthey than by any other thinker.[9] Let me begin, then, by taking account of the influence of Dilthey on the early Heidegger's thinking. Doing so enables us to see that in his early lecture courses, Heidegger was interested in grasping human life *as a whole* and that this was a way of trying to understand the nature of Being. Heidegger is, in some sense, a life-philosopher, but his goal was to view human, historical life from the perspective of Being as such. This is another way of asking, "What does it mean for human beings *to be*?" Looking at Heidegger's reading of Dilthey, we see that the primary object for philosophical investigation in the early Heidegger is life, a claim he makes often in the early lecture courses. In his lectures on Aristotle, St. Paul, Plato, and others, Heidegger's method is to retrieve the factical life context that inspired their concepts and ideas, attempting to develop the context of meaningful relationships from which they philosophized.[10] He was thus as interested in method as he was in philosophical content.[11]

The work of Dilthey is not often the explicit subject matter for Heidegger's lecture courses from the early period.[12] A sustained treatment, though, appears in "Wilhelm Dilthey's Research and the Current Struggle for a Historical Worldview," the Kassel lectures he delivered in April 1925.[13] Clearly, Heidegger was reading Dilthey throughout the early to mid-1920s.[14] Furthermore, in recent years, numerous readers of Heidegger have explicated the specifics of Dilthey's influence. As Robert Scharff demonstrates clearly, what Heidegger saw in Dilthey was that the proper approach to the different modes of being, and thus the proper approach to Being itself, was through life, thus expressing a fundamental and intimate connection between life and Being.[15]

I can isolate two major themes in Heidegger's encounter with Dilthey, both of which demonstrate Heidegger's appropriation of historical life from Dilthey into his own understanding of Dasein as the Being of life. First, through Dilthey, Heidegger wanted to grasp life as a whole. In *Being and Time*, grasping life as a whole means to understand Dasein temporally, as both Being-toward-birth and Being-toward-death. In the Kassel lectures from 1925, which, as Kisiel points out, is one of the first drafts of *Being and Time*, we find one of the first major treatments of the problematic of death. But in the early lecture courses, with Dilthey's help, Heidegger attempts to grasp life as a whole differently. It is not strictly the temporal or even historical structure of life that he intends. Rather, it is the whole of the human being as a worlding being, the historical happening of life as a unified, meaningful context.[16]

The second major element in Heidegger's appropriation of Dilthey is the notion of *Selbstbesinnung*. This notion suggests a kind of self-awareness that is not on the order of consciousness.[17] As Scharff writes, "[Dilthey] shows us *how* life 'is' for us when understood as experienced, instead of merely *what* it looks like as an object when theoretically constituted from the 'Cartesian' standpoint shared by natural science and traditional epistemology."[18] In his confrontation with Dilthey, we thus find both poles of the early Heidegger's method for doing philosophy, called *formal indication*, which

was an attempt to grasp the whole of life together with an effort to apprehend the particularities of the happening of life in its own self-elucidation
and self-awareness.[19]

In the Kassel lectures, there is an identification between life and Dasein.
Heidegger will say, for example, that, "the primal givenness of Dasein is that
it is in a world. Life is that kind of reality which is in a world and indeed in
such a way that it has a world" (S, 163). We see further that he will affirm
that life *is there* (Dasein), as when he claims, "This whole context of self and
world is there [*ist da*] at every moment" (S, 158) and, later, that "all life, on
the other hand, is there [*ist da*] in such a way that a world is also there for it"
(S, 163). Dilthey's efforts to grasp the whole of life provided Heidegger with
a model for apprehending the factical life situation of Dasein as Being in the
world.[20] For Heidegger, existential concerns combine with ontological concerns on the way to *Being and Time*. His genius was to bring together Being
with life, ontology with existence, openness with that which opens.[21] In this,
he is attempting to show how one might achieve a kind of pretheoretical
insight, along the lines of Aristotelian φρόνησις, into life as a whole.

Outline of the Chapters

There are four parts to this book:

Part I: Philosophical Vitality (1919–21): Chapters 1–2
Part II: Factical Life (1921–22): Chapters 3–4
Part III: The Hermeneutics of Facticity (1922–23): Chapters 5–6
Part IV: The Language of Life (1923–25): Chapters 7–9

Since factical life and factical language are themes that Heidegger develops only in the early part of his career, I treat primarily the lecture
courses he delivered from 1919 to 1925, along with letters and manuscripts
from that time.

The approach that I take here is both chronological and thematic.
Chronologically, I am interested in the way that Heidegger's initial understanding of the vitality of philosophy and of factical life as the original
experience of science (1919) and religion (1920–21) unfolds into an analysis of Dasein as Being in a world (1923), whence we see a concerted effort to
develop a language that can capture that experience of living and being in
the world. By taking account of this development, I look at how Heidegger's
interest in Being is intimately related to and develops out of his interest in
life and the effort to develop a language, or a way of thinking about language, that can describe life. Thematically, I am interested in the conceptual
shifts that Heidegger accomplishes in his lecture courses. In many of these

courses, he is showing how our thinking has to change based on the need in philosophy to take account of the facticity of life. This enables him to recast philosophical activity. In 1919, we find him deconstructing the certainties of science down to their origin in factical life. The shift here is from knowledge to what he will call "taking-notice" of the meaningfulness of life. In 1920, again, he deconstructs theological dogma back down into factical life, enacting a shift from religious knowledge to faith. In 1922 he claims that the traditions of philosophy and theology need to be read back down into the facticity of life, to retrieve the vital origins of their development. Between 1923 and 1925, Heidegger sets out on an attempt to rethink language. Here the shift is from propositional grammar to the idea of language as revelation of the world. In looking at these shifts, we see how Heidegger is trying to rethink science (Chapter 1), religion (Chapter 2), the traditions of philosophy and theology (Chapter 5), ontology and hermeneutics (Chapter 6), and language (Chapters 7, 8, 9) according to life's facticity (Chapters 3 and 4).

In Chapters 1–2, I show how Heidegger is interested in deriving the disciplines of science and religion from their ground, which is the original experience of life and its factical vitality. In the course on science (*The Basic Problems of Phenomenology, G* 58), the first course that deals at length with this issue, Heidegger calls factical life a pretheoretical and prerational context of meaningfulness through which one gains access to life in its originality. Chapter 2 takes up two of Heidegger's courses on religious life from *The Phenomenology of Religious Life* (*G* 60). In both courses, but especially in the first one from the winter semester of 1920–21, titled *Introduction to the Phenomenology of Religion*, the originality of life takes on a decidedly temporal-historical character for the first time. Primarily through a reading of the letters of Paul, Heidegger says that in their expectation of the second coming, the early Christians lived temporality. The factical life of the early Christians was characterized by this original experience of their own temporality based on faith.

Chapters 3 and 4 deal extensively with *Phenomenological Interpretations to Aristotle: Introduction to Phenomenological Research* (*G* 61), the lecture course in which Heidegger provides the most sustained treatment of factical life. Chapter 3 is devoted to an explication of the meanings of facticity and factical life. It establishes the cardinal importance of these themes to what Heidegger at that time understood to be philosophy's primary tasks. Heidegger wanted to bring philosophy back to the situation of life as it is lived, namely, as in the world. In 1921–22, when this course was delivered, factical life meant to live in the world. The dynamic between life and world, for Heidegger, is the place from which philosophical questioning must begin.

In Chapter 4, I continue the investigation of factical life in *G* 61 but with attention to the problems that belong to living in the world. Heidegger introduces the term "ruinance" in this course. The term "ruinance" later becomes "fallenness." Ruinance belongs to factical life, and by this Heidegger means that human beings tend to objectify themselves and, in doing so, cover over their temporal-historical constitution. In this chapter, the dynamic between life and world is deepened so that factical life comes to indicate the context of worldly experience within which human beings tend to cover over their temporal-historical constitution but also through which temporality and historicality can be retrieved.

In 1922, Heidegger applied for jobs at the universities of Marburg and Göttingen. As part of the application, he wrote a prospectus of his current and projected philosophical work. The title of this work is "Phenomenological Interpretations with Respect to Aristotle: Indication of the Hermeneutical Situation," and it forecast an exciting new interpretation of Aristotelian philosophy. The problem of facticity figures prominently in this manuscript. In analyzing it, in Chapter 5, I try to show how Heidegger wanted to ground the disciplines of philosophy and theology in the factical situation out of which Aristotle conceptualized. For Heidegger, Aristotle is the critical figure for philosophy and theology. He claims that since German Idealism can be traced back to Reformation theology, and since Luther was influenced as much by Paul and Augustine as he was by an encounter with late scholastic theology, which operates, in large part, with Thomistic concepts, the importance of Aristotelian philosophy, especially his ethics and ontology, becomes manifest. Moreover, Heidegger says that Augustine and Neoplatonism can also be traced back to Aristotle. In all of this the retrieval of Aristotle and, more specifically, the retrieval of factical life in Aristotle becomes the defining feature of Heidegger's early philosophical project of grounding philosophy and theology in facticity. Along with this comes a refined analysis of the need to take account of history in order to interpret factical life in terms of the originality of its sources.

In Chapter 6, I analyze the last course Heidegger delivered at Freiburg before going to Marburg (*G* 63). Its title is *Ontology: The Hermeneutics of Facticity*, and an important transition takes place in it: Factical life becomes Dasein as Being in a world. With this transition, it becomes clear that it is facticity that makes possible life's openness to the world in its meaningfulness and, therefore, life's openness to Being. Heidegger says in this course that the world encounters Being. The facticity of life is such that life has access to Being. Life is, in *fact*, the *there* of Being in the world (Dasein).

One of the most important features of facticity that emerges through the analysis is that the temporality of factical life is dynamized by nothingness. To be sure, Heidegger emphasizes that this nothingness is not absolute nothingness but always the nothingness *of* factical life. We see here the early stages of Heidegger's understanding of Being. For Heidegger, Being is not a being; it is not a thing. In this sense, Being is the no-thingness or nothingness of life. Heidegger's research into facticity leads him into the question of this dynamizing no-thingness that permeates factical life's temporal-historical way of Being in the world. This dynamic no-thingness is factical life's and Dasein's temporalizing origin, which Heidegger wants to retrieve.

A critical dimension of the facticity of life is language. Chapters 7–9 present an analysis of factical speaking. They are devoted to Heidegger's reading of Plato and Aristotle, mainly the latter, because when Heidegger went to Marburg he taught a number of courses on the Greeks, and in these courses he is interested, in large part, in recovering the Greek sense of λόγος as speaking. Although this changes later, during this period of his career Heidegger explains that for the Greeks, λόγος originally meant speaking. This insight, that speaking was the essential way in which the Greeks experienced the world, is, I believe, a critical stage in Heidegger's development of the concept of λόγος and its relation to Being. Since *G 63* explains that factical life means Being in a world, in the chapters on language I try to follow Heidegger's development of factical speaking insofar as this means a kind of speaking that is open to the world and, therefore, open to Being. Following the themes developed earlier on factical life, in the chapters on language I focus on how factical speaking is the λόγος of historical Dasein, which, as such, is a λόγος that encounters the meaningfulness of the world.

Chapter 7 is an analysis of the first lecture course that Heidegger delivered at Marburg. Titled *Introduction to Phenomenological Research*, this course (*G 17*) is mainly on Husserl and Descartes. I focus, though, on the first part of the course, which is on Aristotle and which deals extensively with the facticity of speaking. The purpose of this first part is to clarify the original meaning of phenomenology by tracing its basic terms, phenomenon and λόγος, back to what Aristotle meant by λόγος ἀποφαντικός. In doing this, Heidegger shows that originally λόγος ἀποφαντικός did not just mean judgment. For Heidegger, what Aristotle meant by λόγος ἀποφαντικός points to the original experience of λόγος as a way of speaking that reveals or discloses the world. He then becomes interested in the unity of this λόγος: a unity, he says, that is intimately related to the question of Being. He concludes by saying that the spoken λόγος of historical Dasein, in its unity and thus in its Being, reveals the world and at the same time conceals the world. This concealment is also a deceiving, so that speaking (λόγος) is, he claims, the original source of deception for human beings.

By bringing the themes of historicality, the meaningfulness of the world, Dasein, and Being from Parts I–III together with the themes of speaking (the λόγος of historical Dasein), the unity—and thus the Being—of λόγος, the revealing and concealing of the world, and deception, Chapter 7 shows how Heidegger's interest in factical life and its ruinant fallenness (from Part II) merges with his interest in λόγος as speaking and its deceptions (in Part IV). The final two chapters of this book pursue Heidegger's interest in what are potentially very deceptive forms of speaking: rhetoric and sophistry. Heidegger's reading of Plato and Aristotle focuses, in large part, on how the λόγος of human beings is a speaking that reveals the world and, in that revelation, is not free from deception. These chapters attempt to show how λόγος is the speaking of factical-historical Dasein, who is Being in the world.

For Heidegger, it is really Aristotle and not Plato who captures the speaking dimension, that is, the λόγος, of Dasein as Being-in-the-world. He calls this λόγος the language of life. Chapter 8 presents a detailed analysis of Heidegger's lecture on Aristotle's *Rhetoric*. This analysis focuses on speaking and life and thus on the way that λόγος as speaking permeates Dasein's (factical life's) way of Being-in-the-world. I try to show how the speaking of life is intimately related to two important themes that emerge here: limit and disposition. In this course, Heidegger explains that for the Greeks, the Being of a being was its limit. He includes here the sense of nothingness, so that the limit of a being is that beyond which there is nothing. Nothingness, then, is intimately related to the Being of a being. He then analyzes the importance of opinion, passion, and disposition to speaking through Aristotle's understanding of rhetoric. The passions, he says, are the ground of speaking. Since dispositions frame the passions, disposition is also determinative of speaking. Furthermore, rhetorical speaking is not scientific and theoretical but rather always immersed in opinion (δόξα), which is constantly changing. The language of life, therefore, is a kind of speaking that is passionate, and thus disposed in a certain way, and that deals with that which can always be otherwise. As such, it is suffused with deception. Toward the end of the course, Heidegger brings limit, nothingness, and

Being together with disposition, passion, opinion, and speaking. These phenomena happen together in the context of the rhetorical situation, wherein a person is deciding whether or not to be convinced by a speaker or rhetor. Heidegger concludes that the genesis of speaking is an experience of nothingness. A rhetor appeals to the passions of the listeners, who must then decide whether or not they will be convinced by the λόγος of the rhetor. The rhetor thus brings them to a limit, a moment of decision, wherein they must make a decision about their own lives. In that moment wherein the listeners are trying to decide whether or not they will allow themselves to be taken along by what the rhetor says, they begin to speak. The authentic origin of speaking, therefore, is a confrontation with this limit and the nothingness that is constitutive of limit. Accordingly, the authentic origin of speaking is the confrontation of life or Dasein with its own Being (its own no-thingness). I use the notion of authentic speaking to highlight ways of thinking about politics, authentic community, and even ethical excellence.

Chapter 9, the final chapter, is an analysis of Heidegger's lecture on Plato's *Sophist*. As to Plato's understanding of λόγος, Heidegger is, on the one hand, critical of Platonic dialectic because it involves a seeing of the forms and, thus, a seeing of Being as beings. This is problematic because it makes Being into a being, or rather into many beings (the various forms), and it involves a seeing that passes through λόγος to pure νοεῖν, which Heidegger claims is not possible. On the other hand, Heidegger also says here that despite the problems with dialectic and the forms, Plato construed λόγος in an original way because he recognized how λόγος meant disclosure, and thus the possibility for discourse, and he understood how profoundly this disclosure determines human existence, and thus Dasein as Being-in-the-world.

The conclusion of the book is divided into two sections: "The Problem of Destruction" and "Worlding." In the first section of the conclusion, I identify a certain confusion about how Heidegger understands the importance of factical life. At times, it is a source of deception that needs to be destructed or deconstructed, whereas at other times it is a source of profound meaningfulness. I take account of this confusion in order to demonstrate the importance of both of these tendencies within factical life experience. I criticize the notion that Heidegger is offering a choice between authentic and inauthentic life.[22] My reading of the early Heidegger avoids this dichotomy by showing that if the present situation of factical life is simply inauthentic, then Dasein's destructive retrieval of the past cannot take account of our present situation. It cannot make any sense of what Heidegger means by worlding, which would, on such a reading, be inauthentic. Using the previous chapters in this book, I show how important it is for Heidegger that the world is a context of meaningful relationships, emphasizing the extent to which Dasein is simultaneously both in the truth and in untruth. My reading of worlding and, subsequently, of speaking, which I address in the second section of the conclusion, takes its lead from William Richardson's notion of authenticity. He claims that Heidegger's notion of authenticity acknowledges the darkness in human life, just like the shadows in a Rembrandt painting accentuate the figure in the picture. Accordingly, I argue that Heidegger's notion of factical life as Being in a world captures both the error and the excellence of Dasein, its darkness and its light, and thus presents a realistic and profoundly meaningful way of thinking about human life.

Note on Translation

I have made most of the translations myself. In some instances, where a translation was available, I used it but then adjusted the available translation to fit with how I have been rendering certain German words into English. Translating Heidegger poses special difficulties. I have chosen to make more literal translations, sometimes at the expense of smooth English readability. If there are errors, it is on the side of making literal translations. With the exception of Dasein, a term that has become anglicized, I have translated all German words. Of special note: in every case I translate the German word *Sein* as "Being," with an uppercase "B" and the word *Seiendes* as a "being," with a lowercase "b." Many translators have opted to translate *Sein* as "being" instead of "Being" because the latter suggests that *Sein* is something substantive. Although that is certainly not what Heidegger wants to suggest, I choose to render *Sein* as "Being" because of the importance of the difference, which Heidegger stresses, between *Sein* and *Seiendes*, that is, the ontological difference between Being and beings. In my view, this difference is not captured when both words are translated with "being."

In his early lecture courses, Heidegger often employed Greek expressions in their original language. Keeping with that practice in this book, I have retained the Greek originals of all the Greek words and phrases instead of using their traditional English renditions. The common translations of these terms fail to capture the nuances of meaning that Heidegger wants to draw out of them. The term λόγος, for example, has been translated into English as "sentence," "phrase," "reason," and "composite expression." Heidegger claims, in the early lecture courses and elsewhere, that for Aristotle λόγος meant speaking, which, connected to the innermost existence of the human being, reveals the world. The function of revelation belongs to this word's original meaning, and to translate it as "sentence," "phrase," "reason," or "composite expression" covers over that original meaning. To use another example, the Greek term ἀποφαντικός has been translated as "judgment," "assertion," and "proposition." For Aristotle, every ἀποφαντικός is a λόγος, but not every λόγος is an ἀποφαντικός. The difference between the λόγος and the λόγος ἀποφαντικός is that every λόγος ἀποφαντικός contains either truth or falsity. Heidegger emphasizes that the common understandings of truth and falsity, as correctness and as incorrectness, derive from an original revelation, which lets something be seen, either as what it is (truth) or as other than it is (falsity). As with λόγος, the translation of λόγος ἀποφαντικός as "judgment," "assertion," or "proposition" conceals the nuances of meaning, and thus the force, of the original Greek.

PART I

Philosophical Vitality (1919–21)

Science and the Originality of Life

The strictness of philosophical expression means concentration on the genuineness of the relations of life in concrete life itself.
—**Martin Heidegger,** *Grundprobleme der Phänomenologie*

Reading Martin Heidegger's early lecture courses is exciting and not simply because of the various ways in which they presage concepts and themes in his later work. Many of the initial interpretive forays into these courses have focused on the development of Heidegger's concepts on the way to *Being and Time* and beyond. Identifying how and when various concepts developed is essential to understanding Heidegger's thought, and throughout this book I attempt to show how Heidegger's phenomenology of life develops into an ontology of Dasein. But the early lecture courses, and his other writings and manuscripts from 1919 to 1925, present innovative and provocative ideas in their own right about philosophical problems. Heidegger's students from those years, such as Hannah Arendt, Hans Jonas, and Hans-Georg Gadamer, were influenced not by what they took to be inchoate, developing ideas that would only find completion in their teacher's published works; they were influenced by Heidegger's interpretations of metaphysics, ontology, religion, history, and science, which opened up new ways of thinking about philosophy, and about life.

It is astonishing to see how much Heidegger was interested in the phenomenon of life. He would later claim that he was not an existentialist and that he had never been one. By Sartre and others, he was thought at first to be an existentialist, and reading the early courses, one can see why. There is in these early courses an intense and sustained focus on the phenomenon of life. But what distinguishes Heidegger from both classical life-philosophy and existentialism is that his topic is not just life or simply the movement of life[1] or even temporality. Heidegger's interest from early on was the dynamic happening of life, dynamic in the sense that life is a priori charged with meaning. He is not a life-philosopher because, for him, the flow of life is not simply a flux of sense-impressions. As Heidegger reads it, the flux or flow of life is directional, intentional, and already meaningful. It is not an indifferent flow. Nor is he an existentialist, because it is not simply brute life or sheer human existence that he is investigating but rather that rich, mysterious "something" that motivates and dynamizes the happening of life.

From as early as 1919, we find Heidegger attempting to describe not simply life, but the happening of life, the origin of life, and the intentional directedness of life within our various worlds of experience. In the War Emergency Semester of 1919 (from *Toward the Definition of Philosophy*, *G* 56/57), Heidegger will say that it is necessary to grasp the essence of "lived experience" (*G* 56/57:66/53). Then, during the winter semester of 1919–20, Heidegger discusses at length the concept of factical life in a course titled *Basic Problems of Phenomenology* (*G* 58).[2] In that lecture course, Heidegger explores the relation between phenomenology and factical life in order to determine how phenomenology can justifiably call itself the original *science* of life. He did not adopt the general term "facticity," as distinct from "factical life," until the last few moments of a lecture course delivered one semester later found in *Phenomenology of Intuition and Expression* (*G* 59), from the summer of 1920. Heidegger would then thematize facticity and factical life in much more detail in his next lecture course, *Introduction to the Phenomenology of Religion*, from the winter semester of 1920–1921, which can be found in *The Phenomenology of Religious Life* (*G* 60). In the religion course, facticity names the original experience of early Christian religiosity, which Heidegger extracts from the epistles of Paul. What all of this means is that the concept of facticity, first as factical life and then as the more general term "facticity," in both its scientific and religious interpretations, names an experience of life that is dynamic, a happening of the directions of experience, which has an origin. From the beginning, Heidegger's interest was in the origin or what we might call the originality of life as a dynamic experience.

In this part titled "Philosophical Vitality," which comprises Chapters 1 and 2 of this book, I focus on Heidegger's analyses of science (Chapter 1) and religion (Chapter 2) from 1919 to 1921. In the first chapter, my focus is on the three lecture courses mentioned above: *Toward the Definition of Philosophy* (*G* 56/57); *The Basic Problems of Phenomenology* (*G* 58); and *Phenomenology of Intuition and Expression: Theory of Philosophical Concept Formation* (*G* 59). This chapter is divided into four sections. In the first section, I analyze what Heidegger says about life in that first text (*G* 56/57). Although he does not mention facticity or factical life in his course from the War Emergency Semester of 1919, he does say here that philosophy needs to take account of lived experience and that such experience is primary. In the second section, I look briefly at the closing minutes of *G* 59 (summer semester, 1920) in order to determine the sense in which Heidegger had adopted the term "facticity" as a name for his unique approach to life. The third section constitutes the bulk of this chapter. I step back to focus on *G* 58 (winter semester, 1919–20) to see how factical life is the ground of science (since phenomenology is the original science of life). In doing so, I demonstrate that in Heidegger's analysis of phenomenology as a science, there is a fundamental meaningfulness within life itself. Even in the trivialities of average, everyday life, we find meaningful relations and meaningful contexts. The human being lives within a context of life-worlds. As such, the goal for phenomenology should be to figure out how to grasp the historical and contextual movement of life and then develop concepts that might adequately express that movement. The human being lives within meaningful historical contexts, and it is philosophically valuable, if not necessary, to explicate these contexts. The fourth and final section continues to look at *G* 58 in order to focus on the notion of the self-world and the way in which there is a kind of concentration or intensification of life-worlds layered within the self-world. The self-world is a context, and the different life-worlds have a kind of rhythmic echo within that context. This shows that factical life has an origin through which and out of which it continually renews itself. As such, phenomenology is not a kind of science that devivifies life. It is, rather, original science that focuses on the meaningful contexts and relationships within life.

The Primacy of Lived Experience

From as early as 1919, Heidegger was developing ways of thinking about human life as an active, dynamic context of meaningful relationships. As we will see, this is a theme that continues in his lecture courses up through 1925 and into *Being and Time*. In his course from the War Emergency Semester of 1919, *The Idea of Philosophy and the Problem of Worldview*, as a prelude to his attempt to explore the way in which philosophy is a primordial science, he will identify the various contexts within which and through which life happens.

> Every personal life has in all moments within its particular predominant life-world a relationship to that world, to the motivational values of the environing world, of the things of its life-horizon, of other human beings, of society. These life-relations can be pervaded—in quite diverse ways—by a genuine form of accomplishment and life-form, e.g. the scientific, religious, artistic, political.

The scientific man, however, does not stand in isolation. He is connected to a community of similarly striving researchers with its rich relations to students. The life-context of scientific consciousness expresses itself in the formation and organization of scientific academies and universities. (G 56/57:4/4)

For Heidegger, it was essential that we recognize the extent to which human beings live within meaningful contexts. As academics, scientists, artists, people of faith, and even in our everyday lives, we are open to these contexts, which consist of people, things, and ideas. These contexts constitute a horizon of relationships, and although these relationships are subject to corruption, they can, nonetheless, be transformed: "Life-relations renew themselves only by returning to the genuine origins of the spirit" (G 56/57:4/4). There are various ways in which Heidegger develops these contexts of meaning, in terms of both life and language. In this very early course from 1919, we see how these contexts are manifest with respect to the following: *the pretheoretical understanding, worlding*, and perhaps most importantly in what Heidegger says about the notion of *the historical-I*.

The goal of the lecture course is to determine how philosophy is a primordial science. Such an investigation into the nature of philosophy is, perhaps, not unusual for a novice philosophy professor, although the question of philosophy, what it is, and how it poses questions will remain an issue for Heidegger throughout his life. As phenomenology is, for Heidegger at this time, primordial science, a method for conducting philosophical research and analysis, the course is accordingly devoted to an analysis of method.[3] It is important to see, however, that the method that Heidegger is developing springs from his objects of investigation, which in this course are, first, the nature of philosophy itself and, subsequently, the phenomenon of life, or lived experience, which is the primary object for philosophical research.

There are two methods that emerge in the beginning of the course, (1) the development of a worldview and (2) the critical-teleological method, neither of which, according to Heidegger, is able to grasp living experience. For this reason, neither should be construed as philosophy, as it is the goal of philosophy to disclose and to articulate pretheoretical, lived experience. As to the problem of worldview, Heidegger separates the notion of worldview into two possibilities, a precritical metaphysics, on the one hand, and the critical, scientific development of a system of values, on the other. The history of philosophy develops from the first, metaphysical, sense of worldview. Just as particular people have their own worldviews (Heidegger mentions the factory worker and the peasant in the Black Forest), and political parties have their own worldviews, so, too, philosophers attempt to develop an ultimate perspective on reality and human existence, and thus their own, philosophical worldview, which is nonetheless meant to be universal and absolute.[4] A critical, scientific, post-Kantian sense of worldview will differ from metaphysics in that it is not investigating beyond the realm of experience, but the goal is still the same, namely, the "interpretation of the meaning of human existence and culture" together with "absolutely valid norms which in the course of human development have expressed themselves as the values of the true, the good, the beautiful, and the holy" (*G* 56/57:8/9). Perhaps, then, there is a third sense of worldview, one that separates worldview from philosophy entirely in that it is disconnected from "ultimate questions about humankind" (*G* 56/57:9/11).

In an essay that can be dated to 1920, "Critical Comments on Karl Jaspers's *Psychology of Worldviews*,"[5] Heidegger criticizes Jaspers for his use of mere observation in the development and articulation of worldviews and—in thus showing that the problem with Jaspers is the method he employed, which ended up missing basic philosophical problems— Heidegger will shift the analysis of worldview to a delineation of the meaning of factical life, which begins with the dynamic happening of the "I am." Heidegger emphasizes the sense of Being of the I, which is not simply a region of objects or concepts surrounding an I-object, but rather the historically enacted—and thus factical—self, motivated by anxious concern to deconstruct the tradition with which it is burdened in order to develop "ways and means of explicating our actual experience of the self" (*G* 9:34/29). Thus, in both texts from this period, we see the contrast that Heidegger wants to draw between the tendency in the history of philosophy to construct absolute, universal worldviews on the one hand and, on the other, what Heidegger sees as necessary, and which the development of worldviews has forgotten, namely, the articulation of the historically situated self, which has been buried by tradition and become encrusted by an objectified significance.

In the course from 1919, Heidegger recognizes the enormity of claiming that philosophy should be separated from worldview. He says that such a separation "would imply an entirely new concept of philosophy which would be totally unrelated to all the ultimate questions of humankind. Philosophy would thus be deprived of its most traditional entitlements as a regal, superior occupation" (*G* 56/57:11/9). Even in this very early course, Heidegger is attempting to develop a radical new sense for philosophy, one that is not an articulation of ultimate meanings, but rather one that takes account of lived experience. Neither sense of worldview, as precritical or as post-Kantian, attempts to disclose pretheoretical experience. This is why philosophy must be conceived as primordial science, an attempt to describe experience before it becomes rigidified and theoretical.

The critical-teleological method, like worldview, cannot be primordial science—and, therefore, cannot be philosophy, and for the same reason. It is not able to grasp factical life or factical experience. The critical-teleological method grounds principles of assessment or norms, and as Kant showed clearly, these norms are a priori universal and necessary, and therefore cannot be discerned through experience. Although the apprehension of these norms may make some reference to experience, the goal of the critical-teleological method is to identify those norms that serve as axioms to universally valid truth. If the method can show that those norms are necessary to the achievement of that goal, then the method has been successful. But it is precisely the success of the method that reveals its fundamental inconsistency. Once the goal has been achieved, then the method is no longer necessary. In other words, while the critical-teleological method can identify the standards for moral action, if the standard is discovered, then you no longer need the method that helped you to find the standard. This method is inherently self-defeating (*G* 56/57:44/35).

Moreover, what is important for philosophy is not the establishment of a transcendental, universal and necessary, standard or ought; rather, for Heidegger, philosophy describes the way in which the ought gives itself and, even more importantly, the way that value-relations are experienced in human life. He writes, "The universality and necessity of the *should* is not *factical* and empirical but *ideal* and absolute" (*G* 56/57:36/30). Once we recognize this, then we can develop an approach to philosophy that sees the ought not as a "primordial objectivity" but rather as a mode of factical life. Heidegger says, "I experience it, I 'live' it as an ought" (*G* 56/57:46/37). He finds it best, however, to cast this experience of the ought as an intransitive formulation: "The value 'is' not, but rather it 'values' in an intransitive sense: in being worth-taking, 'it values' for me, for the value experiencing subject. 'Valuing' becomes an object only through formalization" (*G* 56/57:46/37). The German impersonal sentence, which Heidegger uses extensively, such as "there is" or "it worlds" or, as here, "it values," points to a dynamic and original event.[6] In the case of the way in which I experience values, we might say that values are open to me and available to me prior to any attempt to discern, through the critical-teleological method, universal and necessary norms or standards. What makes these values open and available? These values are not simply the experience of an ought. In other words, there is more to value than simply an ought. Heidegger writes, "In the morning I enter the study; the sun lies over the books, etc., and I delight in this. Such delight is in no way an ought; delightfulness as such is not given to me in an ought experience" (*G* 56/57:46/37). Although I may experience delight as a value, I do not experience it as an ought. Thus, the primordial event or happening of life is an event or happening that broadens the experience of life, from a narrow conception of norms discerned through a philosophical method to the value-rich texture of life as it is lived. This experience is not something theoretical, like being-true. "In value-taking there is nothing theoretical; it has its own 'light', spreads its own illumination: '*lumen gloriae*'" (*G* 56/57:49/39).

In using the impersonal sentence Heidegger is trying to replace the objectified subject-thing or I with an I that is thoroughly integrated into the world. It is crucial to see, however, that even though the impersonal sentence lacks a natural subject, Heidegger still emphasizes the extent to which this dynamic happening, of valuing, worlding, giving, or even living ("it lives"), has a reference *to me*. He writes, "In worth-taking, the 'it values' does something *to me*, it pervades me" (*G* 56/57:49/39). He is trying to displace the I into the world, and yet he is trying to salvage some notion of the I at the same time: "I ask: 'Is there something?' The 'is there' is a 'there is' for an 'I', and yet it is not to and for whom the question relates" (*G* 56/57:69/55). In other words, in the question, "Is there something?" there is a relation to an I, but not, in this case, to my particular I. Even here, Heidegger is exploring the non-thingly nature of experience, but he is still maintaining some relation to an I. Kisiel notes Heidegger's distinction between the theoretical I, which is deworlded and removed from experience, and the I that resonates with worldly experience, but Kisiel may go too far when he emphasizes that this latter I essentially disappears into the world and its environment. He claims that, "in fact, in the 'seeing' involved here, my I goes out of itself completely and immerses itself in the world in total absorption. This impersonal experience of the historical I wholly 'given over' to its world is thus the opposite of that of the theoretical I almost totally remote from its objectified *es gibt*."[7] This issue becomes particularly important in *Phenomenological Interpretations of Aristotle: Initiation into Phenomenological Research* (*G* 61, from winter semester, 1921–22), where Heidegger will, indeed, describe facticity's total absorption into the world and call it life's ruination. In both that course and in this course, however, Heidegger is trying to reconfigure the experience of life from that of a subject looking theoretically at objects to an impersonal happening of life, which is, nonetheless, *self-referential*. Although not pivoting around an objectified I, experience is still happening to someone, to a self. So, when Heidegger gives his famous example of the lectern in this course, contrasting the way he sees it and the way in which a Senegal Negro might see it, he emphasizes, "In the experience of seeing the lectern something is given *to me*" (*G* 56/57:72/58).

When Heidegger mentions *Ereignis* in this lecture course, he will affirm that there is a twofold event of appropriation, one that happens on its own and of its own accord and another that happens explicitly to and for me.

> In seeing the lectern I am fully present in my "I"; it resonates with the experience, as we said. It is an experience proper to me and so do I see it. However, it is not a process but rather an *event of appropriation* (non-process, in the experience of the question a residue of this event). Lived experience does not pass in front of me like a thing, but I appropriate it to myself, and it appropriates itself according to its essence. (*G* 56/57:75/60)

Kisiel points out how remarkable it is that Heidegger mentions *Ereignis* as early as 1919.[8] At this early stage, for Heidegger, *Ereignis* indicates the way in which I appropriate lived experience along with the way in which this experience appropriates itself. He uses it in the service of showing that the experience of life is not something external that then becomes internal. It does not consist of objectified images given to the mind. Factical life is, rather, the primordial experience of one's own self, which Heidegger calls here "one's own-ness" (*G* 56/57:75/60).

What do we call this self? In 1919 Heidegger will call it the historical-I, probably the very first incarnation of what he will eventually name "Dasein."[9] What is most important for the sake of the argument that I am trying to make is the fact that this historical-I experiences different levels of intensity. When we experience the world theoretically, as a world of things, then the historical-I becomes both deworlded and dehistoricized, an experience of life that has been devivified and stripped of its vitality. The only way in which experience can be *given* is in the theoretical attitude, wherein the historical-I is bracketed and, essentially, dismissed (*G* 56/57:85/67). Heidegger is grasping here not the givenness of experience, but rather the way in which experience is lived. In factical life, we do not collect data of experience. Lived experience is not the accumulation of sensations. Although that is one way to apprehend experience, it takes a remarkably abstract and theoretical mind to do so. Moreover, such an apprehension would be a derivation of the way life is originally experienced. Admittedly, Heidegger is attempting in this course to show how one can apprehend the vitality of experience. But the situation he is describing is not either/or. He is not claiming that either the world is experienced theoretically or it is experienced factically. His claim is that there are various levels of intensity in the experience of life. He writes, "There are levels of vitality of experience, which have nothing to do with individual chance 'life-intensity', but which are on the contrary prefigured in the essence of modes of life-experience and their worlds, i.e. in the unity of genuine life itself" (*G* 56/57:90/70).

Later, in *Being and Time*, the notion of authenticity will become confused by the way in which Heidegger writes about it. In saying that Dasein can be either authentic or inauthentic, he will seem to suggest that life is a dichotomy between these two possibilities. I address this issue in more detail in the conclusion, but we can see here that in Heidegger's thinking about the experience of life, at least in 1919, he is not suggesting that life is inauthentic and needs to become authentic, nor is he saying that the primordiality of lived experience is not genuine experience. On the contrary, from the beginning Heidegger wanted to develop an approach to the richness and vitality of life in its intensities, and not in *chance* intensities but in the various modes of living, worldly experience.

It is from this perspective of the intensities of life that we need to understand what Heidegger says about worlding in this course. For Heidegger, the question as to whether or not the external world is "real" is an absurd question. In that this question is a question for both critical idealism and critical realism, both succumb to this absurdity. Both positions maintain a theoretical view of the world. Heidegger writes: "This primacy of the theoretical must be broken" (*G* 56/57:59/47). Given the absurdity of the question, what any philosophy would call "real" is thus a theoretical object. These "real" objects are able to "world,'" Heidegger says, but there is more to worlding than simply that which is thought to be "real" (*G* 56/57: 91/71). Worlding, therefore, is a nontheoretical or pretheoretical experience of the intensity of life. That intensity is constituted by contexts of meaning. This is why the lectern, in Heidegger's examples, is seen in such different ways. He writes, "I see the lectern in an orientation, an illumination, a background" (*G* 56/57:71/57). The peasant from the Black Forest sees "'the place for the teacher,'" whereas the Senegal Negro sees "Perhaps something to do with magic, or something behind which one could find good protection against arrows and flying stones" (*G* 56/57:71/57). What none of them would see, except in a purely theoretical, abstract, and deworlded way, is "intersecting brown surfaces" (*G* 56/57:71/57). Apprehending the world in terms of contexts of meaning is how Heidegger conceived of a philosophical life. For him, in 1919, a genuine life is one that is lived, experienced, and such a life "is not achieved by any constructed system of concepts, regardless of how extensive it may be, but only through phenomenological life in its ever-growing self-intensification" (*G* 56/57:110/84). In the years leading up to and including *Being and Time*, in spite of all that Heidegger will say about ruination, fallenness, and inauthenticity, he will always maintain this positive sense of lived experience in terms of worlding, living within contexts of meaning, and undergoing intensification (we might even think of anxiety as it is described in *Being and Time* as the pinnacle of that intensification) prior to the development of a theoretical, pure seeing of phenomena.

In subsequent chapters of this book, I continue to follow what Heidegger says about lived experience, life, and factical life as he moves toward a refined notion of Dasein as Being in the world and into his analyses of language. Throughout, we will see that he maintains an orientation to the positive side of everydayness as a context of meaningful relationships. Through his reading of Aristotle, especially, he develops an acute sense of the negative dimensions of life, its deceptions and masks, but not until *Being and Time* does this take on the character of a dichotomy in the sense of a person being either authentic or inauthentic. But even there, as I intend to prove, Heidegger endeavors to show how the negativity of human life is not something that can be avoided. He presents, rather, a way of grasping human life as riddled with deception but, nonetheless, charged with meaning and open to revelation and insight.

At this point, I continue to look at Heidegger's early lecture courses and turn first, however briefly, to *Phenomenology of Intuition and Expression* (*G* 59), and then, in much more detail, to *Basic Problems of Phenomenology* (*G* 58). We will witness here a shift from his discussion of lived experience, as it is described in *Toward the Definition of Philosophy* (*G* 56/57), to a more through analysis of facticity and factical life.

Self-Concern and the Problem of Origin

If, at the very end of *G* 59, Heidegger names facticity as the primary subject matter of philosophical research, it is not abundantly clear from the rest of the course that he was leading up to this conclusion. Nor is it clear from this course that facticity will take on the importance that it does only two years later, in 1922, when Heidegger says that the traditions of both philosophy and theology need to be reinterpreted according to the hermeneutics of facticity. Indeed, there are very few references to the concept of facticity in *Phenomenology of Intuition and Expression* (*G* 59). Nonetheless, when Heidegger says to his students in the very last hour of this lecture course that facticity has been forgotten amid the regional ontologies of transcendental philosophy and that the factical life of Dasein needs to be retrieved from them, these realizations have a kind of inevitability about them. It seems as though Heidegger's study of phenomenology as a strict science and his research into the history of life-philosophy have pointed him toward a more original experience, the full actualization of facticity, which philosophers, especially Natorp, and even life-philosophers such as Dilthey and Bergson, have left unexplored.

Specifically, this course on philosophical concept formation, together with the previous one on phenomenology and factical life, have led Heidegger to realize that philosophy emerges from concern (*Bekümmerung*) about the self and, furthermore, that that self-concern comes from *factical* life.[10] The full actualization of facticity means that the self experiences life through its own self-concern. He writes,

> The self in the current full-actualization of life-experience, the self in the experience of itself is the primal reality [*Urwirklichkeit*]. Experience is not taking-notice but the vital being involved, the being concerned so that the self is constantly co-determined by this concern. Environing-world, with-world, and self-world are no areas of being. All reality receives its original sense through the concern of the self. (*G* 59:173/132–33)

Indeed, the sense of reality that science and scientific philosophy construct is grounded in the self insofar as the self is *concerned* about itself. Therefore, philosophers need to retrieve that sense of concern that emerges from factical life and bring it into their own research in order to ground philosophy (even philosophy construed as a science) in that original, concerned, factical experience of life from which it originally springs. Through concern the self opens itself to that primal experience that, and this is central for Heidegger, *it always already is*. Facticity is, in this sense, the self's original reality: primal experience, which allows for constant renewal whenever life chooses to take up its own origin in life-experience by becoming concerned about itself. In this way, philosophy is always under way toward its own origin, which is to say, toward itself. Far from being objectified, life's factical retrieval of its own origin is the self's actualization of itself; life does not grasp its origin theoretically but rather participates in that original experience. Factical life is the immediacy of the self's participation in life and in the world; in this sense, life experiences itself and the world in an original and primal way. In other words, when it is concerned about itself, life experiences its own participation in the vitality of primal (living, worldly) experience. The self does not take an objective distance from that experience, rather, the self is life-experience, even though it does not always understand itself in this way. Philosophy, for its part, when it is directed toward the self's being concerned about itself, can retrieve this basic experience (*Grunderfahrung*) and incorporate it into its own research. Philosophy, like the self, participates in the world and in life-experience. Let this stand for what Heidegger says about facticity at the end of *G* 59.

One difference between *Basic Problems of Phenomenology* (G 58, winter semester, 1919–20), and *Phenomenology of Intuition and Expression* (G 59, summer semester, 1920) is that in the earlier course, facticity really does not have the urgent sense of concern that it has in the later course. This is an important point because the sense of concern that opens the self to the primal experiences of life and world, though mentioned only briefly in G 59, will become an extremely important theme for Heidegger in the religion courses and, later, in his projected work on Aristotle. Indeed, the defining trait of Heidegger's unique appropriation of facticity is this particular sense of concern that can only come from the intensification of the facticity of life and that opens the self not just to itself but to the surrounding world and, as we will see, to other people.

Delivered one semester earlier, G 58 describes the relationship between phenomenology as a strict science and the factical experience of life. Here, Heidegger points out that both life and world are centered in self-life (*Selbstleben*). Factical life in G 58 is an indication of the layeredness of the self; the "world-characters" (*Weltcharaktere*) of life, he says, emerge from those layers. Phenomenology, then, is simply a matter of retrieving those layers of the self that have not yet been drawn out. Of critical importance, however, is how phenomenology will approach factical life, and that is no simple matter. Phenomenology is the original science of factical life, but Heidegger emphasizes that "origin" is not simply given to the phenomenologist. The original region must be won. As such, the phenomenologist must investigate factical life in order to determine the sense of origin in which factical life is grounded. Indeed, factical life is not the original region, itself. Rather, factical life provides access to the original region, and in this way phenomenology studies factical life insofar as it emerges from that origin.

In what follows I take a closer look at this relationship between phenomenology and the origin of factical life from G 58. In doing so, I isolate three themes: (1) science's devivification of the life-world; (2) the sense of meaningfulness that constitutes the original, factical encounter with life; and (3) the layeredness of life in the self, and, as part of that, what Heidegger describes as the "rhythmic echoing" between life and world. This last theme will bring us to the importance of history and the "intensification" (*Zugespitztheit*) of the life-worlds in the self-world, both of which will be significant topics in Heidegger's analysis of Christian facticity. All three of these themes will serve to explain how Heidegger understands phenomenology's task of understanding the *origin*ality of factical life as well as phenomenology's status as a science. Clearly, Heidegger is developing his own sense of phenomenology, one that takes account of the origin of factical life and attempts to develop a nontheoretical conceptuality to describe life.[11]

Note that Heidegger's aspirations here are quite ambitious. He says on the first day that the great philosophers, Kant, Plato, and Hegel, among others, need to be brought back into the original situation of life. Since phenomenology is the original science of life, these philosophers must now undergo phenomenological interpretation. The phenomenological method will ground the great philosophers within life. Before that can happen, however, phenomenology itself must be clarified. Specifically, Heidegger sets out to determine whether or not the phenomenological method, construed as a strict science, can in fact grasp life, for perhaps something is lost within that scientific grasping. In this way, the question about how phenomenology is able to bring the great philosophers to the situation of life becomes a question about whether science can adequately grasp life at all.

Science and the Vivacity of Life

Heidegger contends that the approach to life offered by Natorp and the Marburg school of neo-Kantianism does not grasp life as it is originally. For them, consciousness of objects is governed by mathematical rules of thought, to the extent that there is no experience of objects without thinking and, more specifically, thinking's theoretical determinations of objects (*G* 58:132, 224–25). These mathematical laws of thinking can then be made systematic and absolute. As such, the initial encounter with objects takes place in thinking, and then the object is not really experienced, it is only an idea. Indeed, the only "experience" of objects that Natorp acknowledges is sensation (*Empfindung*), which is, itself, grasped only through thinking. Likewise, according to the transcendental philosophy of value, exemplified by Rickert and Lask, the immediate experience of an object takes place through perception (*Wahrnehmung*). Like sensation, perception is governed by theoretical thinking so that the immediate experience of an object is epistemological. Neither school of thought takes its point of departure from factical life (*G* 58:133–35, 226).

We can understand Heidegger's analysis here of phenomenology as a response to neo-Kantianism and transcendental philosophy of value. It is a response that, on a very basic level, simply acknowledges that the self actually experiences something, not according to the laws of thought but, rather, as it is. Phenomenology studies the phenomenon, that which appears, that which shows itself, *in* experience: *as* it appears, *as* it shows itself. The sense of origin becomes pivotal because, in trying to subvert the neo-Kantian idea that we "experience" objects epistemologically and thus strictly according to the laws of thought that govern human knowing, Heidegger must show that that experience of objects has a source, an origin, that is other than the self and its ways of knowing. Hence, the initial question arises as to how the ground of experience is to be won, for when the ground of experience is properly grasped, it points toward that original region.

Heidegger explains that science isolates a particular region of factical life and develops knowledge in the form of concrete logic about the content of that region. He emphasizes that *"science is the concrete logic of its content-region, which grows out of a certain ground of experience in a certain way and in a certain gradation"* (*G* 58:66). With conceptual, methodological means, the scientist will analyze a particular content-region (*Sachgebiet*). This is, for example, the way a botanist looks at a flower: theoretically, analytically, scientifically. The botanist's means of analysis, however, are not self-generating. Science starts as an encounter with the factical life-world, which is the "concrete ground of experience," and then develops theoretical means of analysis to study an aspect of factical life (*G* 58:66). Such means, though, can be developed only in accord with a particular region of things. As a consequence, the theoretical means of scientific analysis devivify the vitality of factical life by isolating a particular region of it. This objectification drains factical life of its vitality (*G* 58:77–78).

But what of that ground of experience? If it is not originally given through scientific means, then how is it experienced? Heidegger wants to retrieve the factical experience of life from which the scientific means of theoretical analysis are initially generated. Three specific problems immediately arise: First, how does the initial experience of factical life happen? In other words, how is the original ground of experience to be won? To use a concrete example: How does the botanist first encounter the plant, or the art historian the painting, or the theologian her religion, before making theoretical determinations about the plant, the painting, or religion? Second, how is that ground going to be interpreted? That is, how is it even understood? Third, how can that ground of experience be brought to expression, especially insofar as simply putting something into words has the tendency to objectify it.

According to Heidegger, having a sense of factical life allows the phenomenologist to develop a way of doing philosophy that participates in life-experience without objectifying it. Paradoxically, Heidegger is trying to fashion a kind of nonobjectifying objectivity: taking factical life as his object without taking the vitality out of it through scientific, theoretical objectification. The first step along that way is Heidegger's response to the first problem. He explains here that factical experience is already there in life. Thus, it is not given but always already pregiven (*vorgegeben*) (*G* 58:70–71). Experience is not simply *available* to the self, as though the self could choose to experience life or not. The self is experience. Factical life is the concrete ground of experience, which, as a precursor to Dasein, Heidegger says, "'is there,' which means that factical life does not first notice Dasein, but rather that it is and lives experientially in a world" (*G* 58:66).

To describe that experience, Heidegger makes reference to Stephan George's poem "The Tapestry of Life." Factical life is an experience of the multiplicity of life, almost in a Jamesian sense of "blooming, buzzing confusion," except that for Heidegger, life's variety, its multiplicity, is already charged with certain directions of experience and concrete motivations: "at one point coming from this life-world, and at another from that one, intertwined, shaken up, overgrown" (*G* 58:68). Factical life, he says, is "speckled"; it is the experience of life in its myriad directions and motivations. In phenomenological terms, this means that factical life is experienced from out of the different life-worlds (the self-world, the with-world, the surrounding-world). According to Heidegger, science actually cannot access these life-worlds (*G* 58:77). Trapped within the logical laws governing systematic thinking, science never encounters those directions of life manifest in the different life-worlds. Only a phenomenological interpretation of factical life can draw them out.

With relation to his response to the first problem, Heidegger addresses the second by explaining that the directions and motivations of factical life manifest in the life-worlds are, at a very basic level, grasped. We can "take-notice" of it. One does not have knowledge of factical life; it is not known, especially not in an epistemological or strictly theoretical sense. But this is not to say that it does not have meaning. Indeed, factical life-experience, in all its multiplicity, variety, and diversity, although not grasped in a theoretical way, is, nonetheless, meaningful, and it can be understood in its meaningfulness. Heidegger writes,

> One must thereby think away all theorizing, and not consult what the epistemologist says about it, but rather see the sense in which factical experience has that which it experiences afresh and always in the character of meaningfulness. Even that which is the most trivial is meaningful, precisely as trivial; even the most worthless thing is meaningful. (*G* 58:104)

Factical life is meaningful simply insofar as it is experienced. Indeed, experience is meaningful, and as such understandable. Heidegger uses the word *Kenntnisnahme* to describe how factical life is grasped. *Kenntnisnahme* involves taking-notice of something. In Heidegger's use of the term, it means taking-notice of the meaningfulness of life. Any claims to validity are rendered impossible by *Kenntnisnahme* because it is a grasping of meaning, and meaning is not subject to epistemological objectification. One does not *know* what is meaningful, rather, one is *convinced* by it. Knowledge here is replaced by conviction (*Überzeugung*). Furthermore, the meaningful dimensions of life are not to be taken in isolation. They are interwoven with one another and form a context. Factical life is this context of meaningfulness.

Adding further support to the basic taking-notice of factical life, Heidegger addresses the third problem outlined above when he says that this context of meaningfulness can be related (*Erzählen*). The factical experience of life can come to expression through discussion about those experiences.

> I can "relate" what I experience, namely, in the general features of factical life. People engage in discussion about some common life-experience and mutually *relate* everything to each other once again. People do not give lectures to each other, and it is, totally apart from the what-character of objectivity, completely different than if I were to describe, in zoology, exactly what I see in the microscope. (*G* 58:111)

Interestingly, there is a footnote here saying that an example of this kind of factical discussion appears in *Antigone* when the messenger relates Antigone's heinous crime. Heidegger does not pursue the possibility of factical speaking any further here, but he has opened the door for inquiry into a kind of speaking that relates the meaningfulness of factical life. Hence, what is important about the spoken expression is its meaning, indeed, *its everyday, factical meaning*. This stands in stark contrast to scientific concepts whose function is not to tell the story of something that happens over time, that is, to relate factical meaningfulness, but to structure things in a static order (*G* 58:143). In later chapters, I will follow Heidegger as he addresses this possibility in more detail.[12] For now, though, suffice it to say that factical life (1) is pregiven (2) in a kind of everyday meaningfulness that is understandable insofar as we take-notice of it and (3) that can be brought to expression when we relate life's meaningfulness in a nonobjective way.

In all of this, perhaps it is difficult to acknowledge that the trivialities of everyday life are meaningful, much less the stuff of philosophical inquiry. It is important to see, however, that Heidegger is working under the shadow of neo-Kantianism here and trying to break out from that shadow by showing that what is experienced in life is not simply an idea structured according to the logical laws of thinking. Rather, what is experienced is meaningful, and, as such, it is real. Furthermore, that meaningful experience is the original encounter of the self and of life-experience, which the self is. As original, that encounter is the self's experience of itself. Again, Heidegger is investigating factical life as emerging from an origin. In that sense, his interpretations here are preliminary ones. Factical life is not the origin; it is an original experience that makes the origin accessible. But what is that origin? To be sure, Heidegger does not explicitly answer that question here. What he does say, however, is that insofar as factical life does emerge from an origin, it will be described *as* emerging from that origin. It is not simply the content of factical life that is at issue here, its what-characters, but rather its emerging characters, its flux and, moreover, its *meaningful* flux in the everydayness of life. In contrast to Bergson, Heidegger says that "life does not just dumbly flow by" (*das Leben fließt nie wie ein Strom dumpf dahin*); nor is factical life "inaccessible to the concept," as the neo-Kantians have claimed. They relegate factical life to the level of irrationality, which is simply the counterpoise to their own sense of rationalism. Factical life is neither rational nor irrational. It is, let us say, prerational and pretheoretical, but, nevertheless, both meaningful and graspable.

Hence, the everydayness of factical life, insofar as it is an original experience of life's meaningfulness, has a positive sense: both as access to the origin and as a direct challenge to the static, theoretical determinations of science, especially neo-Kantianism. There are numerous passages in this lecture course in which Heidegger describes the positive sense of everydayness. Allow me to choose one as being paradigmatic:

> When I see an acquaintance sending me greetings and in factical seeing warmly return his greeting, I saw him greeting; I did not at all see the movement of a material body in objective space, which I interpret as a sign for greeting and thereby conclude: now I must also perform a movement, which is the cause for the other to perceive these special movements and interpret them as *my* greeting; rather, I see him greeting. And the existence of my acquaintance is his particular meaningfulness for me in this situation. If I am in doubt, I do not ask my companion, "Was that arm movement over there real?" rather I ask, "Did that man send a greeting or not?" Or if I jokingly inquire of my acquaintance, "Does he still exist?" and someone answers me, "Yes, I sat down with him the other day in Café Schanz" or: "Today he is having an important book published." Experiencing what is said, I experience his existence, not in such a way that I grasp and, hence, conclude: All right, he really is in space and time, just like Mars or the Feldberg, rather the *experience of existence* terminates in and suffices for the *characteristic of meaningfulness*. (*G* 58:105)

Both trivial and everyday, these examples typify what Heidegger means by factical life, and it holds vital significance for his unique approach to philosophy. Indeed, what we see here is undeniably *a positive understanding of everyday experience*: "What do I experience? Trivialities, the quotidian (*Alltäglichkeiten*)—but that should not concern us. We could also experience important matters. Above all, what I experience really exists" (*G* 58:103). Factical experiences, pregiven in everyday life, are the life that we live. They constitute the ground to which philosophy must return and for which it needs to recover the appropriate language. This is the case for various reasons.

Initially, this factical experience of meaningfulness explains what Heidegger means by the pretheoretical. Again, all the determinations of a particular science—its logic, its strictness, its evidence—spring from an initial, factical encounter with the world of experience (*Erfahrungswelt*). Furthermore, it is the height of presumption for one science to criticize another science from within the parameters of its own content-region (*Sachgebiet*), as when a physicist, based on the determination of objectivity that his or her own science has developed, challenges the "authenticity" of the botanist's determination of objectivity (*G* 58:93–94). What is "authentic" for one science is determined by the methodology of that science and cannot be applied with justification to another science. Hence, Heidegger is showing here that both sciences, botany and physics, indeed all sciences, develop "out of factical situations, which we ourselves are and live" (*G* 58:95). As such, those factical situations are pretheoretical. They precede science.[13]

Furthermore, by establishing factical life as a kind of absolute ground for all the sciences, Heidegger is trying to liberate philosophical thinking (*G* 58:228). Indeed, he explains that this has been the aim of the entire lecture course. Consequently, we can look at factical experience and its average, everyday meaningfulness as an integral dimension of that project. Engagement with the pretheoretical realm of factical life is meant to free philosophy from the strictures placed upon it by science. As a response to Natorp and the Marburg school, factical life will liberate phenomenology from the strict rules of thought that order all experience and prevent any real encounter with the world. The advantage of phenomenology was its ability to concretize abstract problems. By rejecting worldviews as well as all philosophical constructions that buried life-experience beneath principles and axioms, phenomenology penetrated this kind of philosophical overlay down to "the things themselves" (*G* 58:25–26). With regard to life itself, phenomenology makes the experience of life concrete by investigating its motivations and directions. More specifically, phenomenology investigates the particular directions of the self-world, the with-world, and the surrounding-world into which and within which life is moving at any moment. Hence, these life-worlds and the movements of life that are manifest within those life-worlds represent, for Heidegger, philosophical thinking's freedom from scientific objectivity.

Intensification of the Self-World

Having discussed both science's devivification of the life-world and the meaningfulness of factical life, I now turn to the layeredness of the life-worlds[14] within the self-world. The freedom of philosophical thinking requires that those life-worlds be drawn out from the self-world. When Heidegger says that life, *factical* life, is centered on the self-world, he is trying to gain access to the *origin* of factical life. There is something deeper than factical life that he is trying to discover, and going through the laws of thought will not get him there. Factical life is here not the origin, but rather that original experience that makes an understanding of the origin possible. Looking at this closely, we saw that an understanding of factical life demands that no specific area of life be examined. The aim of phenomenology as the original science of life is to grasp the full meaningfulness of factical life in its originality and in its totality.[15]

In all of these interpretations, Heidegger has emphasized that factical life is the self's experience of its own meaningfulness. Hence, the life-worlds that are manifest in factical life are, as such, manifestations of the self-world. There is, Heidegger says, a peculiar "intensification" (*Zugespitztheit*) of the life-worlds in the self-world. The life-worlds are layers of manifestation (*Bekundungsschichten*) within the self-world, and it is the task of phenomenology to draw those life-worlds out from the self. The question that immediately presents itself is this one: In what sense is factical life actually an experience of reality, as Heidegger has insisted time and again throughout this lecture course, if the life-worlds are layers of manifestation within the self-world? Is this not simply a modification of the neo-Kantian position that all experience is structured by the laws that govern thinking, placed into the phenomenological language of the life-worlds?

To answer this question, we must first take a look at why the life-worlds are centered in the self-world. Heidegger says, interestingly, that this peculiar intensification of factical life in the self-world was accomplished by early Christianity.

> The deepest historical paradigm for the peculiar process whereby the main focus of factical life and the life-world shifted into the self-world and the world of inner experience gives itself to us in the emergence of Christianity. The self-world as such comes into life and is lived as such. (*G* 58:61)

Specifically, the importance of "asceticism" and a "denial of worldly goods" (*Weltverneinung*) for the early Christian communities made for new contexts of life-experience that were concentrated on the self. Subsequently, these new contexts led to the modern concept of history (*G* 58:61). A more complete analysis by Heidegger of the importance of the historical does not happen until the next semester (winter semester, 1920–21), which I will come to in the next chapter. Heidegger does say here, though, that the onset of history is tightly bound with this newfound concentration on the self-world. Moreover, both of these developments, the inception of the historical and the concentration of the life-worlds into the self-world, have become intertwined throughout the subsequent history of philosophy with the ancient philosophers, especially Aristotle, and it is the task of phenomenology to untangle them (*G* 58:61).

In carrying out that task, phenomenology must recognize two things: first that the life-worlds are, indeed, centered in the self-world (since the experience of life has the tendency to cover this up), and second, that the life-worlds then need to be drawn out of the self-world. The latter is particularly important because, Heidegger says, the defining trait of the self-world is self-sufficiency (*Selbstgenügsamkeit*). Self-sufficiency will become the defining trait of ruinance in *Phenomenological Interpretations of Aristotle: Initiation into Phenomenological Research* (*G* 61).[16] Here it means that factical life searches for quietude, for it considers quietude to be the fulfillment of itself. Hence, the directions and motivations of the different life-worlds need to be awakened from that quietude. This will be difficult because, as part of its self-sufficiency, "Life speaks to itself in its own language" (*G* 58:231). This twofold process of realizing that the life-worlds are centered in the self-world and then drawing the life-worlds out of the self-world is not in any way linear. One does not simply go through the life-worlds to the self-world and then back to the life-worlds, having then arrived at some fixed point.

In what is almost a poetic description of how this process happens, Heidegger says that there is a rhythmic echoing between the self-world and the life-world: There is "in the life-world an echo of the rhythm of each one" (*G* 58:59). Pursuing this theme he says,

> In the description of the self-life, the life-world manifests itself at the same time, along with its specific rhythm, originating from the self and sketched from there, and vice versa. (*G* 58:59)

The specific example he uses here is biography. Research into the life of a particular person must take account of the life-worlds immanent within that life. In this way, the life-worlds themselves are seen to have a direct and immediate relation to the individual people who live them. Perhaps this is not a particularly startling discovery, for what biographer would not take account of the situations surrounding the life he or she is giving an account of. However, by emphasizing the reciprocity between the self-world and the life-worlds and by explaining that each world implicates the others, Heidegger has established factical life as a ground of experience that constantly renews itself. The self-world always refers to the life-worlds and the life-worlds back to the self-world. Even if there is an intensification of experience in the self-world, the reciprocity of this "rhythmic echoing" between and among the life-worlds is clearly very different from the neo-Kantian position that states that experience is structured by the laws that govern thought.

When we recall that Heidegger is trying to describe factical life as emerging from an origin, we recognize that that origin is what allows for factical life's rhythmic echoing. How so? None of the life-worlds is complete. Because of that incompleteness, each one constantly refers to the others. A person's relation to herself is based on her relations with other people. Her relations to other people depend on how she understands herself. Therefore, the origin of these factical relations is such that it holds something back from each one. The origin is thus always incomplete, and this incompleteness pulls each life-world into the others. This is the movement of time. To understand factical life as emerging from an origin means to understand it as temporal and, therefore, as constantly renewing itself. Heidegger does not say explicitly what that origin is, but he does give an account of it by saying that when phenomenology, the original science of life, investigates factical life, it is, as such, encountering a ground of experience that remains in continual renewal because it is emerging from an origin that is constantly offering new possibilities for the experience of life's meaningfulness. Because of this origin, phenomenology and its investigation of the life-worlds can never be complete. In this regard, Heidegger writes,

> Perhaps the original region has not yet been given to us—but when phenomenology is further along? Not even then—and never. Yes, if it were absolutely complete, it would still be totally hidden from the actual streaming life in itself. (G 58:27)

The originality of factical life is its incompleteness. The importance of constant renewal emerges in the critique of Jaspers, as well, where Heidegger says that the interpretation of hermeneutic concepts must begin constantly anew: "The essential characteristic of the *explicata* involved here is found in the fact that they are *hermeneutical* concepts, to which we have access only in a constant renewal of interpretation that constantly begins anew" (G 9:32/27). A complete system, or science, misses the radical incompleteness of that which it studies. The origin of factical life is thus hidden from science. The original region can be grasped only *through* factical life and from within it. What we know about this original region is that it makes the streaming of life possible: It breathes vitality into factical life by bringing the incompleteness of factical life into view.[17]

In another context, but with explicit reference to life's rhythm, Heidegger says that the self is not an objective "I." The self is, rather, a process of continually winning and losing a certain familiarity with life (G 58:258). From this perspective, it is clear that science devivifies factical life insofar as it constructs systems and other theoretical means, which, in the first place, boast completion, and, in the second, do so by founding those systems on an objective "I," an ego or cogito. These theoretical approaches to life do not grasp life factically, in its *origin*ality. Only phenomenology is able to do that by attending to the streaming character of factical life in its pretheoretical meaningfulness.

Toward the very end of this course, Heidegger says that there are three characteristics to factical life: self-sufficiency, expression, and meaningfulness. I have dealt with each of these traits and thus provided a sense of what Heidegger means by factical life in the winter semester of 1919–20. However, there is one question still outstanding. Heidegger has made clear his contention that science cannot adequately grasp factical life. That being the case, in what sense is phenomenology a science? Heidegger addresses this issue by saying that phenomenology does not have the exactness of the natural sciences or mathematics. The exactness of those sciences is founded on logic, which requires that a particular region within factical life be isolated. Phenomenology, in contradistinction to the particular sciences, is *original* science and, as such, *not a science at all*. Since it grasps the totality of factical life, phenomenology is not science but philosophy (G 58:258). Moreover, to say that phenomenology lacks scientific or mathematical clarity does not mean that it is mysticism, for original science is not in any way arbitrary (G 58:137). Indeed, science and mathematics do not set the standard for strictness. Phenomenology is strict, just not in a scientific or mathematical sense. Its strictness "means concentration on the genuineness of the relations of life in concrete life itself" (G 58:231).

The lecture courses that I have analyzed in this chapter are the first real statements of those concepts that will develop, eventually, into Heidegger's mature thought. The first of these courses, G 56/57, *Toward the Definition of Philosophy*, commenced less than three months after Heidegger was discharged from military service in November 1918. At this point, the young professor, only thirty years old, is keenly interested in questions about the meaningfulness of life. He had met Husserl in 1916, and what we see in these courses is a concerted attempt to show how phenomenology can apprehend the factical experience of life in all its richness and vivacity. But it is not just brute life that the young Heidegger is investigating in these early courses. He sees something deeper in factical life, its origin. These courses are filled with vivid examples of trivial, everyday life, which he uses as instances of meaningful, philosophical experience. Phenomenology needs to focus on these experiences and draw out their vitality. As such, it is not an ordinary science because it does not attempt to objectify its subject matter.

In *Toward the Definition of Philosophy* (G 56/57), Heidegger affirms the primordiality of lived experience over theory. *Basic Problems of Phenomenology* (G 58, from the winter semester, 1919–20) continues this analysis, conveying Heidegger's first extended treatment of factical life. In both courses Heidegger establishes the vitality of lived experience and factical life as the ground for theory and all of the sciences. Theory and science, he claims, devivify life. Phenomenology, by retrieving this ground of original experience, can revitalize scientific research. A number of important themes emerge here: the meaningfulness of life, the concrete reality of factical life-experience, the pretheoretical and prerational characters of factical life, the rhythmic echoing between life and world, the different life-worlds, and the issue of history. Perhaps most important, though, Heidegger's research into factical life as the ground of theory and science has led him to probe the original vitality of factical life or, we might say, the origin of factical life's vitality and the intensity of life experience. This questioning into the origin of factical life reveals the crucial issue of the temporal-historical structure of life.

2

Christian Facticity

For Christian life there is no security; constant insecurity is also the characteristic for the basic meanings of factical life. Insecurity is not incidental, but necessary.
—**Martin Heidegger,** *The Phenomenology of Religious Life*

We are trying to understand concerned Dasein out of our own experience of life.
—**Martin Heidegger,** *The Phenomenology of Religious Life*

In the last chapter we saw that because factical life emerges from an origin, it remains in constant renewal. This renewal of factical life is such that phenomenology, the original science of life, would always experience its vitality in myriad ways. Heidegger refers to this as the tapestry of life, and science can restore that sense of vitality to its own research through an encounter with the factical richness of that tapestry, which, with reference to the scientific world, Heidegger called the pretheoretical. In his lecture courses on the phenomenology of religion, Heidegger is still investigating factical life, but we see now that facticity is not just a prescientific experience. Hence, to say that factical life is pretheoretical should not suggest that it can only then become scientific. Inasmuch as one can ground science in factical life, the richness of facticity is such that its vitality is bestowed on all the academic disciplines as well as on all modes of life. This includes theology and religious life.[1]

The majority of this chapter focuses on Heidegger's readings of Paul and the methodological considerations that precede them. As such, I limit most of my analysis to section 1 of *The Phenomenology of Religious Life* (G 60). Section 1 is titled *Introduction to the Phenomenology of Religion* (winter semester, 1920–21). In the next semester (section 2 of *G* 60) Heidegger held a lecture course on Augustine's *Confessions*, titled *Augustine and Neo-Platonism*, which briefly, though in no unimportant way, addresses the problem of facticity. I address that later text toward the end of this chapter.[2]

This chapter contains four sections. The first section takes up Heidegger's method of formal indication. My main concern in this chapter is with how the early Christians lived factically. For Heidegger, to live factically means to have an acute awareness of the historicality of life and, therein, a sense of coming closer to life and, thus, closer to Being. By making a formal indication of factical life, Heidegger can maintain the temporal vitality of the historical. The second section looks at the facticity of the Pauline situation. I emphasize the way in which Heidegger captures the temporal nature of Paul's relationship with his people. Section 3 takes up the structures of early Christian facticity that Heidegger discerns in Paul's letters: knowledge, παρουσία (the second coming of Christ), and faith. These structures indicate the way in which the early Christians lived temporality. The fourth and final section addresses the notion of hardship (*molestia*) in the lecture course on *Augustine and Neo-Platonism*. As with the structures of early Christian facticity, Augustinian hardship is an indication of the temporal experience of history. In all of his analyses of religion at this time, Heidegger is trying to recapture the temporal, historical facticity of religious experience.

The Factical History of Human Dasein

In an extended methodological consideration about how to approach religious phenomena, taking up the first half of this lecture course,[3] Heidegger describes certain philosophical positions that fight against the historical (*das Historische*). They are (1) the Platonic approach, which is a renunciation of history; (2) the exact opposite of this, namely, an unqualified acknowledgment of the process of history and its formative determinations (Spengler, also pragmatism); and (3) a compromise between the two whereby absolute truths are immanent within historically contingent values (*Werte*) (Dilthey, Simmel, Rickert). Plato's Theory of Ideas, perhaps the most well known example of the three, dismisses history by relegating historical contingency to mere appearance. The latter two examples, perhaps less well known, are both based on epistemological theories that objectify history. Even the second example, although it is the opposite of the Platonic position, is actually Platonic in orientation because it maintains that even though the human being is the product of nature and history, these are also at the human being's absolute disposal. In spite of their radically contingent formative powers, history and nature are still objects that can be manipulated. Insofar as they either objectify history or renounce it altogether, all of these approaches are motivated by the need to secure philosophy against the disturbance of history.[4]

Indeed, Heidegger remarks that none of these approaches acknowledges that history is disturbing. Not only that, they quell all concern about history by making concern into an objective historical reality. (The terms "concern" (*Bekümmerung*) and "disturbing character" (*Beunruhigung*) are taken in the same way here, and Heidegger uses them interchangeably.) As an alternative to all three of these approaches and, indeed, as an alternative to any attempt to objectify history and its intrinsic concern, Heidegger proposes that "we are trying to understand concerned Dasein out of our own experience of life" (*G* 60:52/35). This will require, of course, that the phenomenon of concern in factical life be brought to light, and this, Heidegger suggests, can be done negatively by determining what the three approaches to history just mentioned are fighting against. They are securing philosophy against the historical. More specifically, though, they are fighting against "human-historical reality" (*G* 60:53/36). Therefore, the phenomenon of concern will emerge once we engage the meaning of the historical and its concrete, explicit relation to the factical life of Dasein.

In trying to understand the historical facticity of human Dasein, we must make the right approach to it. The approach should be determined by that which is being approached (the factical-historical reality of human Dasein) and by how that approach is to be made (in such a way that what is being approached not be objectified). Heidegger calls this approach formal indication (*die formale Anzeige*). Formal indication is a radicalization of the Husserlian distinction between generalization and formalization. Both of these have a relation to the universal (*Allgemein*) and are, as such, theoretical determinations of objects. Generalization is a universalizing on the order of genus and species; it is a way of organizing bound to a particular content-region (*Sachgebiet*). As such, it must remain within that particular region. Formalization, on the other hand, is not so bound; it depends, rather, on the relational attitude (*Einstellungsbezug*). This relational attitude is neither an "ordering" nor a "region" (*G* 60:61/42). Heidegger's examples:

> generalization = red is a color; color is a sensual quality
> formalization = sensual quality is a being (*Wesen*); a being (*Wesen*) is an object.

Formalization marks a shift to "something in general" (*etwas überhaupt*). Heidegger attempts to ground both of these determinations in a more original sense of "formal," which has nothing whatsoever to do with the universal.[5]

Heidegger developed formal indication as a response to philosophy's theoretical determinations about what objects are. This method sought to hold phenomena open in their relational senses, recognizing that the relational sense is pretheoretical and that these pretheoretical, relational phenomena could easily become theoretical objects.[6] In this way, the phenomena would not be fully actualized and not tied to a particular *Sachgebiet*. Nor would they be put into an order. In a particular and concrete sense, formal indication is meant here as an approach to the historical. Indeed, Heidegger means to make a formal indication *of* the historical. As such, the historical will not be objectified: It is not simply "what happened in the past," a set of historical facts. Rather, the historical will be viewed in its temporality, so long as "temporal" remains wholly undetermined and not a constitutive character of consciousness. Rather, formal indication will try to interpret historicality from out of the factical experience of temporality.

> The problem of time must rather be understood as we originally experience temporality in factical experience—completely apart from all pure consciousness and all pure time. It is the other way around. We must rather ask: What is temporality originally in factical experience? What do past, present, and future mean in factical experience? Our way proceeds from factical experience, from which the sense of time will be won. In this way, the problem of the historical will be shown. (*G* 60:65/44–45)

From this passage it is clear that the formal indication of history designates the factical experience of temporality. Furthermore, this factical experience of temporality is the originality of the historical.

In this lecture course, after these brief analyses of formal indication, Heidegger abruptly breaks off his methodological considerations and delves into the biblical texts. The methodology that has been sketched here, though, will become pivotal as Heidegger proceeds to gain access to the New Testament by making formal indications of religious phenomena. In doing so, he retrieves the original, factical experience of temporality, which the early Christians *lived*. These experiences had previously been considered only insofar as they were *objective* historical realities.

The Facticity of the Pauline Situation

Heidegger's abrupt turn away from methodology was occasioned by some of his students complaining to the dean of the University of Freiburg that the course, *Introduction to the Phenomenology of Religion*, lacked theological content. If Heidegger was relatively unprepared suddenly to start making explicit interpretations of the biblical texts, his extensive treatment of methodology proves to have been justified once he proceeds to make a formal indication of the factical temporality of original Christian religiosity. By way of introduction to this section of the text, I will make two preliminary observations that place the present considerations into the context developed from what I said in the last chapter about science. The factical experience of life was meant to apply equally well to science, religion, or any of the humanities. There is a similar dynamic between this excursion into religious life and the previous analysis of science. At issue is how religious experience presents itself, how it can be understood, and how it can be explicated. In this course, this trio appears as showing (*Darstellung*), understanding (*Einfühlung*), and explication (*Explikation*) (*G* 60:89/62). As was the case with science, this method will not offer mathematical exactitude, but Heidegger points out that mathematical precision does not in any way guarantee that an understanding of the phenomena has been achieved (*G* 60:77/53). As such, the Pauline situation will be interpreted according to the factical directions of experience in Paul's self-, with-, and surrounding-worlds. Any systematic approach to Paul must be dismissed. As it was with science, Heidegger's approach is pretheoretical; he claims here that the early Christians actually *lived* in pretheoretical, predogmatic religious experience. Indeed, they *were* the pretheoretical insofar as they preceded the objectification of religious experience into theological dogma. Perhaps most important, they preceded the intertwining of religious dogma with the metaphysical system of ancient Greek philosophy. Hence, it is not so much a matter of grasping the temporality implicit within Pauline teachings but rather recognizing through Paul's letters how "Christian experience lives time itself" (*G* 60:82/57). Whereas the scientist must retrieve the sense of pretheoretical anticipation (*Vorgriff*) within objective theories, Heidegger wants to show how Paul and the early Christians actually lived in anticipation. For this reason, Paul's letters are especially enlightening.

With these considerations as pre-text, I turn now to Heidegger's analysis of the facticity of the Pauline situation. Heidegger starts with the self-world of Paul. In doing so, however, Paul is not being isolated, because it is not just his self-world as a solipsistic entity that is at stake here, but rather Paul's self-world in its relation to his with-world and his surrounding-world. In this sense, the communication (*Mitteilung*) between Paul and his congregation becomes critical. Heidegger's focus on the self-world of Paul is, in fact, an analysis of Paul's preaching (*Verkündigung*). Certainly, preaching is a dimension of Paul's self-world. It is Paul who preaches. At the same time, however, this dimension of Paul's self-world brings into view the factical immediacy of Paul's relation to his congregation and to his surrounding-world. Hence, the facticity of the Pauline situation, the directions of experience manifest in his self-, with-, and surrounding-worlds, is brought to light through an understanding of how he communicates with others (*G* 60:80/55–56).

If we start with the How of communication in Paul's letters, we are able to grasp the original conceptuality of his situation. This is the critical shift from an object-historical context to the full historical situation that emerges from the factical experience of life (G 60:90/63). Paul spoke to his congregation in concepts informed by the language of that situation. Therefore, we must try to understand Paul and his situation from within his own conceptuality and the factical situation that forms the ground for his conceptuality (G 60:89/62). To do otherwise would mean that external concepts, completely foreign to Paul's situation, would be used, and such concepts could make only objective determinations about that situation. They can look on at Paul's situation only in a detached and theoretical sort of way, instead of trying to understand that situation according to its own factically charged directions of experience, which is exactly what Heidegger is trying to do. In a way that, interestingly, is not hermeneutic, facticity here marks the attempt to understand Paul as Paul understood himself.[7] Communication makes this understanding possible by giving us access to Paul's more original conceptuality and the directions of experience that inform it.

Pursuing the original conceptuality of Paul's factical situation, Heidegger asks about how Paul stood in relation to his people: "How did he have them?" This is an important question because it directly addresses the problem of how factical immediacy is manifest in our relationships with others (G 60:93/65). Heidegger explains that Paul experienced himself in his people. Note that Heidegger does not in any way suggest that Paul's experience of himself in others is inauthentic or dominated by the publicness of the "they." On the contrary, Paul's relationship with his people is grounded in a shared factical experience of temporality. This is manifest on two levels. First, Paul experiences that his people are as having-become (*Er erfährt ihr Gewordensein*); second, "he experiences that they know (*ein Wissen haben*) that they are as having-become. This means that their Being-as-having-become is also Paul's Being-as-having-become" (G 60:93/65). What binds Paul together with his people is the temporal meaning of having-become a Christian. Indeed, Paul's own experience of conversion (changing before God, turning to God, in short, *becoming*) is intimately and irrevocably bound with that of his people.

Furthermore, it is clear that Being-as-having-become involves no ordinary sense of time.[8] It is, rather, factical temporality insofar as the experience of having-become is there in the present and the experience of the present is there in having-become. Both current Being (*jetziges Sein*) and Being-as-having-become (*Gewordensein*) are experienced together in life (G 60:94/66). Adding the element of the future, Heidegger says that the facticity of Paul's situation, in that it involves changing before God, is also a matter of awaiting (*Erharren*) God's coming again. With these temporal determinations, we can conclude that facticity is an experience of current Being, the present, within which having-become and awaiting are also experienced. This factical temporality binds Paul together with his people. These two experiences, factical temporality and the immediacy of Paul's experience of himself in his people, prepare the ground for a description of the structures of Christian facticity. In the following, I look at knowledge (which is based on acceptance), the second coming or παρουσία (especially the question of when it will happen), and, most important, faith and hope. These structures need to be understood from within the facticity of Paul's situation. They are informed by the facticity of the Christian experience of life.

The Structures of Christian Facticity

Knowledge: I noted above Heidegger's claim that Paul knew that his people had become, that they had changed before God. This knowledge that he had is not to be taken in an epistemological or theoretical sense. But if that is the case, then in what sense did Paul know? We know that the early Christians lived within the pretheoretical. As such, Heidegger claims that knowledge (*Wissen*) and facticity were originally experienced together (*G* 60:94/66). Therefore, there is very little theoretical dogma in what Paul writes in his letters. Dogma and theological concepts spring from the full actualization of the Christian experience of life; and as I just noted, that experience is grounded in factical temporality. The knowledge that Paul has, insofar as it is grounded in factical temporality, comes from a context of becoming (*Werdenszusammenhang*) and, therefore, from whether or not his people accept God and accept that God will return. The facticity of knowledge does not depend on epistemological truths that can be scientifically or logically proven, but rather on the notion of acceptance (*Annehmen*). Paul *knows* that his people have become only if they *accept* what he says to them about God and take it up in their own ways of life.

With reference to Paul's first letter to the Thessalonians, particularly 1 Thessalonians 1:6, Heidegger describes acceptance as a context of activity (*Wirkungszusammenhang*) with God. This context is based on the word of God (λόγον θεοῦ), which, Heidegger says, should be taken in the sense of both the subjective and objective genitive (*G* 60:94/66). The Thessalonians accept the word of God and then, by accepting, submit to a context of activity with God. This context of activity is the How of factical life, the different ways in which they carry themselves (*Sich-Verhalten*) within that relationship. Factical life is the experience, both temporal and meaningful, of this context of activity.[9]

Παρουσία: One critical dimension of that active context is the experience of urgency (*Not*) that Paul impresses upon the Thessalonians in his letters. That urgency is motivated by the proclamation that God will return and that Satan, the Antichrist, will precede Him. This is the second coming (παρουσία), which, notably, is the Greek word for presence. To accept the word of God (in both the subjective and objective genitive senses) means not only to accept the fact that He will return, but also to accept the urgency that accompanies the realization that that return is imminent. Here, again, Paul's self-world is inextricably bound to the relationship he has with his people: "His life hangs between God and his calling" (*G* 60:100/70). The urgency that Paul wants them to recognize communicates his own experience of distress and torment (*Bedrängnis*). This torment disturbs him so much that it interrupts his work. Of course, as it interrupts him, it also informs what he is writing. Torment, even though it reveals Paul's weakness, is inextricably part of who he is and what he is writing and communicating.[10] By holding himself in "absolute concern," he is able to take account of the "authentic How" of the Thessalonians (*G* 60:145/103). In this way, Paul communicates facticity; indeed, facticity is fully there in what he writes, and this language of the factical experience of life that Paul communicates is, Heidegger says, "not the polish and detachment of theory, but rather the turns and refractions of factical life in its afflictions" (*G* 60:145/103). This, he says, is the origin (*Ur-sprung*) of theology.

As such, Paul does not know when the second coming is going to happen. Indeed, not knowing when is the motivation for Paul's urgency. Again, knowledge is placed into the context of factical temporality. There is no precise "when" at all; the question of when is wholly insufficient. When asked when it will happen, Paul turns the question back on to those who asked it and says that those who are asking the question already have the answer. By answering in this way, Paul does not mean, of course, that the person who asks knows precisely when it will happen. Rather, his answer places the person into a critical moment (*Augenblick*) wherein he or she must make a decision (*Entscheidung*), indeed, a momentous decision upon which his or her own life depends. If, like Paul, they decide to accept the word of God, then they agree to live within that active context which opens them to the urgency of life and, most important, to a more original understanding of temporality, whereby they *are* as *having become* and as *awaiting*.[11] That active context relies on not knowing when. It is informed and dynamized by that lack of knowledge which, as we will see shortly, is a profound negativity in their lives.[12]

Those who want to know exactly "when" the second coming is going to happen, on the other hand, are still working with an objective conception of time. They are searching for "peace and security" (G 60:103/72). Knowing when they need to be prepared is calming. Indeed, knowing when makes them complacent. I should note that, according to Paul, peace and security are certainly ways in which people can carry themselves within the context of activity that constitutes their relation to God. As such, peace and security are elements of factical life. There are two directions of factical life that Heidegger points out here. Once you have accepted the word of God and begun to live in a relationship with Him, then you have two choices: either to seek peace and security within that relationship or to experience the urgency of that relationship. Those who want to know exactly "when" the second coming will happen fall into the former group. Thus, it is not enough that one simply live factically. Factical experience can be that of peace and security or factical life can make an experience of urgency possible.

This brings up an important point. If there is nothing about factical life that causes one to become distressed, tormented, or disturbed (*beunruhigt*), then in order to achieve that sense of distress, one must recognize how factical life emerges from out of an origin. Distress comes not from life but from its origin. We see here a development in Heidegger's thinking of the dynamic that we encountered in the last chapter with regard to science. There we saw that the specific directions of factical life, on account of their incompleteness, form a ground of experience that is constantly renewing itself. Here we see that that incompleteness is actually an experience of nothingness. Once again, there are two ways to experience the nothingness of factical life. In the first case, there is the apocalyptic sense of nothingness, whereby everything is simply destroyed. Here, the nothingness is objectified: All things, all objects, are annihilated. There is another experience of nothingness in factical life, though, which is much more profound (G 60:108/77). Heidegger makes the observation that for Paul, either one was saved by accepting the word of God or one simply came to nothing. The different levels of hell were developed later in theological dogmatic. For Paul, damnation did not mean that you were cast into hell; it meant absolute nothingness (*absolutes Nichts*) (G 60:114/80).

The latter, recondite sense of nothingness is, Heidegger says, the "fully actualizing Not" (*das vollzugsmäßige Nicht*) (G 60:109/77). It is a critical dimension of the more urgent sense of factical life. I have already explained that acceptance of the word of God places the believer into a context of activity that constitutes one's relationship with God. Here, although

Heidegger's treatment of the nothingness is not extensive, he does explicitly say that the relationship with God depends on an experience of nothingness. Indeed, there is no relationship without the nothingness. Furthermore, Heidegger says that the nothingness must be understood from within a historical context. Drawing some conclusions, I can surmise, first of all, that this experience of the nothingness in factical life is what dynamizes its distress and insecurity. Also, this experience of nothingness seems to be the driving force behind formal indication. Heidegger says explicitly that to indicate something formally means to hold it in its relational sense. Here, the fully actualizing Not holds the believer in his or her relationship with God. What Heidegger has accomplished, then, is a formal indication of early Christian faith. *Faith is a living context of one's relationship with God, informed by urgency, which is grounded in nothingness.*

Faith: The determining character of early Christian faith was, in fact, insecurity, distress, torment. This is the dimension of faith that Heidegger is trying to draw from these texts. Faith demands acceptance of the word of God. Historically, the early Christians developed out of that acceptance. Their history as Christians begins with that acceptance. The word of God that they accepted, however—and the word or proclamation (*Verkündigung*) was Jesus, himself—was not simply a fact. It was not a memory they carried with them: At such and such a time, they accepted the word of God. Rather, their acceptance was an experience that they lived perpetually. Heidegger explains here that "it is essential that the word (*Verkündigung*) always remains there with you in a vital (*lebendig*) way" (*G* 60:117/84). Faith is a vital experience of one's relationship with God. As such, the experience of the nothingness and its urgency is critical to keeping the word of God vital and alive within one's faith. This was how the early Christians lived their faith, and it is closely tied to the experience of factical life. Heidegger says in this regard:

> For Christian life there is no security; constant insecurity is also the characteristic for the basic meanings of factical life. Insecurity is not incidental, but necessary. (*G* 60:105/73)

An important dimension of that vital experience is that one's relationship with God is not in any way a relationship with an object. Heidegger wants to restore insecurity and urgency to Christianity by placing the problem of eschatology in the center of Christian life. This problem, he says, whose basic direction came from late Judaism (specifically, Esra), was lost even by the end of the first century, and then, with the infusion of Plato and Aristotle into Christianity, the eschatological problem was completely concealed. As a consequence, "The apex of confusion has been reached today by projecting the concept of validity into God" (*G* 60:104/73). When God is made to hold reason, rationality, and validity firmly in place, then God has become merely an object for theoretical speculation, and this objectification of God amounts to "falling away [*Abfall*] from authentic understanding" (*G* 60:97/67). This was the very problem that Luther was fighting against, and it explains why Luther hated Aristotle (*G* 60:97/67).

An objectified God, the God of validity and theoretical speculation, quells the urgency that is a vital experience of Christian facticity. Faith is the experience of absolute concern, which Heidegger, at one point, calls *existentielle* concern (*G* 60:144/102). Faith means to accept the word of God and live as the early Christians lived, namely, "authentically to live temporality," "preserving concern," which is an "authentic appropriation of the factical experience of life" (*G* 60:137/97). This is certainly the way that Paul lived his own faith, and it is the faith that he communicated to his people. In that communication, he did not in any way show his people proofs that the word of God was true. Faith is not theoretical knowledge, but knowledge of disquiet (*Wissen der Unruhe*). With this knowledge, one can know that God is eternal, but knowledge of God's eternity is disquieting. Christians do not yet rest in God, as Augustine has pointed out. They do not simply have faith in the fact that they will not die. Rather, they experience God's eternity factically: hoping, because of Him, that they *are* as *having become* as they *await* His return. This is the knowledge that the early Christians had and which Paul was trying to awaken within them.[13] It was, and is, a knowledge of hope, a knowledge of how to live, a knowledge of awaiting (*Erharren*), which Heidegger calls, "an essential determination of the How of factical life" (*G* 60:149/106).

The Facticity of Augustinian Hardship

In the final hour of his course *Augustine and Neo-Platonism* (summer semester, 1921), Heidegger affirms that "life" is a basic phenomenon with which philosophy has not yet been able to come to terms (*G* 60:298/226).[14] To be sure, Augustine had advanced our understanding of life by recognizing that whatever certainty we can have about the self must be placed into the context of factical life, which submits all self-certainty to the uncertainty of history. Facticity here indicates that the self is *there* in the world in a historical way (*G* 60:252/189). What Augustine accomplished, however, has since been covered over by Descartes, who unburdened the cogito of its factical foundations and thus placed the self into an ahistorical framework. We can read Heidegger's interpretations of Augustine as an attempt to probe the factical, pre-Cartesian, historical foundations of the self.

This is not to say, however, that Augustine was explicitly concerned with the problem of the historical. For Augustine, the self was not, as such, an experience of the historical, but rather an experience of hardship (*molestia*). Looking at this more closely, we see that *molestia* is an intensification of the self, which happens in two ways: "the more life lives" and "the more life comes to itself" (*G* 60:242–43/182). The first intensification is a determination of the directions of experience (*Erfahrungsrichtungen*) that are there within life: As life lives, indeed, the more life lives, the more intense its directions of experience (the self-world, with-world, and surrounding-world) become; in Heidegger's words, those directions of experience become fully actualized (*vollzogen*). The second intensification is a determination of the Being of life. The more that life comes to itself, or tries to come to itself, the more its own Being becomes an issue for it. Heidegger affirms here that "more" is a "measure" only in the sense of the "Being of 'life'" (*G* 60:243/182). It is not quantitative, but rather, in both cases, an indication of the intensification of life's hardship. As the directions of life become intensified, Being *becomes* more acutely an issue for life. Hence, the intensification of hardship reveals this sense of becoming, which is then seen to be grounded in life's temporal-historical constitution.

Insofar as life experiences the intensification of hardship, it *becomes*, and so it must be grounded in historicality. Moreover, it must be grounded in historical facticity (*G* 60:243/182). If we look at this in specific, concrete terms, then we see that the facticity of life is the care (*curare*) that it takes in its directions of experience. Life's care for the self, its care for others, and its care about its surrounding-world would all be examples of this. These cares are life's everyday activities (its forms of meaningfulness, its facticity) and are experienced, of course, in varying degrees. As they become intensified, that is, as life cares more intensely in its different directions of experience, it comes closer to itself and, thus, closer to its own Being. For through the intensification of these concrete cares (that is, through hardship), life's Being matters to it more and more. Heidegger adds another element here, endangering (*Gefährdung*). With the intensification of care, the hardship of life is increased, and as such, life is aware of its own endangerment. That endangerment does not come from any outside source, but from itself, indeed, from its own Being insofar as through the intensification of care and hardship, life's own Being matters to it more intensely. Being shows itself in hardship; and since hardship involves intensification, and intensification is historical (temporal, the "more" of becoming), Being shows itself in the historical.

Even though Heidegger maintains that the Being of life is revealed through the intensification of hardship, he is well aware of the possibility that this view may seem solipsistic. Preempting this charge, he says that what he is proposing here is not in any way "a hyper-reflective solipsism or the like"; rather, "The self 'is' the self of full historical facticity, the self in its world, with which and in which it lives" (*G* 60:254/191). This brings up two points. First, history and the self come together through facticity or, rather, through the full historical facticity of the self which *is*. In this sense, it is the Being of the self (the self insofar as it *is*) that makes it historical. The self can be ahistorical (Descartes), but the self in its original Being is the self in its full historical facticity.

Second, the question arises as to how this intensification of the self in its historicality is experienced. Since the self is historical insofar as it cares about its Being, then history relies on intensification, hardship, and endangerment. Once that happens, however, once the intensification of cares reveals care for Being, how is that awareness of Being in its historicality experienced? Heidegger says in this regard that expectation or anticipation is tantamount to that intensification. With intensification, the self moves closer to Being, but it *is not yet* there. Hence, there is an anticipation of the future. Moreover, there is a sense of becoming implicit with that intensification. This is a recognition of the past: becoming, having become, having been. Facticity, then, is the intensification of the present in the intensification of its everyday meaningfulness that makes possible an awareness of the self as both becoming (and, hence, having been) and as anticipating. In this way, the temporality of facticity comes into view.

Heidegger's religion courses span the years 1920–21. Even though Heidegger (and his wife) had split with the Catholic Church in December of 1918, he still considered himself a Christian as well as a Christian thinker. His now famous claim about still being a "Christian theo*logian*" comes from a letter he wrote to Karl Löwith on August 19, 1921. The whole context of the quote shows the extent to which Heidegger views factical life as the intensity of historical life-experience in a way that includes the intensity of Christian experience.

> I work concretely and factically out of my "I am"—out of my spiritual and thoroughly factic heritage, my milieu, my life contexts, and whatever is available to me from these, as the vital experience in which I live. This facticity, as existentiell, is no mere "blind existence"—this Dasein is one with existence, which means that I live it, this "I must" of which no one speaks. The act of existing seethes with this *facticity of Being-thus*, it surges with the historical just as it is—which means that I live the inner obligations of my facticity, and do so as radically

as I understand them. This facticity of mine includes—briefly put—the fact that I am a "Christian theo*logian*." This implies a certain radical self-concern, a certain radical scientificity, a rigorous objectivity *in* this *facticity*; it includes the historical consciousness, the consciousness of the "history of spirit."[15]

Factical life means *living temporality*, experiencing its urgency so that the concrete directions of life in the with-, self-, and surrounding-worlds manifest that sense of urgency. For Heidegger, this is exactly what the early Christians experienced. In this chapter, I have tried to describe the context of activity of the early Christians and to explicate some of the concepts that emerge from the urgency of Paul's factical situation. Heidegger was trying to develop a new approach to conceptuality by indicating concepts formally, grasping them from within the temporality of the factical situation to which they belong. There were two ways to experience factical life, one that quelled its sense of urgency and one that heightened it. It is the latter experience of factical life that Heidegger wants to recover from Paul's relationship with his people by placing eschatology and its profound sense of negativity into the center of factical Christian experience.

Later on, in Chapter 5, I examine how Heidegger had intended to bring together the traditions of theology and philosophy by grounding them both in the more original experience of the facticity of life, from which both disciplines draw their concepts. In a sense, Heidegger has to mediate between Luther and Aristotle. Luther hated Aristotle because the infusion of Aristotelian concepts into theology caused God to be made into an object for theoretical inquiry. It buried the factical experience of life beneath theological dogma, which had been informed by the theoretical understanding of Aristotle. Heidegger sees himself as a kind of philosophical Luther, freeing philosophy from the systematic view of Aristotle as Luther had attempted to free religion from the system of theology. First, though, I will look directly at *Phenomenological Interpretations of Aristotle: Initiation into Phenomenological Research* (G 61). Heidegger's analysis of factical life in this text is more sustained and in-depth than in any of his early lecture courses.

PART 11

Factical Life (1921–22)

3

Grasping Life as a Topic

"Retrieval": on its sense hangs everything. Philosophy is a basic How of life itself, so that in each case it authentically re-trieves life, taking it back from decline, and this taking-back, as radical research, is life.

—Martin Heidegger, *Phenomenological Interpretations of Aristotle: Initiation into Phenomenological Research*

It is clear that for Heidegger, philosophy is a way to live your life so that it can be retrieved from its tendency toward decline. As he says, philosophy is a How of life, which is constantly taking life back—indeed, taking itself back—from decline. In the lecture course *Phenomenological Interpretations of Aristotle: Initiation into Phenomenological Research* (*G* 61), which Heidegger delivered in the winter semester of 1921–22,[1] the third and final section undertakes an extended investigation of the problem of factical life; so in this chapter and the next I provide a thoroughgoing analysis of this particular section in the hopes of acquiring a more complete understanding of this complex, yet philosophically rich, concept.[2]

To reiterate, the aim of my analysis is to discern the significance of factical life for the early Heidegger. More explicitly, I am trying to determine the way in which factical life is an experience of life that bears philosophical merit in itself. In other words, I am trying to determine the points of connection between life and philosophy in order to discern those interpretative nexuses where life and philosophy implicate each other. How and where do life and philosophy meet? In the appendix of the course, Heidegger says that he is trying "to bring the bindingness [*Verbindlichkeiten*] in the object of philosophy to life" (*G* 61:169/127). There are vital, living possibilities within philosophy that are drawn from the factical experience of life. Life is, thus, a well of vitality that can rejuvenate philosophy. As such, the concrete, factical experience of life carries within it the possibility of a radical recasting of philosophical interpretations.

We have seen already how Heidegger reinterpreted the study of science (Chapter 1) and religion (Chapter 2) in terms of factical life. In this lecture course, *G* 61, he calls facticity "the main point of philosophy" (*G* 61:99/74). There are a number of important shifts taking place in this lecture course. First, Heidegger focuses on life itself. Instead of explaining how science or religion needs to be interpreted in terms of factical life, he investigates life directly. Clearly, he sees philosophical possibilities within the phenomenon of life. Second, those possibilities are opened up by the expression "life." I take up the theme of life in this chapter in four sections. In the first section, I make a critical distinction between Heidegger's approach to life and traditional approaches to the same topic. The traditional approaches have made the term objectively ambiguous, rendering it impossible to understand. For Heidegger, there is a factical ambiguity (as opposed to an objective ambiguity) to life that he is actually trying to retain. In making this distinction, I hope to demonstrate some of the differences between systematic philosophy and historical philosophy in order to argue that a philosophy of life must take account of the historical (since life, itself, is temporal and, therefore, historical). In the second section, I explain how Heidegger makes a factical retrieval of the Being of life through Descartes. Both thinkers start with the notion of the "I am," but Descartes focuses on the "I" whereas Heidegger focuses on the "am." In this way, Heidegger can open up the temporal-historical dimension of life in ways that Descartes did not. In the third section, I look at the profound connection in phenomenology between what something is and the words that express what something is, that is, between *phenomenon* and *logos*. I show here how Heidegger's analysis of the expression "life" opens up the phenomenon of life and the relation between "life" and world. In the fourth and final section, I will begin to engage in a preliminary way some of the specific characteristics of factical life, namely, speaking, questionability, care, wanting, disquiet, and concern. As I will show, these are structures that emerge from the factical interpretation of life and which make possible a vital, living philosophizing.

The Ambiguity of Life

At the outset of Heidegger's investigation of factical life in section three of this lecture course, life is shown to be a *terminus technicus* that can be, and certainly has been, subjected to exhaustive philosophical analysis. Indeed, the expression "life" has been investigated too often and too facilely.[3] Such analyses, however, have not served to sharpen our understanding of life, rather they have only demonstrated the multiplicity of interpretations that the expression "life" can yield, all of which claim to have discovered its meaning, so that, according to each one, further investigation of this term is no longer required. This multiplicity is not limited to the sphere of philosophy. There are numerous treatments of life in religious, literary, and artistic fields; it has been investigated zealously and in exceptionally diverse ways (*G* 61:81/62). As a consequence, its virtual obscurity has been assured, and this warrants a renewed investigation of it.

Such an analysis, however, must approach the topic in the right way. A renewed investigation of it, one that does not take the matter lightly (*sich der Sache leicht bemächtigen*), ought not to proceed in the traditional fashion if it does not want to add to the obscurity of its meaning. Thus, the interpretation of life that Heidegger provides in this course cannot claim to achieve perfect clarity either, certainly not in the sense of universal validity (*G* 61:87/66). By the end of the course the concept of life is still unclear and even ambiguous. Heidegger will say that since life itself is hazy and circuitous, it cannot be rendered unambiguously. There is an important distinction to be made, therefore, between the ambiguity of traditional interpretations and what Heidegger means by life's basic ambiguity. Because life is unclear, hazy, and even ambiguous, it resists objectification and philosophical systematization. This will prove important as Heidegger develops a nonobjective and nonsystematic approach to life.

What I would here like to call *objective ambiguity* has been imposed on the expression "life" by those philosophical approaches that intend to achieve an objective or systematic interpretation of it. Heidegger is arguing that such an interpretation is only possible when life is denied its most basic, factical tendencies. The ambiguity of objectivity emerges from competing systems, all of which claim to have made complete or final interpretations of what life really means. This kind of ambiguity is not clarifying but obscuring because it prevents us from looking into the expression "life" at all. The vitality of the expression is ignored, buried as it is beneath axioms and principles about how to live. A systematic analysis that tries to be objective prevents an investigation into the word's most basic meanings.

Factical ambiguity, in contrast, is not obscuring because it proceeds directly from life itself. Indeed, life is ambiguous, and necessarily so. Heidegger even says that life is "circuitous" (*umwegig*) and "hazy" (*diesig*): "Life itself is to account for [*verschuldete*] this haziness; its facticity holds itself in this indebtedness [*Schuld*] and is always falling into it in new ways" (*G* 61:88/67). A proper approach to the phenomenon of life acknowledges this haziness. What does this mean? Basically, it is a determination of life's temporality. Hans-Georg Gadamer explains that for Heidegger, life is hazy because it is temporal: Life stands between two expanses of darkness (*Dunkelheiten*), the past and the future. For all that we can know and learn about ourselves, life will never be transparent. We are at all times inflicted with these expanses of darkness.[4] Of course, life's haziness is not simply a matter of not *knowing* the past and the future, that is, that we do not know what the future holds or that there are dimensions of the past that we have forgotten. Life's haziness is more profound than that. Hidden meanings from the past and deep uncertainties about the future conceal disturbing possibilities for life. Facticity is an experience of life that acknowledges the ways in which life is hazy because it is temporal and, as temporal, subject to the ambiguous and disturbing possibilities of its own past and future. The factical present is thus charged not only with mystery, but also with disturbance and ambiguity.

By contrast, life has been robbed of its vitality (disturbance, ambiguity) by those philosophical *theories* of life that have tried to construct absolute principles about it. By Heidegger's reading of the situation, philosophy at the time when he was giving this lecture course had become complacent— not disturbed at all, totally unambiguous—and through this complacency (*Bequemlichkeit*), it had lost touch with those matters that are "authentic, fundamental" (*eigentlich, grundsätzlich*) (*G* 61:163/123). Indeed, philosophical theories that strive toward absolute knowledge have actually relinquished the possibility of philosophizing: "To be sure, it is most comfortable to place oneself outside of the world and outside of life directly into the land of the blessed and the absolute. I just do not understand why one philosophizes at all, when one is already 'that far along'" (*G* 61:99/75). The tendency toward complacency, which Heidegger claims to be the bankruptcy of philosophy (*Bankrott der Philosophie*), reached its term in the choice to do away with the expression "life" entirely (*G* 61:89/67). Heidegger says, "The high point of complacency or [in other words] the bankruptcy of philosophy is when one pleads for the 'word' [life] not to be used anymore. One gets this uncomfortable reminder off of one's back—and writes a system!" (*G* 61:89/67) This is not to say that philosophers have opted not to use the word. Quite the contrary, the word is and has been used and analyzed vigorously by philosophers.[5] What Heidegger means here is that through systematic analysis they subsequently suppressed the word's most fundamental meanings, and, in effect, have done away with the expression entirely by not following its most basic tendencies. The search for absolute knowledge has caused life-philosophers to miss "life's" fundamental meanings.

A systematic or objective analysis, which attempts to achieve absolute clarity about life, fails to take account of life's temporality and, as such, it avoids or covers over life's hazy, essentially ambiguous, and sometimes even disturbing meanings. Heidegger says,

Secure objectivity is insecure flight from facticity, and that objectivity misunderstands itself insofar as it believes that its objectivity increases because of that flight. (*G* 61:90/68)

The search for absolute knowledge, motivated as it is by systematic thinking, is, in fact, an avoidance of facticity. Indeed, philosophical systems become possible only *through* the avoidance of factical life's disturbing possibilities. This was the case for Kant who, Heidegger says, rewrote the *Critique of Pure Reason* because he was scared off by something he saw (Being) while completing the first draft. At any rate, the investigation into the criteria for the validity of absolute knowledge is grounded in factical life even as that investigation covers over factical life. Instead of following those disturbing possibilities, one writes a system, and, thereby, ignores them or even covers them over.

The cardinal difference, therefore, between Heidegger and the tradition is this: Heidegger maintains that while the ambiguity of the expression cannot be eliminated, it can still be understood in its ambiguity, and this is better than trying to construct a perfectly clear system that then suppresses life's native ambiguity. Instead of attempting to clarify the concept of life "once and for all," as occurs, for example, when one writes a system, Heidegger seeks to achieve a proper analysis of "life," one that embraces the ambiguity of the expression and, thereby, attempts to take hold of and show the ambiguous tendencies immanent within it. What this means is that an approach to life is not made proper through the attempt to explain the meaning of life by way of a few trenchant but objective principles. Such attempts suppress basic meanings in the interest of a philosophical simplicity that does not let the phenomenon of life be seen as what it is.

Opening the Way to Life as an Object of Philosophy

Of the utmost importance is that we approach the phenomenon of life in the proper way. We cannot simply accept the traditional interpretations of life that have been passed down to us from those thinkers who have led the way. However, we should also not simply write something "up-to-date and refurbished" (*G* 61:167/126). In the appendix to this lecture course, Heidegger provides a brief sketch of the approach that he will make to the problem. He claims there that the investigation of facticity is an inquiry into the possibility of a philosophy that is living (*lebendig*). This can only come from a direct confrontation between philosophy and life: Philosophy must confront life, and it must confront life as life really is, in its facticity. In faithfulness to a factical understanding, we will not begin simply with the domain of the human being (*das Gemächte des Menschen*), that is, the cultural and traditional life-contexts of the human being (*G* 61:167/126). Rather, we must direct our investigation "to the human being himself *in the How of his Being*—as the origin of his domain" (*G* 61:167/126). In this way, we will not simply be looking at cultural and traditional contexts but at How the human being lives (is) within these contexts. Hence, the first stage of the analysis is to take account of How the human being lives within certain historical and cultural traditions, be they religious, philosophical, scientific, or even literary. Traditional and cultural contexts are grounded in How the human being lives within those contexts.

Insofar as we intend to take account of How the human being lives its traditions and its culture, we cannot lose sight of the question of the meaning of the Being of the human being. Heidegger is investigating "the human being insofar as he is comprehended in terms of 'What he is and how he is,' what determines his sense of Being [*Seinssinn*]" (*G* 61:168/126). Heidegger's approach in this second stage of the analysis is perhaps best understood in these terms:

> Existenz (Facticity) *becomes* [how it is] in increasingly radical questioning of life; not reflection upon the I, the ego, or the logic of the ego. This questioning [is] a concrete interpretation of facticity. (*G* 61:168/127)

A factical analysis studies the relation between Being and the human being. As such, facticity does not grasp the human being as an "I" or an ego, which can only be analyzed by way of an initial distance that is established between the self and its immediate surroundings. Facticity studies How the human being lives in its most concrete life-contexts, and these contexts must be comprehended in terms of the sense of Being of the human being. The situational context of the human being is not simply a world that is interpreted as being drawn out from a central "I." Rather, the sense of Being of life is the origin of life's relation to its situational contexts. The Being of life makes possible the relationship life has to culture, tradition, and history. Facticity, then, involves philosophical research into the "specific existence" of the Being of the human being.

> Philosophical research is only proper and is thereby factical, in so far as it develops the specific existence of concrete researching-questioning Being in its full actualization [*Vollzug*]. (*G* 61:169/127)

We have reached the third stage in this brief structural outline of the analysis, namely facticity. Hence, life is sought (1) in How the human being lives in its traditional and cultural contexts; (2) from the sense of Being of the human being; and (3) through philosophical research that is authentic (*eigentlich*) only insofar as it is factical. I take this correlation between philosophy and the concept of facticity to be what Heidegger means when he says that life itself is radical research. In other words, factical life is the philosophical investigation of the sense of Being of the human being within its traditional and cultural contexts (*G* 61:169/128).

In trying to retrieve the sense of Being of life, Heidegger finds it necessary to go back to Descartes, whose investigations into the cogito as the foundation for knowledge suppressed the Being of the human being beneath epistemological concerns. Descartes, like other philosophers who missed the problem of Being, treats life and world as distinct regions that can be separated out from each other (*G* 61:174/131). Interestingly, Heidegger first allies himself with Descartes by claiming that his own research into the question of the sense of Being of factical life also begins with the question regarding the meaning of the expression "*I am*" (*G* 61:172/130). Keeping that question, Heidegger shifts its weight from the "I" to the "am" by claiming that "in the peculiar character of the Being of 'I am,' it is the 'am' which is decisive and not the 'I'" (*G* 61:174/131). By making this shift, Heidegger achieves critical distance from Descartes as well as from that tradition of transcendental philosophy that, like Descartes's grounding of absolute knowledge in the *cogito*, is founded upon the transcendental ego.[6] Although Descartes starts with an analysis of the "am," he subsequently avoids an investigation of the Being of life by not questioning "the pregrasping of the sense of Being" (*den Vorgriff des Seinssinnes*) of the "I," namely, the "am." For Descartes, the "*sum*" of "*cogito ergo sum*" was from the beginning unquestionable and indubitable, "*Unbezweifelbar*," and, therefore, never became problematic, and so he misses the way of Being of the human being. Thus, the starting point for Heidegger and for Descartes is the same, only for Descartes the "I am," "*sum*," does not need to be questioned, whereas for Heidegger, it is the very questionability of How the human being *is* that makes possible a proper investigation of the Being of life.

Descartes did not treat the meaning of the expression "I am" as a question. By contrast, Heidegger submits the Being of life to radical philosophical questioning. For Heidegger, philosophical research depends on the character of the questionability of factical life (*der Fraglichkeitscharakter des faktischen Lebens*). That questionability makes the full actualization (*Vollzug*) of philosophical research possible, so that the questionability of factical life is crucial to the entire undertaking.[7] Indeed, it is this questionability that makes possible the opening up of the object under investigation, life, in its sense of Being. A factical approach to life is a questioning approach, one that holds the object open to the possibility of being encountered in a truly genuine way. Starting with the Cartesian question of the meaning of the "I am," Heidegger achieves a radical questioning by making the Being of life into a question, "am I?," and then investigating that question in its full actualization.

As a consequence, that full actualization demands that the "I" be taken in the context of its worldly and historical situation (*G* 61:174/131). A factical understanding of life is one that respects the worldly and historical situation of the human being by taking up the sense of Being of life in its concreteness. It stands to reason that since Heidegger has taken an altogether different approach to the meaning of "I am" from Descartes, he would then achieve a very different understanding of the meaning of the sense of Being of the human being and of the endeavor of philosophical research. Instead of reaching the ground of absolute knowledge, as Descartes claims to have done, Heidegger recognizes that a full actualization of any knowledge of the sense of Being of the human being must be understood in terms of its own historical constitution. The knowledge that we acquire about the human being will not be absolute knowledge. Life is the "object" of philosophy, but insofar as the analysis is factical and insofar as we are investigating the Being of the human being, the subsequent knowledge of that "object" will be imbued with the same temporal and historical character that life and the human being intrinsically and ineluctably have in their Being. This is part of the great promise that Heidegger's investigation of facticity holds, namely being able to bring to light life's historical-temporal constitution. Life needs to be "indicated" in its basic historical possibilities, as we saw in the last chapter. It is held in its historical character, thus preventing its objectification into theoretical propositions. As such, there is here an intrinsic "indeterminacy of the object 'my life'" (*Unbestimmtheit des Gegenstandes mein Leben*), but that indeterminacy,

> is not a deficiency in method, rather it ensures the free and ever new means of getting at factical life in its temporal, forward development; this is an indeterminacy which does not blur its object, but rather secures for it the possibility of being genuinely encountered and indicated without ever being pre-determined. (*G* 61:175/131–32)

Again, life is ambiguous and even indeterminate, but that is not at all a deficiency. Life must come to us from its ownmost possibilities, from out of itself. In this way, the categories of life will reveal themselves, but not theoretically. Any determinations of life must be held within their indeterminacy in order to preserve the freedom of their historical possibilities. Hence, the object will not even be determined; it will be *indicated* in its temporality. This indication provides a philosophical analysis that lets the object under investigation *be*. The investigation must proceed from life itself in its historicality. There are two elements to that indication that Heidegger mentions here: "openness" (*Aufgeschlossenheit*) to the object and "allowing the object to spring to you" (*sich zuspringen lassen*). In describing the "living effect and appropriation of *phenomenology's basic attitude*" (*die lebendige Auswirkung und Aneignung der **phänomenologischen Grundhaltung***), he says,

> it is not [a matter of] allowing the traditional opinion or idea of the objective validity of knowledge to be professed, i.e. moving unclearly and rashly therein and then [just] arguing; rather, it is a matter of allowing the character of fairness to the object and of the objective commitment of philosophical research to spring to you [the researcher] within the openness for the sense of objectivity which springs out of the full actualization of philosophical questioning itself and out of the objectivity which is intended therein; this is to say, we want to bring the character of this commitment to a spring, "springing-to," and at the same time to take and hold that character so that it does not contradict the full actualization of philosophizing, but rather itself determines a moment of full actualization of the temporal development of philosophizing. (*G* 61:166–67/125–26)

This passage describes in the most explicit terms found in this lecture course the address of factical research to its object. Research into facticity is an approach to research objects, but this approach attempts to preserve them within the "spring" that they make from out of themselves to the researcher. Factical research is at the same time research into the temporal ("springing-to") constitution of objects; it preserves their vital (temporal) tendencies. Fairness to the object demands that it be preserved in that springing movement in order for the "full actualization of philosophical questioning" to be achieved. In this way, the temporality of the object is acknowledged and respected. The responsibility of the researcher is to engender the possibility for openness (*Aufgeschlossenheit*) within which that springing-to can take place. Indeed, the researcher must, through radical questioning, catalyze the spring, and allow himself or herself to be sprung-to. It is radical questioning, here the full actualization of philosophical questioning, which reveals the object in its springing movement. In the openness of allowing the object to spring and holding it in that spring "a moment of full actualization of the temporal development of philosophizing" becomes possible.

Through the Expression "Life" to World

What I have shown so far in this chapter is that factical life and philosophical research implicate each other. Philosophy retrieves its vitality through a confrontation with life, while life comes to an understanding of its own temporal, historical constitution through the endeavor of living philosophical research. Facticity, therefore, names that reciprocal implication between life and philosophy; in facticity philosophy becomes lived (better: it achieves its lived and living possibilities) and life becomes philosophical, but philosophical in the sense that it comes to an understanding of its temporal and historical foundations. Thus, in investigating factical life philosophy engages the factical rootedness of life in its temporal and historical possibilities. As I mentioned before, life's basic tendencies proceed directly from life itself. Hence, we must first confront life *as it is in itself*, allowing it, so to speak, to "spring to" us. Since Heidegger's analysis is phenomenological, we do so by starting with the way in which the word "life" is used.

Heidegger's research into factical life attempts to break free from any reification or objectification of life's tendencies resulting from the determination of what valid knowledge the human being can have. He maintains that this reification comes from the self's distancing itself from its sense of Being. The result is an unbalanced if not exclusive emphasis on the self and its knowledge, while the sense of Being of the self has been avoided if not simply forgotten. The self has been construed to be a transcendental ego or cogito, which must first be isolated or bracketed in order to be investigated. As soon as that bracketing takes place, however, an understanding of the sense of Being of the human being, that is, *How* the human being lives, is forfeited, because human being has been separated at the very start from its temporal dimension. Any determinations about the temporality of the human being are passed over in the interest of an analysis of the self that has the clarity of absolute knowledge. But human being *is* temporal, and so Heidegger tries to investigate human being in its temporality. Therefore, in starting out from the word "life," Heidegger says that the investigation will get its direction from the "intransitive-verbal meaning" of the verb "to live" (*die intransitiv-verbale Bedeutung "leben"*), which is to say, from living itself (*G* 61:85/65). The intransitive-verbal meaning of "to live" yields the meaning of human being in its temporality, and this provides a sharper indication of *How* the human being lives and is. The *How* of human being indicates the way that the human being *is*, how he or she goes about in life. Through this temporalizing *How*, the analysis comes closer to the sense of Being of the human being. Heidegger is investigating the *How* of the human being by following the intransitive meanings of the verb "to live," in order to remain faithful to the temporality of "life." Thus, it is not some static thing, "life" per se, which is being investigated, but "living," the vital tendencies contained within the expression "to live." In this way, that is, by following the living tendencies of "life," we make the pivotal shift from the expression "life" to the phenomenon of world.

Heidegger explains that when we follow the intransitive meanings of the verb "to live," then a particular phenomenon emerges as intrinsically related to the expression, namely, world. He writes,

> The intransitive-verbal meaning of "to live" explicates itself, concretely visualized, always as to live "in" something, to live "out of" something, to live "for" something, to live "with" something, "against" something, to live "on" something, "toward" something, to live "from" something. The "something," which the manifold relations of "to live" indicate in these seemingly only casually gathered and enumerated prepositional expressions, we fix with the technical term, "*World*." (*G* 61:85/65)

There are a number of important points to be drawn out of this passage, all of which hinge on the transference from a grammatical/semantic interpretation of the intransitive meaning of the verb "to live" to an indication of a phenomenon, this "something" that we call world. The analysis of the expression indicates the immediacy of this phenomenon within the expression. This is the deep sense of Heideggerian phenomenology, namely that the expression (*logos*) and the phenomenon determine each other; they are inextricably interrelated.[8] Whenever we talk about life, that is, whenever we use the expression "life," in its living sense of "to live," there is an immediate and essential living phenomenon already present in the word, whether we are aware of it in our use of the word or not. When we say the word "life," we are encountering the phenomenon of world. (This becomes thematized in the later Heidegger in its much deeper ontological character, as when he says that when we pass through a forest or brook, we are passing through the word "forest" or the word "brook.") Here he says, "With the phenomenological category 'world' we are at the same time talking about— and this is important—that *which* is lived, from which life is thought of, on to which life holds" (*G* 61:86/65). It is impossible to separate life from the phenomenon of world that makes living possible. Nonetheless, it is possible to speak of life and not be aware of its intrinsic relation to the world, and in fact this tendency to delete world from "life" occurs often. Indeed, the Cartesian separation of "I" from "am" is effectively a separation of "life" from world. For Descartes, the living "I" is worldless. A proper analysis of the word *as it is* brings those living meanings to the fore, it brings the "I" and the "am" together, and, thereby, it implicates the living phenomenon with which the word itself is ineluctably connected, namely world. Moreover, this immediacy of world within "life" makes "life" become life. When we pursue the word "life" factically, we see that it is no longer just a word but an experience of the world. "To live" means *to live* in the world.

Further, we see in this passage a validation of the average, everyday usage of the word "life." This is an important point. The initial foray into a phenomenological investigation of "life" passes first through the average, everyday use of the word. Heidegger's analysis proceeds by way of common prepositional expressions, which then prove to be critical to our understanding of the way in which the human being relates to the world. These expressions, which are "seemingly gathered and enumerated only casually," are of cardinal importance to the investigation into the intrinsic relation between "life" and world and, thereby, to the sense of Being of the human being. As the point of access to life, these prepositional expressions cannot be overemphasized in their importance. Taking account of the concrete facticity of life prevents a theoretical interpretation of life's possibilities, and these prepositional expressions provide critical factical direction. Perhaps most important, these prepositional, verbal expressions temporalize the human being's relation to the world. To say that the human being lives is to say that he or she lives in, on, with, against, from, toward the world. These are temporal directions of living. Any philosophical interpretation must return to these initial factical possibilities, always keeping them in mind, if it wants to take account of the temporality of the human being in the world.

Also, the importance of the concept of *Wiederholung* emerges here. When Heidegger claims, as in the epigraph to this chapter, "Retrieval, on its sense hangs everything," one dimension of this is that there are deeper meanings within our average everyday use of language. When words are analyzed properly and allowed to speak for themselves, those deeper meanings emerge and make a claim on us. The point of access to life, like the point of access to the object of any phenomenological investigation, bears all the interpretative weight. This is to say that "life" must be approached in the proper way. Only then does anything like world speak to us from out of its genuine possibilities. It seems clear, then, that (1) the word "life" is tied to the phenomenon of world and that (2) we see this connection through language, that is, through words and speech. Retrieval involves the recovery of these connections.

But what of the transitive meanings of "to live"? One can say, for example, "he knows how to live" (intransitive) or one can say "he lives life" (transitive)

(*G* 61:82/63). Do such transitive meanings not complicate our understanding by objectifying the very phenomenon that we are trying to keep from being objectified? To be sure, the expression "life" contains within itself an "intransitive-transitive equivocalness" (*Zweideutigkeit*); Heidegger says, though, that this ambiguity is something "which we do not want to cross out, but rather leave in the expression and keep a firm hold on" (*G* 61:82/63). What is important is that even when "life" is taken transitively, there is still a verbal sense that is retained. Indeed, the verbal (temporal) sense is what accounts for the ambiguity! The verbal sense can be understood transitively or intransitively, and these verbal expressions of the word, despite their equivocalness, provide a critical starting point to Heidegger's analysis.

The goal is not to achieve a mere "grammatizing" of the expression "life" but rather to achieve a deeper understanding of the phenomenon of life through the way in which the expression "life" is used. How the word is used in actual, living speech is important to the analysis. Grammatical categories originate in "living speech, in the immanent speaking of life" (*G* 61:82/63). Hence, by passing through grammar we are led back (retrieval!) to a critical dimension of the factical experience of life, that is, to the more original sense of speaking that precedes all theoretical articulations of life. If we start with a grammatical analysis, we do not become trapped within philosophy of language.

Heidegger's interpretation of life tries to proceed directly from life itself. His goal is to articulate the factical immediacy of life. Insofar as life is itself unclear, so too any analysis of life is sure to reflect that same lack of clarity. Factical immediacy is inherently ambiguous. The factical use of the expression, in both its transitive and intransitive meanings, provides us with a basic understanding of the phenomenon, and if we follow the tendencies that the expression contains, then we can, thereby, determine how those semantic tendencies "express particular basic tendencies of Dasein."[9] In other words, we follow the tendencies in the expression "life," how we speak of it, to the temporality of Dasein. Along the way, we encounter speaking, which is in close proximity to Dasein's temporality, since speaking precedes all theoretical, objective, or logical determinations of life. In this way, we have entered life through language, that is, we have entered the phenomenon of life (world) through the expression, "life." This was made possible by the immanent relation between living speech and those most basic, fundamental directions of concrete, factical life in its world. When we let phenomena "spring forth" as they are, we listen to the words that bring them forth, that is, the words with which we speak about them.

The Meaningfulness of Life's Basic Categories

So far, I have demonstrated the important shift from the expression "life" to the phenomenon of world, and this has revealed the immediacy of language and phenomena. Facticity is the place where language and life meet.[10] Deeply immersed within this relation is the human being, who lives in language. Of course, language does not cause the human being to be related to the world. The human being is not worldly because he or she uses language. Rather, the human being's use of language holds and, when investigated in the proper way, reveals an essential relatedness between being human and living in the world. Language is thus an essential dimension of the human being's relation to the world; it dynamizes the connection between life and world.

The livedness (depth, vitality: *Lebendigkeit*) of the human being is central to the phenomenological relation between the verbal expression of phenomena and phenomena themselves. A phenomenological analysis is a factical interpretation that pursues the temporal, historical constitution of the human being as an integral, guiding aspect of its research. Since phenomenological research is factical research, then phenomenology is a philosophical method that investigates life in its temporality, and, thereby, in its historicality. Having seen that we gain access to the phenomenon of world through an investigation into the expression "life," the world-relatedness of life comes more sharply into focus. Again, "Life is in itself world-related" (*G* 61:86/65). I will pursue the world-relatedness of life in this section in order to show that that world-relatedness is dynamized and indeed made possible by a profound and essential *movement*. Movement is central to the concept of facticity. A factical understanding of life is at the same time an understanding of the deep sense of life's movement because the factical concreteness of life is experienced only through and within that movement. This will allow us to take account of what Heidegger means by the meaningfulness of life's basic categories, because meaningfulness is grounded in the origin of the human being's movement.

The understanding of the life of human being that I reach in this section is, according to Heidegger, categorial. A categorial understanding is one that is aimed at a factical interpretation of life.

> "*Categories*" means: something, which according to its sense, interprets a phenomenon in a directional sense [*Sinnrichtung*] in a certain way, *prinzipiell*, which brings the phenomenon as what-is-interpreted [*Interpretat*] to understanding. (*G* 61:86/65)[11]

The basic categories of life are categories in the sense that they attempt to capture the phenomenon of life in its directional-sense, and they do so in a *prinzipiell*, which is to say factical, way. The *How* of life is researched with regard to the depth of its directionality. In this regard, the categories are concepts that grasp the "springing to" (*Zusprung*) or moving-character of life. They are concepts that capture life's facticity. Heidegger says, "Categories only come to understanding insofar as factical life itself is forced into interpretation" (*G* 61:87/66). Heidegger's categorial research here is and remains factical because the profound movement of life and the concrete factical existence of the human being as a temporal-historical being are under scrutiny. What is of consequence is the relation between the human being as moving (temporal) and that which makes movement (temporality) possible, that is, the origin of its movement. The dynamic that Heidegger is trying to capture here is difficult but necessary if a nonmetaphysical, nontranscendental understanding of the human being, one that proceeds directly from life itself, is to be achieved. The direction that the sense of life takes is grounded in a deeper sense of movement. We gain access to this origin through facticity, but still we are constantly interpreting and reinterpreting the sense of life in and through this origin.

This constant process of the reinterpretation of life's factical possibilities is *Wiederholung*. This retrieval is a process of taking up the factical possibilities of life in the depth of their originality, reinterpreting them in terms of their origin. One important consequence of this process is that it places the interpreter in his or her own historical-temporal situation. Phenomenological research, when understood as factical, recognizes not only the historical temporality of the object that is under investigation but also the historical situation of the interpreter or researcher. There is a movement surging through both that which is interpreted as well as the human being who is accomplishing the work of interpretation. That movement is historical-temporal. This relation will become clearer as I proceed through Heidegger's analysis of ruinance and the basic categories of life in the next chapter. It is important to recognize here, though, that facticity indicates the vitality of historical-temporal research. In order for the vitality of that relation to be sustained, then, an understanding of life must be reached that holds on to the temporality of life as a concrete, factical phenomenon. Heidegger is seeking categories that grasp the temporal *How* of life. To do that, he must first determine the way in which life relates to the world. His question: What is the concrete relation between life and the world? In other words, what dynamizes the prepositional expressions that I just said are so important?

Life's relation to the world is one of care. In short, life cares for the world. This is the case because life is always on a search for *meaningfulness*. For this reason, the world is not simply an object or concept. The world is meaningful, and life cares for the world insofar as it is meaningful. We could say, in fact, that life's care for the world is a search for meaningfulness. Heidegger writes, "Meaningfulness is a categorial determination of the world; the objects of the world, the worldly, world-like objects are lived in the character of meaningfulness" (*G* 61:90/68). Moreover, life's care for the world in its search for meaningfulness is imbued with an essential wanting (*Darbung*), and this wanting dynamizes life in its care. " 'Wanting' (*privatio, carentia*) is the relating- and actualizing basic How of the sense of Being of life" (*G* 61:90/68). This means that there is a profound lack (*privatio*) in the human being that manifests itself as wanting. Care, then, is more than just a search for meaningfulness; it is a need for meaningfulness dynamized by lack and wanting. As such, care is not an ethical category. It does not mean to like something or to be fond of it. It means that life is in want of the world. Furthermore, in its wanting, life's care is concerned about the world. As a category, care means to be concerned about[12] the world in such a way that the world is held open in a caring encounter (*Begegnis*). Heidegger writes, "Category means interpreting and is only interpreting, namely factical life, appropriated in *existentiell* concern" (*G* 61:87/66). Care is a relational category dynamized by an essential wanting, through which and on account of which life searches for meaning. It provides access to the world by being concerned about it.

This, I argue, is what it means to make a factical investigation of the Being of life, that is, to interpret the world insofar as the world is opened up by the wanting and lack that dynamize the human being's care for the world. This is the facticity of phenomenological analysis, which experiences the world through the relating sense of care. Factical phenomenology attends to the experience of the meaningfulness of the world as it is encountered through the wanting of care. In this way, life's experience of the world is understood with regard to the lack (*privatio*) and wanting at the core of the human being.

It seems that we have at this point come to a definition of factical life. Simply said, factical life is an interpretation of the dynamic relation between life and world. That relation, as we have already seen, is care in the sense of concern. Life relates to the world through concerned care. Even more, life's concerned-caring relation to the world is one of meaningfulness. As such, life's care for the world is not simply a manipulation of objects but rather an encountering of the world's meaningfulness. The meaningfulness of the world is important in the analysis that follows, because the basic categories of life as Heidegger describes them are determined according to the meaningfulness of life's care. Heidegger stresses that meaningfulness in this sense does not mean worth or value (*G* 61:91/69). The factical experience of objects is an encountering of objects in their reality (*Wirklichkeit*). Objects are there in the world and are to be encountered as they are in concrete world-experience (*aus konkreter Welterfahrung*), that is, in their facticity. This concrete encountering is in no way a "naked reality" that is ready to be dressed with some kind of value (*G* 61:91/69). The world is meaningful simply insofar as it is encountered.[13]

It is important to recognize that the concept of meaningfulness follows directly from life itself, that is, from the way that life is lived. This interpretation of life yields an understanding of what it means "to live factically 'in' meaningfulness" (*G* 61:93/70). To live in meaningfulness means to live in, out of, through, against, and from the world.

Closely related to the understanding of meaningfulness as a direct experience of encountering the world is the sense of movement that characterizes factical life in its going about its tasks in the world. The world could not be encountered in its meaningfulness if not for the movement of the human being. As I have already shown, the relational sense of life is care for the world, whereby the meaningfulness of objects is lived in concrete experience. What we have not yet seen, however, and what is pivotal to the understanding of facticity, is that the movement that makes care for the world possible in the first place is characterized not just by wanting but also by disquiet (*Unruhe*). Heidegger evokes Pascal's *Pensées* to demonstrate that there are disquieting tendencies deep within the human being which then also dynamize the movedness of factical life. Heidegger writes, "The How of this disquiet as full phenomenon determines facticity" (*G* 61:93/70). The more deeply we investigate factical life, the closer we come to the motivating, disturbing, *disquieting* tendencies of life. The movement of life is disquieting. Coming on the heels of his analysis of meaningfulness, the description of disquiet can be read in tandem with that analysis. In this regard, the disquiet of factical life is also meaningful, better: Disquiet makes meaningfulness possible. Indeed, the disquiet of life is enlightening.

The disquiet-enlightening, the enlightened disquiet; dis-quiet and questionability; the domain of temporal development; disquiet and the where-to. The disquieting aspect of disquiet. The not drawn out, not decided Between of the aspect of factical life: between surrounding-, with-, self-, pre-, and afterworld; something positive. The overall

seeping through of disquiet, its forms and masks. Quiet—disquiet;
phenomenon and movement (compare the phenomenon of movement
in Aristotle). (*G* 61:93/70)

Heidegger's writing here is aphoristic and even somewhat cryptic. Nonetheless, there is, indeed, an enlightening aspect of disquiet that he is trying
to convey. In the first place, there is the suggestion here that the disquiet of
movement is a manifest aspect of questionability, and we saw earlier that
this questionability is an important characteristic of the kind of factical
philosophizing that makes it possible for the sense of Being of the human
being to be revealed in a proper way. The relation that Heidegger suggests
here between disquiet and questionability indicates that the human being
is questioning precisely because of disquiet. There is a basic disquiet to life
that causes us to question, and far from being suppressed this experience
of disquiet needs to be retrieved.

In this sense, the dogmatic, objective *life* and dogmatic, objective *philosophies* are the same. Both attempt to quell the essential questioning of
disquiet, and in doing so, they either ignore or suppress basic tendencies of
the human being. This suppression of life's basic tendencies amounts to an
abnegation of the facticity of life. Moreover, this suppression effectively
brings an end to the questioning of the human being. As such, it brings
about a darkening of the world. Disquiet is questioning, and that questioning is an en-lightening that reveals the world as it really is. The disquiet of
life, which is the basic character of its movement, impels the human being
to experience the world in a questioning, en-lightening way. We experience
the world only when we inquire about it, when we question it with rigor and
intensity, and do so constantly. This rigorous questioning is, for Heidegger,
philosophizing, and in this sense philosophizing has its roots in the factical
disquiet that is ingredient to the most basic and essential structures of human being. To suppress that disquiet summarily brings an end to the human
being's factical experience of the world: its questioning, its disquiet, its enlightening, its concern, its openness, its speaking.

One final point: When fundamental disquiet en-lightens the world
through questioning, it thereby enlightens the world in the powers of its
temporal development. The world is thus opened up in its temporal character. This point is not to be overlooked. The temporality of the world is to
be dis-covered through the investigation into the factical disquiet of life.
To be sure, the disquiet of life will not be easy to find. Although everywhere (*überall*), it also has its forms and masks (*Gestalten und Masken*). As
Heidegger advises, we must look into the Between, "the not drawn out and

not decided Between" of the various directions of life in the world. I follow this line of argument in the next chapter.

In this chapter, I have shown how Heidegger attempts to restore basic fundamental meanings to life through an investigation of the expression "life." We have yet to see what the basic categories of life are, but I have prepared the ground for an investigation into those basic categories. The preparation of that ground demands that the research into life be approached in the right way. This point is capital: The life of the human being must be allowed to show itself from itself as it is. Insofar as phenomenology helps us to carry out the investigation, it must attend to the factical relationship between "life" and world. An analysis of the word "life" immediately opens up the phenomenon of world. To be in the world is, thus, the sense of Being of the life of the human being.

The worldly dimension of life has revealed that there are certain tendencies within life that all philosophies that strive for absolute clarity, especially systematic philosophies, either ignore or cover over. Two important structures have been revealed here, the historical and temporal dimensions of life. These dimensions of life have been shown to be dynamized by care, which is the fundamental relation life has with the world. Life cares for the world. Through care, the meaningfulness of the world reveals itself. But care, in turn, reveals a fundamental wanting in the human being. That wanting is the origin of disquiet, which is itself the origin of questioning, which informs all philosophical research. In this way, we see that systematic philosophies actually shut down the questioning that impels philosophizing in the first place. The wanting and disquiet of life are here embraced as the enlightening of philosophical questioning.

To circumvent a philosophical situation that is dominated by the search for absolute clarity, the basic tendencies of life must be investigated through a retrieval of the facticity of life. Heidegger reaffirms the importance of facticity in the section of the course immediately preceding the concrete investigation of life's basic categories. With reference to the categories, he says that they are

> in life *in facticity*, which means then that [life] establishes factical possibilities in itself, which are never (and thank God never) to be released; [this means], therefore, that a philosophical interpretation— which has seen the main point of philosophy, facticity, insofar as [that interpretation] is real (*true*)—is factical, insofar as it radically professes possibilities of decision as philosophical-factical, and

thereby [radically professes] itself. But it can only do that when it is there—in the way of its Dasein. (*G* 61:99/74)

Facticity is "the main point of philosophy" because, by placing the human being into question in a radical way, it opens life up to its world and thereby opens up the manifold of possibilities for a vital interpretation of the Being of the human being in the world.

4

Ruinance

Ruinance takes time away, i.e., from out of facticity it tries to destroy the historical. The ruinance of factical life has this fully actualizing sense of the destruction of time.

—Martin Heidegger, *Phenomenological Interpretations of Aristotle: Initiation into Phenomenological Research*

In this chapter, I am still looking at *Phenomenological Interpretations of Aristotle: Initiation into Phenomenological Research* (G 61, from winter semester, 1921–22), the text on factical life, but my focus is now on the relationships among factical life, its world, and what Heidegger describes as factical life's ruinance.[1] With ruinance, Heidegger is showing the various ways that life is weighed down by the world and distracted by worldly concerns. There is thus an important shift that takes place in this course from the notion of factical life as a source of vital and intense life-experience to the ways in which factical life experiences the world as a burden and a distraction from its true self. Indeed, ruinance is the precursor to what Heidegger call fallenness. But I do not view ruinance in a simplistic sense as the degradation or abasement of life. Rather, Heidegger's descriptions of life's ruinance demonstrate not just how life falls into the world of its concern, loses itself, and avoids itself by identifying itself with the world. He is also showing here how certain positive dimensions of factical life can be retrieved from within life's fallenness and inauthenticity, such as its openness to the world, its temporal-historical constitution, and its capacity to engage in rigorous philosophical questioning. By retrieval, I mean here the recovery of these positive dimensions from those modes of life that tend to cover them over.[2] The factical situation includes both a tendency toward decline as well as the richness and vitality of life-experience. Ruinance indicates the ambiguity of life in both of these tendencies.

In this chapter, I develop a sense of ruinance that accents life's temporal dimension by capturing the concrete, factical temporality of this falling movement. The chapter is divided into four sections. In the first section, I look at the triadic structure of the life-world, namely the self-world, the surrounding-world, and the with-world. I emphasize the temporal structure of these worlds by showing the caring movement of life into these worlds. In the second section, I analyze the basic categories of life. These are Inclination, Distance, Blocking-off, and Making Things Easy. These categories indicate the ways in which life identifies itself with the world so closely that it ends up losing itself in the world and its distractions. Each category, however, delineates the way that life is in a temporal relation with the world and the way in which that temporality gets covered over. This, I argue, is the real meaning of ruinance, namely, the concealing of life's temporal constitution. In the third section, I analyze two critical structures, relucence and prestructuring. These are directions of life's facticity that show how the temporality of life is enlightened within the categories of ruinance, so that temporality emerges, it is still *there*, relucent within the ruinant concealing of temporality. In the fourth and final section, I take up the structures of counter-ruinance, which are openness, care, wanting, and questioning. If ruinance is the destruction of life's temporality, then counter-ruinance is an opening of life's temporal relation with the world. In a moment of insight, a *kairos*, these counter-ruinant structures point life back toward itself and its original caring movement toward the world.

From World to the Basic Categories of Life

Heidegger differentiates among three different kinds of world: surrounding-world, with-world, and self-world (*Um-, Mit-, und Selbstwelt*).[3] These worlds are determined according to the direction in which life's caring moves. The direction of care decides which world is being experienced at any particular time. What is the direction of care? There are always numerous possibilities with which the individual life is presented. Those possibilities can be experienced only in time. The character of those possibilities and especially the sensitivity of those possibilities to time is what Heidegger means by direction of care. Care has a directedness, and that directedness has a certain shaping or molding (*Ausprägung*), which is determined according to particular, concrete, temporal possibilities. Life is always caring in some particular direction, for example, about a person, idea, or plan, and these caring directions are always given in the form of possibilities that are afflicted with time constraints. Considering the close relationship between care and world, indeed, because life relates to the world through care, Heidegger refers to these worlds as care-worlds (*Sorgenswelten*). The differences among these worlds depend on the factical ways in which that caring manifests.

Heidegger begins with the self-world. Of the three worlds, the self-world is the most significant. This is not to be taken in an egoistic or solipsistic sense; to say that the self-world is the most significant of the three care-worlds is not the same as saying that the self in its own self-reflection is more important than the self in its relation to others or in its relation to its surroundings. Heidegger is not prioritizing the self here in order to claim that the isolated self should be the sole object of philosophical inquiry. On the contrary, his analysis of facticity in this course endeavors to situate the self, and, more precisely, the factical life of the self, in the full experience of the life-world. As such, he insists that the self-world can be understood only in, through, and out of the other two worlds. Indeed, without a with-world and a surrounding-world, there would be no self-world. Therefore, the life of the self-world cannot be construed in terms of reflection on an I, ego, or cogito, because that would presume that the world is not necessarily encountered in that reflection. When Heidegger prioritizes the self-world, he is developing a way to think about the self so that it cannot be extricated from life and world. It is with this understanding of the self-world that we should understand the following passage:

> The "I," a category of complex form [*Ausformung*], does not as such need to encounter me at all in my care for the world, in my care for "myself" in the factical sense. The "myself," for which I am in care, is experienced as self-world in certain forms of meaningfulness [*Bedeutsamkeiten*], which open up [*aufgehen*] in the full life-world, in which the with-world and the surrounding-world along with the self-world, is always there. The life-world is in each case experienced in this shaping, whether expressly or not. Shaping [*Ausprägung*] is a How of facticity. (*G* 61:94/71)

The self-world is a factical category. Moreover, it is not an "I." The "I," taken in either the Cartesian sense or in the sense of the transcendental ego, is a complex category in its own right, but it does not encounter the facticity of life. The concrete, factical sense that is intrinsic to the self-world is, therefore, not an "I," but rather an experience of the self in its factical meaningfulness as "myself." This factical "myself," then, "is experienced as self-world in certain forms of meaningfulness," which, and this is of critical importance, "open up in the full life-world." The self-world is a relation to the self as a meaningful encounter with the life-world in its fullest and richest sense. This seems contradictory, because it sounds as though the self-world were both a relation to the self and a relation to the world. That is precisely the case, but there is no contradiction. Once the relation that the human being has to itself is construed factically, as self-world in the

Heideggerian sense, that self-relation is seen to be an experience of concrete, factical meanings that open up when they are understood in, through, and out of the larger context of the life-world and, hence, out of the with- and surrounding-worlds. These three worlds must always be taken together, for they are inextricably interrelated

The life-world, Heidegger says, is the triadic structure of with-, self-, and surrounding-world. It is the complex of care-worlds, but these worlds are not three districts (*Bezirke*), differentiated according to various groupings of objects, things, and humans (*Gegenstände, Dinge, Menschen*). This complex of worlds must be understood as relational and complementary both to each other and to life itself. When we try to understand ourselves factically, we are immediately confronted with concrete meanings that emerge through these care-worlds. These meanings are not values, but concrete realities. What Heidegger shows here is that those concrete realities *are* meaningful, even if they are not meaningful in the traditional sense of being valuable or worthy. The meaningfulness of something is the concrete experience of it. Meaningfulness is a determination of encountering something and not of valuing it or establishing its worth. As such, we do not simply encounter objects in the different care-worlds; we encounter directions of meaning.

Looking at the other two care-worlds, which open up through the self-world, we see that the with-world, which Heidegger calls a "part" of the self-world, is an encounter with other human beings. There is a caring relation between the self and others, who are thus a part of that self. That encountering with others opens up possibilities of life for that caring relation. The surrounding-world is a determination of those possibilities that pertain to the care that one takes for those meanings that are in the world which do not belong to the with-world relation. All three of these worlds, Heidegger says, are grounded in the temporalizing character of every life (*Zeitigungscharakter jedes Lebens*) and need to be interpreted accordingly (*G* 61:97/73). Thus, there is a temporal dimension that guides the three directions that life can take—toward the self, toward others, and toward its surroundings.

In explicating the temporality of life's caring directions, I am trying to prove that that life must be determined according to its concrete relations with the world. Heidegger is trying to bring to light certain meanings within those directions that have thus far remained latent. There are dimensions of the relation between life and world that have not been drawn out (*Unabgehobenheit*). An analysis of the temporal constitution of life's care-worlds reveals those hidden dimensions. Insofar as these not-drawn-out dimensions of the world are care-relations, they constitute the basic categories of life in its relational sense. I turn now to those categories in order to determine more precisely how life and world interrelate.

The Categories of Caring Movement

There is a caring relation between life and world. The relational sense of life is care, and that care can be understood in terms of the self, others, and its surroundings. Further, that care is temporal such that the caring directions of life are temporally constituted. That being the case, the relation between life and world involves a certain movement. This point is capital: The basic categories in the relational sense of life are concrete manifestations of life's caring movement.

1. Inclination (*Neigung*): This, the first of the basic categories, is a determination of the way that life cares about forms of meaningfulness in such a way that it is weighed down by them. Insofar as those forms of meaningfulness are orientations toward the world, life bears the heaviness of the world. This means that life is constantly immersing itself within new inclinations toward more forms of meaningfulness, which ensconce life firmly within its worldly inclinations. Life is inclined toward new determinations of worldly meaningfulness, and so it understands itself strictly in terms of those inclinations. As a consequence, life becomes self-sufficient (*Selbstgenügsamkeit*) within its world. Normally, one would not think of self-sufficiency as a temporal phenomenon. It suggests rather a kind of stability amid the flux of life: One is self-sufficient with the way things are and does not want them to change. Heidegger shows, however, that self-sufficiency is temporal and thus constituted by a certain movement because it is based on life's propensity constantly to weigh itself down with new distractions. The self-sufficiency of inclination is always an inclination *toward* the world and its distractions (*Zerstreuungen*). Self-sufficiency is thus the defining and sustaining character of inclination. By immersing itself within distractions, life becomes self-sufficient and thus understands itself strictly in terms of those distractions. In this way, the temporal dimension of inclining gets covered over by the aura of perpetuity afforded by self-sufficient.

2. Distance (*Abstand*): The second basic category of the relational sense of life builds on the first. If inclination is an indication of the heaviness of life in its many distractions, distance is a determination of how life hides the fact that it is held in distraction. Heidegger says that even though life's forms of meaningfulness are always "in front of" it as possibilities, life tends to destroy that distance. The defining dimension of distance as a category of life's relational sense is thus the destruction of distance (*Abstandstilgung*) between life and world. Here, Heidegger gives the first indication of life's ruinance. Life is ruinant when it fails to recognize that its forms of meaningfulness stand before it as possibilities. In its caring movement toward the

world, life catches up with its meaningful possibilities and thus identifies itself with them, destroying that distance.

The consequence is that life fails to see itself (*es versieht sich*) and, more significantly, it mismeasures itself (*es vermißt sich*), and in doing so it misses itself (*G* 61:103/77). Heidegger uses the term *vermessen* here to indicate the way that life mismeasures itself by chasing after worldly achievement: "rank, success, position in life (world), catching-up, advantage, calculation, bustle, noise, style . . ." (*G* 61:103/77). The self transfers the distance between life and world into life, itself, identified now as world. Instead of having concrete forms of meaningfulness before itself, life allows itself to be carried away by the world, rendering distance as a worldly phenomenon. In this way, distance becomes measure, worldly measure, and life comprehends its own importance only through that measure. Hence, Heidegger suggests that striving after material success in life can be traced back to the relation between life and world and, more specifically, to the covering over of that relation and the subsequent interpolation of that relation to the world into life, along with its composite forms of meaningfulness.

With that shift, life regards itself as hyperbolic, and this hyperbole, Heidegger says, is the genesis of science. We have just seen that life seeks after distances within the forms of meaningfulness in which it lives, thus engaging in the measuring of life, instead of understanding itself in its distance *from* those forms of meaningfulness. In other words, life identifies itself with worldly distractions. These distractions are apparently limitless. Thus, when life identifies itself with those distractions, it thinks of itself as being limitless, too, that is, it ignores all limits. This is what Heidegger means when he says life thinks of itself as hyperbolic: It identifies itself with the apparent limitlessness of worldly distractions. Heidegger does not say so explicitly, but this seems to be the case because life is temporal. In its cares, life moves toward the world. When that distance is eliminated, life's temporalizing takes place as a seemingly endless series of new distractions. The hyperbolic limitlessness of life's worldly distractions is based, however implicitly, on temporality. Insofar as science investigates worldly meaningfulness, it, too, is grounded in hyperbolic distraction. As such, science fails to recognize the temporal distance between life and world, thus misinterpreting meaningfulness as hyperbolic and, thus, excessive (limitless).

Heidegger does suggest in this analysis of distance/destruction of distance that there is "the possibility of a true interpretation of life-related contexts," and that is by way of "phenomenological discovery" (*G* 61:104–5/78). Without explicitly "correcting" the problem of distance by directing life away from its distractions, phenomenology is able to draw out these categories of life's relational sense so that the distractions of life in its world are recognized as distractions. Phenomenology indicates how life becomes entangled in its world. It focuses not on how life grasps itself but rather on those ways in which life becomes distracted and avoids itself. Life's evasion of itself is thus the proper theme of phenomenological research.

3. Blocking off (*Abriegelung*): As life continues to become weighed down by the world, eliminating the distance between the world and itself, life blocks off access to itself. Yet, at the same time that life avoids itself and looks away from itself, it is, nonetheless, still *there*. Heidegger's argument here is strangely Cartesian; Descartes says, even if I am being deceived, I still am. Heidegger is saying that even when life avoids itself, it still *is*. But Heidegger is not trying to ground all knowledge in the ideal ego. He is showing the brute facticity of life in all of its various deceptions and distractions. Thus, in very non-Cartesian fashion, Heidegger impels us to look for life in those places where it blocks itself off, where it is deceptive and hides behind different masks. Whereas Descartes tells us to avoid that which is deceptive, Heidegger says that in those places where life is most deeply hidden one will find its most primordial meanings. Indeed, the temporalizing of factical life (*die Zeitigung des faktischen Lebens*) is most originally *there* where its masks are the most difficult to discern and uncover. This third category is thus meant to show that even where life blocks itself off from itself, it is still *there*. He writes, "In constantly new ways of looking away from itself, it [life] always searches for itself and encounters itself precisely there where it does not suppose, in its masking [*larvanz*]" (*G* 61:107/80). Life's masks thus contain philosophical import. In its avoidances, its masks, its evasions, life is concretely and factically *there*. The most well-hidden mask is that of life's endless possibilities. He writes,

> Limitlessness is the mask which factical life factically places before itself, i.e. before its world and holds there. This concept of limitlessness, without itself being clear, plays a decisive role in the assessment and anticipation of modern life philosophy. (*G* 61:107–8/80)

These possibilities seem limitless because life is constantly identifying itself with the world's distractions. When life then understands itself as being identical with the world, it views itself as being limitless, too. Heidegger says here that factical life is elliptical. This is a determination of its temporal movement: By blocking itself off from itself, life is constantly moving around itself, being drawn in by itself yet avoiding itself and being drawn into the world at the same time. This being-drawn-in and turning-away account for the temporalizing of life's elliptical movement around itself.

4. Making things easy (*das "Leichte"*): In direct reference to Aristotle's *Nicomachean Ethics*, Heidegger claims that we tend to make things easier

for ourselves. As Aristotle says, "Virtue is difficult, vice is easy." This is the most basic of the four categories, for the first three are all modes in which life attempts to establish some measure of security for itself by making things easy. Avoiding itself and looking away from itself, life secures itself in a kind of carelessness (*Sorglosigkeit*), and this is an abiding state in which it lives. It belongs to life's care for its world that it constructs a world for itself in which it does not need to make any decisions about itself. In being careless, life avoids the difficulty of having to be decisive.

With these categories Heidegger is trying to determine how to go about philosophical research. He insists, as we have already seen, that the most important task for philosophy is to determine how its object will be approached. Insofar as philosophy's "research object" is life, Heidegger makes the determination that life will be approached factically, which is to say that it will *not* be treated as an object at all. Facticity is an indication of philosophical research that attempts to subvert the categories of subject and object by investigating the Being of life, indeed, by investigating "The Being of life as its *facticity*" (*G* 61:114/85). Facticity is an element of the unobjectifiable Being of life. Heidegger can make this claim because, through a factical interpretation of life, the temporalizing movement of life is taken into consideration, and movement belongs essentially to life's Being. By taking account of its facticity, life recognizes its own caring movement. The relational categories outlined above are, then, modes of access to life's caring-temporalizing movement and, thus, to the Being of life.

Relucence and Prestructuring

By investigating the different ways in which life gets taken away by the world in distraction, the ways it avoids itself, and the ways it makes things easier for itself, philosophy can grasp its own temporality in its most concrete primordial indications. The four categories listed above are temporally constituted, even though they do not seem to be at first glance. Indeed, it is precisely because they do not seem to have a temporal constitution that Heidegger maintains that life's most original temporalizing can be found through them.

Hence, through these categories, the problem of the historical can be concretely grasped according to a *prinzipielle* knowledge of history. The categories of life's relational sense will deconstruct the idealities of philosophy—its systems and its historical ideals, such as worth and values or the atemporal thing-in-itself—by providing concrete, *prinzipielle* knowledge about life from within our factical experience of it. Through an adherence to *prinzipielle* knowledge, in this context, Heidegger lauds the practice of philosophizing over the discipline of philosophy. "Philosophizing," he tells us, "as *prinzipielle* knowledge is nothing other than the radical full actualization of the historical dimension of the facticity of life" (*G* 61:111/83). The project of investigating the historical is a factical endeavor because knowledge of history is, for Heidegger, a concrete, *prinzipielle* knowledge of historical *movements*. If we take the example of science, as Heidegger does here, we see that it should not be interpreted systematically, according to its logical structure. Rather than constructing a metaphysical system out of Aristotle's texts, as Aquinas has done, for example, Aristotle can be viewed according to his factical, philosophical-historical situation. The "problematic of facticity" can be understood as a "discussion of the living historical situation" of a science (*G* 61:115/86). Facticity is not science but rather the historical situation of a science that makes possible concrete scientific research.

If we say that facticity is an indication of life's movement which is determined through concrete historical knowledge, this means that movement needs to be rethought according to the factical, temporalizing movement of that kind of knowledge. Heidegger describes this sharper understanding of movement through the terms "relucence" and "prestructuring."[4] These are the specific dimensions of movement appropriate to the basic categories of life's relational sense. They indicate how, in life's relation to its world, there is both an *enlightening* that takes place, whereby the world is revealed (this is relucence), as well as a *structuring process*, whereby life secures for itself that which has been revealed (this is prestructuring). Through the latter process, life stabilizes certain meanings and fixes their determinations. Factical movement is constituted by both of these processes. Through the explication of how these categorial movements function within each of the relational categories of life, Heidegger says that the Being of the world will open up. The relucence and prestructuring of inclination, destruction of distance, and blocking off reveal more precisely how life relates to the world. This relation is characterized by that double process of being revealed and solidifying what is revealed into fixed determinations. Retrieval is necessary to recover that which remains hidden, yet relucent, within those rigidified structures. The movement of revelation and solidification is a temporal process of constantly retrieving relucent meanings from within prestructured determinations. This movement belongs to the Being of life.

Looking first at inclination, we know already that life weighs itself down with various distractions. Insofar as it is life itself that is being distracted, however, life is still relucent within that distraction. It is life that is enlightened in that distraction because it is life that is being distracted. In its caring movement toward the world, in its distractedness, life lights itself up. In this way, life, which is hidden within distraction, is actually enlightened by that distraction. The fact that life is *there* within distraction becomes apparent through the distraction, itself. Thus, even while avoiding itself, life illuminates that caring region within which it dwells. Life, "constructs the enlightening-region in each case for its next caring-contexts" (*G* 61:119/88–89). In this sense, life illuminates the world because that relational distance between life and world is the caring region.

As relucent, however, life also guards itself: "As caring, life is also protecting, in its relucence it is at the same time prestructuring" (*G* 61:120/89). This is to say that if life as caring is relucent, it is also prestructuring insofar as caring life protects itself by identifying itself, Heidegger says, with cultural objects. Life is prestructuring insofar as it protects itself against itself within cultural experience. The prestructuring understanding of life, therefore, is cultural life, which Heidegger defines as the "prestructuring organized inclination of the worldly relucence of caring life" (*G* 61:120/89). By protecting itself within cultural objects, life confers a certain value upon itself, and it interprets itself according to that value. Life then *becomes* a cultural object so that all dimensions of experience are thought to emerge from life as an objectified, cultural thing. As thus objectified, life becomes secured as a cultural value. This is what is often referred to as Reality, the reification of life into a cultural object that can be evaluated and assessed according to its worth. All positive and negative estimations about the value of life emerge from this object. Again, in this prestructuring acculturation of life, the possibilities for life are endless because there are always new forms of life, new cultures, new forms of knowledge through which life can understand itself.

With regard to the destruction of distance, we know already that life transfers the distance between itself and the world into itself as the world, becoming hyperbolic. Heidegger explains here that as hyperbolic, life is prestructuring. He writes, "The hyperbolic is a How of the expression of the specific prestructuring movedness of factical life" (*G* 61:122/90). As prestructuring, life constructs worldly distances such as rank, position, and success. Those distances are hyperbolic because they reflect the limitlessness of life's worldly meaningfulness. In this regard, the theoretical attitude of science is prestructuring insofar as it places an objective value upon life. The theoretical attitude is a prestructuring measuring of life in its scientific objectivity. Even this prestructuring objectification of life, however, is relucent because life is still there in that objectification. The "in front of" which runs ahead of life, between life and its worldly distractions, returns to life in the form of scientific objectification so that life is relucent within objectification;

in a sense, it is life that enlightens objectification. Objectification is grounded in factical life as a relucent, enlightening process.

In blocking off, life again manifests relucent and prestructuring movement. Life's elliptical movement is prestructuring insofar as life evades itself and looks away from itself. At the same time, however, because life is evading itself, that prestructuring elliptical movement is also relucent within it. The ways in which life flees from itself will determine how it goes about in the world. Although its ways of fleeing are masks, so that for the most part life does not know that it is fleeing, those masks are temporally constituted because they are modes of fleeing. Life is relucent within those masks because in its fleeing life it is thereby able to look back upon itself. Although it does not have to, life can look back and see itself as it flees from itself.

These interpretations are meant to show that facticity is a determination of both the movement of life as well as a determination of those masks whereby life's movement remains unexpressed. Indeed, within those relational categories wherein life seems most secure (inclination), most objective (distance), and most hidden (blocking off), the most primordial determinations of life's movement, its fundamental temporal constitution, can be discovered.

> The interpretation of life with regard to its relational sense, care, more precisely, the interpretation of the movedness character of care (life), aims toward coming closer to the sense of movement, as factical, in an explicative and categorial way in order to make the factical itself in some way accessible and therefore appropriate "facticity" in a categorial way. (*G* 61:124/92)

Facticity is thus an indication of life's movement. We have seen that the categorial interpretation of life's movement consists of dual structures: the relucent and prestructuring movements of life, in other words, both the manifestation and the hiddenness of life's temporality. In its relation with the world, life expresses that movement, and it conceals that movement, so that *factical* movement encompasses *both* life's caring movement and its hiding of that movement.

By focusing on this relucent/prestructuring process, one can see how life relates to the world. Heidegger says that "factical life lives the world" (*G* 61:130/97). As relucent, life is open to the world, it moves about the world in certain directions. In this sense, there is a certain priority given to the "surrounding" dimension of worldliness. Both the with-world and the self-world can be understood, Heidegger says, as the surrounding-world. It is the surrounding-world that is factically enlightened by all of life's caring movements. Being-with-others and Being-with-oneself indicate the surrounding-world in some way because "the world is such that relucence is factically possible, i.e. the world as surrounding-world" (*G* 61:130/96). But the "surrounding" dimension should not be taken in a strictly objective sense here. The relucent dimension of factical life is a determination of life's openness, its outward direction toward the world prior to its identification of itself with the world. Relucence is an enlightening dimension of life's factical movement by which life *can* encounter the world. It indicates life's openness to the world. At the same time, however, life's movement is pre-structuring insofar as it secures itself in its world. That prestructuring-securing movement covers over life's relucence even as life continues to be relucent. In this sense, life, in this relucent/prestructuring process, "is."

The Temporality of Ruinance

In the following, I argue that what Heidegger describes as the ruinance of life needs to be interpreted from the context of the relucent/prestructuring dimensions of life's temporal-caring movement. Hence, by describing it as ruinant, Heidegger is not passing a strictly negative judgment on factical life. Ruinance is not the degradation of life or of the world. Rather, ruinance is a determination of life's temporal movement. As such, ruinance emphasizes life's fallenness in order to show that fallenness, too, is a dimension of life's movement. Indeed, the term "fallenness" captures the sense of temporal movement within it. *Ruinanz*, as the precursor of *Verfallenheit*, fallenness, has a decidedly temporal character. My goal in this section is to emphasize the temporal dimension of ruinance in order to rid ruinance of its connotative sense as the degradation or abasement of life.[5]

In turn, I also argue that there is a relucent dimension within ruinance that makes possible a counter-ruinance. In this regard, ruinance is an indication of life's temporality that enables it to effect a countermovement against ruinant fallenness. As such, those counter-ruinant structures are grounded in temporality. They emerge from life's ruinance, and they cannot be dissociated from that ruinance. Insofar as life's movement is factical, it is a caring movement toward the world, such that life's counter-ruinant structures are determinations of that caring, worldly movement. Let us look at this more closely.

Heidegger describes ruinance as a "crash" (*Sturz*) through the "emptiness" (*die Leere*) (*G* 61:131/98). This crash, which is the basic sense of movement for factical life, occurs within an emptiness. Ruinance is thus "the movedness of factical life" that "'fully actualizes' factical life *in* itself, *as* itself, *for* itself, *out of* itself, and in all of this *against* itself," which is another way of saying that the factical movement of life "is" (*G* 61:131/98). Since emptiness is what makes the crash possible, it seems clear that the temporal movement of life is grounded in that emptiness. Insofar as life's ruinant crash takes place within an emptiness, what possibility is there of a countermovement? What Heidegger points out is that since life is always moving against itself, as the relational categories of life's movement have shown, the countermovement is a movement back *toward* life. This countermovement is a matter of grasping life as it is enlightened (relucent) within those relational categories.

In every interpretation of life there are certain prerequisites, inexplicit assumptions that are made. Life lives in a certain interpretedness. The countermovement of life moves backward through that interpretedness in order to grasp that dimension of life that cannot be pursued any further, in other words, its brute facticity. The countermovement can thus be described as the dismantling of life's assumptions down to the factical immediacy of life, which Heidegger at one point describes as its wanting (*Darbung*). With regard to its caring movement, that wanting becomes manifest as life's openness to the world. Life is open to the world because it is in need of the world; it is in want of the world. Both wanting and openness, however, are grounded in that emptiness that makes possible life's caring-temporalizing movement. The countermovement of life against ruinance, therefore, is in fact a matter of grasping that dimension of emptiness upon which life stands and which informs all of its caring movements. There is, then, in facticity a tracing back (countermovement) of life's determinations toward that original emptiness. Because that emptiness is the ground of life, i.e. because it makes the crashing-temporal movement of life possible, this tracing back leads to life itself in its most original determination. This, we can say, is part of life's facticity, the retrieval of life's care in accordance with that emptiness which forms the ground of its temporal-caring movement. Life's openness, its care, its wanting are dynamic modes of that temporalizing emptiness.

The most critical dimension of life's counter-ruinant movement is its ability to question (*G* 61:153/113). This questioning is not simply a matter of always having the maxim on hand: "Make sure to ask questions." That kind of questioning is purely mechanical. Counter-ruinant questioning, in contrast, recognizes that there is a question built into every answer. Answers are thus never free from radical questioning. It is, in turn, a questioning that is based on factical experience. Counter-ruinant questioning is thus grounded in the "basic experiences of factical life and its sense of Being [which] remain in factical, historical vitality" (*G* 61:153/114). This counter-ruinant questioning is thus not the construction of an epistemology, but a matter of putting the historical (temporal) vitality of factical life into question. Since factical life temporalizes as a crash through the emptiness, counter-ruinant questioning is directed toward that emptiness. This questioning emerges from emptiness: We question because of that emptiness. Human beings are incomplete (finite) and so want to know. Wanting to know, of course, is based in wanting (*Darbung*), which comes from emptiness. Deeper still, Heidegger writes that factical life crashes not just within emptiness but within the nothingness (*das Nichts*). As such, counter-ruinant questioning is grounded in that nothingness, because factical life is temporal. It is oriented toward that nothingness insofar as it wants to know what it is (a being grounded in nothingness). This questioning out of and toward life's nothingness is counter-ruinant because it intensifies life's crash and, thereby, reveals the origin of its own temporality in that nothingness. It shows human beings who they are.

Nothingness, Heidegger says, co-temporalizes (*mitzeitigt*) factical life. As such, nothingness here is not absolute nothingness, but rather always the nothingness *of factical life*. In questioning back to that nothingness, factical life is taking account of the way in which nothingness dynamizes factical life's temporalizing. From the argument so far, it is clear that factical life tends to objectify itself, and, in doing so, it tends to objectify its own temporality. As such, factical life's temporality is negatived: When it objectifies itself, factical life denies or says "no" to its own temporality. Counter-ruinant questioning grasps back into factical life's nothingness in order to take account of its own temporal dynamic.

Following counter-ruinant questioning back to that original nothingness, we come across two important features of factical life: taking-care (*Besorgnis*) and kairotic time. Καιρός refers to a decisive moment. "Kairotic" time, therefore, is factical life's temporality insofar as that temporality is decisive for factical life. It is factical life's temporality insofar as that temporality is grasped. These two structures are indications of the intensification (*Steigerung*) of life's ruinance. Since ruinance is based on life's temporal crash through the emptiness, an intensification of that crash causes life to become aware of its own fundamental temporality. Again, life is both prestructuring and relucent. As prestructuring, life avoids itself and evades itself; it is not aware of its own ruinance because it is too busy caring for its world. It holds itself in its cares, and care is overwhelmed by cares. In other words, life's openness to the world (care) is covered over by those things to which life is open: its cares, concerns, and preoccupations, that is, those things that it takes care of. Care, *Sorge*, becomes overburdened by cares and so becomes preoccupied, *be-sorgt* (*G* 61:136/101). The etymological relationship among the words care (*Sorge*), preoccupied (*besorgt*), and taking-care (*Besorgen* or

Besorgnis) is clear.[6] The intensification of life's taking-care of objects reveals its original openness to those objects, which is care itself.

Through the intensification of its cares, life announces itself to itself in its care for the world. This happens because as life's cares become intensified, something begins to torment life. Heidegger describes this as the Being-to-me of the tormenting (*Mir-Sein des Quälenden*) (*G* 61, 138/103). There is something gnawing away (*Nagen*) or eating away (*Fressen*) at life, and this corrosion announces itself to life when it is taking-care of the world. It is not, however, an object or entity that announces itself as gnawing away at life but rather some "thing" which is not explicitly worldly but which is also not "categorially other" (*G* 61:138/103). What thus announces itself in the intensification of cares is life itself (!) and, more explicitly, the temporality and historicality of life.

Temporality and historicality are dimensions of life's facticity that emerge from the intensification of life's cares. They are indications of life because life is both temporal and historical. They emerge through life's cares because it is by taking-care (of the world) that life realizes that there is something intrinsic to it (its own temporal-historical constitution), which is gnawing away at it. With reference to temporality, Heidegger writes that "factical life *has its time*; 'time,' which is entrusted to it, which it can 'have' in different ways: keeping in expectation, preservation" (*G* 61:139/103–4). Time is an intrinsic dimension of life. According to Heidegger, καιρός means time, the time that is proper and appropriate to factical experience (*G* 61:137/102). Hence, to say that factical life is kairotic is to say that it is temporal and historical in its own way, that is, in the way that is proper to it. As I have made clear, life's time can be had in various modes, that is, as reluctent (open, enlightening) and as prestructuring (objective). Factical life is kairotic when its temporality and historicality have become properly enlightened— not when they have been objectified.

With regard to history, life is historical insofar as life's time "allows itself from itself to be had" (*G* 61:139/104). Thus, facticity is an indication of how the historical is given to life. This, too, can be taken in different ways because, as ruinant, life covers over that historical givenness. Heidegger writes, "Ruinance takes time away, i.e. from out of facticity it tries to destroy the historical. The ruinance of factical life has this fully actualizing sense of the *destruction of time*" (*G* 61:140/104). I take this to be the most crucial meaning of ruinance. Far from signaling the degradation of life, ruinance is more properly an indication of the way that life is so engrossed within its world that it fails to accept its own temporal-historical constitution. Ruinant life destroys time.

But since life is also reluctant, at the same time that it destroys its own temporality, the possibility emerges that it recognizes itself as temporal and, more specifically, as historical. Heidegger says here that even in the destruction of time, "the historical is still there in life, it is in all ruinance always factical (the historical as *Konstitutivum* of facticity)" (*G* 61:140/104). The temporality of life is an enlightening within life that emerges when life's cares become intensified. Temporality is an enlightening because life is open to the world, only because it is temporal. Factical care is a temporalizing process through which life encounters the world. Ruinance is thus founded on that temporalizing that is also an enlightening and an openness to the world. Insofar as ruinance is an indication of the destruction of life's time, it is a fleeing away from time. Ruinant life does not want to acknowledge the fact that it is historical. Ruinance is thus a modification of historicality (let us say, it is a fallen reification of historicality) whereby life becomes complacent within its world and thus destroys its own time. Nonetheless, temporality emerges within the destruction of time because ruinance is a fleeing from temporality. In that fleeing, temporality is still *there* in life, however unexpressed.

Facticity, therefore, indicates life's concrete movements within its world, in other words, the temporalizing process of care. *As such, facticity is a determination of life's ruinance insofar as within that ruinance the possibility of grasping life is also there.* Life is ruinant because it is factical; life is also kairotic, that is, it can grasp itself as temporal and historical, because it is ruinant and, therefore, factical. By recognizing the temporality of ruinance, Heidegger is showing not only life's evasions and masks but also the factical dimensions of καιρός. Inclination, the destruction of time and distance, blocking off, and making life easy, what we would call the ruinant dimensions of life, are modes that belong to life's facticity. By the same token, temporality, openness, and historicality, what we would call kairotic dimensions of life, are also modes that belong to life's facticity. Facticity provides access to the dimensions of relucence and prestructuring that delineate both life's ruinance and its enlightening and kairotic openness. Facticity shows life's immediacy, how it (life) is *there, within* ruinance.

In this lecture course from 1921–22, *Phenomenological Interpretations of Aristotle: Initiation into Phenomenological Research* (*G* 61), Heidegger seems to present a very different notion of factical life than he had in his earlier courses from 1919–21. Factical life, it seems, is not primarily a context of meaningful relationships and, thus, a source of vitality and intensity, as was the case in *Towards the Definition of Philosophy* (*G* 56/67), *Grundprobleme der Phänomenologie* (*G* 58), *Phenomenology of Intuition and Expression:*

Theory of Philosophical Concept Formation (*G* 59), and *Phenomenology of Religious Life* (*G* 60). He now describes factical life in its basic categories of Inclination, Distance, Blocking off, and Making Things Easy. One might think that his initial sense of the richness and vitality of life has changed fundamentally into a belief that factical life is so weighed down by the world that it no longer retains temporal and historical vitality. In a letter to Georg Misch, however, dated June 30, 1922, Heidegger provides the following summary of all the courses he delivered from 1919 to 1922:

> The investigations upon which the fully elaborated lecture courses are based have as their goal a systematic, phenomenological, and ontological interpretation of the basic phenomena of factic life, which in its sense of be-ing is understood as "historical" and is to be brought to categorical definition in keeping with the essence of its basic comportment of coping in and with a world (environing world, communal world, self-world).[7]

We can see from this quotation that Heidegger's project throughout these early years has been the same: to explore the worldly and historical dimension of factical life. What has changed, therefore, is his emphasis. He has shifted his perspective from descriptions of the vitality of factical life, which can become devivified by objective science and theological dogma (1919–21) to the need to apprehend that temporal, historical vitality from ruinance, which, in its objectivity, destroys time.

My goal in this chapter was to show that life is always both relucent and prestructuring at the same time: both caring and complacent; both kairotic and destructive of time; both revealing of itself and concealing of itself within that revelation. The duality of factical life suggests that ruinance is more than a pessimistic description of life's abasement or degradation. When it is read against both the relucence and prestructuring of life's temporality, ruinance can be viewed as Heidegger's way of situating life's fallenness into its proper temporal dynamic, and this allows for the retrieval of that which is relucent and enlightening within those ruinant categories: temporality, historicality, openness, and care. In the next chapter, I show how Heidegger intended to reinterpret philosophical and theological concepts in terms of the facticity of life. This involves the retrieval of those temporal-historical meanings, that is, the caring movement and radical questioning, that are relucent within the historical traditions of philosophy and theology.

PART III

The Hermeneutics of Facticity (1922–23)

5

The Retrieval of History

Thus the phenomenological hermeneutics of facticity sees itself as called upon to loosen up the handed-down and dominating interpretedness in its hidden motives, unexpressed tendencies, and ways of interpreting; and to push forward by way of a dismantling return toward the primordial motive sources of explication.

—Martin Heidegger, "Phenomenological Interpretations with Respect to Aristotle: Indication of the Hermeneutic Situation"

"Phenomenological Interpretations with Respect to Aristotle: Indication of the Hermeneutical Situation,"[1] known as Heidegger's "lost manuscript," is the prospectus that he sent to Marburg and Göttingen for the purpose of attaining teaching positions at those universities. It is both historically and philosophically important because in it Heidegger outlined his current and projected philosophical interpretations of Aristotle. Gadamer, in his introduction to the subsequent publication of the manuscript (1989) after its rediscovery, titled *Heideggers "theologische" Jugendschrift* (*Heidegger's "Theological" Youthful Writings*), maintains that there are two impulses motivating the young Heidegger's interest in Aristotle: (1) a critique of Aristotle's understanding of Being and (2) a retrieval of the facticity of Dasein through Aristotle. It is the latter impulse, Gadamer claims, that is partly theological insofar as Heidegger affirms that Christian theology moves within concepts that originated in Aristotelian ontology.[2] Since Reformation theology provided a critical impetus to Kant and the development of German Idealism, Heidegger's interpretations of Aristotle can be understood as an attempt to redirect current philosophical and theological traditions toward Dasein's facticity. In that sense, facticity involves both the retrieval of certain lost traditions and the reinterpretation of current traditions through that retrieval.

Considering that Heidegger was providing a sketch of his current research and drawing up plans for future work, the prominence of facticity as retrieval and reinterpretation in this brief yet enlightening and provocative text confirms its centrality to Heidegger's project. I show here how Heidegger intends to makes a retrieval of Dasein's facticity through Aristotle and how he believes that attention to facticity can bring about a radical reinterpretation of philosophical and theological research. My claim is that Heidegger does not simply want to retrieve ideas from the past. Rather, he is interested in the *current* state of philosophy and theology, which, he tells us, is operating with Aristotelian concepts but without a proper orientation toward Aristotle's philosophical-historical (factical) situation. If philosophy and theology can be traced first to scholasticism and then, on the one hand, through St. Thomas and St. Bonaventure back to Aristotle, and, on the other hand, through Augustine and Neoplatonism back to Aristotle, then Aristotle is certainly a pivotal figure. Philosophy and theology have lost sight of certain critical insights into ontology and logic that Aristotle had made through his own analyses of the facticity of life. For philosophy and theology to reclaim those insights, they need to recognize that Aristotle's philosophy was a description of the meaning of factical life, which, Heidegger claims, is the proper object of any philosophical research.

In this chapter, I analyze this text in four sections. The first section shows how the present can take hold of the past. It can do so only by taking account of the *radical questioning* of the past and the *caring movement* of traditions immanent within the past. This radical questioning and the caring movement that belonged to the past need to be brought into current research. The second section addresses the problem of σοφία. In this text, as Gadamer claims, Heidegger seems to privilege σοφία over φρόνησις. This is puzzling since σοφία is an understanding of the eternal and φρόνησις is concerned with action. I argue, however, that Heidegger only privileges σοφία over φρόνησις because Aristotle does so and that we can see in this text how Heidegger is critical of σοφία because it is an unconcerned pure beholding that cannot take account of the facticity of life. For Heidegger, it is φρόνησις that, in a moment of insight, can bring the facticity of life into a truthful safe-keeping (*Verwahrungsweise*). That truthful safe-keeping does not mean that facts about the past will be analyzed or even that the results of historical research will be interpreted. Rather, what needs to be grasped is the temporalizing movement of history. That is the subject of the third section, where I show that the factical life of the past, the How of its temporal movement, needs to be retrieved in order to renew a discipline's current traditions and concepts. The fourth and final section describes the structures of factical life: caring, falling, the How of having death, as well as the countermovement against falling, what Heidegger here calls *Existenz*. As a countermovement, *Existenz* can resist fallenness by taking account of the Being of life in its temporal movement.

The Radical Questioning and Caring Movement of Facticity

It is, of course, possible simply to view Aristotle as a significant historical figure, who, at one time, was of particular importance philosophically. If Aristotle's research is going to speak to us today, however, we need to recognize that an illuminating dimension of Aristotle's philosophical experience endures within our own philosophical and theological traditions. Aristotle thus becomes relevant only when the issues with which he struggled are seen to be imminent and of critical importance to our own lives. The commonality of Aristotle's experience with our own becomes palpable to us through what Heidegger describes as the hermeneutical situation: the ability of contemporary research to grasp the past and bring it thoughtfully and appropriately into the present. Heidegger writes, "The past opens itself only according to the resoluteness [*Entschlossensein*] and force of the ability-to-lay-open [*Aufschließenkönnen*] which a present has available to it" (PIA, 237/358). The present must open the past using those resources it has available to it, so that the past can then emerge as properly historical and not simply as a set of facts or results. In this regard, Heidegger explains that history can never be "false" because, "it remains effective in the present" (PIA, 239/360).

When the retrieval of the past is properly historical, it is, Heidegger says, a recalling of the concreteness of primordial questioning, which did serve then and can serve now as a "problem-awakening model" (PIA, 238/359). The past is then viewed and even evaluated according to the primordiality of its questioning, because it is this, radical questioning, that the hermeneutic situation retrieves from the past and brings into truthful safe-keeping in the present. Heidegger affirms, and this is of the utmost importance, that no epoch should be robbed of the "burden" of having to ask its own questions. He says, "Philosophical research is also something that will never want to claim to be allowed to, and be able to, take away from future times the burden and concern of radical questioning" (PIA, 238/359). The "effectiveness" of Aristotle's (or of anyone's) philosophical research will depend on the primordiality of its questioning (PIA, 238/359). Hence, the object of philosophical-historical research must be such that it can retain the "burden and concern" of radical questioning within its research. For Heidegger, that research "object," indeed the proper object of any philosophical research, whether explicitly historical or not, is human Dasein. When human Dasein is placed into question, the rigor of primordial questioning can be sustained. This is because human Dasein is factical, and it belongs essentially to Dasein's facticity that it is concerned about (*Bekümmerung*) its own Being.

In and through that concern, the temporalizing of Dasein's Being is made manifest. Heidegger writes: "Factical life is in such a way that in the concrete temporalizing of its Being it takes-care of its Being [*um sein Sein besorgt*]" (PIA, 238/359).[3] If philosophical research is directed toward the facticity of Dasein, then it recognizes that Dasein's own Being is an issue for it in such a way that that taking-care is only possible because Dasein's Being is concretely temporalizing. Dasein can take-care only because it is temporal. If it were not a finite and temporal being, Dasein would not be able to take-care of its Being. It can only recognize that it is temporal, though, through taking-care and this means that Dasein will grasp its finite temporality *through* taking-care.

The factical life of Dasein is such that it cares about (*Sorgen*)[4] the world, and that caring is fundamentally a movement. Dasein cares for the world in and through its dealings with the world, that is, in its "tinkering about with, preparing of, producing of, guaranteeing through, making use of, utilizing for, taking possession of, holding in truthful safe-keeping, and forfeiting of" (PIA 240/362). All of these dealings are ways in which factical Dasein is in a basic movement with the world. That movement is only possible because Dasein is temporal. It is thus the temporality of Dasein in its dealings with the world that is to be questioned fundamentally. Questions about Dasein's facticity are questions about Dasein's Being, because movement is a fundamental dimension of Dasein's Being.

Philosophical research, when oriented toward the historical, retrieves the temporalizing movement immanent within past philosophical research. This is important because Heidegger claims that to understand something, you must "repeat (*wiederholen*) primordially that which is understood in terms of its own situation and for that situation" (PIA, 239/360). Factical life is the a priori, the unavoidable reality of human existence. Nonetheless, factical life is not an absolute a priori because it is not the same for every historical period; rather, it is, in each case, its own: "Factical Dasein is what it is always only as its own, and not as the general Dasein of some universal humanity" (PIA, 239/360). Factical life needs to be understood on its own terms by bringing to light the ways in which it actualizes the temporalizing movement of its worldly dealings within an historical epoch. What are philosophically and historically relevant are not the answers that a certain historical period passes along but the ways of questioning, the "problem-awakening models," that it cultivates and that give impetus to the development of new relations to factical life in future historical periods.

In concrete terms, the object of philosophical research is the temporalizing movement between Dasein and the world. This is the meaning of factical life so long as the relation between Dasein and the world is not that of subject and object. Factical life indicates that temporalizing, caring movement that is actualized in and through the Dasein-world relation. Heidegger repeats here that world can mean the surrounding-world (*Umwelt*), the with-world (*Mitwelt*), and the self-world (*Selbstwelt*) (PIA, 240/361). All of these worlds are possibilities for Dasein's Being. They are world-relations that provide structure for Dasein's facticity. As such, they provide directions of meaning through which philosophy and theology accomplish their research insofar as life itself is the constitutive "object" for these disciplines. Heidegger says in this regard that life, *vita,* is "a basic phenomenon, upon which the Greek, the Old Testament, the New Testament-Christian, and the Greek-Christian interpretations of human existence are all centered" (PIA, 240/361). Since life is factical and, as such, an indication of the radical questioning and temporalizing movement of the Being of Dasein in its world, the philosophical and theological meanings of human existence can potentially be rethought in these more radical, more fundamental terms.

The Deconstruction of Σοφία

A critical moment in Heidegger's retrieval of Dasein's facticity through Aristotle is the deconstruction of σοφία. In his introduction to this manuscript Gadamer writes that he is surprised by the importance that Heidegger gives to σοφία over φρόνησις in this text.[5] Indeed, Heidegger does say that φρόνησις and σοφία are "the concrete ways of actualizing this truthful safe-keeping-of-Being (*Seinsverwahrung*)," and he says that "on account of the authentic movement which is available to σοφία, the Being of life must be seen exclusively in the pure temporalizing of σοφία as such" (PIA, 258, 260–61/381, 383). These statements would seem to justify Gadamer's thesis that Heidegger was more interested in σοφία than he was in φρόνησις as a mode of temporalizing that explains life in its Being.

It must be recognized, however, that Heidegger was not only attempting to retrieve the facticity of Dasein from the texts of Aristotle, he was also showing how Aristotle has been appropriated by the tradition. In that light, he first situates the pure beholding of σοφία into the temporal context provided by the factical movement of care in order to show that σοφία has a temporal structure. But Heidegger then goes on to say that σοφία is an "*unconcerned*, time-possessing [σχολή], pure beholding Tarrying-by the ἀρχαί of the always existing beings" (PIA, 261/384). It is a pure beholding, a pure understanding (νοῦς, θεωρεῖν) which "has its concrete possibility of being actualized in Being-free from the preoccupations [*Besorgnisse*] of the routine-directive dealings," and as such is manifest in "purely observational dealings," which "no longer see that very life itself within which they are" (PIA, 263/386). By describing σοφία in these terms, Heidegger is not only showing how σοφία has come to be an indication of the highest possibility of human existence, that is, as a pure beholding of always existing beings, he is also showing how that interpretation has lost sight of the factical life situation that is its own ground.[6]

Heidegger is thus criticizing the notion of σοφία when he says that it is an *"unconcerned* pure beholding." As unconcerned, σοφία actually obstructs radical questioning. This is no unimportant matter insofar as it is the primordiality of radical questioning that is at stake in philosophical research, as we just saw. Concern makes possible a proper understanding of history. Heidegger even describes his endeavors here as "an appropriation of history through concern" (PIA, 239/360). If present historical research is concerned, which is to say that it addresses the Being of factical life, then it allows thereby for the past to emerge in the present as concrete historical understanding. Heidegger describes that understanding as the "radically simple *things worthy of thought*" (PIA, 239/360). Since σοφία is unconcerned it blocks philosophy's access to history and to that within history that is most worthy of thought.

With σοφία, there is a subtle yet consequential shift that takes place from the temporalizing care of factical life to an "observing for its own sake" (PIA, 262/385). In the routine-directive dealings of factical life there is, Heidegger claims, always a "More of observing," and when factical life attends to that "More," it relinquishes the "care of routine-directing," and this amounts to nothing less than an abandonment of life itself (PIA, 262/385). The displacement from the concrete dealings of life to an observing of those dealings emerges from the appearances that the dealings of factical life offer. The interpretation of those appearances is not theoretical, it is practical, but still it offers a certain surplus in the observational tendencies of its practicality. As observational, that surplus takes a subjective stand toward factical life. Factical life, thus objectified, is denied its temporal and historical character.

Σοφία is founded on those ahistorical appearances that emerge in the "More of observing." As such, it grasps movement but only the pure movement of beings that always are. This sense of movement has provided Christian theology (as *actus purus*) and scholastic ontology (as prime mover) with significant theories for the understanding of Being, but the categories that these traditions are using have been borrowed from that surplus of appearance, the objectifiable "More of observing" immanent within Dasein's factical life. Without gainsaying the obvious richness of those interpretations, which have guided Western ontological and theological speculation for so long, Heidegger suggests that philosophy and theology need to reappropriate their own historical foundations by retrieving a concrete understanding of human existence through the same factical dimension of life that proffered that surplus in the first place.

When certain interpretations become rigidified or solidified, as is the case with σοφία, the facticity of life can always be retrieved from that interpretation. That retrieval is accomplished here in Aristotle through the other concrete actualization of the truthful safe-keeping of Being, φρόνησις. Heidegger describes φρόνησις as "the way of truthfully safe-keeping the full moment of insight" (PIA, 259/382). In that moment of insight, a certain truth into the meaning of human experience is revealed. Thus, tantamount to φρόνησις is Heidegger's understanding of what Aristotle means by truth, ἀλήθεια. He insists that by ἀλήθεια Aristotle did not mean anything like "agreement," "valid judgment," "representation theory," or the epistemological sense of "critical realism,"[7] all of which either directly or indirectly have been attributed to him. Heidegger understands Aristotle's ἀλήθεια as an active process, ἀληθεύειν, which means "to take the being which is intended, and which is intended as such, as uncovered into truthful safe-keeping" (PIA, 256/378). Ἀληθεύειν is constitutive of φρόνησις in a special way; φρόνησις is a "truthing" and, therefore, an uncovering and a bringing into truthful safe-keeping of the πρακτική. Hence, φρόνησις is the ἀλήθεια πρακτική,

> the uncovered, full moment of insight into factical life in the How of its decisive readiness for dealing with its own self, and it is such within a factical relationship of preoccupation [*eines faktischen Besorgensbezuges*] with respect to the world which is thus encountered. (PIA, 259/382)

In contradistinction to σοφία, which grasps beings that always are in a beholding of their pure movement, φρόνησις grasps in a moment of insight beings that can be otherwise in the How of their encountering. Φρόνησις is concerned with action, as Aristotle claims, and Heidegger interprets these actions as the concrete relations that take place in and through Dasein's factical interaction with its world.

Φρόνησις is a determination of life's praxis; it reveals the πρακτόν. As such, λέγειν is a part of that process. Heidegger writes that "Λέγειν gives the being in its own self" (PIA, 257/379). There is intrinsic to λέγειν an "as-what" structure that makes revelation possible. Insofar as φρόνησις reveals what to do in a practical situation, it uncovers the action as πρακτόν, something to be done. This "as-structure" manifests in φρόνησις through λέγειν. *Discussing* what to do in a situation and, thereby, actualizing the

How of that situation—the concrete relational dealings between Dasein and the world—is intrinsic to the process of φρόνησις. Heidegger explains here how εὐβουλία, good counsel, is a dimension of φρόνησις; it is, in fact, "the concrete way of actualizing λέγειν which is immanent to φρόνησις" (PIA, 260/382). This kind of discussing happens in and through the moment of insight, and it happens by bringing out the concrete "what" of the situation: through λέγειν, "a what pushes forth" (PIA, 257/379).

This "what," which emerges through the as-what structure of λέγειν, is, in φρόνησις, the situation in its uncoveredness. As uncovered, the truth of the situation has been revealed by φρόνησις. That uncoveredness, however, is not free from deception (ψεῦδος) because the truth of the situation emerges only by way of a "detour" through ψεῦδος. According to Heidegger, ψεῦδος does not mean "false," but rather "remaining-concealed, the Being-covered." Concealedness, therefore, is determinative of both ψεῦδος and αλήθεια.

> Here, the *remaining-concealed*, the *Being-covered*, is fixed explicitly as that which determines the sense of ψεῦδος, and thus the sense of "truth." Aristotle sees Being-concealed as something positive in itself, and it is not a coincidence that the sense of "truth" for the Greeks is characterized privatively—and this according to its meaning and not just grammatically. (PIA, 257/379)

When φρόνησις reveals the truth of a situation, it is only uncovering the How of an action. In the sense that truth is uncovering, φρόνησις uncovers that which it uncovers, and nothing more. Ψεῦδος is intrinsic to truth. Thus, there is always a dimension within that which is uncovered that remains concealed: "The being in the How of its Being-uncovered, ὄν ὡς αληθές, is that which must be taken into truthful safe-keeping against possible loss" (PIA, 257/379). This is to say that the uncovering work of φρόνησις is a revealing of the How of a situation insofar as *that* is revealed which can in that moment be revealed. Φρόνησις protects that which is revealed "against possible loss" because Dasein is consistently in a condition of loss. Dasein, as fallen, is always falling (temporal). Φρόνησις protects, however momentarily, the How of Dasein in its factical situation; it brings the How of Dasein into truthful safe-keeping for a particular moment. Thus, there is no complete truth revealed by φρόνησις, only a momentary truth that is always afflicted by ψεῦδος.

Gadamer is not wrong to say that Heidegger put σοφία in a higher position than φρόνησις. Heidegger did do that, but he did it only to the extent that Aristotle also did so. Heidegger is trying to retrieve that ground of factical life that has given rise to both σοφία and φρόνησις. At the same time, however, as he retrieves factical life from Aristotle, he finds that φρόνησις provides more penetrating insight into facticity because it does not obfuscate the concerned questioning of Dasein, as σοφία does, and, more positively, it brings the concrete temporal structure of Dasein into view through an understanding of its way of grasping the truth immanent in the How of Dasein's concrete dealings with the world. If φρόνησις provides critical insight into factical life, that is because it recognizes the movement that is intrinsic to the concrete How of beings in their Being. Σοφία forgets the factical life situation in which it is grounded, whereas φρόνησις recognizes and embraces it. For this reason, it is through φρόνησις that the factical movement of history can be fully actualized. Through facticity, philosophy and theology can retrieve life and thus allow the historical to emerge within their research.

Temporalizing History

In this section I look at how philosophy and theology can be redirected toward factical life without having to relinquish their own concepts and, thereby, their own histories. Factical structures are not absolute principles that can simply be applied to various fields of research. Rather, facticity is the concrete reappropriation of history through its sources, which means that there are factical structures already there within every field of research, and those structures stand in need of retrieval. We have already seen how radical questioning and temporalizing movement are important to that retrieval. We can see here that facticity is implicitly yet unavoidably a historical stimulus that allows the present to recollect history and bring the originality of its own sources into the truthful safe-keeping of the present. To put factical life into question, therefore, means to return to the sources of that very questioning process so that the reappropriation of history will profoundly influence the present.

The problem of facticity is the problem of the historical; it is a matter of gathering traditions back into the present so that they can speak from themselves, that is, from the facticity of their own situations. As such, this process of the factical retrieval of the historical requires some measure of deconstruction. That deconstruction is, in a sense, violent, but only insofar as Dasein's refusal simply to accept theories and propositions that have been handed down to it without the rigorous scrutiny of radical questioning is violent. Through this deconstructive process, a historical attitude is constructed. Without being skeptical, this attitude toward history scrutinizes "the handed-down and dominating interpretedness in its hidden motives, unexpressed tendencies, and ways of interpreting" (PIA, 249/371). Historical research is thus by nature deconstructive when it essays to return to the primordial sources of meaning for human existence. Heidegger calls this retrieval of history a "dismantling return . . . toward the primordial motive sources of explication" (PIA, 249/371). He accomplishes that return through the phenomenological hermeneutics of facticity.

If Heidegger is right to say that "the Being-character of today's situation (with reference to the problem of facticity) is to be described as the Greek-Christian interpretation of life," then the task of a phenomenological hermeneutics of facticity is first to determine the constitutive components of factical life and then to trace the concepts of that Greek-Christian interpretation back to their advent in factical life (PIA, 250/371). Based on what I have already shown about factical life, we can see that those Greek-Christian concepts are grounded in a temporalizing process. Insofar as they are revealed in a phronetic moment of understanding, those concepts are true only to the extent that they are uncovered (αλήθεια) in and through that temporalizing process.

Hence, the phenomenological hermeneutics of facticity involves a retrieval of that which has remained concealed within that process. As I have already mentioned, the factical movement of care is the Being of Dasein. Philosophy investigates factical life in its Being-character. It is not just an analysis of Dasein's daily dealings but rather an attempt to understand what makes those dealings possible. As such, philosophy investigates the Being of factical life, which Heidegger thus describes as the ontology of facticity. In other words, philosophy is "prinzipielle Ontology," which is to say that it is research into Being as the factical ground of this temporalizing process. Philosophy situates ontology in facticity. By the same token, philosophy must take account of the way that Being has been interpreted already. Dasein always exists in an interpretedness of its own Being, which is determined by the claims that have been made and are being made about it. Insofar as Dasein must attend to those interpretive claims, philosophy is as much about logic as it is about ontology. The claiming and interpreting (logic) of Being (ontology), let us say, the logic of ontology, must be factically reinterpreted. Heidegger says, "Ontology and Logic are to be brought back into the primordial unity of the problematic of facticity," which is to say that the histories of ontology and logic will be reappropriated and thus reinterpreted in terms of that temporalizing process of uncovering and concealing (PIA, 247/368).

Facticity is, in one sense, an indication of how to approach a research "object." This is not to say that it is simply a historical methodology because that presumes a certain model of interpretation through which one understands history. Facticity's approach is to dismantle such models. As such, this dismantling of research models reveals the co-temporalization of the research itself with its object. "Philosophy," Heidegger writes, "also stands within this movement of facticity, since philosophy is simply the explicit interpretation of factical life" (PIA, 248/369). It belongs to the primordial unity of facticity that it ground not just ontology and logic but research subject and research object within its temporalizing movement. Specifically, though, to bring ontology and logic back to facticity thus implicates philosophical research itself within that retrieval. Appropriating those histories according to their factical determinations is effective insofar as it changes the living present. Therefore, philosophy as the factical reappropriation of history must contend with those historical interpretations that have been handed down to it. Philosophy cannot relinquish its own history; rather, it must rethink its own history.

Heidegger is situating Dasein ineluctably *within* its own history. He is not interested in developing fully clarified philosophical concepts that stand outside of the temporalizing movement of history. To break free from predetermined concepts is to release oneself *into* various modes of life's facticity. This is what prevents facticity from becoming a dominant theory: It does not move within perfectly clear concepts. Its concepts are temporal ones that encourage radical questioning into that which has been concealed in every revealed moment of understanding. Factical life is fundamentally temporalizing; it is the "How of the movement of life," which, when understood properly (as *Existenz*), "can never become a matter for the general public or for the 'they'" (PIA, 245/367). Dasein is a task that remains in continual renewal; there is always more work to be done; there are always further dimensions of human experience that can be explored. The question for Dasein is whether or not it will engage in the difficult work of radical questioning by searching for the primordial historical sources of its own present. That, I would say, is the authentic work of philosophy.

The Constitutive Structures of Factical Life

If Dasein so chooses to take up its own history, there are three constituent features of factical life with which to work. They are, Heidegger says, (1) caring; (2) the tendency toward falling; and (3) the How of the having of death. Caring, as we have already seen, is the concrete temporalizing movement of Dasein in its dealings with the world. I have also alluded briefly to the second feature, the tendency toward falling, but without situating it into its proper temporal context. Temporality is a critical dimension of the phenomenon of fallenness. In its caring-temporalizing movement, Dasein is preoccupied with the world. It encounters the world and is engaged with it. In that movement, Dasein becomes world-laden and, as such, it loses itself within the world. Dasein ceases to see any self other than those world-laden preoccupations that constitute its they-self or, let us say, its world-self. Heidegger describes this tendency toward falling (*Verfallensgeneigtheit*) variously as falling away from one's own self (*Abfallen von sich selbst*), falling prey to the world (*Verfallen an die Welt*), and the falling apart of oneself (*Zerfall seiner selbst*), all of which are unified by the root meaning of falling prey to (*Verfallen an . . .*). In a historical context, Dasein loses itself in those traditions that constitute it without thinking through those traditions in terms of the primordiality of their original sources. In this case, Dasein is simply the traditional-self.

Thus, to say that Dasein is fallen is to say that it has fallen into its world and understands itself in and through the world. As such, Dasein tends to make things easy for itself. This is the clearest indication of the fact that Dasein "finds its own self difficult to bear" (PIA, 238/359). The world and traditions are used by Dasein to cover itself over, to hide itself from itself. "Metaphysical assurances" are also placed into this determination of how Dasein makes life easier for itself. Other tendencies of Dasein's facticity emerge from the tendency toward fallenness, all of which hinge on the fact that fallenness is a movement of Dasein toward the world of its preoccupation. Since Dasein is temporal, it is moving, and as moving it falls into its world in various ways. There is the movement of tempting, whereby Dasein relaxes into a kind of idealized self-displacement; as tempting, life can also be comforting, whereby certain locations of "unconcerned security" become fixed; as comforting, factical life is then alienating, such that Dasein moves further and further away from ever possibly understanding itself as itself and not as the world-self or they-self. Perhaps most pernicious of all, through these movements, Dasein loses its own language and speaks only the "*language* of the world" (PIA, 243/364). In all of these falling movements, the possibility of concern becomes increasingly remote. Along with concern goes the possibility of radical questioning because Dasein engages in such questioning only when it is concerned about its own existence.

It should be noted, though, that inasmuch as the they-self or world-self is characterized by Dasein's falling movement into the world, that falling movement is at the same time a fleeing from the world. Heidegger says that "it is typical of flight from the world rather to [imaginatively] insert life into a new, comforting *world*" (PIA, 245/367). As Dasein falls into the world, it engages in so much distraction and hides itself to such an extent that it not only fails to see the world as it is, but it also actually falls into a "new" and "comfortable" world of its own design and artifice. The world thus properly understood is not the world into which Dasein falls but rather the world that Dasein as falling is fleeing from.[8]

According to Dasein's own inclinations, if it wants to bring its own history into truthful safe-keeping in a moment of insight, that is, if it wants to counter, somehow, its falling movement and, thereby, grasp the world in a proper way, it will have to make life more difficult for itself (PIA, 238/360). It does so by rethinking its world, its traditions, its concepts, and its metaphysical ideas in terms of the primordial historicality of their original sources. It is here where the third feature of facticity, the How of the having of death (*das Wie des den Tod Habens*), becomes prominent because it is through an understanding of death that Dasein can bring its life into view and, thereby, properly interpret temporality. Heidegger explains here that factically, death is not an issue for the metaphysics of immortality; it is, rather, the certainty of one's own end. Death is immanent to life: It is always there, both when it is grasped and when it is avoided. The avoidance of death manifests as a fleeing into worldly preoccupations. The grasping of death, however, places life before its present and its past. To grasp death is to acknowledge its certainty, and this acknowledgment puts life into perspective. It shows life to itself by bringing it before its present and its past. In other words, through an understanding of death temporality is grasped in explicit, concrete terms as the temporality—the present and the past—of human Dasein (PIA, 244/365–66). Since historicality is founded on temporality, the How of the grasping of death is determinative for history as well.

When Dasein avoids its own death, it fails to grasp the meaning of its own life. This is not an existential argument but rather an ontological one insofar as Dasein's Being is the temporalizing movement of care. By grasping life through death, Dasein does not, existentially speaking, achieve perfervid individualism. On the contrary, the life that emerges through the proper grasping of death recognizes its finite emplacement within a conceptual historical genealogy. When Dasein does not avoid death but rather grasps it, recognizing itself as finite and, thus, accepting that it is what it is—a finite and temporal being—then Dasein becomes properly historical. In contrast to an ahistorical or metaphysical interpretation of Dasein, which resists its own historical constitution, factical Dasein acknowledges its historicality when it understands its own temporality through the proper grasping of death.

The recognition that it is historically constituted allows Dasein to take up its own history in an authentic way. Authenticity here is an indication of what Heidegger calls the countermovement against falling care, or *Existenz*. This is a problematic possibility for Dasein because it suggests that Dasein can actually resist its own temporality in the manner of those very same metaphysical philosophies that Heidegger says obstruct radical questioning. Heidegger insists, however, that the countermovement of *Existenz* is not a reversal of or even a resistance against temporality. Indeed, how could it be? Heidegger explicates the "counter" of "countermovement" in terms of a "not" which "expresses a primordial achievement which is constitutive of Being" (PIA, 245/367). "Negation," he tells us, "has a primordial primacy over position," such that the countermovement of *Existenz* is, in fact, a retrieval of that primordial negativizing movement (PIA, 245/367).

Existenz is a countermovement that works against Dasein's falling care insofar as it is trying to protect Dasein against inevitable loss. Dasein's fallenness is a given. *Existenz* resists fallenness only through the concerned appropriation of Dasein's Being. Concern is the critical and defining aspect of *Existenz* because so long as Dasein is concerned about its own Being, so long as its own Being is actively and rigorously an issue for it, Dasein can engage in radical questioning and, thereby, protect itself as much as possible against lapsing into those falling movements that have been enumerated above. Heidegger writes, "This counter-movement, as life's being concerned about not becoming lost, is the way in which the possible and apprehended authentic Being of life temporalizes itself" (PIA, 245/366). Dasein loses itself in and through those falling movements, but *Existenz*, a possibility of Dasein's facticity, brings Dasein's temporalizing into truthful safe-keeping. This takes place through an understanding of the primordial negativizing of Dasein's temporality.

Heidegger clearly says that *Existenz* and facticity are not the same. *Existenz* is one possibility of Dasein's facticity, among others.[9] At the same time, however, Dasein's other factical possibilities, the modes of fallenness, do not preclude *Existenz* either. On the contrary, insofar as Dasein's falling movements are temporalizing movements, they provide access to *Existenz*. This is an extremely important point, and Heidegger stresses that even when Dasein is making life easier and more comfortable for itself, it is still temporalizing in its possibilities: "Factical life takes-care of its Being, even when it avoids itself" (PIA, 238/359). Even when Dasein is distracted away from itself, lost and absorbed in the world (in fact because of that distraction and absorption), it is afforded a view of itself.

> Like every movement of factical temporality, the "absorption-in" has in itself a more or less expressed and unacknowledged view-*back* toward the thing *from which it flees*. (PIA, 244–245/366)

The countermovement of *Existenz*, therefore, is a movement toward the Being of the life of Dasein. It brings Dasein face to face with its own death, its own finitude, and, therefore, with its properly understood primordial origins, which is to say, with that "negation" that is, he says, more original than position. The concerned questioning of *Existenz* is both made possible by that negation and it is directed toward that negation insofar as Dasein is concerned about its own Being. Since Dasein is concerned about its own death, it is concerned about that primordial negation.

On the level of history, traditions and concepts that are handed down can then be reinterpreted according to the negativized temporalizing movement of facticity. Heidegger does not then do that work of reinterpretation in this essay, which, after all, is only a prospectus of his future research plans, albeit a very rich and provocative one. Also, Heidegger did not pursue a reinterpretation of Christian concepts to the degree that this text might suggest. What he has accomplished, however, is an indication of how the disciplines of philosophy and theology can retrieve their own histories by recognizing the factical-historical genesis of their own concepts.

The most important insight into that factical-historical retrieval is that every attempt to understand philosophy or theology starts with a certain interpretedness. As the phenomenological hermeneutics of facticity then goes about the work of retrieval, it does so by investigating that which is not said within that interpretedness, that which is so "obvious" about it ("what is not discussed about it, what is assumed not to require any further clarification") that it need not be said (PIA, 248/370). Indeed, what is not said is what motivates that which is said so that the unsaid needs to be said. This need to say the unsaid motivates speaking, and it does so through concern because the retrieval of that negative dimension, the unsaid, is what authenticates the interpretedness of what is handed down by opening it to the concerned speaking of radical questioning. This is the way in which a present can bring about radical change through its own past. Retrieval opens the present to its temporalizing ground. What is said thereby is thus a kind of temporalizing speaking. Even though Dasein cannot ever fully avoid the temptations of fallenness, it can resist fallenness by submitting to its own temporality, revealed through death, which brings Dasein face to face with its present and its past, and speak about its own Being. The ways that Dasein speaks about Being, Heidegger says, are "the ways in which factical life temporalizes itself and speaks with itself in such temporalizing (κατηγορεῖν)" (PIA, 246/368). Through this temporalizing speaking, which is a speaking about Being, factical life, as *Existenz*, is "brought into a temporalizing truthful safe-keeping" (PIA 250/371).

It is well known that this manuscript, written in 1922, is one version of what was meant to be the introduction to a book that Heidegger planned to write on Aristotle. In the coming years, Aristotle becomes an increasingly pivotal figure, and in this text we can see why Aristotle was so important to Heidegger's project. As a philosopher who was also intensely interested in Christianity, Heidegger believed that the traditions of both philosophy and theology needed to be traced back to the notion of factical life in Aristotle. With the retrieval of factical life, Heidegger is not establishing absolute, a priori factical principles that one can then apply to any philosophical-theological research field. Factical structures are already there within a field of research, in the present case that of Aristotle. This means that every researcher must make his or her own way through what they do. They must ask their own questions. Heidegger is pointing out how researchers can lose their way in that research by not taking account of the temporal, historical constitution of the Being of factical life. But still, the decisive possibilities of factical life, which need to be brought into philosophical and theological research, can emerge only through that research. When that happens, that is, when factical life is made into a research "object," then the worn-out and borrowed concepts of these disciplines can be rethought in terms of that negativizing and temporalizing movement of Being, which both conceals the world and uncovers it.

Through temporalizing speaking, Dasein is able to retrieve itself, returning to the primordial sources of interpretation for itself. Dasein thus discovers itself "in rooted possession" within a history that emerges factically in and through the negativized temporalizing of Being (PIA, 250/371). Since they are grounded in the facticity of life, the borrowed concepts of Greek-Christian ontology and logic are rooted in a primordial facticity that is neither Greek nor Christian. The goal of current philosophical research, for Heidegger at that time, was to bring the Aristotelian traditions of ontology and logic back to the factical life situation that Aristotle was himself trying to explicate. This will not at all destroy that philosophical tradition but rather allow it to recognize where it has fallen prey to certain metaphysical assurances so that it can enliven and renew its research through radical questioning. Therefore, even though those original factical structures are neither explicitly Greek nor Christian, they can emerge only insofar as they have been interpreted within certain Greek-Christian contexts.

But what is this temporalizing speaking? In Chapters 7, 8, and 9, I demonstrate how Heidegger focuses on factical language, especially in Greek philosophy. In doing so, he pays close attention to the Greek language itself. For what makes the Greeks to be Greek is, in large measure, the Greek language itself. For Heidegger, the average, everyday language of the Greeks, as described in Aristotle and Plato, had both a revelatory function and a concealing one. He looks at rhetoric in Aristotle and sophistry in Plato as ways of uncovering the temporal and historical context of human beings speaking to each other in the world (in the *polis*) in order to renew philosophical concepts. Thus, temporalizing speaking is nonsystematic. It is the average, everyday speaking of factical life and is a source of both deception and insight. But before looking at factical speaking in the Greeks, I analyze the last course that Heidegger delivered as Husserl's assistant in Freiburg. This course represents the culmination of the early Heidegger's focus on factical life before he shifts toward a more sustained interest in factical language in Plato and Aristotle.

Facticity and Ontology

The "they" has something definitely positive; it is not just a phenomenon of fallenness, but as such a How of factical Dasein.
—**Martin Heidegger,** ***Ontology: The Hermeneutics of Facticity***

In *Ontology: The Hermeneutics of Facticity* (G 63), from the summer semester of 1923, we find a remarkably illuminating analysis of the richness and vitality that emerge from a factical interpretation of life.[1] Heidegger offered this course one semester after he had written the prospectus outlining his plans for future research (Chapter 5). That makes this lecture course the last one he delivered while still Husserl's assistant in Freiburg before traveling to Marburg to become an assistant professor. What we see in this course, quite explicitly, is that because life is factical, its way of being is Being-in-the-world. Facticity emerges here as the nexus wherein Being and life co-implicate each other. In this sense, facticity is an indication of the concrete *there* of the human being in its Being; in other words, facticity indicates the *da* of *Sein*, synthesizing Heidegger's existential and ontological interests. This lecture course is thus a culminating point in a number of respects. Biographically, it marks an important transition in Heidegger's own life. Intellectually, the notion of Dasein crystallizes in this text. The facticity of life and the meaning of Being clearly come together in the structure of Dasein.

As the relationship between facticity and ontology is brought more sharply into focus in this lecture course, certain factical structures that we have already seen, such as historicality, meaningfulness, and openness, are clarified, while others, which we have not yet seen, come out, specifically, the Today and the particularity of Dasein, curiosity, average everydayness, Being-in-the-world, and Being-with-others. All of these structures are placed in the context of a hermeneutics of facticity. Since the hermeneutics of facticity serves the history of ontology, these structures are factical indications of Dasein's understanding of Being. Drawn from average everydayness, they are the concrete ways that factical Dasein is in the world in such a way that through them Dasein can achieve access to an understanding of its own Being.

There are six sections in this chapter. The first section explains how Heidegger understands the importance of hermeneutics. The interpretations of phenomenology and ontology remain within a specific region of objects, whereas a hermeneutic ontology puts factical life into question. The second section of this chapter follows up on what Heidegger means by hermeneutics. I show how, through a hermeneutic analysis of factical life, Dasein can achieve a better understanding of itself because hermeneutics involves a kind of vigilant self-awareness of one's own life. The third section explains what it means to live in a pre-having of Being. I show here how the hermeneutics of facticity involves an understanding of Dasein in its particularity and in its Today, as a factical, living being, and thus not as an objectified thing, such as a person or as a rational animal. The fourth section contrasts the structure of curiosity with philosophical and historical consciousness. In *Being and Time*, curiosity is simply a mode of fallenness. I show how in this lecture course philosophical and historical consciousness take an objective and objectifying distance to what they study, whereas curiosity, although it is a mode of Dasein's average everydayness, is actually a positive phenomenon that indicates the temporality of one's interest in a subject. The fifth and sixth sections follow up on the notion of average everydayness. I demonstrate in these sections how Heidegger does not view average, everyday life as purely negative. On the contrary, his factical interpretations indicate the ways in which average everydayness opens Dasein to the meaningfulness of objects and of people in our lives.

The Need for a Redefinition of Phenomenology and Ontology

This course is actually quite short, a one-hour a week lecture course consisting of only about a hundred pages. Nonetheless, Heidegger's designs are characteristically ambitious as he suggests that the traditional and accepted interpretations of ontology and phenomenology need to be redefined according to the hermeneutics of facticity. These disciplines, he says, as they have been handed down to us, provide only a kind of knowledge that is specific to a certain area. That knowledge is certainly accurate but only within the scope of that area. As such, ancient ontology has been marked off from metaphysics, and modern ontology has been marked off from a theory of objects (*G* 63:3/2). For that matter, modern ontology has been taken over by the specific criteria of phenomenology. Ontologies of nature and culture as well as material ontologies demarcate specific fields of objects that phenomenologists then analyze within the limited scope of consciousness. In this way, ontology has become an understanding of the consciousness of objects (*G* 63:2/1).

Hence, traditional ontologies have buried Dasein and, more specifically, Dasein's historicality, underneath the scientific analyses of natural and cultural objects. Nature and culture thus become objectified significations of the world. Indeed, Heidegger says here that nature can be taken to mean both "world" and "object-region" (*G* 63:3/2). At the same time, however, Dasein is itself reluctant within the scientific analyses of the consciousness of objects. Nature construed as an object springs from Dasein and its historicality.

Dasein has been objectified and thus made into a natural, cultural, or material object through phenomenology. Heidegger explains here that Husserl effectively radicalized Brentano's concept of intentionality. In doing so, he demanded that the question of how one gains access to objects be brought into the consideration of consciousness. The incredible breakthrough that Husserlian phenomenology had made, therefore, was to develop a radical approach to the study of how objects are analyzed by consciousness. At the same time, however, Husserl does not change the area that phenomenology investigates: "The sphere of things remains the same; all that has changed is the *How* of inquiring and determining: description over and against a method of constructing and arguing" (*G* 63:71/56). Husserlian phenomenology thus remains a theory of objects delimited within a specific region (consciousness of natural, cultural, and material objects) that does not address the factical dimension of Dasein. Furthermore, Husserl used mathematics as a model for phenomenology and tried, thereby, to bring the criterion of mathematical exactitude into the method of phenomenological description. According to Heidegger, it is a mistake (*ein Irrtum*) to think that a phenomenological analysis is insufficient when it has not achieved the level of mathematical precision (*G* 63:71/56).

For Heidegger, then, the problem with Husserlian phenomenology is not what Husserl *accomplished* by radicalizing Brentano's sense of intentionality but rather what Husserl left unchanged in Brentano, namely, the object of phenomenological description, that specific region of things that consciousness is meant to analyze. By remaining within a specific, objectified region, phenomenology lends itself to the mathematical model. Mathematics *can* be a model for phenomenology only insofar as brackets are placed around what is being investigated, thus making it into an object-field. This phenomenological bracketing objectifies the area so that its content can then be manipulated, evaluated, and even controlled in such a way that absolute certainty about it can be achieved. In no way, however, does this bracketing do justice to factical life. Factical life is precisely not a specific region of objects; factical life can be bracketed, but once it is, then it is no longer factical.[2] In order to remain faithful to life's temporality, therefore, phenomenology must put factical life into question instead of just investigating a regional ontology. In doing so, a factical ontology develops whose basic structures, Heidegger says, are hermeneutic.

Ontology, Hermeneutics, Facticity

If ontology is, for Heidegger, neither metaphysics nor a theory of objects, what is it? Moreover, what role does facticity play in Heidegger's redefinition of ontology? In what sense does factical Dasein retrieve ontology? On a preliminary level, I can start with the course's title and say that ontology is the hermeneutics of facticity. This title suggests, in the first place, that facticity and Being are somehow related. Furthermore, it indicates that that relationship between facticity and Being is hermeneutical. Let us look at the relationships among facticity, ontology, and hermeneutics more closely.

The first line of the course reads: "As a comment on the first indication of facticity, its closest description is: ontology" (*G* 63:1/1). Heidegger then pursues the "closeness" of ontology to facticity by saying,

> *Facticity* is the denotation for the Being-character of "our" "own" *Dasein*. More precisely, the expression means: this *particular* Dasein (phenomenon of "particularity"; compare whiling, not-walking-away, *There*-on-hand (*Da-bei*), There-Being), insofar as it is "*there*" in its Being-character *according to its way of Being*. To be there *according to its way of Being* means: never to be there primarily as an *object* for examination and clear determination, simply acquiring knowledge about it; rather, Dasein is itself *there* in the How of its ownmost Being. The How of Being opens and surrounds the particular possible "there." (*G* 63:7/5)

Heidegger makes two observations about this definition of facticity. First, he explains what it means to say that Dasein is "in each case its own" (*je eigenes*). "Ownedness," he maintains, is a "How of Being, the indication of the way of the possible being-aware" (*G* 63:7/5). When Dasein is its own, it is aware of its own Being. Perhaps more aptly put: As its own, Dasein becomes aware of *itself* in its own Being. Ownedness is a How of Being; it is a Being-character. Here, to be its "own" does not mean that Dasein becomes isolated, *solus ipse*. Rather, when it is its own, Dasein becomes aware of its Being, and, as such, it recognizes that it is what it is only in and through

Being. Dasein depends on Being. Rather than isolating Dasein, ownedness brings Dasein into an understanding of itself, its own Being. We will see shortly what that means.

The second observation Heidegger makes here is that if " 'life' " is "a way of 'Being,' " then, " 'factical life,' " accordingly, means "our own Dasein as 'there' in any sort of expression [*Ausdrücklichkeit*] of its Being-character according to its way of being" (*G* 63:7/5). This is a difficult and even somewhat cryptic claim. Nonetheless, it seems to suggest that factical life is an indication of Dasein insofar as Dasein is the *there* of Being. This is a tautology, but what it means is that Dasein can both be itself and not be itself. It can grasp itself (in its temporality), and it can evade itself (by seeing itself as an object). Factical life, then, is a determination of Dasein when it is what it is, the *there* of Being, in such a way that it can understand itself as such.

That Dasein *understands* itself as the *there* of Being is an important point. Factical life is not an object to be taken up and examined. There is no explicit knowledge that can be derived from it. Indeed, we cannot have knowledge about factical life *because* it is not an object. That being the case, Dasein's understanding of itself will not be on the order of knowledge. Rather, Dasein's understanding of itself must be moved into the theme of hermeneutics. Dasein understands itself hermeneutically. Dasein will have, instead of knowledge, a heightened "awareness about itself" (*das Wachsein des Daseins für sich selbst*) so that it can recognize those Being-characters immanent within its own alienation (*G* 63:15/12).

> Hermeneutics has the task of making the Dasein which is in each case its own [*das je eigene Dasein*] accessible to Dasein itself in its Being-character, to communicate [the Being-character to Dasein], to pursue the self-alienation with which Dasein has been struck. In hermeneutics the possibility develops for Dasein to become and to be *understanding* for itself. (*G* 63:15/11)

Interestingly, "communication" (*Mitteilen*) is Heidegger's translation of the Greek word ἑρμηνεύειν (*G* 63:14/11). Hermeneutics pursues Dasein's alienation from itself by retrieving its own Being-character from its specific forms of self-alienation and then communicating, transmitting, that sense of Being back to itself. Hermeneutics is not knowledge of the self but rather Dasein's way of "being and becoming *understanding* for itself." It is an awareness (again, *Wachsein*) of the self in terms of its own Being.[3]

Insofar as factical life is placed into a hermeneutic context, hermeneutics is the "self-interpretation of facticity" (*G* 63:14/11). Heidegger is not saying here that hermeneutics, as a subject, grasps factical life, its object.

Hermeneutics interprets facticity in terms of its Being-character. As such, hermeneutics is Dasein's interpretation of itself as it is under way toward itself. As being under way, factical life cannot be objectified, for in that case it would no longer be under way but rather observing itself from outside itself. There is some sense of constancy to Dasein's awareness of itself. Heidegger describes hermeneutics here as a "rooted awareness of itself" (*eine wurzelhafte Wachheit seiner selbst*) (*G* 63:16/12). Nonetheless, that constancy of awareness is still not knowledge of an objectified self. It is not a way that Dasein has taken hold of itself. To have taken hold of oneself is to have a certain objective self in view. That would mean that one is not under way toward oneself but rather that one has reached oneself already. Hermeneutics understands the self as being under way toward itself by placing factical life into the pre-having (*Vorhabe*) (*G* 63:16/13). In this pre-having, Dasein exists (*Existenz*!), prior to any possible objectification.

Any objectification is preceded by a questioning. Hermeneutics, therefore, is a method of tapping into Dasein's basic questioning (its *Fraglichkeit*), because that questioning is Dasein's pre-having. As such, Dasein understands itself according to those structures that emerge from that questioning. Heidegger briefly mentions a few of them here: "caring, disquiet, anxiety, temporality" (*G* 63:17/13). These are structures of questioning relucent (Chapter 4) within Dasein's pre-having. Many of them we have already seen. It is important to recognize now, though, that they are Being-characters that emerge from the hermeneutic interpretation of facticity. To conclude this section, I can say that hermeneutics, through a kind of vigilant self-awareness, situates facticity in the pre-having that is prior to objectification in order to retrieve those Being-characters relucent within itself. As such, the hermeneutics of facticity is always under way toward the Being of the self. Hermeneutics is an understanding of the self in its Being, whereas facticity is the way that Being is *there* within the human being.

To Live in a Pre-having of Being

How is Being *there* within the human being? As I have already shown, factical life is not simply an "object" for hermeneutic inquiry. Moreover, hermeneutics interprets facticity as the *there* of Being from within human being. As such, factical life will not be objectified *because* it is an indication of the there *of Being*. The Being-character within the human being is what prevents objectification. The hermeneutics of facticity asks about the Being of the human being; the human being, as such, is here not taken as an object because the Being of that (human) being cannot, according to Heidegger, be objectified. Perhaps this is better said in this way: The Being of the human being *can* be objectified, but when it is, then what is being asked about is no longer Being. When that happens, Being becomes objectified and, thus, a being.

The human being, of course, is a being, but when it is understood factically, the human being is a being that *lives* in a *pre-having* of its own Being. The hermeneutics of facticity interprets factical life by asking how Dasein lives in a pre-having of Being so that it might then retrieve Being-characters from that pre-having.

Even though Heidegger is asking about the "Being of the human being," he purposely avoids that language (*G* 63:21/17). He prefers rather to say "facticity" in order to distinguish his own investigation of Dasein from traditional interpretations of the Being of the human being, such as person, personality, or even ζῷον λόγον ἔχον (rational animal, an essence endowed with reason), all of which have developed from out of a specific object-region: that of "plants, animals, humans, spirits, God" (*G* 63:21/17). These definitions objectify the Being of the human being. Facticity, in contradistinction to these traditional interpretations of the human being, is able to grasp Being as it is *there* within the human being. It grasps the Being immanent within objectification. That is the case because insofar as facticity is an indication of Dasein, that is, insofar as Dasein is its own, it asks about the particular *there* of Dasein. Heidegger writes, "The own Dasein is what it is only in its particular there" (*G* 63:29/24).

Expounding upon this meaning of facticity, Heidegger says that Dasein's particularity (its *Jeweiligkeit*) is the *Today* (*das Heute*) (*G* 63:29/24). To be sure, my translation of "*Jeweiligkeit*" as "particularity" unfortunately does not capture the sense of whiling (*weilen*) that this term has. As *je-weilig*, however, Dasein is not just whiling, but whiling in its particularity (*je*), as its own. *Jeweiligkeit* is the particular whiling of Dasein in its concrete present. For this reason, Heidegger calls it the Today, which is the concrete present. This Today will then be analyzed according to its ontological character. As such, Dasein is construed in terms of the "present which is closest, the they [*man*], Being-with-others" (*G* 63:30/24). These are ontological structures within Dasein's facticity. These structures are the ways that Dasein lives in a pre-having of Being.

The task of a hermeneutics of facticity is to grasp in the most original way possible how Dasein lives in a pre-having of Being. It can do that, Heidegger says, by attempting to understand those structures according to their temporality. Temporality, coming to pass historically, is the basic phenomenon of facticity (*G* 63:31/25). That much is clear from the fact that factical Dasein "lives" in its own pre-having of Being. Living is temporal. As living, factical Dasein is temporal; it is in the process of becoming itself.

We gain access to that temporality through the facticity of Dasein, that is, through the fact that Dasein is living. Dasein does not *have* life; Dasein lives! The originality of the factical structures that emerge within Dasein's pre-having of Being will be determined by how well they are grasped in the light of their own temporal constitution. I turn now to the temporality of Dasein in its own Today.

Philosophy, History, and Curiosity

If Heidegger is going to make the claim that we live in a pre-having of Being, that means that Being is already *there* within life. As already *there*, Being must somehow have been interpreted for us. Dasein lives in an understanding of Being that has in some way already been interpreted for it. That interpretedness is a mask behind which Being hides. The hermeneutics of facticity, then, must engage that mask by looking into it. How can one know what that mask looks like? It is, according to Heidegger, that which seems to require the least investigation, that which is already so understood that it has become common sense. Indeed, Heidegger says that philosophy challenges common sense, so that Dasein needs to be investigated precisely *there* where one would not expect to find it.

Philosophy (phenomenology) does not need to be taken in some new direction. What he proposes, rather, is that philosophers look for Dasein *there*, where it is thought already to have been found. This is the impulse that causes him to research the Greek thinkers. It is, in fact, the presiding impetus for the entire project of fundamental ontology, namely, to retrieve the Being of Dasein (the Being of the human being) from within those disciplines that have claimed already to have found it, be it philosophy, psychology, metaphysics, ontology, or theology. These are disciplines that claim to have the self already in their grasp, as soul, spirit, personality, or rational animal. Heidegger wants to uncover the Being-characters hidden within those disciplines. In this sense, he wants to get back to the basic and fundamental questioning which originally informed the conclusions that those disciplines subsequently made. As such, he is recovering the original experience these disciplines had with life, factical life, as they were struggling with that experience, before it became objectified or systematized, hardened, into a science, dogma, discipline, or code.

The two disciplines through which Dasein already understands itself are history and philosophy. Historical consciousness and philosophical consciousness, Heidegger tells us, are the Today of Dasein. They are the ways in which Dasein believes that it has hold of itself already. The aim of hermeneutics, then, according to Heidegger, is to ask this question: "Which

Being-character of Dasein shows itself in these ways of having hold of itself?" (*G* 63:49/39). Like ontology and phenomenology, historical and philosophical consciousness are objective sciences that emerge from the study of specific object-regions.

Historical consciousness, for its part, studies the past by maintaining a certain objective distance from it. Heidegger takes Oswald Spengler's book, *Untergang des Abendlandes*, as an example of historical consciousness. Here, Dasein has a full view of its own historical past in an objective sense, as "what happened." By looking at its own past in this way, Dasein consequently objectifies its own present, viewing its Today as an object. The present is simply what is happening, the past simply what has happened. These objective fact*ual* happenings may be interpreted, but the human being is nonetheless construed as an object and certainly not with regard to its Being-character. Philosophical consciousness, likewise, takes an objective view of the human being by attempting to draw a picture of reality that is scientific and, as such, totally free of all standpoints (*G* 63:63/49–50). It constructs "pure truths" about the human being that admit of no prejudices (*G* 63:63/49). They are purely objective, static, and they conceal the temporality of factical life.

Both historical consciousness and philosophical consciousness attempt to establish pure, objective agreement in their research: in history, agreement about the "objective having-been"; in philosophy, agreement about the "unchangeableness of always being in such and such a way" (*G* 63:65/51). By creating absolute agreement, however, they submit their work to the "everywhere and nowhere" of timeless, objective knowledge. Such knowledge is certainly secure (*G* 63:62/48–49). It has already been decided upon, proven, and thus accepted as absolute knowledge, so it can be assumed. That makes it valid, objective, and, hence, everywhere. However, because it shuts out all opinions, protecting Dasein against the indeterminacy of skepticism, it quells Dasein's need to question. This knowledge is never asked about, never called into question, always simply assumed. As such, it is not just everywhere, it is also nowhere.

But even though the objective knowledge of Dasein in historical and philosophical consciousness is both everywhere and nowhere, it is also a determination of the present of Dasein, its Today. As being everywhere and nowhere, this objective knowledge is present, *there*, within Dasein in such a way that Dasein is not even aware of it. This is a kind of knowledge that is assumed and, as assumed, it structures and determines the way that Dasein lives in the world, albeit in a concealed way. This assumed knowledge needs to be drawn out and examined. When it is, then its basic temporality emerges, a temporality that calls into question the very objectivity of that knowledge.

The temporality of objective knowledge is, Heidegger says, the basic phenomenon of curiosity. Although this is a fallen mode of the understanding, that is, it is how Dasein, "finds itself in its (fallen) way" (*in seiner (abfallenden) Weise [sich] findet*), curiosity is still a way in which Dasein lives its own Being. This is important because curiosity is a dimension of Dasein that shows itself even in the objectivity of philosophical and historical consciousness. Even if one does not submit objective knowledge to the rigor of radical questioning, one is at the very least curious about it. There is an active sense to Dasein's curiosity that Heidegger is trying to bring out. Heidegger calls curiosity "something like a movement of Dasein itself . . . movement: a How of temporality, of facticity" (*G* 63:65/51). It shows that Dasein is in some small way concerned about its own Being; it shows that philosophy and history are not just dead or anesthetized "cultural wares" (*Kulturegüter*) that one might find in a book somewhere (*G* 63:65/51). Rather, curiosity is a way that Dasein actively lives in a pre-having of Being.

One can recognize the activity of Dasein's curiosity in the opinions and standpoints that one has about objective knowledge. One never simply starts with objective knowledge. There is a whole process of questioning and examining, trying to figure something out, which is *there* within objective knowledge. Curiosity is a vestige, a trace, of that radical questioning, which we can then follow back (retrieval!) to that more original sense of questioning. Hence, the suggestion that objective knowledge is subsequently free from all opinions, all standpoints, all need for questioning, amounts to a denial of the historical development of that knowledge. For this reason, Heidegger says that being free of all standpoints (*Standpunktfreiheit*) is itself a prejudice (*G* 63:82–83/63–64). The recognition of one's own curiosity immediately subverts the objectivity of the knowledge one has about oneself by submitting Dasein in a preliminary way to the origin of objectivity in radical questioning and, thus, to the history of that knowledge.

Curiosity, then, is a factical and, therefore, temporal dimension of Dasein. To be sure, it is a fallen mode of Dasein, but it is still a phenomenon that needs to be grasped because, thereby, the basic temporality of objective knowledge, that is, the fundamental questioning that went into it in the first place, can be drawn out of it. Curiosity is hidden within the objective knowledge that Dasein has. It is a factical dimension of those objective determinations about itself within which Dasein lives. Viewed factically, the objectivity of that knowledge is seen to conceal this basic movement.

Factical Being in the World

Using phenomenological terminology, we can say that the objective knowledge produced by philosophical and historical consciousness covers over, conceals, "the things themselves." As that objective knowledge is handed down by tradition, the concealed thing is taken to be the thing itself (*G* 63:75/59). The hermeneutics of facticity, which travels the same way as phenomenology by trying to bring the things themselves into view, might replace phenomenology and, thus, as a kind of radical phenomenology, "place philosophy once again before the decisive contexts" (*G* 63:75/59). It can do that by way of deconstruction (*Abbau*). The retrieval of curiosity from behind the mask of objective knowledge marks one small step along the path of deconstruction insofar as it brings Dasein closer to its own Being.

But why is curiosity closer to Dasein's own Being than objective knowledge? Heidegger answers this question by saying that "it belongs to the *Being*-character *of Being . . . to be in* the way of *concealing itself* and disguising itself—and not in an accessory sort of way, but rather according to its Being-character" (*G* 63:76/60). We have seen already that Dasein understands itself in terms of philosophical and historical consciousness and that curiosity is concealed within the objective knowledge that those disciplines proffer. We see here, though, that the process of concealing curiosity behind objective knowledge belongs to Being itself. Indeed, as Heidegger pursues curiosity, he draws the conclusion that curiosity is itself the concealing of care. Curiosity is a "*How of care*"; it is one of care's masks (*G* 63:103/80). Hence, by grasping objective knowledge, one is led back to curiosity and, further still, to care. Recognizing Dasein's masks and what lay behind them is an ontological endeavor insofar as the process of concealing belongs to Being itself.

Heidegger describes the effort of the hermeneutics of facticity in this way: "We need to move away from that which lies closest and proceed to that which grounds it" (*G* 63:77/60). Is not Being that which grounds everything? It is, to be sure, but we can reach Being only by starting with that which lies closest. That which lies closest, as we have seen, is the objective knowledge of historical and philosophical consciousness, the ways that Dasein understands itself. This objective knowledge is everywhere and nowhere. Furthermore, according to Heidegger, that objective knowledge that lies closest must be grasped in its originality, namely, in its temporality. What Heidegger is describing here is the way that objective knowledge needs to be approached in order for that knowledge to then be grasped in its prehaving. Dasein lives in a pre-having of Being, but that is not to say that it is aware of that pre-having. Dasein must enter into that pre-having of Being in the right way. Heidegger calls this the construction (*Ausbildung*) of the pre-having. Therefore, deconstruction can be placed into positive terms as the construction of Dasein's pre-having.

The "destiny" (*Schicksal*) of a hermeneutics of facticity comes down to this moment wherein Dasein tries to approach itself in such a way as to make its own pre-having of Being accessible to itself in the right way (*G* 63:80/62). Curiosity plays an important role in that approach. Heidegger writes, "The pre-having should identify itself precisely in the analysis of curiosity" (*G* 63:80/62). He emphasizes that curiosity does not determine whether or not the pre-having has been grasped in an original way. Curiosity only shows that there is more there within objective knowledge that can be uncovered. The full interpretation of Dasein's pre-having demands that that pre-having be entered into factically. This is another way of saying that Dasein will be understood as Being in a world. Heidegger says quite explicitly,

Dasein [factical life] is Being in a world. (*G* 63:80/62)

The world is that which lies closest to factical life. We saw this in the third chapter: To say the word "life" brings one immediately to the phenomenon of world. Here, that analysis is refined so that the move from factical life to world brings Dasein, which factical life *is*, closer to its own Being. As Being in a world, factical life (Dasein) encounters Being (*G* 63:85/65).

As a description for factical Dasein's way of Being in a world, Heidegger uses the term everydayness (*Alltäglichkeit*). Everydayness is the particularity (*Jeweiligkeit*) of Dasein. Through the analysis of everydayness, Dasein's pre-having can be constructed in the most original way, that is, with regard to its own temporality. Heidegger explains, "Everydayness characterizes the temporality of Dasein" (*G* 63:85/65). This is an important point because Heidegger is trying to undermine the objectivity of the knowledge that emerges from historical and philosophical consciousness. Through the analysis of everyday Dasein, he is showing how life, factical life, is relucent within that objectivity. He accomplishes that by submitting this objective knowledge to its own temporality, which is to say, to its own escape from temporality. As Heidegger does this, he recognizes that there is a certain averageness that characterizes everydayness. The phenomenon of the "they" emerges in this regard. Insofar as Being in a world grounds objective knowledge, everydayness, Dasein's way of Being in a world, generates that objective knowledge. Philosophy and history emerge from out of Dasein itself.

I noted above that objective knowledge is both everywhere and nowhere. As objective (universal, absolute, scientific), it is everywhere, yet as unquestioned (assumed, implicit, simply "understood"), it is nowhere. The reason why it is both everywhere and nowhere is that this objective knowledge, without being placed into question, is then passed around from person to person. It becomes disseminated without being fully considered. Hence, its objectivity is not based on any scientific principles but rather on the averageness of that knowledge handed about by the "they." The objectivity of historical and philosophical knowledge, indeed the objectivity of all knowledge that makes such a claim, is based on this everydayness of knowledge and, therefore, on the way that Dasein tends not to submit the knowledge that it has of itself to the rigor of radical questioning. To be sure, this is itself a radical claim. But if we can believe Heidegger when he says that objectivity is a prejudice because no knowledge is free from its own historicality and, therefore, from those standpoints and opinions that informed its development, then the "aura" of objectivity that this knowledge has must come from somewhere else, namely, the average everydayness of Dasein's Being in a world.

Therefore, we can read average everydayness in a positive sense as submitting objective knowledge to its own historicality. Heidegger suggests this reading of everydayness when he says, quite explicitly, that the "they" is something positive:

> Interpretation begins in the Today, i.e. in the particular [*bestimmten*] average understanding [*durchschnittlichen Verständlichkeit*], out of which philosophy lives and to which it *speaks back*. The *they* has something definitely [*bestimmtes*] positive; it is not just a phenomenon of fallenness, but as such a How of factical Dasein. (*G* 63:17/14)

Clearly, facticity and fallenness are related. Nonetheless, facticity admits of something positive that the phenomenon of fallenness, for whatever reason—Heidegger does not say—does not. From the foregoing analyses we can say that as a "How of factical Dasein," the "they" submits objective knowledge to its own historicality. It makes objectivity a worldly phenomenon. Everydayness is the passageway from science to factical Dasein. Viewed negatively, the "they" is accountable for the fallenness of objective knowledge. This is to say that objective knowledge is knowledge that has fallen from its factical-historical (temporal) situation into objectivity. Viewed positively, an understanding of the "they" brings that knowledge back to its original facticity, that is, back to the temporality of Dasein's Being in a world.

Factical Openness to Being

If we pursue this positive-negative dimension of the "they," we recognize that the primary way in which the "they" is accountable for the fallen condition of knowledge's objectivity is by way of speaking. Specifically, the way that "they" speak is in idle talk (*Gerede*), which Heidegger describes as the "public-average way in which Dasein takes itself and keeps itself" (*G* 63:31/25). By addressing itself in this way, Dasein communicates an interpretedness of Being to others. That interpretedness is, as we have already seen, philosophical and historical consciousness. These are the ways that Dasein understands itself on an everyday level, how it addresses itself and speaks to itself: historically, as an objective having-been (*seines objektiven Gewesenseins*) and philosophically as an object that, in its unchangeability (*in der Unveränderlichkeit des Immersoseins*), will always be an object: an I, ego, or cogito (*G* 63:65/51).

Again, though, in a more positive sense, in addition to explaining how these interpretations of Dasein came to be seen as objective (that is, through the averageness of everydayness), idle talk is also a How of Being through which ontological meanings emerge. As such, this way of speaking is not just average; it is also Dasein's way of being open to the world and to Being. Through this way of speaking, Dasein is not enclosed (bracketed) within a specific object region; it is, rather, open to the world. (Perhaps more aptly put: Dasein becomes open to the world and to Being by going through that specific object region and retrieving that sense of Being that opens Dasein to the world and, therefore, to Being.) For this reason, Heidegger says that Dasein in its everydayness encounters (*Begegnen*) Being. Indeed, Being is only encountered in our factical experience of the world. In its idle ways of speaking, Dasein is open to the world, and since the world encounters Being, Dasein's idle talk is an encountering of Being. Let us look at this relation more closely in order to determine the meaning of Dasein's openness.

First, we need to establish that the world does, indeed, encounter Being. What Heidegger says here is that Dasein encounters the world by being preoccupied with it (*Besorgen*). In that preoccupation there is a kind of carelessness (*Sorglosigkeit*) insofar as the world that is thus encountered seems simply to be *there*. As simply *there*, though, the world is encountered as something meaningful. As *there*, the world simply is, and insofar as it simply is, the world admits of meaningfulness. Hence, by being preoccupied with the world, Dasein encounters meaningfulness. Dasein as Being in a world encounters Being as the meaningfulness of the world. Moreover, since Dasein is preoccupied with the world, and since to be preoccupied with something means to encounter its factical meaningfulness, to be preoccupied with the world is to be preoccupied with Being as Being in a world: Heidegger writes, "This, *being preoccupied with world-Dasein—Being*, is a way of Dasein of factical life" (*G* 63:86/66).

Heidegger presents two elements of openness: the present-at-hand (*Vorhandenheit*) and bringing others to light (*der mitweltliche Vor-schein*). With regard to the former, Heidegger says that when objects are present-at-hand, their temporality becomes accessible. Indeed, Dasein in its everydayness is open to the temporality of objects that are *there*, present-at-hand, in the world. He provides an excellent example of this to his students by making two analyses of a table, one analytic, the other factical. In the analytic analysis, he looks at a table, any table, which is just a thing, a thing in space, with certain qualities: It is flat and made of wood or stone; it has some value; it is beautiful, practical, and so on. As such, the table is, in its Being, "a material, spatial thing" with value tacked on to it (*G* 63:89/68). In the factical analysis, however, where the table is described according to the way it is encountered in its meaningfulness, Heidegger describes not just any table but this table here in this room (again, facticity is *je unser eigenes Dasein*, hence the particularity of the table): It is a table for "writing, eating, sewing, playing," located in this or that part of the room, it gets good light; a friend sat there; we worked there; we had a party there; my friend and I made a decision there (*G* 63:90/69).

Heidegger calls these descriptions the table's "factical spatiality" (*faktische Räumlichkeit*). The table is viewed not simply according to what it is, as an object, but rather according to How it used: Who is using it?; for what purpose?; when?; why?; why now?; where did it come from? These determinations are not insignificant or trifling. They are the stuff of philosophical analysis in its factical temporality and its factical spatiality. These descriptions bring into view the particularity (*Jeweiligkeit*) of the table's "historical everydayness" (*geschichtliche Alltäglichkeit*) and thus its temporality (*G* 63:98/75). Moreover, this factical spatiality, by opening Dasein up to these kinds of questions in its experience of the table, is an encountering of Being. In this factical analysis, the objective determinations about the table, while certainly not false, break down in the light of a kind of thickening of factical meaning within the temporality of everydayness, where objective truth and falsity are somehow inappropriate. Is it simply "true" that we eat at the table? In a way, it is true, but the factical experience of eating there with family and friends is certainly more than just true. It is meaningful. It *is*.

Preoccupation (*Besorgen*) is a mode of care within which care (*Sorge*) lies hidden beneath that with which we are preoccupied. The etymological connection is certainly evident. As such, to be preoccupied with something conceals within it the more essential, ontological structure of care itself, through which and because of which being preoccupied with something or, for that matter, being curious about something, is made possible. Without explicating the meaning of care in great detail, Heidegger does say that care encompasses the multiplicity of ways in which Dasein is in the world: "producing, performing, taking-into-possession, preventing, protecting from failure, etc." (*G* 63:102/79). All of these are ways in which Dasein is preoccupied with the world. Only when the world is interpreted in this way, as an encountering of the world's meaningfulness, is it possible for the openness (*Erschlossenheit*) of Dasein, its care, to be grasped.

Furthermore, Dasein in its everydayness is open to others. Others are *there* for Dasein in their meaningfulness. Factical Dasein is not *solus ipse*. Interpreting factical life in terms of its own Being does not isolate Dasein. Heidegger says explicitly that it would be a misunderstanding to believe that facticity, one's own Dasein, means brooding about an isolated I. On the contrary, facticity opens Dasein to those ontological structures *there* in Dasein's pre-having of Being. Dasein is, on the one hand, open to the meaningfulness of the world, and, on the other hand, it is open to Being-with-others.

As open to others, Dasein brings others to light. There are others in the everyday with-world who are thus encountered in their meaningfulness. These are the people who are there in the everyday life of Dasein: people with whom we work and play, neighbors, the friends who sit down with us at the table to eat. They are the people whom we care for in our everyday world. They are, in other words, those people with whom we are familiar. Dasein brings others to light by encountering them in their meaningfulness and thus recognizing the familiarity that Dasein has with them.

This openness that Dasein has to objects in the world and to other people in the world is, as I said, Dasein's everydayness. In a negative sense, that everydayness is marked by averageness. Even this familiarity is a kind of averageness, so that when Dasein brings others to light, they carry the "they" with them. In a positive sense, however, Dasein can grasp its own temporality through everydayness. The temporality of Dasein is unfamiliar to it. For the most part, Dasein does not understand itself temporally but rather, as I have already stated, in terms of the objective knowledge of philosophical and historical consciousness. The familiarity of everydayness makes possible the grasping of temporality by preparing Dasein to recognize what is unfamiliar to it. By appreciating the familiar, Dasein is then able to accept the unfamiliar. In this way, everydayness subverts the objectivity of knowledge by allowing that which is unfamiliar to that knowledge, its own temporality, to emerge from within it.

In everydayness, Dasein has, Heidegger says, a kind of fixity (*Feststellbarkeit*) to it. This experience of everydayness is neither one of pure Being nor of pure objectivity. It is, rather, that moment when the two come together, as Da-Sein. In this moment, Dasein has the opportunity to make itself into an object—*Da*-sein, or it can grasp itself in terms of its own Being—Da-*sein*. In the latter case, Dasein recognizes that it encounters the world in its meaningfulness. As such, the world is not experienced as an object or object-region but rather in its Being, and Being is not an object; it is not a being. When the world is encountered in its meaningfulness, then Dasein's openness to the world is grasped. That openness, he says, works against the objectivity of Dasein and, thus, against the objectification of Being by bringing the temporality of Dasein's everydayness into view.

In this chapter, I have attempted to trace the development of facticity into Being in a world. In doing so, I have tried to accentuate the positive sense of everydayness. At the same time that average everydayness accounts for the objectivity of knowledge proffered by philosophical and historical consciousness, the retrieval of everydayness, that is, the way that Dasein lives factically in a pre-having of Being, actually submits that objective knowledge to its own temporality. Dasein, in turn, is shown to be not simply a being but rather a being that lives in a hermeneutic understanding of its own Being. Dasein is Being in a world, which, insofar as it encounters the meaningfulness of the world, encounters Being. The analysis has thus revealed Dasein's essential openness to the world and to Being. In that openness, Dasein encounters the meaningfulness of objects, and it brings other people to light.

In the years immediately following this course, as he starts a careful and incredibly detailed, often line by line, reading of ancient Greek texts, Heidegger will discuss the explicit mechanics of facticity less and less. This is not to suggest, however, that he abandons the concept. What happens is that instead of describing what facticity is, he will, in a sense, engage in a factical method of studying philosophical texts. He makes factical analyses of Greek thinkers, thus shifting from the portrayal of what facticity means to a retrieval of factical meanings. Central to this endeavor is the attempt to discern the speaking relationships that people have with each other in the world and how speaking informs philosophical concept formation. In *Introduction to Phenomenological Research*, *G* 17 (Chapter 7), he will look at the Being of speaking to show how language admits of profound deception and, at the same time, reveals the richness of the world. In *Basic Concepts of Aristotelian Philosophy*, *G* 18 (Chapter 8), he analyzes Aristotle's *Rhetoric* in order to understand Aristotelian concepts from within Aristotle's factical-historical situation, the Greek marketplace, wherein citizens of the city, in average everydayness, spoke to each other, talking, debating, refuting, and engaging in dialogue. This is quite similar to Heidegger's earlier attempt to understand Pauline concepts from within Paul's own factical-historical situation, as we saw in Chapter 2. In *Plato's Sophist*, G 19 (Chapter 9), Heidegger analyzes Aristotle's *Ethics* and the Platonic dialectic in order to present a new understanding of language based on the disclosive power of words to show what Being-in the world means.

What is at stake in Heidegger's turn toward the Greeks is a focus on speaking and on Being. As we saw in the last chapter, Heidegger believes that philosophical and theological research need to retrieve the temporality and historicality (facticity) of their own traditions by taking account of factical life in Aristotle. It stands to reason, then, that when he goes to Marburg, he would analyze the Greeks, especially Aristotle, in terms of their facticity. He delves into an intense analysis of the factical meanings that emerge within Greek Dasein, analyzing the Greeks as they are, that is, within their own factical-historical situation. Since the Greeks lived so profoundly in the spoken word, Heidegger focuses on the phenomenon of speaking in his readings of Plato and Aristotle.

Furthermore, the study of factical life brings Heidegger to refined ontological concerns about the specific relations between life and Being. Ontology is the hermeneutics of facticity insofar as the retrieval of factical life from Aristotle's texts makes possible an understanding of how the Greeks understood Being. Since philosophy and theology stand in a tradition that dates back to the Greeks, the retrieval of how they understood Being will certainly influence those disciplines. Since world encounters Being and since factical life means to live in the world, facticity provides access to Being. In this way, the specific mechanics of facticity begin to yield to ontological determinations about the Being of the human being that are relucent within factical structures. Thus, the present course *Ontology: The Hermeneutics of Facticity* (G 63), marks an important transition: The dynamic of facticity reaches a certain culmination here just before Heidegger begins to use it as a method to read the ancient texts of Greek philosophy.

PART IV

The Language of Life (1923–25)

7

Factical Speaking

> The Being of the world and of life have a very specific interconnection
> through the Being of speaking.
>
> —**Martin Heidegger**, *Introduction to*
> *Phenomenological Research*

During the winter semester 1923–24, in *Introduction to Phenomenological
Research* (*G* 17), Heidegger sought a clarification of phenomenology. The
purpose of the lecture course was first to define the constituent terms of
phenomenology, that is, φαινόμενον and λόγος, through a return to Aristotle. That analysis establishes a ground upon which to evaluate Husserl's
conception of phenomenology and, further, his appropriation of Descartes.
For the purposes of this chapter, the explicit mechanics of Husserl's use of
Descartes are not as important as Heidegger's analysis of phenomenology
via Aristotle. However, a brief glance at Husserl's Cartesian insistence on
certainty and validity as the true goal of philosophical reflection makes
clear the radical shift that has taken place in philosophy from Aristotle's
uncovering of the basic tendencies of the human being to a search for evidence that will guarantee epistemological certainty about human being.
Heidegger calls our attention to this shift and at the same time recovers an
original experience of λόγος through a return to Aristotle.

This renewed investigation of phenomenology brings a factical understanding of language to the center of Heidegger's thinking. It takes place
through a retrieval of speaking in the Greek world. In this and subsequent
lecture courses, all of which preceded the publication of *Being and Time*,
Heidegger investigated the extent to which speaking determined the way
that the Greeks lived in their world. Heidegger points out (one semester
earlier) that Aristotle's definition of the human being as ζῷον λόγον ἔχον
proves this. For Aristotle, λόγος did not mean reason; it meant speaking
and discussing with others.[1] Facticity means "Being-in-a-world," which
Heidegger established in his earlier lecture course titled *Ontology: The*

Hermeneutics of Facticity (*G* 63), and since "Being-in-the-world," for the Greeks, meant speaking, facticity involves speaking. Factical language is the speaking of human beings with each other in the world. Moreover, since world encounters Being, speaking (as "Being-in-a-world") is a discursive encounter with the Being of the human being. Although most of this course is devoted to Husserl and Descartes, Heidegger will spend the following year investigating the factical dimension of language as a kind of speaking that encounters the world and, therefore, encounters Being. The purpose of the present chapter is (1) to show that Heidegger discovers and defines the factical dimension of language through a retrieval of Aristotle's conception of λόγος and (2) to demonstrate that the facticity of language is the primary source of both showing and deception for the human being. The latter idea is of primary importance. Heidegger's point here is that language not only shows objects as what they are but that in that showing language is also deceiving. Thus, language shows objects both as they are and as they are not. Revealing and concealing are both essential to language, and since language is an essential dimension of the human being, revealing and concealing are both essential elements of the human being.

In this chapter, I deal with the topic of revelation and concealment in five sections. Heidegger bases his analysis of λόγος on the facticity of Dasein, which indicates the Being of the human being as living in a world with others. In the first section, then, we see that λόγος as speaking will serve as the ground for Heidegger's analysis of language. The second section includes the following: λόγος as showing and λόγος as concealing. Here we find Heidegger's retrieval of Aristotle's conception of λόγος as revelation. In that retrieval, he discerns the primacy of the λόγος ἀποφαντικός, which is the λόγος of science. The λόγος ἀποφαντικός conceals the revelatory character of λόγος, but it is only by going through the λόγος ἀποφαντικός that we can uncover that revelatory character. The third section attends to the unity of the λόγος ἀποφαντικός. There we find the source of human deception—and thus of concealment—in speaking. The fourth section looks more closely at that deception to see that there is, for Heidegger, a lie built into the structure of speaking itself. The fifth section shows that this deception arises only through the disclosure of the world and its richness.

Factical Dasein as the Ground for Any Investigation of Language

A genuine attempt to understand the Greeks must take into account the fact that the Greek way of Being was thoroughly grounded in language. Again Heidegger points to Aristotle's description of the human being as ζῷον λόγον ἔχον, an animal that speaks and discusses, to demonstrate this. For the Greeks, language was an essential dimension of the human being. With reference to the concept of λόγος in Aristotle, Heidegger says, "Language is the Being [*Sein*] and becoming [*Werden*] of the human being himself" (*G* 17:16/12). This is to say that the Greeks did not simply believe that words were tools. Certainly, the objects of the Greek world were viewed as πράγματα, practical objects, and words were to a certain extent practical objects that served their purposes. Aristotle's treatise on rhetoric, when read in a specific, theoretical way, will attest to this as will the philosophies of language, grammar, and logic that date back to the Hellenistic period. Heidegger explains, however, that for the Greeks a word could not be considered exclusively in terms of its practical value as a tool (*Werkzeug*), for it did not have the fixed meaning (*feste Bedeutung*) or purpose that tools have. Tools are designed to accomplish specific tasks. The task determines the meaning and purpose of the tool. The meaning of a word, however, does not emerge quite so cleanly from the object or experience that the word is meant to identify or describe. The generation of the word depends on the factical experience of human beings in the world. This means that the opinions and viewpoints of human beings as they encounter objects and have experiences go into the meaning of a word (*G* 17:16/12). There is a worldly (*weltlich*) encounter that takes place with the inception of a word, and that encounter must be a determinative factor in any explanation of the word and its meaning. As a result, the human being and the impulses, motivations, and tendencies that determine how human beings are in the world are implicated directly in the meaning and development of language. The Greeks were very much aware of this.

Words are not simply tools to resolve practical, everyday tasks. This pragmatic view of language does not take account of how deeply the human being is immersed in the relation between language and the world. Certainly, humans are practical beings who engage in tasks and solve problems. In this sense, the human being cares for the world. But how are we to conceive of this practicality? Earlier lecture courses, as we have seen, provide clues as to how to answer that question. The intensification of life's cares (construed variously as concern, distress, and torment) opens Dasein to the more original dimension of care (*Sorge*) in such a way that Dasein realizes that its own openness to the practical, everyday, world is care itself. Care is Dasein's openness to the world. Further, that intensification causes Dasein to realize that its care and openness are dynamized by temporality. Dasein can care and be open because it is temporal and, as such, historical, as we saw in *The Phenomenology of Religious Life* (*G* 60:241–46/181–84). Moreover, Dasein's temporality is a crash through the nothingness (or emptiness), and what Heidegger calls counter-ruinant questioning emerges from and is directed toward that emptiness, as we saw in *Phenomenological Interpretations of Aristotle: Initiation into Phenomenological Research* (*G* 61:131–55/98–115). Therefore, the pragmatic view of language must be viewed from these structures of human being, the historicality and the nothingness of Dasein.

Heidegger claims that the λόγος of the Greeks was thoroughly historical, since it derives from the ways of speaking of historical human beings. Traditional meanings are contained within words. A scientific view of the Greek language, that is, to say that they constructed a theory of language or a philosophy of language, covers over this historicality. The Greek approach to language was historical because the language of the Greeks proceeded directly and genuinely from the Being of the human being. Again, for the Greeks λόγος meant speaking, which was the everyday way in which they lived in their world. As everyday, their speaking was factical. Therefore, retrieving the Greek sense of λόγος is a retrieval of the facticity of Dasein. Since Heidegger says, "*The theme is factical Dasein as such, which as such is historical*," investigating Greek λόγος (speaking) brings us to the factical and, therefore, historical experience of Dasein as "Being-in-a-world" (*G* 17:304/231). How they spoke gave their world its character.

One remarkable comment that Heidegger makes here is: "The Greek lived in an outstanding way in language and *was lived by it*; and that was known to him" (*G* 17:18/13). Although this observation is not explicitly developed at this time, it suggests that language belongs to the origin of factical-historical human Dasein.[2] We do not simply manipulate words; words do things with us. This confirms that for Heidegger human beings do not simply use language as a tool. Language lives human beings. We are thus impelled to explore that origin to determine how and to what extent language belongs to it. The analysis of the historical character of Dasein, insofar as world encounters Being, brings us closer to that origin.

Human beings do not just create words to solve practical, everyday tasks. The genesis of a word does not involve the meticulous, theoretical study of an object or experience in order to determine *the* word that corresponds to that object or experience; it does not involve a subject determining the name for an object. The genesis of a word does not take place in the human being as scientist but rather through the human being as "Being-in-the-world." There is an encounter between an object and factical-historical human Dasein, and in that encounter there is a naming that takes place. Words emerge from that encounter, when things are named. Heidegger explains, "The genesis of the word is not sustained by the physiological Being (*Sein*) of the human being but rather by his authentic existence" (*G* 17:16/12). Further, he claims that "insofar as the human being is in the world and, with it, *wants* something in it and for itself, he speaks. He speaks, insofar as something like world is *revealed* for him as what needs to be taken care of and [insofar as] in the 'for him' *he* is disclosed to himself" (*G* 17:16/12). Thus, words do name objects, but that is not all that they do. Words are the names for objects insofar as those objects are encountered in the world by a factical-historical (speaking) human Dasein.

I now turn directly to Heidegger's interpretation of Aristotelian λόγος. He first describes λόγος as speaking that shows the meaningfulness of the world. This leads to the fundamental importance of the λόγος ἀποφαντικός, through which we can uncover a deeper understanding of λόγος itself.

The Retrieval of Aristotle's Conception of Λόγος

Λόγο ς as Showing: A genuine understanding of the philosophical discipline of phenomenology demands that we understand the origin of its key terms. Heidegger explains that φαινόμενον means "self-showing," from φαίνω, which means "to bring something into the daylight" (*G* 17:7/4). This is to say, simply, that an object, a being, is brought into the light of the day and thereby seen as that which it is. But if phenomena can be seen because of the daylight, what is that light which allows them to be seen? The sun, of course, "whose presence is brightness" (*G* 17:9/6). The light of the sun lets beings be seen. Phenomena let themselves be seen in the sunlight. They are present, showing themselves within that light and showing themselves according to How we encounter them (*ein Wie des Begegnens*). It is not just light, however, which lets something be seen. Darkness contains within it the possibility of light, the possibility that something may come into presence that is not currently there. The darkness is a lack, στέρησις, but it is a lack that looks toward the presence of an object. Heidegger insists that to say that "light is that, which lets-be-seen; darkness then is that which does not let-be-seen" would be a misreading of what Aristotle says about light and dark, for "darkness also lets-be-seen" (*G* 17:10/7). In this sense, darkness is a δυνάμει ὄν, being potentially.

Heidegger's purpose here is not to construct categories of the night to respond to those of the day. Rather, the dominance of categories of the day must first be investigated to see why they have such privilege. The privilege of day-categories is closely associated with the disposition of science, which investigates beings only in the light of the day. The scientific disposition is one that does investigate phenomena as they show themselves, but it then attempts to force them into a certain "fundamental placement" (*fundamentale Stellung*) and hold and keep them there (*G* 17:12/9). This purifies phenomena of their non-being, their lack. To be sure, the scientific disposition encounters beings in the world, but in trying to grasp them as objects and in trying to prove that they have certain properties, those beings are "placed" into a rigid framework that runs counter to their historical character. As Heidegger says, "The Being of the scientific human being is a certain being-placed [*Gestelltsein*] over and against the Being of the world" (*G* 17:12/9).

By investigating the darkness as a way of showing, Heidegger accomplishes two new ways of thinking about language. In the first place, he demonstrates that the original function of language is not, as science holds, to establish what something is. Rather, the original function of language is to show what something is *as it is encountered* by historical Dasein. As such, objects are encountered not just in their actuality but also in their possibility. What something could be is part of what it is. But what something could be resides in the object as a lack, as what it is not. Possibility shows itself only in and through lack, which is to say, in and through darkness. In this way, Heidegger opens up the possibility for thinking about lack as a dimension of what something is. What something *is not* is as much a part of what it is as what it is. Naming an object considers only that which it is. The same holds true for science, which forces an object into certain categories about it, that is, about the way it shows itself openly in the light, and holds it there. This sort of knowledge is of the kind that perpetuates the science because this kind of knowledge can be taught. It is a rigidified knowledge that can then easily be passed on. Of course, this is not to say that science does not take the possible into account when it does its research. Indeed, science attempts to take account of all possibilities. As such, the goal of science is to establish absolute knowledge. Thus, it aims to eliminate the merely possible. It tries to exhaust the possible in order to draw a complete picture of what something is. The scientific method proceeds by eliminating the ways in which something could possibly be in order to determine that which it is and must be: its reality. The scientific disposition pursues the valid and certain, and in doing so, it covers up the worldly and historical character of the object.

Heidegger admits that it will be impossible to determine exactly the way in which the Greeks lived in their own language (*G* 17:17/12). Still, this is a question, he maintains, that has not yet been posed and that needs to be posed. In posing this question, it is necessary that we not think rigidly. The investigation of how the Greeks lived in their language and how they were "lived by" language is not simply a matter of determining what "name" and "verb" meant for the Greeks. It is not an analysis of grammatical structures or any kind of theoretical philosophy of language. What we are looking at is the worldly—and thus factical—character of the Greek λόγος. Therefore, the analysis will focus on meaning rather than on naming. Heidegger has discovered an experience of language that is prior to naming. That prior and more original experience is the showing of the object as that which it shows itself as. "One will not arrive at λόγος if one wants to start simply with naming. The original function of meaning is showing" (G 17:25/18). The worldly character of language will thus embody these two elements: showing and meaning.

When Aristotle maintained that "having speech" was an essential dimension of the human being, he meant that this was the Greek way of "Being-in-the-world." Therefore, the interpretation of the human being in terms of language requires that the way in which the Greeks experienced language be investigated. The primary way in which the Greeks had language was by way of speaking. Certainly, this does not answer our question regarding the way the Greeks lived their language. It does insist, however, that access to the way the Greeks lived their language is gained only by looking at the way in which they spoke with each other. It is not language as such that is at issue but rather language insofar as it is spoken.

> Talking [Reden] is not a property like "having hair." Talking co-determines the specific Existenz of the human being: the human being is in the world in such a way that this being [the human being] talks with the world and about it. (G 17:21/15)

Speaking was central to the life of the Greeks and, thus, to how they encountered the world. Speech is a how of encountering. This understanding of λόγος comes from Aristotle and causes Heidegger to recognize that "λόγος is articulated Being, which means something, it is voice: Λόγος δέ ἐστι φωνή σημαντική" (G 17:14/10, quoting from Aristotle, De Interpretatione 4.16b26). Recall Heidegger's remark from the winter semester of 1921/22 (Phenomenological Interpretations of Aristotle: Initiation into Phenomenological Research, G 61) that logical, grammatical rules find their origin in the way that people talk with one another. Strict grammatical structures developed out of the loose, even casual ways people spoke to each other in the world. Speaking is the origin of those structures that then determine the way that objects are to be spoken of. Indeed, not just language but the φωνή of language, its voice and sound, is an essential dimension of the Being of the human being that emerges through Heidegger's analysis of what Aristotle means by λόγος.

So, we have, at this point, achieved a basic outline for Heidegger's conception of Aristotelian λόγος. "A λόγος is there," he says, "when speaking is a speaking with the existing world [*mit der daseienden Welt*]" (*G* 17:20/15). This is to say that the original experience of *phenomenology* for the Greeks, which Heidegger derives through the texts of Aristotle, is a matter of letting-be-seen through speaking that which shows itself in its meaningful, worldly character. But this λόγος does not simply show, it also conceals, and I will look at that concealment now.

Λόγος as Concealing: Deception is the primary way that the human being lives in the world. Therefore, we need to look at how the primacy of deception determines and guides the analysis of world and, thereby, guides the analyses of facticity itself and the facticity of language. Note first that Heidegger's recognition of the primacy of deception is heavily influenced by Aristotle.

> In *de anima* Aristotle emphasizes that the early philosophers had taken too little heed of the fact that the human being spends the larger part of his time in *deception* [*daß der Mensch den größten Teil seiner Zeit sich in der Täuschung bewege*]. Because the human being is much more at home in deception [*Trug*] than we generally believe, it does not suffice to leave deception by the wayside and not make it into a problem, and do so in a *prinzipiell* way. (*G* 17:25/18–19)

Since we are looking at λόγος, the deception ingredient of λόγος needs to be investigated. The critical question is how that investigation is going to be carried out. From the previous analysis of λόγος, we already have our answer, that is, through an investigation of λόγος as a showing through speaking of that which shows itself in its meaningful, worldly character. In this return to Aristotle Heidegger not only recovers a dimension of λόγος that Aristotle had revealed and that was subsequently covered over by the λόγος of science; we also see, in that retrieval, an even deeper dimension of λόγος than Aristotle himself had discovered. I will first attend to the λόγος of science.

The Λόγος of Science. To begin, we have to recognize that for Heidegger a genuine appropriation of "the things themselves," the explicit goal of phenomenological research, is rendered impossible from the start by the scientific search for evidence and certainty. Science investigates objects in order to make determinations about the knowledge in particular scientific regions. Science develops particular methods to investigate those regions and verify certain forms of knowledge about them. Therefore, a predetermined "idea of fixed knowledge determines the theme of the investigation" (*G* 17:44/34). The goal of science is to achieve certain and verifiable knowledge about the object under investigation. Insofar as every λόγος is a showing, we recognize that scientific phenomenology does, indeed, show objects, but it shows them from within the limited perspective of scientific method. The λόγος of science reveals objects researched within the parameters of a particular methodology. Within a specific scientific region, the methodology that is distinctive of that region is able to make clear certain valid truths about those objects that it investigates.

A genuine appropriation of the things themselves demands that the situation be reversed, so that the theme of the investigation—here, factical Dasein—determines the character of whatever knowledge is going to be attained. In taking factical Dasein as his theme, Heidegger has no particular object in view, nor any particular scientific region. No knowledge of the content of Dasein will be set forth. Rather, Dasein must show itself as it is in the How of its own Being. Whatever determination of Dasein is made will be a determination of this How.

Since How Dasein *is* is to be in the world, the λόγος that emerges here will reveal itself as more original than the scientific, objectifying λόγος of science. This is because it displays the primacy of deception, whereas in science, which would claim certainty, deception, as such, is suppressed. When the purview of research is limited to a particular region, as scientific research is, then valid knowledge is, indeed, acquired. When factical Dasein becomes the theme of research, however, certainty and validity become impossible, because deception is an essential and ineluctable dimension of Dasein. This dimension is revealed by the facticity of Dasein's language. I will come to this in more detail shortly. At this point, we need to look at the concealment ingredient of λόγος.

Transition: Λόγος as Λόγος Ἀποφαντικός. The primary way in which λόγος shows beings is by way of λόγος ἀποφαντικός. This holds true for science as well as for the way in which Aristotle construes λόγος. What is the λόγος ἀποφαντικός? We have already seen its basic features. Indeed, when Aristotle describes λόγος as a speaking which lets-be-seen that which shows itself, he, in fact, means that this takes place primarily through λόγος ἀποφαντικός. Heidegger points out that "the λόγος ἀποφαντικός is a discourse with the world through which the existing world is shown as existing [*die daseiende Welt (wird aufgezeigt) als daseiende*]" (G 17:21/15). This is the way in which we should understand the sense of λόγος that Heidegger derives from Aristotle: showing the beings of the world as meaningful.

What is most characteristic of the λόγος ἀποφαντικός, however, is that it makes determinations about the world that are considered to be either true or false. Indeed, the λόγος ἀποφαντικός is the place where truth and falsity become possible. This is because when the λόγος is λόγος ἀποφαντικός, something is said about the world. Saying something about something presupposes that an interpretation is being made, and what is said about the world can be evaluated in terms of its accuracy. The word "true" is applied to those expressions that correlate with the world as it is, whereas the word "false" is applied to those expressions that describe the world inaccurately. Further, the λόγος ἀποφαντικός has been particularly pervasive as a way of evaluating questions of human existence. And this is not just the case in science. Heidegger explains that the λόγος ἀποφαντικός has played the decisive "role" in "the history of the self-interpretation of thinking in all questions which have to do with speaking, the determination of concepts, and the interpretation of existence" (G 17:25/18).

What progress is there, then, in a return to Aristotle? How is Aristotelian λόγος different from the λόγος of science if both construe λόγος as λόγος ἀποφαντικός and, thereby, in terms of the truth and falsity of expressions made about beings in the world? We have to recognize that the determination of λόγος ἀποφαντικός in Aristotle acknowledges that λόγος is essentially a revealing. Although truth and falsity may reign within the scientific interpretation of λόγος ἀποφαντικός, the Aristotelian interpretation shows that both truth and falsity are *revealed* by the λόγος. In any λόγος ἀποφαντικός, something is *revealed* as true or *revealed* as false. Without that original character of revelation, there could not be any claims of truth and falsity. Even a false expression reveals something: It reveals that which is false. The false is *revealed* as false, in which case, the false is not simply false, but rather the deceptive revealing of something as other than it is. Science, therefore, is based upon the λόγος ἀποφαντικός, but it covers over the more original dimension of λόγος as revealing. The λόγοι of science are judgments. They are estimations about the properties of objects delimited within a specified scientific region, and they are evaluated strictly in terms of truth and falsity.

By returning to Aristotle, Heidegger is able to retrieve the original dimension of language as revealing. It would be going too far to say that the apophantical structure of λόγος that Aristotle uncovers takes account of the ontological difference, that is, the difference between Being (*Sein*) and a being (*Seiendes*). This is because the λόγος ἀποφαντικός does not attempt to show the Being of a being (*das Sein eines Seiendes*), rather the λόγος ἀποφαντικός "shows a being as a being," that is, it shows "*Seiendes als Seiendes*" (G 17:20/14). But we also have to take into consideration the fact that the recognition of λόγος as λόγος ἀποφαντικός makes it possible for us to uncover the more original, revelatory character of λόγος. This is a deeper sense of λόγος than the λόγος of science, which covers over that originary dimension of revelation by interpreting λόγοι as judgments that strive for certainty within a particular scientific region and by interpreting them according to the methodology of that particular region. To be sure, the λόγος ἀποφαντικός provides the ground for scientific research, but in carrying out that research science subsequently covers up its own ground. The recognition of λόγος as λόγος ἀποφαντικός is, therefore, a pivotal and necessary step toward the uncovering of the ontological structure of language, that is, its revelatory character. We can discern that ontological structure by investigating the unity of λόγος.

Speaking and the Unity of Λόγος

The recognition of λόγος as λόγος ἀποφαντικός serves a transitional purpose. Although it could be demonstrated in detail how scientific inquiry is derived from the λόγος ἀποφαντικός and how that scientific research has buried the original revelatory character of λόγος ἀποφαντικός beneath its refashioning as true and false judgment, that is not my purpose here. Following Heidegger, I pursue the revelatory character of λόγος that is hidden within the λόγος ἀποφαντικός. In doing so, I attempt first to demonstrate the main structural features of the λόγος ἀποφαντικός in their unity. I do this in order to show, second, that the unifying ground of the λόγος ἀποφαντικός is not made up of apophantical structures but rather the more original meaning-functions of λόγος as revealing and deceiving. Third, I show that it is the recognition of deception as an essential dimension of the λόγος ἀποφαντικός which makes access to that unity possible. Importantly, we will see that the facticity of language is essential to that unity. This analysis will not only provide us with a sharper characterization of factical language, but also demonstrate the more original possibilities contained within λόγος that are opened up by the recognition of its facticity. Indeed, what we will see is that the original ground of λόγος, its unity, can be discovered only by investigating the possibility of deception within the λόγος ἀποφαντικός. Research into the unity of λόγος is guided by the facticity of speaking, wherein the showing and deceiving of language are manifest. That unitary dimension, as we will see, is λόγος itself in its revealing and concealing character. The analysis of deception will have led us into the basic unity of λόγος. More explicitly, though, it is the analysis of speaking as the condition of the possibility of deception that will reveal that basic unity.

Heidegger stresses the importance of recognizing that it is the speaking-dimension of λόγος that reveals λόγος in its unity. Note first Heidegger's contention, following Aristotle, that not every λόγος is a λόγος ἀποφαντικός. There are λόγοι that are prior to the apophantical region where judgment, truth, and falsity take place. Here Heidegger uses the verbal form of λόγος, λέγειν.

> Not every λέγειν (questions, orders, requests, and bringing [something to someone's] attention) is "true and false." To be sure, however, every [λέγειν] is revealing [*offenbarmachend*]—δηλοῦν-, which should not be confused with theoretical disclosure [*Aufdecken*]. These days everyone tries to understand all knowledge from the perspective of judgment as a modification of it [judgment]. (*G* 17:20/14)

He then affirms that speaking, in its worldly character, is prior to judgment. He says, "Speaking is a Being with the world; it is something original and precedes judgments. Judgment must become understood starting from this," that is, the speaking situation (*G* 17:21/15). From this we see two things: First, that the original meaning of λόγος is not judgment but revealing, δηλοῦν. Second, we see that speaking is fundamental to that original meaning insofar as it, too, precedes judgment. We can surmise that speaking is more original because it expresses the encounter with beings in the world (hence worldly) prior to any judgments about their truth or falsity. Speaking itself, therefore, is a "Being-with-and-in-the-world."

When the unity of the λόγος ἀποφαντικός is placed into question, the λόγος shows itself as a unity that reveals the unity of a being. Heidegger explains:

> The question of unity is tightly bound to the question of Being, Being in the sense of existing. The question about the unity of the λόγος ἀποφαντικός is the same as the question: What characterizes the λόγος ἀποφαντικός as *one*? It is the unity of revealing (ἓν δηλῶν); this means that the meaning-function of λέγειν, wherein a being is shown as existing [*Daseiendes*], determines the oneness of a being. (*G* 17:25/18)

The question of the *unity* of the λόγος ἀποφαντικός is, therefore, an ontological question because that unity reveals a being in its Being. The unity that Heidegger is describing here is the original unity of λόγος, a unity that then determines (*bestimmt*) the oneness of a being. A better way to explain this unity, perhaps, is to say that Heidegger is interested in how λόγος is unified, that is, the active process of how it comes to be a unity. The active, unifying process of λόγος, he says, is λέγειν, speaking, and this active sense of unifying determines the oneness of a being in its Being. If we recognize that speaking is linked fundamentally to the unity of λόγος, then the importance of speech becomes manifest, too. Speaking is pivotal to the ontological determination of a being. Moreover, if we recognize that the being that we are taking as our theme is Dasein, then we see that speaking is essential to the ontological understanding of Dasein.

Heidegger points out that the unity of the λόγος ἀποφαντικός was, indeed, a matter of importance for Aristotle (*G* 17:22/16). In this recovery of Aristotle, the "unity" of the λόγος ἀποφαντικός must be considered with regard to two components: "what is meant" (*das Bedeutete*) and "factical meaning" (*die faktische Bedeutung*) (*G* 17:22/16). For Heidegger, the worldly character of beings in the world is retained only when the meaning of those beings is interpreted according to how factical-historical Dasein encounters them. What we see here is that, when considered with regard to their unity, the words that describe those beings are preceded by a relational context composed of other meanings, and this relational context belongs to Dasein. That relational context of meanings, of a name (ὄνομα), for example, or a verb (ῥῆμα), determines the meaning of the name or the verb (*G* 17:23/16–17). A name or a verb gets its meaning from a relational context consisting of different pre-opinions and views from which it has been drawn. Heidegger says that, "Dasein = speaking, which speaks in [certain] regards, particular pre-opinions" (*G* 17:298/226, drawn from Aristotle's *De Anima* III). The meaning of the name or verb emerges from that relationship between it and the context of opinions and perspectives of the speaking Dasein that give it shape and determination.

Therefore, factical speaking determines the λόγος ἀποφαντικός in its unity. More specifically, the "specific unity of the λόγος ἀποφαντικός" is determined by affirmation (κατάφασις) and denial (ἀπόφασις), which Heidegger describes as factical ways of speaking about the beings that Dasein encounters in the world (*G* 17:23/17). Affirmation and denial are more original ways of λόγος than are truth and falsity. In the first place, they presuppose speech: To affirm or deny something is to speak about it in some way or another. Thus, affirmation and denial are ways that Dasein is in the world. They are ways of describing original, factical experience. Further, to affirm or deny something is not the same as making a determination about whether it is true or not. Heidegger explains affirmation and denial in these terms: Affirmation is "to attribute something from something else to something" (*etwas von etwas anderem auf etwas zu sprechen*) and denial is "to take something away from something in speaking of it" (*etwas von etwas weg sprechen*) (*G* 17:23/17). Attributing and taking away are ways that Dasein encounters beings and experiences in the world and speaks about them.

When we look at truth and falsity in this light, then we see that truth means that someone has affirmed that something can be attributed to something else. This understanding of truth relies not on correspondence (i.e., that what I say corresponds with an actual state of affairs) but on conviction, namely, the conviction, which Dasein has, that what is being attributed to something is warranted. Moreover, this sense of truth relies on Dasein's expressing that conviction to others. Falsity, likewise, is not based on correspondence but on Dasein denying that something can be attributed to something else. Both affirmation and denial place Dasein and, more specifically, Dasein's expression of its own convictions into the structure of truth. In this way, truth and falsity are traced back to the factical life of Dasein, who encounters beings and other people in the world and speaks about and with them.

Going further back, we see that both of these ways of speaking (affirmation and denial) are grounded in perceiving. Indeed, speaking is a kind of perception. Heidegger brings speaking (*sprechen*) together with perception (αἴσθησις) by showing that in both speaking and perceiving, something is drawn out against a background. Heidegger says, "The αἴσθησις is as such a *drawing-out* of something against something else (distinguishing)" (*G* 17:26/19, referencing Aristotle directly from *De Anima* 3.2.426b8–10). To perceive is to set something into relief (κρίνειν) against something else. The relational context of Dasein's views and opinions gives meaning to names and verbs, as I just noted. We see, then, that drawing something out against something else, setting into relief, is the structure of speaking, and it is a speaking *from* certain views and perspectives. Those views and perspectives determine how what is said will draw something out. There is never a pure perception, and by the same token never a pure speaking. Absolute truth, a pure ego, and certainty are here rendered meaningless so long as Dasein is speaking, which it always is in its basic structure.

> The αἴσθησις is in a being [*Wesen*] of such nature that it has language. With or without speaking aloud, this being is always in some way speaking. Language does not just speak alongside of perception, but rather it *leads* it; we see *through* language. Insofar as language is appropriated in a traditional and not in an original way, it *conceals* things, the very same language which also has the basic function of showing things. Thus it becomes understandable that in the Dasein of the human being, insofar as it has a *Dasein*, insofar as it has *language*, the *possibility of deceiving* [*Trug*] *and deception* [*Täuschung*] is also there along with it. (*G* 17:30/22)

From this we recognize that speaking is a basic dimension of language and that language is a basic dimension of Dasein; indeed, to have Dasein is to have language. For this reason, deception is also a basic dimension of Dasein. Speaking suffuses Dasein with the inevitability of its being deceived. Again, perceiving is a speaking ("we see through language") because it (perceiving) is a setting into relief of one thing against the background of another. Heidegger says, "Speaking is one with the way of perceiving" (*G* 17:28/21). Speaking is a setting into relief of one thing against another thing. Since setting into relief is the original determination of speaking, speaking is subject to the same deceptions as perceiving.

What Heidegger is saying here is that the structure of perceiving is the same as the structure of speaking. To perceive something is to set it into relief (κρίνειν) against something else, against a background. In the same way, to speak is always to speak about something, so that what is said is set into relief against that which it is being said about. In both cases, Dasein is bringing meaning out from an original unity, what Heidegger calls unitary Being. Within that difference between what is said/perceived and unitary Being, deception arises. In other words, speaking conceals that original unity within what is said. Even as it brings meaning out, providing Dasein with an understanding of the world, speaking conceals that original ground from which a world emerges. In that concealment, there is a deception taking place. What is said is supposed to be providing access to that unity, saying what it is. And yet what is said is not that original unity. This is where Heidegger finds the deception both of perceiving and of speaking: What is said is not what it purports to be saying.

If there is concealment in the structure of speaking, then there must also be withdrawal. Unitary Being withdraws from what is being said about it. That withdrawal obscures any claims that might be made about that which is withdrawing. Moreover, that withdrawal is itself concealed. So, the concealment is compounded insofar as it conceals its own concealment. Speaking is normally construed differently. Speaking claims to say something about something in such a way that what is spoken about does not withdraw. This is precisely the meaning of predication. Speaking says something about something and, in doing so, claims that what is spoken about is predicated and so has not withdrawn. Thought in terms of predication, the withdrawal of unitary Being is concealed by speaking, so we find in speaking a more profound deception.

Further still, Heidegger points out that setting into relief also governs understanding (νόησις). He says,

This κρίνειν is not only constitutive for αἴσθησις but also for νόησις. These two possibilities distinguish the Being of the human being. The human being is a being such that in its fashion it has its world there by making-it-accessible through drawing-out. It stands within the possibility of *moving* [κίνησις κατὰ τόπον] in this drawn-out and articulated way. (*G* 17:26/19, quoting from Aristotle's *De Anima* 3.2.427a18)

Hence, deception penetrates every manner in which the human being goes about his or her way in the world. This is manifest because only by setting into relief is the human being able to gain access to the world. The human being moves within the difference between what has been drawn out and that limit against which what has been drawn out comes to a stand. Since that difference is where deception takes place, the human being is suffused with deception and error.

Speaking is central to this deception because it is through speech that human beings are able to lie. In a fundamental sense, though, the lie pervades all speaking. I turn now to the facticity of speaking, which contains the lie.

The Facticity of Speaking

With the recognition that setting into relief guides perceiving, understanding, and speaking, the fundamental ground of deception has been shown. Deception (ψεῦδος) is a fundamental dimension of the human being because of how it goes about its way in the world, such that that deception pervades Dasein through and through. When we take account of the fact that the λόγος ἀποφαντικός has been the primary way in which the interpretation of the human being has been carried out throughout history, and when we remember that the interpretation of the λόγος ἀποφαντικός has been strictly in terms of truth and falsity, then we are now ready to see that the basic ways in which the human being can be false are determined by the facticity of speaking. Although deception contaminates every way in which the human being is in the world, the deception of speaking is more fundamental than that of perception and understanding. This is the case because one must speak in order to lie.

Heidegger says that there is a lie built into the basic structure of Dasein, and this lie characterizes the facticity of language: "In the facticity of language resides the lie" (*G* 17:35/26). Thus, when we talk about "the *facticity of speaking*," which Heidegger says needs to be brought closer to the investigation, we have to recognize that there is a lie that is built into the human being's power to disclose the world through speaking (*G* 17:35/26). There is a lie that is hidden within speech. This lie derives from the fact that speaking always speaks about something. Heidegger says, "Speaking as such, the factical dimension of speaking [*das Faktische des Sprechens*], is grasped from the outset as this: *something* is talked about," and there is always a difference between that something and what is said (*G* 17:35/26). The lie is in that difference. Speech is fundamentally disclosive, but that disclosiveness deceives as much as it discloses; it conceals as it reveals. I emphasize: The lie of factical speaking covers more than the intentional lie. This is because the more basic meaning of lying is that whenever something is talked about, that is, whenever there is speech, that which is spoken about is in some way hidden by what is said. In this sense, all speaking be-lies that something that is being talked about. Dasein is inextricably bound to deception because Dasein speaks, and speaking is the real and proper source of deception.

There are three ways of being false for Aristotle: as false thing (ὡς πρᾶγμα ψεῦδος), false speech (λόγος ψευδής), and false human (ὡς ἄνθρωπος ψευδής) (*G* 17:31/23). There is a priority, however, accorded to false speech. For a thing to be false or for a human to be false is grounded in the way in which speaking draws out the world by setting it into relief.

> How are the three meanings of ψεῦδος dependent on one another? To this end we take into consideration concrete λόγος as that of a human being who lives in a world and whose πράγματα have the possibility of being spoken of as ψεῦδος. We are placing the meaning of ψεῦδος into the sphere of *factical Dasein*. (*G* 17:34/26)

We recognize first that the "concrete λόγος of a human being who lives in a world" is the λόγος of "factical Dasein." Factical Dasein, as we see here, is shot through with deception. This is revealed through the speech that Dasein uses, that speech being a fundamental dimension of factical Dasein. Although Aristotle certainly recognized the manifold ways in which the human being can be deceived, he did not recognize their unity in λόγος ψευδής. There is deception intrinsic to human life. Dasein is essentially a speaking being, and since deception follows from speaking, Dasein is victimized by error. Heidegger emphasizes that *"the factical Dasein of speaking as such, insofar as it is there and simply insofar as it is there in speaking, is the actual source of deception. That means that the Dasein of speaking carries within itself the possibility of deception"* (*G* 17:35/26).

To conclude, there are three ways that speaking leads human Dasein into error. First, speaking is always about something. As such it draws out meaning from unitary Being. Speaking thus conceals that original unity, the unitary Being, from which it emerges. What is said is different from that about which it is said. There is always something concealed within what is said, and that concealment is deception. Second, that concealment is itself concealed. Although there is a withdrawal of unitary Being from what is said, that withdrawal is itself concealed, by speaking. So, there is in speaking both concealment and a concealment of that concealment. Third, Dasein always speaks from within particular contexts. Its speaking is tainted by opinion and prejudice. Since there is no speaking which is free of standpoints, opinions, prejudices and the like, deception will always be a part of what Dasein says. A pure and objective, prejudice-free conversation is impossible. Deception is always there.

Although deception belongs essentially to the λόγος (speaking) of factical human Dasein, it is important to remember that that deception arises through disclosure. Human beings are deceived because they are able to disclose, through speaking, the world and the richness of meaning that world offers. I take account of that richness of meaning now.

The Richness of the World

It is important to recognize that even though the human being is characterized here as fundamentally suffused with deception, this is not meant only negatively. It is not a degradation or abasement of the human condition. Rather, speaking is the ground of deception precisely because it is fully engaged with the world. Concealment and so deception are necessary in order for meaningful aspects of the world to be drawn out. In fact, we can make an identification here between deception and worldly engagement. To live (facticity) is to speak and be engaged with the world. This living-speaking-worldly engagement submits human beings to the inevitability of deception. Two basic components of speech emerge here. The first is that every speaking is also a disclosing of something that brings it into an open realm. Speaking situates what is said about something out into the open. Second, that open space wherein speaking takes place is composed of other people. Heidegger explains, "Speaking is from the outset with the Dasein of speaking human beings there, and it is taken in advance to be the showing of something" (*G* 17:35/26). Speaking is a disclosing of something within the world to others. Further, it is a disclosing that is always at the same time subject to deception.

It must be kept in mind that Heidegger is working from within the confines of a scientific view of the world while trying to break out from that view. The quest for validity and certainty has prevented science from grasping objects in the world in their character as worldly and thus prevented it from grasping Dasein in its original situation. He is trying to penetrate the scientific attitude and get down to its ground. He is trying to reclaim the richness of that original ground. At the same time, however, he wants to recognize the evolution of the scientific attitude from that ground and show

how science has covered up the inevitability of deception. He wants to uncover the original dimension of λόγος as revealing and as concealing, and he wants to show how those more original determinations developed into scientific judgments of truth and falsity. Since the things of the world elude the scientific investigation of existence, "This existence of things [in the world] is much richer and offers more changing possibilities than the thematically prepared existence [of science]" (*G* 17:37/28). He continues, saying that "because the world in its richness is only there in each case in the concretion of life, the elusiveness [of the world] is that much more extensive, and consequently, the *possibility of deception* is there. The more concretely I am in the world, the more authentic is the existence of deception" (*G* 17:37/28).

The experience of the world is gained here at the price of deception. I take this to be the most important contribution to the understanding of factical speaking (λόγος) that Heidegger makes in this section of the lecture course. Deception is fundamental to human experience because deception is fundamental to speaking, and speaking is fundamental to human experience. It cannot be avoided, despite the presumption of science, which claims that deception can be overcome. If science and scientific philosophy intend to grasp the world as it really is, they must submit their research to the inevitability of deception.

Insofar as Dasein is open to deception, it is in the world with others, speaking with them. This is the proper counterposition to the scientific interpretation of existence. Existence is shown here as it is in its average everydayness (*Alltäglichkeit*). This average everydayness is factical, to be sure, but it is a genuine grasping of Dasein in its Being, that is, as "Being-in-a-world." The subversion of the scientific search for certainty requires first that Dasein be seen in its average everydayness. This average everydayness has been revealed by the facticity of Dasein and, more explicitly, by the factical speaking of Dasein. "*Facticity* is not a concretion of the general, but rather the original determination of its specific Being as Dasein" (*G* 17:289/221). Facticity is Dasein in its here and now, in its average everydayness.

Another aspect of Dasein's facticity emerges here, namely the uncanniness (*Unheimlichkeit*)[3] of Dasein. Heidegger explains that "uncanniness shows itself in the average everydayness of Dasein" (*G* 17:289–90/221). This uncanniness threatens Dasein because it shows Dasein what it is in its Being: "Uncanniness is when one asks what he is, *nothing*, where he is, *nowhere*" (*G* 17:290/221). Dasein is "nothing" and "nowhere." The uncanniness of Dasein is the realization that it is grounded in nothingness. Indeed, the experience of nothingness is the origin of Dasein's speaking. Since uncanniness is an experience of Dasein's nothingness, speaking is grounded in that nothing-ness inasmuch as Dasein's speaking is Dasein's average, everyday (factical) experience with the world.

The scientific interpretation of Dasein blocks off the nothingness of Dasein. It protects Dasein within that which is familiar, turning it against itself. Dasein evades itself, it evades its own Being, refusing to see what it is, by fleeing into the certainty of the familiar. *"That before which* Dasein *flees* in the way of its *care for certainty* is *uncanniness.* Uncanniness is the authentic threat under which Dasein stands" (*G* 17:289/221). Dasein is protected from that threat by blocking itself off from its own Being. In contrast, Dasein is opened up to that threat when it is considered in its average everydayness. In this sense, average everydayness is a subversion of science because it opens Dasein to the possibility of experiencing uncanniness.

What I have tried to accomplish in this chapter is an understanding of Heidegger's deconstruction of the scientific approach to Dasein through an investigation of the λόγος that is intrinsic to Dasein's Being. What we have seen is that λόγος is fundamentally a speaking and that since speaking is the authentic ground for deception, Dasein, too, is suffused by deception. In this way, Heidegger has not *proven* anything about Dasein, rather he has simply shown the way that Dasein is as "Being-in-the-world." This has served to undermine the emphasis on certain and valid knowledge, which the sci-entific disposition hopes to attain with regard to Dasein. Further, it has shown that the quest for certainty is a fleeing in the face of Dasein's Being. In this sense, science is a fleeing toward the familiar, a fleeing that is also a protecting. Heidegger has attempted to let Dasein show itself in its worldly character by investigating the λόγος that is a fundamental dimension of Dasein. He concludes:

> The Being of the world has the character of *self-showing-itself,* the Being of life is a basic possibility in the way of *speaking* about Dasein; the Being [of Dasein] *is shown* through speaking. The Being of the world and of life have a very *specific interconnection* through the *Being of speaking.* The Dasein of the world in this self-showing-itself has the possibility of changing into a *giving-itself-out-as. Life is in itself the pos-sibility of concealing the existing world* [*die daseiende Welt*]. (*G* 17:44/33)

Because of speaking, Dasein is equally able to show itself as it is able to hide itself. Dasein is, therefore, the possibility of showing and concealing through speaking.

By investigating Aristotle's understanding of φαινόμενον and λόγος, Heidegger has uncovered an essential unity between the two words. That unity is Dasein, whose basic structure includes the showing and conceal-ing through speaking of beings that show themselves in and through the world, because Dasein is in-the-world. This has been accomplished as a way of releasing λόγος from the stranglehold of science, which aims to secure a certain location and placement (*Gestelltsein*) of beings by describing those beings in a language that strives toward certainty and validity. By investigat-ing the λόγος of Dasein through the Greek experience of λόγος as λόγος ἀποφαντικός, Heidegger has uncovered speaking as the ground for decep-tion. This discovery is an essential one for Heidegger in his development of an even more original understanding of λόγος than Aristotle had brought about. Most important, though, the deception ingredient of the factical speaking of Dasein has revealed the richness of Dasein as a being that is "Being-in-the-world."

8

Rhetoric

The λόγος has at its disposal the particular revelation and openness of the world. It gives to us the directions in which Dasein can question the world and itself.
—**Martin Heidegger,** *Basic Concepts of Aristotelian Philosophy*

In his work on rhetoric, Aristotle provides an articulation of the philosophical facticity of λόγος by making the language of Being-in-the-world concrete. The worldly dimensions of λόγος emerge quite explicitly in a lecture course Heidegger delivered on Aristotle's *Rhetoric* in the summer of 1924, *Basic Concepts of Aristotelian Philosophy* (*G* 18).[1] As the title of the course suggests, Heidegger is trying to interpret some of Aristotle's most basic philosophical concepts (he lists thirty of them on the first day of the class) from within Aristotle's own philosophical-historical, and thus factical, context. Interestingly, Heidegger claims that the course is not, as such, philosophical, if philosophy means the investigation of the history of philosophy or the history of philosophical problems. It is, rather, philological in the sense that philology means "the passion of grasping what is said" (*die Leidenschaft der Erkenntnis des Ausgesprochenen*) (*G* 18:4/4).[2] Thus, we *can* say that the content of this course is philosophical if we recognize the passion of speaking and call philosophy the investigation of the milieu of human beings speaking with each other that constitutes the conceptuality of our concepts. As Heidegger says here, "The basic concepts [of Aristotle] should be considered according to their *specific conceptuality*" (*G* 18:4/4).

In what follows, I move through this analysis of the relationship between speaking and conceptuality in order to develop a sense of authentic speaking in Heidegger's reading of Aristotle.[3] Heidegger is investigating the *Rhetoric* in order to retrieve a sense of authentic language from the Greek world and, importantly, from the Greek language in its average everydayness. Again, what makes the Greeks to be Greek is that they spoke Greek. From a historical context, Heidegger points out, Aristotle's *Rhetoric* marked the attempt to resuscitate language from its fallen condition. Greek Dasein was speech-laden. Much of that speech was sophistical, which Heidegger describes variously as discussion (*Gespräch*) and, more perniciously, as prattle (*Geschwätz*) and idle talk (*Gerede*). Aristotle meant "to take speaking back," (*das Sprechen zurückzuholen*) from those discursive ways in which Dasein becomes entangled in its own language, a possibility to which Greek Dasein was acutely susceptible given that the Greeks lived profoundly in speech. What is decisive, though, for Heidegger, is that Aristotle attempts to retrieve language from the perniciousness of sophistry by recovering a "possibility of existence" (*Existenzmöglichkeit*) latent within Greek life itself. He says, "*The Rhetoric is nothing other than the interpretation of concrete Dasein, the hermeneutic of Dasein itself.* That is the intended sense of rhetoric for Aristotle" (*G* 18:110/75). Hence, the development of authentic language, the recovery of speaking from mere prattle and idle talk, requires, in Heidegger's view, an explication of the ordinary ways in which human beings speak with each other in the world. Heidegger focuses here on the language of the Greeks and how the everyday world of Greek life resonated in Aristotle's philosophical terms. There is a positive content within ordinary speaking that Heidegger wants to bring to light. In this chapter, I explore that possibility of authentic speaking, with respect to the specific language of Greek factical life, and then extend it to notions of Being-in-the-πόλις, authentic community, and even to ethical excellence and the good of human life. Based on what he says in *Being and Time*, Heidegger was often criticized for not ever developing possibilities for authentic language, authentic speaking, or ethical excellence. We see here that *he had already done so* before *Being and Time* was ever published. His reading of Aristotle here is an attempt to synthesize the rhetorical possibilities of everyday speaking with ontological insights into human life.

This chapter is divided into five sections. In the first section, I show how Heidegger is interested in the everyday language of the Greeks. He is interpreting Aristotle's *Rhetoric* because he views the everyday language of the Greeks as essential to the development of his philosophical concepts. There are ontological meanings embedded within language because Dasein's way of Being-in-the-world happens fundamentally through speaking. The second section focuses on what Heidegger says about the *there* of a being. At this time, he claims that ontological research into the meaning of Being must be based on beings and that the meaning of Being protrudes within beings as those beings are *there*. The ontological comes together with the ontic and shows their mutual dependence on each other. The third section follows this line of thought by showing that the *there* of a being is disclosed in speaking. I develop a sense of authentic speaking in this third section, a possibility of Dasein that is not elaborated in *Being and Time*. Through this reading of Aristotle's *Rhetoric*, Heidegger draws on the way in which the passions are operative in the rhetorical situation. The speaker or rhetor conveys the passions in what she says; the listener is then taken along by the passion of the speaker. The listener can experience fear or, alternatively, anxiety or uncanniness because of what the speaker is saying. This happens because the listener is brought to a moment of decision about who she is. In that moment of anxiety or uncanniness, the listener begins to speak. Anxiety and uncanniness are the origin of speaking, and in that moment authentic speaking about who one is becomes possible. In the fourth and fifth sections, I use this notion of authentic speaking to shed light on other parts of this lecture course, where Heidegger suggests ways of thinking about authentic Being-with-others and even ethical excellence. Since human beings live together in the πόλις, in speaking relationships with others, speaking must be the ground for Being-with-others. Authentic Being-with-others will involve a modification of how the "they" live together in average everydayness, and it will involve attentive listening as well as an insight into the particularity of life, its here and now. Although Heidegger is certainly not writing an ethics in this course, he does follow up on the notions of particularity and the here and now in order to draw ontological conclusions about the good of the human being. In the fifth and final section of this chapter, I show how Heidegger construes ethical excellence, the human good, in terms of the Being of factical life as a καιρός or moment of insight into Dasein's own orientation in the world, which is its ἦθος.

On Speaking and Being

Heidegger returns to Aristotle in order to retrieve an understanding of definition and, thereby, an understanding of the conceptuality of the concept that precedes the dominance of traditional logic. Specifically, he says that this return to Aristotle will show that definition once meant "the *basic possibility of the speaking of human beings*" (G 18:13/11). Human beings simply talking to each other and trying to understand what things are is prior to the logical senses of definition and concept; this impels Heidegger to investigate speaking-with-others as the ground of definition and, thereby, as the ground for the determination as to what something is in its Being. Since the authentic function of a concept is to say what something is, then both "conceptuality and the meaning of the concept depend on how one understands the question about *what* something is and where this question actually finds its origin" (G 18:11/10). Definition, concept, and conceptuality all take root in that ground that is constituted by the speaking-together of human beings, and Heidegger returns to Aristotle here to reclaim that ground. Speaking provides the directive for an answer to the question regarding what something is, its "origin," its Being. Speaking and Being, in that they both are determinations of what something is, belong together in close ontological proximity.

According to the Greeks, the most basic and fundamental way of Being-in-the-world for human beings is language. The language of Being-in-the-world, however, is not abstract or theoretical; it is the concrete way in which human beings speak with each other about the world, and that speaking is a speaking-out. As the ground of conceptuality, this speaking-out is a wholly nontheoretical understanding of objects. Heidegger calls this original conceptuality "thing-giving basic experience" (*G* 18:18/15). When we look at language in this way, as the concrete speaking with others about the world, then we see how speaking is a fundamental aspect of life. Life here does not mean anything biological or psychological because speaking is prior to those sciences. Life here means οὐσία, Being, Dasein as Being-in-the-world. This λόγος, as speaking-out, "is the *fundamental determination of the Being of the human being as such*" (*G* 18:18/14). Since definition (ὁρισμός) is a λόγος, "a 'speaking' about something, a speaking-to the matter 'itself as what it is,' καθ' αὐτό" (quoting Aristotle, *Metaphysics* 4.8.1017b22 and 7.1.1042a17), then what is at stake in speaking/defining is "becoming intimately acquainted with a being in its Being" (*G* 18:17/14). In a remarkable passage where Heidegger is speaking directly to the students in his class, we hear,

> *The Being-in-the-world of the human being is basically determined through speaking.* To speak with the world, about it, from it is the fundamental way of life of the human being in his world. Thus the human being is determined precisely through λόγος, and so you see, if definition is a λόγος, this matter of definition has its ground. The λόγος as ὁρισμός says: the being in its οὐσία, in its Dasein. We need to come to an understanding about οὐσία. (*G* 18:18/14–15)

Heidegger moves through the logical meaning of definition to speaking and, by necessity, to Being, to the Being of a being. What is at stake in the speaking of life is the comprehension of the Being of a being, the ontological difference.

The facticity of speaking reveals a better understanding of definition and of conceptuality, and, more importantly, of life and Being. Thus, the factical speaking of life is central to any investigation into the question of Being.

The Greek term that Heidegger identifies as indicating the authentic function of language for the Greeks is λόγος οὐσίας. Λόγος οὐσίας, the speaking of Being, is the primordial meaning of definition, so that when we clarify what λόγος οὐσίας means through Aristotle then we will arrive at the basic ground, the conceptuality, of the concept. In its basic sense λόγος means: speaking, speaking-with-others, speaking about something with others, letting-be-seen (ἀποφαίνεσθαι), disclosing (δηλοῦν); it also means that which is spoken (*das Gesprochene*). Heidegger points out that both of these modes of λόγος, as speaking and as what is spoken, can become worn out and average through the general understanding. The language we use has a way of ceasing to belong to the person who is speaking, in which case what is said no longer refers directly to the matters themselves. Rather, what is said belongs to the general understanding; it refers strictly to what other people say, indiscriminately, and without the intent of engaging the matters at issue. This is a kind of speaking that is not thought through; it belongs only to others and not to oneself. Clearly, we see here the dimension of idle talk as it appears in *Being and Time*. It is noteworthy, however, that in this description of idle talk, Heidegger maintains that the averageness of language is a possibility precisely because human beings live in language, because they grow up within a certain understanding of language and of the world (*G* 18:20/16). Language can become worn-out precisely because of the fact that it is worldly. As a consequence, the averageness of language is founded upon the existence (the Being-in-the-world) of the human being, who grows into an understanding of the world and of language. We see, then, a relation between that pre-understanding within which human beings always find themselves and the averageness of language. Human beings *are* always already in a language and in a world. Averageness is always a possibility. We could say, then, that without that possibility of averageness the hermeneutical pre-understanding could not be investigated.[4]

Heidegger is not disparaging human speech here; idle talk is not the degradation or abasement of language. On the contrary, Heidegger is pointing out that human speech is prone to average, everyday meaning; it can become worn-out and exhausted, and that can happen only insofar as speaking is fundamentally a speaking with others. If you do not accept that averageness, then you are not analyzing human existence, because human existence is prone to error and deception. In the same paragraph in which he describes the possible averageness of human speech, Heidegger explains that, "Life is a *How*, a *category of Being*," and that, "Life is Being-in-a-world" (*G* 18:21/16). The leveling down of human speech to the averageness of the general understanding can occur only insofar as speaking is considered within that context of Being (*Seinszusammenhang*) that belongs to the life of the human being (*Leben des Menschen*). As such, "language belongs to the *authentic Being-drive* of the human being" (*G* 18:21/16). If you take away the possibility for the averageness of speech, you take away the possibility of life.

For the same reason that human language is prone to averageness, it is also prone to deception. There is a basic ambiguity that is built not only into λόγος but also into οὐσία. Speaking-with-others is a basic determination of Being; this speaking of Being, the λόγος οὐσίας, discloses a basic multiplicity (*Vieldeutigkeit*) intrinsic to οὐσία. Heidegger says that οὐσία is "*absolutely the most basic concept of Aristotelian philosophy*" (*G* 18:22/17). It is the ground not just of definition, ὁρισμός, but of all of Aristotle's concepts. Still, it resists clarification. This resistance to clarity can, Heidegger admits, emerge from (a) confusion about the meaning of the word or even from (b) an inability to recognize levels of meaning within it, but more profoundly this resistance comes from (c) *a genuine relationship with the matters themselves*. The investigation of Being is made difficult by the fact that οὐσία can mean a being, the How of a being, the How of Being, Being, or even Dasein in a twofold sense as there-being (*Daseiendes*) or the Being of there-being (*das Sein des Da-seiendes*) (*G* 18:25/19).

Recognizing that basic ambiguity, Heidegger investigates οὐσία in terms of the ontological difference. He says that "οὐσία does not primarily describe a being, but rather the How of Being of a being, whereby a particular being is co-meant" (*G* 18:27/20). Significantly, Heidegger arrives at this determination of οὐσία by analyzing the natural meaning of the term in the everyday language (*Alltagssprache*) of its Greek usage. The common and familiar meaning of οὐσία was such that it meant property, possession, house and grounds (*Vermögen, Besitz, Anwesen*). This is not to deduce the terminological from the common; rather, it is a recognition of how the terminological meaning of οὐσία (Being, a being) and the common meaning (property, possession, or house and grounds) must be taken together to indicate the way in which beings are factically there in their Being. It is a way to understand a being, such as a household (*Hausstand*), so that "in an explicit way, [it] is *there:* the very being which in the first place and for the most part is there in life, within which Dasein for the most part moves factically, out from which, in the same way, life ekes out its existence" (*G* 18:26/20). A being *is* in such a way that it is *there* in an explicit way. It is not there simply as present; it is *there*, it is present, *in its Being*. That presence is not simple presence but factical presence; a being is factically present when it is *there* in the factical *movement* of life. This factical presence indicates the way a being is *there* in its Being. In this way, the terminological meaning of οὐσία comes to be either (1) "a being in the how of its Being" (where there is an emphasis on the ontical dimension of the ontological difference) or (2) "the How of Being of a being" (which places an emphasis on the ontological). This, the ontological difference, is the manifest multiplicity (*Vieldeutigkeit*) or ambiguity that comes from a genuine relationship with the matters themselves.

In true Aristotelian fashion, Heidegger is reclaiming the substantive ground of ontological research: beings.

> Should there be a research which has Being as a theme, then that research, which has the Being of a being as a theme, will somehow be held also to visualize a being, because in the end a being is itself only read from the character of its Being, so that by necessity a being must also be placed into consideration. (*G* 18:27/20)

According to Heidegger, Aristotle determined the proper ground for ontological research when he said that it must be based on beings. In any investigation of Being, one has to start with that pre-understanding of Being that is *there* already in beings. Because we grow into language and world (later, in *Being and Time*, because we find ourselves *thrown* into language and world), we always already have that pre-understanding. On Heidegger's account, Aristotle established a ground for ontological research that Plato, in his groundless speculations about Being, had no idea about. The λόγος οὐσίας is a determination of how beings are disclosed (λόγος) in the How of their Being (οὐσίας) as either "a being in the how of its Being" (ontic) or "the How of Being of a being" (ontological).

Σώματα and Οὐσία: Securing Beings as the Ground for Ontology

By drawing out the common (average, everyday) meanings of οὐσία that are contained within the terminological meaning of οὐσία, Heidegger is showing that this concept, the most primary of all of Aristotle's basic concepts, is an indication not just of simple presence but of the immediacy of the *there* of beings present to us in life. That immediacy bespeaks a determination of the Being of beings. Thus, the investigation of Being must be an investigation into the urgency (*Dringlichkeit*) that is *there* within beings. Perhaps even more radically, this is an urgency that is in the *there* of presence. Heidegger looks at Aristotle's descriptions of the σώματα to penetrate this Being-dimension of beings more thoroughly. He points out that the Greek word σῶμα, normally translated as body, bodiliness, or materiality, actually refers to the "peculiar *obtrusiveness* (*Aufdringlichkeit*) of a being" (*G* 18:28/21).[5] Hence, by insisting that ontological research must first investigate beings in order to have a ground under its feet, Heidegger is not ontifying the Being question. He is interested, rather, in the obtrusiveness of Being that shows itself in beings. Even though beings serve as the point of access to Being, the Being-character of beings is always there in the first place.

When a bodily being (σῶμα) is perceived, that perception (αἴσθησις) is of "a being that in the first place and for the most part is there in the everydayness of life" (*G* 18:28/21). Such beings—animals, trees, earth, water, air, the heavens—are not dead; they show life and, in that life, Being. In the perception of the σώματα, it is the "Being of that being" (οὐσία) that is really at stake. Interestingly, Heidegger translates αἴσθησις, perceiving, as *Vernehmen*, which more accurately means hearing or listening (*G* 18:29/21). The natural, everyday perception of the σώματα is not in any way a mere receiving of sense data, a sensitivity (*Empfindung*) to sense data (*Sinnesdaten*), but a matter of listening to the Being-dimension there within beings. Insofar as we listen to speaking, that speaking, which is an addressing of beings in their Being, contains within it ontological indications. In listening, we hearken to those indications, and this is possible because even in the everyday way of speaking with others, those indications are there.[6]

To conclude this section: By exploring definition, Heidegger retrieves the more fundamental meaning of it, namely, the speaking to, with, and about the Being of beings by recognizing that Being "obtrudes" in the *there*. This is the that-there of the being, its here and now, which is thus disclosed in speaking.

Authentic Speaking

Authentic speaking with others: Speaking is a λόγος, which, while it entails audibility, is not only audibility. Both animals and humans have the power of φωνή, audibility, but only humans have λόγος, which includes both sound and understanding. At stake in both φωνή and λόγος are the ways in which life encounters the world. For both animals and humans, the world is always there; it is encountered by living beings, and as such, it has to do with them (*Angehen*). Specifically, the encountering of animals, apropos of φωνή, occurs through ἡδύ and λυπηρόν, the pleasant and the distressing, whereas the encountering of humans, apropos of λόγος, occurs through συμφέρον and ἀγαθόν, the useful and the good. This "having-to-do-with" is not always readily apparent; in fact, it is often not apparent because, for the most part, everyday activities do not seem important. Even then, however, when we say that the world has nothing to do with us, we are admitting that "Dasein interprets the world as something, in the character of something, that it has to do with" (*G* 18:51/36). The character of the world is such that it is always and ineluctably *there* whether we recognize it or not. As such, the world manifests different levels of uncoveredness, so that the *there* of the world is determined by

> how much life is *shut in* on itself or how much life is *awake*, how much Being-in-the-world is *uncovered*, how much it has the character of the *revealed There*, how much the world itself and Being-in-it are *revealed*. (G 18:52/37)

φωνή and λόγος are levels of uncovering; better: They are dimensions of the world in its uncoveredness, and as such they are possibilities of Being.[7]

For Heidegger, the possibility of authentic speaking develops out of the rhetorical situation. The listener, when moved by the language of the speaker, begins to speak. Authentic speaking depends on a certain kind of ontological movement. The movement of becoming belongs to the Being of any being. In any movement of becoming, as when wood becomes a table, for example, there is a directedness-toward (πρός), and that directedness-toward belongs to Being. Interestingly, Heidegger explains directedness-toward in terms of thinking. Thinking manifests a *Wozu*, a toward-which, that is a directedness-toward others: "Thinking demands according to its own sense: *to be open to the other*" (G 18:234/157). Being open to others is a determination of living beings, and insofar as living beings think, they are, by thinking, *there* in an open relation to others. By openness to otherness Heidegger means that living beings are always *there* with other beings. Openness to others means Being-in-the-world with other beings.

Pre-Aristotelian philosophers investigated movement, but in doing so they determined that it is fundamentally something unclear and undetermined (ἀόριστον); a category of indeterminateness had to be created.[8] For the Greeks and for Heidegger, life means to be in a relation to other beings; it means to be in a world. Movement is, therefore, a unifying relation for us. Heidegger uses Aristotle's example of teaching. For Aristotle, there is a unifying movement that takes place in teaching and learning; this relation is not of two distinct movements, one of teaching, the other of learning. Rather, teaching-learning is a single actualizing movement. Heidegger expands this example to include the importance of speaking.

> The authentic Being of a teacher is: to stand before an other and speak to him such that the other follows along with him. It is a unified context determined through κίνησις. (G 18:327/221)

The oneness of movement as a unifying relation based on the fundamental openness we have to others is critical. In the rhetorical situation, where we find the possibility of authentic speaking, the passions of the listener are moved by what the speaker is saying. This movement of the passions depends on the listener's experience of pleasure and pain. Pleasure and pain are determinations of the life of Dasein. Life has these two possibilities that are thereby intrinsic to Dasein's very Being. On the one hand, there is pleasure (ἡδονη) in the disposition of grasping (αἵρεσις), whereby Dasein takes hold of itself; while on the other hand there is pain (λύπη) in the disposition of fleeing (φυγή), whereby Dasein runs away from itself. Pain in the life of Dasein is co-primordial with pleasure. Both belong to the original ontological determinations of the life of Dasein (*G* 18:247/166).

By recognizing that grasping and fleeing are ontological determinations of Dasein, Heidegger is showing how movement functions within Dasein, itself. Movement is intrinsic to the Being of a being, indeed, it determines the authentic There-character of a being in its limitedness. The πάθη, pleasure and pain as grasping and fleeing, are determinations of Dasein's movement. Dasein is moved in its passions, as, for example, when a person is moved to tears or moved to anger. Further, that movement is a unifying determination between action and passion. There is a singular, unifying movement that determines Dasein in its Being. There is here a moment of decision, where the passions *happen to* Dasein: Dasein is moved. The πάθη, he says, "are *ways of being-taken-along* (*Mitgenommenwerden*) *with regard to Being-in-the-world*; the possibilities of orienting oneself in the world are essentially determined by the πάθη" (*G* 18:242/162). Hence, there is a change that takes place with regard to how Dasein orients itself in the world only insofar as it is taken away by the passions, *or not*. Dasein must decide (κρίνειν) whether or not it will allow itself to be taken away and, thereby, changed. Decision provides the context for πάθος and λόγος. When Dasein makes a decision about how it is going to reorient itself in the world (how it is going to live), it then allows itself to genuinely listen to the λόγος of the speaker who is making an appeal to it. To listen means to allow to speak. Thus, by listening, Dasein allows that λόγος to speak to it.

When is Dasein ready to be advised? When is Dasein ready and willing to allow itself to be convinced? In a remarkable passage, Heidegger says that that moment takes place in and through fear. In fear, Dasein shrinks back from that which it is afraid of. In order for someone to fear, that which is posing a threat must be imminent. The threatening must be directly and immediately there, such that the person being threatened must recognize and care about the fact that something is about to happen to him. Thus, loss of hope (οἴεσθαι, *glauben verloren zu sein*) accompanies fear. At the same time, however, there is also a profound hope (ἐλπίς, *hoffen*) that takes place within loss of hope. He says, "In this 'hope of being rescued' the peculiar disposition reveals itself, that I care about that which I am afraid of: It must concern me, it cannot be something neutral" (*G* 18:260/174). There is a hope for rescue (ἐλπὶς σωτηρίας) immanent within the loss of hope that accompanies fear insofar as one fears and cares about that which is threatening him. This condition, whereby hope and fear occur together, Heidegger calls disquiet (ταραχή, *Unruhe*). In that condition of disquiet, Dasein fears the annihilation of its own existence (*Vernichtetwerdenkönnens*); it fears the distinct possibility of its own not being, but at the same time, it experiences hope that it not be annihilated, that it *not* not be.[9] In this sense, Dasein fears its own Being: "The possibility of being saved, in short: *to be*, is there; nonetheless *I shrink back from Being*" (*G* 18:260/174). In this moment, the fleeing and grasping, (φυγή and δίωξις, pursuit), of pain and pleasure (λύπη and ἡδονή) occur together in the disquiet of hope and fear-as-loss-of-hope (ἐλπίς and φόβος as οἴεσθαι). In this condition of disquiet a person is ready to be advised. More than that, *this is the moment when a person seeks discussion*.

In the rhetorical situation, fear is conveyed insofar as the speaker is advising his listeners to become something that they know they can become but which they are not already. The rhetoric of the public gathering is oriented toward the future. Fear is of the new, that which is unfamiliar, because one can only take advice about that which he is not already doing. The hope therein is the recognition that what the speaker is advising you about is something that you decide that you will do even though it frightens you. The listener can come to a decision through discussion about what the speaker is saying; he decides to accept it when he trusts what is being said and the ἦθος of the one saying it.

On an even deeper level, Dasein does not fear anything in particular but rather is anxious about the nothingness of its own Being.[10] Heidegger says here that anxiety is a phenomenon *that occurs in the everydayness of human existence*. When Dasein is anxious, when it does not know what it is afraid of, that is, when fear is taken in this peculiar other sense as being the fear of nothing, which is anxiety or horror (*Angst* or *Grauen*), it experiences uncanniness. And this, says Heidegger, the uncanniness of anxiety, is the origin (γενεσις) of speaking.

> When we experience uncanniness, we start to speak. That is an indication of the *γενεσις of speaking which is peculiar to Dasein*, the way that speaking interconnects with the basic determination of Dasein itself, which is characterized through *uncanniness*. (*G* 18:261/175)

In *Being and Time*, Heidegger does not say that the uncanniness of anxiety is the genesis of speaking.[11] On the contrary, he says that when Dasein is anxious, it is silent, taciturn. It seems clear from this lecture course, however, that the same dynamic that takes place within Dasein itself in its everydayness through the disposition of anxiety, and which is well-known from *Being and Time*, can occur in the rhetorical situation between and among people in the public gathering. As in the case of anxiety, Dasein's uncanniness manifests in a confluence of hope and loss of hope. Authentic speaking with others recognizes that Dasein is in the world in speaking relations with other people. What is decisive in this situation is that the listener, who, in listening, lets speak, comes to a decision about what is being said. For that to happen, the listener must be placed within a certain disposition. That disposition determines whether or not the listener will be convinced by the speaker. The decision that takes place within that disposition is, then, practical insofar as Dasein comes to a decision about itself, that is, about its own life. The good of Dasein is τέλειον, life itself. In the rhetorical situation, Dasein makes a decision about itself, and that decision involves its being resolute regarding that which is being said to it. In the rhetorical situation, Dasein comes to a decision about the meaning of its practical life.

Authentic λόγος is attuned to that nothingness that Dasein experiences in the uncanniness of anxiety. Such a λόγος is a kind of speaking that recognizes that the πάθη are ontological determinations of Dasein's orientation to the world. It is a λόγος that is grounded in that confluence of hope and loss of hope that comes only when Dasein *in its average everydayness* experiences its own nothingness, its limitation, its profound finitude, which is fundamentally a part of who it is. When Dasein is struck with the uncanniness of its own nothingness, it searches out conversation. This is the point at which it is ready to engage in discussion about who it is. Dasein's speaking in that moment is an authentic speaking, an authentic conversation, because it is trying to come to terms with who it is, that is, it is trying to confront its own nothingness.[12]

Authentic speaking about things: Heidegger takes seriously the distinction between ἐντελέχεια and ἐνέργεια, full presence and presence. In both of these concepts, the Being of a being is at stake, but there is a difference between them that needs to be recognized. Both are indications of the presence of a being. With ἐντελέχεια, however, that presence only recognizes the way that a being holds itself, unmoving, in its finishedness. ἐνέργεια, however, indicates the presence of a being such that movement is still a dimension of that being. This ἐνέργεια-ic presence indicates the way in which a being is both finished and not finished. It is present; it is there, but it is also still becoming; it is potentiality (δύναμις). ἐνέργεια-ic presence recognizes, then, the possibility that a being can (1) not be and (2) become.

Since κίνησις is only a determination of the ἐνέργεια-ic presence of a being and does not belong to ἐντελέχεια, the proper presence of a being is such that it can also not be there. Heidegger believes that Aristotle made an important advance in ontological research over Plato by situating absence (στέρησις) in the there of a being. Looking at the *Physics*, chapter 8, Heidegger points out that Aristotle recognized the possibility that something can come from nothing and that this "not" remains within the being. Only by looking at beings in this way is it possible to recognize that a being can become and, thereby, change. Hence, Heidegger explains in this course that, "κίνησις [determines] *the authentic There-character of Being*," insofar as movement is a determination of δύναμις, ἐνέργεια, and στέρησις, which are essential to a being (*G* 18:287/194). The most important of these determinations is στέρησις, absence, which Heidegger also calls διχῶς, the "doubling" (*Zweifachheit*) of a being. Something that is cold, he says, is not warm, but it is potentially warm, and this absence is a potentiality belonging to the object even as cold. This absence/potentiality is the doubling, the διχῶς, of the being. Hence, it belongs essentially to a being that it is not there in its fullness, in its full presence; absence is constitutive of a being. As a "not yet" or "no longer," this absence is fundamental to its movement and, thereby, fundamental to its presence.

This possibility of not being poses a distinct threat to Dasein. Pre-Aristotelian philosophers failed to recognize these Being-characteristics of beings (δύναμις, ἐνέργεια, and στέρησις) out of fear (φόβος) that beings could possibly not be. As such, the highest possibility of human existence according to the ancient philosophers, the pleasure (ἡδονή) that comes from a consideration of the world in its full presence (ἐντελέχεια), indeed, the pleasure of pure θεωρεῖν, is actually grounded in fear of the absence or non-being of beings. The true pleasure of science, Heidegger claims, is actually an avoidance of the fear of the threat that the non-being of beings poses (*G* 18:289–90/196–97).

There is, however, another kind of pleasure (ἡδονή) that is based in a proper consideration of pleasure and pain (ἡδονή and λύπη), not one where pleasure means simply the avoidance of fear. This new sense of pleasure is still a matter of enjoying the presence of beings, but it is pleasure in the ἐνέργεια-ic presence of beings wherein the passion of movement within presence is recognized. That pleasure is the pleasure of life itself, insofar as life means Being-in-the-world with beings that have the possibility of not being. Since truth as ἀλήθεια means the revealedness or uncoveredness of beings, this pleasure is pleasure in the truth of beings. Perhaps most important, this pleasure is prereflective. This is not to say that it is sheer enjoyment in the pleasures of life as those pleasures are construed by everyone else, the pleasures of the they. On the contrary, Heidegger claims that the prereflective pleasure in life is a disposition that is able to take life back from the everydayness within which it dwells. This pleasure that works against everydayness is the pleasure that emerges from the interpretation of Dasein (*G* 18:277/188). Perhaps this sounds peculiar, but insofar as Dasein means life, the pleasure taken in the interpretation of Dasein is the pleasure of life itself. Heidegger brings the passions, the πάθη, back to life, back into Dasein, and back to their proper philosophical significance.

Since the πάθη indicate Dasein's movement in a fundamental way, the λόγος which attends to the πάθη will recognize the δύναμις, ἐνέργεια, and στέρησις that are the constituent characteristics of the movement of a being in its Being. Heidegger explains that the πάθη are determinative of speaking; they form the ground for speaking, and as such, they are the primary way in which Dasein orients itself in the world through language. The πάθη determine the way Dasein finds itself, the way it is in the world, and "Within this so characterized self-finding and Being-in-the-world the possibility is in the first place given to speak about things in such a way that they are stripped of the look they have in their first contact" (*G* 18:262/176). This is not, to be sure, apodictic, scientific truth of what the thing is but rather a kind of speaking about it that takes account of how it is in its *there*: the limitedness, absence, negativity, potentiality, and temporality of its presence.

Authentic speaking is true in the sense that it reveals the uncoveredness of a being.[13] Heidegger explains here that λόγος is wholly dependent on the world and that "the uncoveredness, the revealed Being-oriented [of λόγος] in Being-to-itself and in Being-to-others is characterized through ἀλήθεια and more explicitly through ἀληθεύειν as a ἕξις" (*G* 18:265/178). This truthful speaking is a revealing of the world as it is. Dasein has access to the world because Dasein is Being-in-the-world. Aristotle claims that the one who speaks the truth, the ἀληθευτικός, resides in the mean between excessive and deficient πάθη and has, therefore a true relation (*die Echtheit des Verhaltens*) to himself and to others. His way of speaking (ὁμιλία, συζῆν) is non-hiding, non-concealing. Heidegger takes that understanding and recognizes its ontological determinations. The one who speaks the truth is the one who has an understanding of Being-in-the-world such that what he says, the words he uses, reveal the world. Authentic language has the function of revelation. The world, construed even in a more natural sense as earth, is the "absolute center of orientation" for Dasein (*G* 18:266/179).

Authentic language is, therefore, a speaking that reveals Dasein as Being-in-the-world. Heidegger concludes that

> The consideration of the *Dasein of the human being as Being-in-the-world* has been brought to a conclusion of sorts. This Being-in-the-world has the *basic character of its Being* in λόγος. Λόγος permeates Being-In. In λόγος there is kept the way that the world and Dasein are revealed, opened up in it. The λόγος has at its disposal the particular revelation and openness of the world. It gives to us the directions in which Dasein can question the world and itself. (*G* 18:269/183)

If we then return to Heidegger's original question regarding the conceptuality of concepts, then we see that to interpret concepts in accord with their original conceptuality means to interpret them in accord with Dasein as Being-in-the-world, such that Dasein is itself conceptuality. Since Dasein as Being-in-the-world means speaking with others, the conceptuality of concepts is determined by speaking. Since Dasein begins to speak through the uncanniness of anxiety, authentic λόγος is grounded in the nothingness of Dasein, which is the origin of Dasein's anxiety. To make a move that Heidegger does not explicitly make here: since the nothingness of Dasein is its no-thing-ness (i.e., not-a-being but Being) then λόγος, Dasein itself, and conceptuality are all grounded in Being.

It must be kept in mind that this return to the world does not in any way guarantee that the truth of speaking can avoid error (*Irrtum*). Insofar as authentic speaking reveals Dasein and world, it also reveals the negativity that is intrinsic to Dasein and world. As I have already mentioned, anxiety and uncanniness are possibilities of everyday Dasein. As such, Dasein is ineluctably fallen; anxiety does not remove Dasein from that fallen condition. Error belongs to Dasein. The authentic λόγος that reveals world and Dasein always reveals some error (*G* 18:280/190). Anxiety and uncanniness reveal Dasein as fallen. Heidegger insists, however, that the showing of beings—through λόγος—by fallen Dasein through προαίρεσις (described variously as the *Augenblick*, καιρόσ, anxiety, uncanniness, excellence, ἦθος) is a "positive grasping" of Dasein insofar as Dasein has, thereby, "*the possibility to determine the there-being* (*Daseiende*) *as it is*" (*G* 18:280–81/190). The showing of beings as they are is only possible insofar as the imminent possibility for error is there within that language whose function it is to reveal the world as it is. The revealing of language is, thereby, a revealing of the negativity and limitation that are *there* in Dasein and in world.

A concrete example of authentic speaking would be Aristotle's categories. Heidegger challenges those critics of Aristotle who claim that because

Aristotle did not propose a determinate number of categories his philosophical work is sloppy (*keine saubere Arbeit*) (*G* 18:302/205). A living interpretation of Dasein, which Aristotle accomplished, demands that there not be a fixed and determinate number of categories. Heidegger explains that many interpreters of Aristotle forget that the categories are fundamentally related to λέγειν. They are ways of speaking, the natural speaking that took place in the Greek marketplace (ἀγορεύειν) where people talked with each other, argued, tried to be convincing, which, Heidegger says, are "not simply talking" but are "*ways of addressing a being in its Being*" (*G* 18:303/205). This is the kind of speaking that Heidegger is here trying to recover from Aristotle. It is an authentic speaking that addresses beings as they are in their Being and that is consequently opened up to the possibility for error because authentic speaking is always an addressing of the limit and negativity of beings. Heidegger says in this regard that there is a "doubling" (διχῶς) intrinsic to all of Aristotle's categories because each category is a "way of the Dasein of the world, of the encountering of the world" (*G* 18:311/210). The categories are ways of speaking about the world, and as such they contain an essential absence. They are how people speak about worldly beings, and those beings manifest a διχῶς, a doubling. They can always be otherwise, and this otherness is an absence that belongs to the presence of the being. The categories, which speak about beings, are thus also διχῶς. They, too, manifest this doubling. Aristotle claims that there is no good in itself. Heidegger points out here that Aristotle makes this claim because he interprets Plato's good in accord with the categories. Aristotle interprets the good in terms of absence and doubling, στέρησις and διχῶς. Through these speaking-categories, he situates the good in the practical world of human Dasein. In this way, the good is seen to be an indication of Dasein's Being-in-the-world.

Authentic Being-with-Others

Heidegger is interested in speaking because he wants to understand the existence, the Dasein, of human beings, the way that they *are* in the world, and speaking is a basic determination of Dasein's Being-in-the-world. He says explicitly, "*We need to understand the basic concepts of Aristotle in concrete Dasein and in its basic possibilities of speaking with its world*, within which Dasein is" (*G* 18:41/29). In order to explore the meaning of Dasein, he retrieves the Aristotelian sense of the human being as ζωὴ πρακτική τις τοῦ λόγον ἔχοντος, "a life, and namely a practical life, of such a being that has language" (*G* 18:43/31, quoting the *Nicomachean Ethics* 1.6.1098a3–4). As such, hearing and listening are essential to ontology.

"Hearing," ἀκούειν, which corresponds to speaking, is the fundamental way of "listening," the genuine possibility of αἴσθησις. In hearing I am in communication with other human beings insofar as being a human being means speaking. (G 18:44/32)

He says further:

Although seeing in the context of θεωρεῖν reveals the world in the authentic sense, it is actually *hearing*, because it [hearing] is the *perceiving of speaking*, it is the *possibility of Being-with-others*. (G 18:104/72)

Heidegger admits that the emphasis that Aristotle places on hearing is peculiar considering the importance of θεωρεῖν and ὁρᾶν to Greek ontology. Heidegger is showing here that for Aristotle, hearing and speaking are basic ways in which human beings are together with each other in the world.

As such, hearing and speaking are determinative of the city, the πόλις. Aristotle affirms the importance of the city when he says that one is only a human being insofar as he lives in the πόλις. This is not because being human is a basic possibility that living in the πόλις offers, but rather because the πόλις itself is a basic possibility of human beings. Heidegger says, "In the Being of the human being himself lies the basic possibility of Being-in-the-πόλις" (G 18:46/33). The πόλις is the place wherein human beings are together with one another. In that human beings are speaking beings, they are together with one another, such that the πόλις itself is grounded in speaking. That basic dimension of speaking reveals what Heidegger says is a "fundamental character of the Dasein of human beings . . . *being-with-one another* . . . in the sense of *speaking-with-others* in the way of communication, refutation, debate" (G 18:47/33).

Speaking provides the foundation for being-together. Hence, politics is grounded in speaking because politics investigates the ways in which human beings can be together.[14] More specifically, politics investigates the way that human beings can strive together toward that which is good for all: the greater good. Politics and the good toward which politics strives, the good of the human being, as well as ἦθος, ethical excellence (ἀρετὴ ἠθική),[15] happiness, and deliberation—all of which depend on the being-together and speaking-together of human beings—will be interpreted through those structures that are revealed within the basic character of speaking. The πόλις is grounded in λόγος.

In the beginning of one of his class sessions from this lecture course, Heidegger reiterates what he has already said about the averageness of language. He reaffirms that language is determinative of Being-in-the-world. For the first time, however, he introduces the idea of the "they" and makes the astonishing claim that "the they is the authentic How of every-dayness," and this is because the human being, in the everydayness of our Being-with-others, basically is other people, and is, thereby, prone to aver-ageness (G 18:64/45). Addressing his students directly, Heidegger makes this even more astonishing claim about Being-with-others:

> Through a sharper comprehension [*Fassung*] of the they you will see that it [the they] is at the same time the possibility from which an authentic Being-with-others can in a certain way grow. (G 18:64/45)

This is a thought-provoking idea; it affirms that the possibility of Being-with-others authentically will not at all be a matter of negating the "they" because the "they" is always already a way of Being-with-others and authen-ticity does not eliminate that. Authentic Being-with-others will be a modi-fication, cultivation, and development of the inauthentic way of Being-with-others.

Further, Heidegger says that "*the authentic carrier of the they is language*" (G 18:64/45). Thus, the possibility of an authentic sense of Being-with-others must involve a renewed understanding of language. Authentic lan-guage makes authentic Being-with-others possible. Heidegger says here, interestingly, that averageness actually comes from universality or univer-sal validity. The "they" is an expression of the way universal validity, pro-pounded and passed along by the "they," is appropriated by individuals in and through language. Universal validity invades the self in such a way that the self becomes a they-self. The counterpoise to the averageness of universality is, then, the Here and Now, *Jeweiligkeit*, the καιρόσ that is revealed in a particular, concrete situation, the Being of a being in its *there*.[16] The critical and defining moment of the Being of the *there* is limit, πέρας. The Greeks understood Being in and through Dasein in its limitedness.

Ἦθος and Ἀγαθόυ

Heidegger suggests that although the good is the authentic character of Being for the human being (indeed, because of that explicit relation to the human being), it needs to be interpreted in terms of limit. Dasein is fun-damentally practical; he says, "The Being of the human being is deter-mined as taking care" (taking care = *Besorgen*, which is Heidegger's trans-lation of πρᾶξις) (G 18:65/46). Further, Heidegger explains that every πρᾶξις ends in a τέλος, and "the τέλος of every πρᾶξις is ἀγαθόν as πέρας" (*G* 18:65/46). The good is here a practical good, the concrete good of Dasein, which is, thereby, fundamentally limited by the profound limitation of Dasein itself. Further, the good is "a *How of Dasein, itself*," which manifests in the way that human beings handle themselves with others (*G* 18:69/49). There is clearly a political dimension being explored here, which involves a kind of practical knowledge, what Heidegger calls the know-how (*Auskenntnis*) of something. This is significant because it addresses the problem of ethics. Both ethics and politics are manifestations of Dasein as Being-with-others. To know the good is to know how to carry yourself in the world, how to be with others. Political knowledge is a practical knowledge of Being-with-others; it is a manner or posture (*Haltung*) that is, in other words, an ἦθος. Ethics is not, therefore, a dimension or section of politics. Rather, ethics and politics involve "learning the know-how about the Being of the human being in his authenticity" (*G* 18:69/48). They are both grounded in ἦθος.

Heidegger is not trying to subsume the good under Being; he is not trying to ontologize the good as a way of destroying the practical dimension of the good of human action, as many have claimed. Rather, he is reinterpreting ethics and politics through Aristotle so that these disciplines are oriented toward the human being and, more specifically, toward the Being of the human being. The former is basically Aristotelian, the latter thoroughly Heideggerian. What he discovers is that Aristotelian ethics is, fundamentally, an analysis of the ἦθος which is indicative of the Being-dimension of the human being as authentically Being-with-others. Thus, ἦθος is a manner or posture that involves know-how with regard to that ontological dimension wherein human beings speak together with each other authentically in the world. Heidegger says that ἦθος is "how a human being is there, how he presents himself as a human being," basically a way of carrying oneself with others (*G* 18:106/73). With regard to a speaker or rhetor, Heidegger says that ἦθος refers to the posture that a person takes with regard to those things about which he is speaking. Further still, Heidegger points out that Aristotle makes an etymological correlation between ἦθος and ethical excellence (ἀρετὴ ἠθική) to show that ἦθος refers to the genesis of ethical excellence in the temporal sense (*G* 18:191–94/129–31). Time here is not linear: One does not become more and more ethical with time. Rather, ἦθος is the ground of ἀρετὴ ἠθική, and through the repetition of actions one develops an ἦθος, but the temporal dimension here is indicative of a certain calmness or composure (*Gefasstsein*) that one attains with maturity: It is "the authentic composure within Dasein [which] the human being wins as a man, not in youth and not in old age" (*G* 18:194/130–31).

Clearly, Heidegger is following Aristotle when he says that what needs to be investigated is not simply the good in itself but rather the concrete good of the human being. Heidegger is going further than Aristotle, however, by making determinations about the ontological meaning of the good of the human being by emphasizing that the concrete experience of individual goods, *as limited goods*, is directly related to (and a result of) the Being of the human being as Being-in-the-world. Dasein is practical because it *takes care* in its daily practices. This presumes that what Dasein takes care of is *there*; taking care is not worldless; it is not a grasping into an emptiness, but is always a taking care of that which is *there* in the world. This is the case because taking care is fundamentally determined by limit. To be in the world means to be limited in our cares and experiences, and it had that meaning for the Greeks. Dasein is a being that is essentially limited. It can fully actualize a situation and take care of something only because it is fundamentally a being that is limited in its Being. Dasein takes care in such a way as to determine the end of something. To take care of something is to realize its end, to finish it, to bring it into its *there*; by the same token, Dasein can take care because it is itself a being determined by its own end and for which its own end is an issue.

Heidegger maintains, therefore, that the good of the human being (ἀνθρώπινον ἀγαθόν) is an end for the sake of itself (τέλος δι᾽ αὐτό); it is a τέλος that "we take care of 'on account of itself'" (*G* 18:72/51). The good needs to be interpreted in terms of limit. *In that way, the good is understood according to the Being of the human being.* As such, the good is both a limit and an end. What emerges here in the determination of the concretion of Dasein and the corresponding concretion of the good is an understanding of the life of Dasein. Ethics and politics strive after the good, but they do so in order to determine how to live well (εὐζωία). The good, therefore, is the good of human Dasein; it is a "How of life," where the end is to live well. To be sure, Heidegger is following Aristotle quite closely here, but he does so in order to break down the idea of an impossible ethics. There is no good in itself, only individual goods that, thought more radically, have an intrinsic relation to the Being of the human being. The exploration of ἦθος as the ground of ἀρετὴ ἠθική demands that the Aristotelian understanding of ethical goods be retrieved and grounded. Ethical goods must be construed in terms of their concrete Being-there in the world, for only then can their full ontological meaning be explored.

Indeed, by situating the good in the concrete world of human Dasein, Heidegger emphasizes the defining characters of limit and end. The good is an end. More specifically, though, it is a τέλειον, which is defined by Heidegger as "something complete." Heidegger examines *Metaphysics* 4.16, though, and gathers together eight points regarding the meaning of τέλειον from that text. He affirms that τέλος and τέλειον mean limit (*Grenze*) and not just "something complete," and he goes further and says that these are also ontological determinations about the Being of something. As such, they do not just mean limit, in the sense that the garden gate marks the end of the path; rather, they mean "beyond-which-nothing" (*das Worüber-hinaus-nichts*). In this latter sense, τέλειον is a determination of the Being of a being.

> τέλειον is not a being, a piece of a being, whose end it determines, rather τέλειον is *Being*, a *way of Being itself.* . . . The τέλειον is a *determination of the Being of a being*, and not any kind of property like something black or white. The beyond-which-nothing has the character of limit in the sense of a determination of Being. (*G* 18:89/61–62)

For Dasein, the τέλειον is death, the no-longer-Dasein, and this no-longer-there belongs to the *there* of Dasein. Hence, death is a part of who Dasein is, as its limit: not as the garden gate, but more profoundly as *the beyond-which-nothing*. That nothing is essentially a part of Dasein. Moreover, Heidegger has said, through Aristotle, that the good is a concrete good. Since that concrete good is indicative of the end or limit of a taking-care, then the good is an end, a limit. As a consequence, the good is intrinsically related to the nothing. There is a negativity built into the structure of the good that is apparent only when the end and limit characters of the good are recognized and fully actualized. Further, that "beyond-which-nothing" is a determination of the Being of a being. As such, it is a recognition of the *there* of a being and, more explicitly, a recognition of the relation between what is there and what is not there. The not or nothing of a being is intrinsically *there* within it.

For a community, therefore, an authentic Being-with-others can take place and does take place when certain boundaries to the community are recognized. Heidegger picks up on Aristotle's example of friends and relatives. Being-with-others belongs essentially to Dasein's Being, but that does not mean that a person is a friend to everyone. He says, "The authentic Being-with-others loses itself when it is a wild Being-with-everyone," that is, when it extends to friends of friends and relatives of relatives (*G* 18:96–97/66). Authentic Being-with-others requires that certain limitations be recognized. Even so, that is the case because of intrinsic limitations within the human being. The boundaries of authentic Being-with-others stem from the essential limitation of Dasein.

But what is the good of the human being? For Aristotle it is εὐδαιμονία, happiness. However, Aristotle's sense of εὐδαιμονία involves a multiplicity of actions that can be summed up, and the τέλειον of Dasein is a determination of its Being, not a summation of its actions. The τέλειον is not the what of a being (the summation of its actions throughout the course of a lifetime) but the How of a being in its Being (ἦθος). Thus, the τέλειον or good of Dasein, the ἀνθρώπινον ἀγαθόν, is an ontological determination of the Being of πρᾶξις . *Thus, the good or τέλειο ν of Dasein is life itself.* Heidegger explains that the good or τέλος of any πρᾶξις is its ἔργον, the finished work. The ἔργον of the human being is itself, and "Insofar as the τέλος of the human being does not lie outside of itself but rather *in itself as a possibility of Being*, the ἀνθρώπινον ἀγαθόν is ζωή itself, 'life' itself" (*G* 18:100/69). Dasein is essentially a work in progress; it *is* possibility and, more specifically, possibility of Being, which is to say that its own Being is an issue for it.

It has been suggested through Aristotle that excellence requires the repetition of good actions, but this explanation suggests routine (*Routine* and *Betrieb*). This is problematic because according to Heidegger the disposition of excellence is not and cannot be based on routine: Routine actually destroys the *Augenblick* (*G* 18:190/128). Excellence is a repetition (*Wiederholung*), but not in a mechanical sense of doing the same thing over and over again. It is a repetition of προαίρεσις, a matter of repeating, "the concrete resoluteness and appropriation of the *Augenblick*" (*G* 18:191/129). Dasein is temporal, and so it cannot achieve some routine that holds it perfectly in the state of excellence. Dasein can always be otherwise. One must achieve practical know-how about the world in each particular situation. It is not enough that one just get angry; one must determine how to be angry in each particular situation. Excellence is, therefore, not a relation to an ethics a priori but is, rather, a practical determination of the posture or orientation of Dasein in its world. In this way, excellence has an intrinsic relation to ἕξις, which determines Dasein's authentic way of Being-in-the-world.

Excellence is determined by the transformation that comes over a person in that change of disposition that adjusts a person's orientation to Being-in-the-world. In Aristotelian terms, excellence means determining the mean in a certain situation. Heidegger casts the mean in ontological terms and calls the mean a καιρός, a moment of understanding about Dasein's orientation in the world. Since Dasein is oriented in its world through disposition, excellence is a disposition, and since this excellence is a special disposition wherein Dasein understands that it can choose its own future, excellence is a "prohairetic" disposition. Finally, since Dasein is fundamentally a Being-and-speaking-in-the-world-with-others, excellence is a "prohairetic" disposition that takes place in language (ἀρετή is ἕξις προαιρετικὴ μετὰ λόγου) (G18 209/140). The λέγειν of excellence is, then, the kind of speaking that corresponds to Dasein insofar as Dasein is in the καιρός or *Augenblick*. Heidegger has shifted the emphasis on excellence from an ethical context to the ontology of the life of Dasein. Determining the whole of the human being, therefore, is not a matter of measuring the good actions that a person has performed over the course of a lifetime, as is the case in Aristotle. Rather, the whole of the human being is a determination of life, that is, of Being-in-a-world.

> The whole of the human being must be understood with regard to its Being as life, ζωή, as Being-in-a-world. So understood, the authentic theme is not psychology but rather *discussing the Being of this being* [*Erörterung des Seins dieses Seienden*]. (*G* 18:192/129)

At the very end of this lecture course, Heidegger says, "It is not necessary to say anything new, but rather to say that which the Ancients already meant," and much of what Heidegger says in this course is an explication of Aristotle (*G* 18:329/222). It is, after all, a lecture course that was intended for students who were interested in listening to a professor who could breathe new life into the ancient texts of Aristotle. In doing so, however, Heidegger says more in this course than is there in the Aristotelian texts. Many have called Heidegger's readings of Aristotle interpretive violence. I accept this expression only if it is taken in a positive sense to mean that Heidegger was trying to bring out what is implicit in what Aristotle said but which Aristotle did not and could not say. Heidegger is clearly searching through Aristotle for something. That something is the Being of beings.

My contention is that in and through his search for the Being of beings, Heidegger has retrieved a more original understanding of λόγος that is based on Dasein's average, everyday way of Being-in-the-world. He has shown that the authentic function of speaking is to reveal or uncover Dasein and as it is *there*, in the world. In the disposition of anxiety or uncanniness, which take place in the rhetorical situation, Dasein experiences a moment of understanding, a καιρός, about its orientation in the world. It recognizes itself as limited and as fallen. At that moment, Dasein begins to speak. It seeks out conversation about who and what it is as a finite and limited being. This is why the notion of authentic speaking contributes to our understanding of authentic Being-with-others and ethical excellence. Heidegger is interested in the way that Dasein is engaged in speaking relationships with others. The πόλις, or city, is the place where these dialogical relationships of speaking and listening, debating, refuting, and arguing occur. Aristotle's

Rhetoric presents us with the average, everyday way in which the Greeks communicated with each other in the marketplace, and that is why Heidegger is analyzing this text. An authentic sense of community and Being-with-others happens through the average everydayness of life, speaking with others in the πόλις.[17] The good of human life, ethical excellence, is thus not a routine, but rather a posture or orientation that Dasein takes to life itself.

9

Sophistry

The matter at issue, what is properly visible in it, word, word-sound—
beings, world, disclosure of beings, discourse, manifestation. This is nothing else than the universal context of phenomena within which man, the
ζῷον λόγον ἔχον, ever exists. This context is ultimately grounded in Being-in, in the antecedent uncoveredness of the world.

—**Martin Heidegger,** *Plato's Sophist*

An understanding of Plato's dialogue the *Sophist*, Heidegger tells us, demands that we acquire the proper vantage from which to understand Plato.
That standpoint comes from Aristotle. By going through Aristotle to Plato,
and not from Plato to Aristotle, Heidegger claims that he is simply adher-
ing to the hermeneutic principle of proceeding "from the clear into the
obscure." This way, Plato can be interpreted in the most proper way, from
out of his own historical situation. In addition to being hermeneutic, Heidegger's method is also factical. Factical research respects the concrete,
historical situation of a particular thinker. By engaging Plato through Aristotle, Heidegger is trying to get his students attuned to the facticity of
Plato's situatedness within his own philosophical-historical context and,
more specifically, to the Greek experience of λόγος.

Heidegger claims in *Plato's Sophist* (G 19) that Plato was able to prepare
the ground for Aristotle's later investigations into rhetoric. Moreover, he
claims that in the *Sophist* (one of Plato's later works) there is evidence that
Plato was influenced by the young Aristotle. Heidegger admits that he is
only surmising this possibility, but he nevertheless makes his case that there
are elements from the young Aristotle in Plato, which suggest that Plato
recognized certain difficulties with his own understanding of the Ideas. By
watching the development of Plato's Ideas, we can get a better look at the
Platonic insights into Aristotle's understanding of rhetoric as well as delineate those areas where Aristotle had made advances over Plato in doing
ontological research, even to the extent that Aristotle may have urged Plato
to change how he thought about the Ideas.

In his analysis of the *Sophist*, Heidegger recognizes the central position of λόγος within Greek Dasein, in both the Platonic and Aristotelian senses. Heidegger's interpretations of the Greeks were essential to his development of fundamental ontology, but at the same time he often demonstrated a kind of ambivalence toward the Greek thinkers. He recognized the primordiality of their thinking, but he also discovers clues in these texts of even more primordial ways of thinking. Therefore, in this chapter I argue that Heidegger is trying to determine the positive contributions to philosophical research (ontology—ὄν, ὄντα, and λόγος: Being, beings, and language) which can be retrieved from both of these pivotal thinkers of the Western tradition.

One guess as to why Heidegger made such an exhaustive analysis of Plato's *Sophist* comes from the claim that Plato makes there, that we find the philosopher by searching for the sophist. For Heidegger, the basic questions of philosophy emerge through an understanding of the possibility of deception, here the possibility of sophistry. As we saw from Chapter 7, human beings spend most of their time in deception. Insofar as philosophy investigates the existence of the human being, deception, as the primary mode of existence for the human being, must be placed in the center of that investigation. As we have seen from earlier chapters, philosophy must engage life in its deceptions and masks. The guiding line for Heidegger's explications in this course is a concrete analysis of the ontological work of Plato. Both the dialogue itself and the course have as their theme the relationship between being (ὄν) and non-being (μὴ ὄν). That relationship is probed in order to determine the possibility of the being of non-being. If non-being is, for Plato, an ontological possibility, that is, if it is possible for non-being to be, then the possibility of the existence of the sophist has been proven. This is because the sophist dwells in non-being by engaging in deception, λόγος ψευδής, the presentation of something as other than it is, that is, the presentation of it as it is not. The fundamental question here is of being and non-being, especially in terms of λόγος, and that is the way toward philosophizing. The question of the philosopher is as important as "the question of the *negativum*, the sophist" (*G* 19:577/400). As Heidegger emphasizes on the last page of the course, in searching for the sophist, "the *philosopher* has become transparent in himself, and that has happened uniquely by way of concrete philosophizing itself " (*G* 19:610/422).

In keeping with the thematic investigation of the relationship between deception and existence, this chapter will demonstrate that the deception that is ingredient to language is necessary to understanding the existence of the human being. I take existence here to indicate an ontological dimension of the human being whereby Dasein is Being in a world (which, as we saw from Chapter 6, encounters Being). One major theme that emerged from Chapter 7 was Heidegger's endeavor to undermine science's fantastical search for certainty by submitting that search to the concrete existence of Dasein in the world. In this course, we will see a further development of that theme. In turn, Heidegger places the investigation of λόγος at the very center of the analysis of human existence. What is at stake in this course, as he traverses the analyses of Being, truth, and rhetoric, is the concrete existence of the human being, that is, temporal and historical Dasein (Being in a world), and the expression of that existence in speaking.

Again, I return to the task of trying to investigate the facticity of language. Heidegger does not emphasize the facticity of language here, indeed, he does not use the expression "the facticity of language" at all. But if we take the facticity of language to indicate the concrete speaking of human beings in the world (as we saw in Chapter 8's analysis of rhetoric) and the way in which that way of speaking is prone to error and deception (which we saw clearly from Chapter 7), then factical language is still a central concern of Heidegger's researches at this point.

There are four sections in this chapter. In the first section, I explain Heidegger's complex reading of Aristotle and Plato. It is often thought that Heidegger simply dismisses Plato as the father of metaphysics. I show in this first section that that is not the case. Heidegger believes that Aristotle made advances over Plato in terms of ontological research and in terms of his understanding of language. He even believes that Plato changed his theory of the Ideas based on the influence of the young Aristotle. But Heidegger thought that Plato had a more original relationship to Being and to language than we do today. In the second section I pursue this original relationship by analyzing the dimension of speaking within Platonic dialectic. Although dialectic is intended to surpass speaking toward a seeing of the Ideas, which are themselves beings and not Being itself, dialectic does involve speaking and, thus, the temporality of human existence. In the third section I focus on the essential relationship between human existence and speaking. Heidegger looks at two views of rhetoric in Plato, a negative view from the *Gorgias* and a positive view from the *Phaedrus*. By examining these two views, I am able to show that for Heidegger, it is the facticity of human life that would prevent one from ever being able to see the Platonic Ideas. Nonetheless, Heidegger sees how Plato's view of rhetoric in the *Phaedrus* is positive because of its concern with substantive and meaningful speaking about factical human existence. In the fourth and final section, I look at Heidegger's analysis of the structure of λόγος. I show here how Heidegger rethinks our understanding of language from analyses of propositions to the disclosure of meaningful contexts in factical human life. The original function of λόγος, therefore, is to disclose the ways that factical human Dasein is in the world.

Plato and Aristotle on Being and Λόγος

I will begin with some preliminary observations about Heidegger's Aristotelian critiques of Plato. Most of this chapter, though, will be devoted to the way in which Platonic dialectic is grounded in speaking and, therefore, in an experience of Being-in-the-world. To reiterate: Heidegger investigates Aristotle first in order to prepare the ground for research into Plato. His stated reason for doing this is that he is laying the foundation for the proper investigation of truth in Aristotle, so that Plato's ontological investigations are considered from Aristotle's treatment of truthing (ἀληθεύειν). Heidegger proceeds in this fashion because he believes that Aristotle delved more deeply into the question of Being than had Plato and that Plato actually recognized the problems that Aristotle's investigations posed for his (Plato's) own understanding of ontology. Specifically, Heidegger saw that even though Aristotle conceived of Being as a being, in the same way that Plato had, Aristotle "saves himself when he says: Being and the manifold of the characters which pertain to Being καθ᾽ αὐτό are ὡς φύσεώς τινος, like something ὡς φύσις τις, 'something already present by means of itself'" (G 19:210/145). This is to say that Aristotle was more attuned to the possible way that beings come to presence by their own means, in their own Being, than was Plato, whose ontological investigations were directed toward Being itself in a separate realm of Ideas and not toward the Being *of beings*. Aristotle, for his part, suggests the possibility for investigating the temporal unfolding of objects that makes them present in the first place. The basic distinction: For Aristotle, the temporal unfolding or coming into presence (movement) of beings belongs to beings themselves; for Plato, the forms are true Being, and they are distinct from beings. Hence, for Heidegger, Aristotle was a provocative thinker who suggests the possibility of thinking the Being *of beings*. Since Plato conceives of Being (the Ideas) as in another realm altogether, so that beings participate in Being, he did not think of beings as coming into presence under their own power and thus in their own Being. This distinction between the two thinkers becomes clearer when we take account of how Plato may have adopted some of Aristotle's insights.

Heidegger surmises that there are two elements in the *Sophist* that are quite clearly Aristotelian in orientation. The first element is that of bodies, σώματα. Plato, for the first time, bases his ontological investigation on the σώματα or αἰσθετά, perceived things, which were, in fact, "the proper impetus of Aristotle's research" (G 19:484/335). Hence, Aristotle was researching Being through beings, through bodies and perceived things, and, "Plato is obviously taking this determination into account, with the result that the σώματα in fact do provide a basis for a discussion of Being" (G 19:484/335). Second, Heidegger claims that Plato makes δύναμις into an ontological problem precisely because he was being influenced by the young Aristotle. To be sure, Aristotle ultimately conceived of δύναμις in a much more radical way than Plato, who was trying to incorporate δύναμις into his theory of the Ideas. Whereas Aristotle, from the start, conceives of δύναμις as "an ontological category in connection with ἐνέργεια," so that potentiality (as we have already seen from *Introduction to Phenomenological Research* [G 17], potentiality is darkness, negativity, δυνάμει ὄν) is an essential dimension of the coming into presence of beings, Plato tries to accommodate δύναμις into the Ideas (G 19:484/335). This accommodation of δύναμις, however, is insufficient because Plato concludes by saying that the "dunamic" powers, φρόνησις, νοῦς, κίνησις, and ζωή, are also beings. For Plato, prudence, understanding, movement, and life are not so much powers of Being that dynamize the coming-to-presence of beings as they are themselves beings that "keep company with the genuine beings" (G 19:482/334). Plato construes Being as beings whereas Aristotle suggests the possibility that prudence, understanding, movement, and life are not beings but nonobjective, elemental forces or powers, in which and through which the Being of beings is manifest.

Hence, for Heidegger, Aristotle's first philosophy attempted to exhibit the Being of beings through δύναμις. Moreover, Aristotle attempted to do this through speech, rhetoric, the everyday ways that people speak with each other. As such, Aristotle's treatment of λόγος was a marked improvement in ontological research over Platonic dialectic. To be sure, both of their philosophical approaches aim at the whole (ὅλον), and they are both properly philosophical in that sense; neither involves the study of just a particular region of Being. They both have Being as their aim. But dialectic is fundamentally inadequate, and it is inadequate because, even though it strives toward Being, it leads, ultimately, toward a beholding of Being as a manifold of beings (the Ideas) (G 19:214/148). This is how Aristotle realized that the dialectical conversation is fraught with difficulties. A dialectical conversation is grounded in pure νοεῖν, a beholding of the truth of Being construed as beings that can be seen. What Plato means here by Being—prudence, understanding, movement, life, even soul or the creative powers—he construes as beings, which are co-present with the genuine beings, the Ideas.

In an explanation of Aristotle's radicalization of Platonic dialectic, Heidegger says:

Aristotle did deprive dialectic of its dignity, but not because he did not understand it. On the contrary, he understood it more radically, because he saw Plato himself as being under way toward θεωρεῖν in his dialectic, because he succeeded in making real what Plato was striving for. *Aristotle saw the immanent limits of dialectic, because he philosophized more radically.* . . . Aristotle could do this, of course, only because he understood the function of λόγος and of διαλέγεσθαι within scientific reflection and within human existence in general. Only on the basis of a positive understanding of the phenomenon of λέγειν within life (as can be found in his *Rhetoric*) did Aristotle acquire the foundation for interpreting λέγεσθαι in a wholly concrete way and thus for seeing διαλέγεσθαι more acutely. (*G* 19:199–200/138)

Some interpretations of this passage suggest that Heidegger believed that Aristotle understood dialectic more radically because Aristotle was able to realize fully the θεωρεῖν that Plato was striving for but could never accomplish.[1] I would argue otherwise. Heidegger claims that Aristotle understood Platonic dialectic more radically precisely because of his concern with the concrete speaking of human existence, what he calls the λέγειν within life.[2] For Aristotle, the theme of philosophy *was* human existence, and Plato's dialectic, ultimately, attempts to submit human existence and being-with-others to a kind of θεωρεῖν that meditates Being as beings. Platonic dialectic takes Being as a being because it remains focused on human knowledge. It finds the source, the ἀρχή, of Being in human knowledge. It does not consider how beings *are* by means of their own power. By providing a "positive understanding" of the manifold ways in which human beings speak with each other, the concrete ways of speaking in the world, Aristotle, in the *Rhetoric*, is able to show that Platonic dialectic is not so much a conversation wherein two or more people who are in the world speak with each other about the Being of the human being (*about* Being in the world, *about* factical Dasein), as it is a seeing (and thus not a speaking) that is grounded in knowledge of the Ideas. The *Rhetoric*, as we saw, opens up human beings to their Being as Being in the world, unlike the Platonic dialectic, which, even though it is a conversation that thinks about Being, is ultimately not a matter of speaking about how human beings are in the world but a matter of seeing the Ideas; it is a matter of "bringing one's partner in the argument to open his eyes and see" the genuine beings: prudence, movement, life, understanding, the soul, the good, the beautiful, and so on (*G* 19:200/138).

Even Aristotle construed genuine λόγος as ἀποφαίνεσθαι, letting-be-seen, but according to Heidegger, Aristotle considered λόγος more radically than Plato because he recognized that the ἀρχή of the Being of a being is not at all in human knowledge but in the being itself. The *Rhetoric*, as we saw, considers the manifold ways of speaking as a way of going about one's way in the world in such a way that one experiences or encounters Being. There is a practical dimension in Aristotle's ontology, not only because he founds the thinking of Being on beings, σώματα and αἰσθετά, but also because he was more concerned with how human beings speak with each other than was Plato. Aristotle's understanding of λόγος is, thus, richer than Plato's because he (Aristotle) thinks of language as the addressing of something as something, the λόγος ἀποφαντικός, in terms of what it is, "its ontological provenance, namely that which already resides in it, what it itself in a certain sense is, although this is indeed prior to itself" (*G* 19:510/353). We would go too far in saying that Aristotle meditated the ontological difference, but it is not an exaggeration to suggest that Aristotle considers the Being of beings more radically than Plato precisely because he founds his ontology on σώματα and αἰσθετά, (beings), conceives of λόγος as addressing the ontological provenance (movement, temporal unfolding, Being) of those beings, and because he grasps the λόγος (λέγειν) more radically than Plato.

Still, it must be kept in mind that Aristotle's research into διαλέγεσθαι, dialectical discussion, is what allows him to accomplish a radicalization of Platonic dialectic, and this radicalization is not simply a reproof of dialectic and its problems. On the contrary, Heidegger believed that Aristotle recognized the positive contribution of dialectic by seeing that it was concerned with the substantive content of the matters themselves. In this sense, Aristotle understood what subsequent interpreters of Plato did not understand, namely, that dialectic is not of itself theoretical but dialogical, even though its goal is ultimately θεωρεῖν. Aristotle was able to provide a positive understanding of λέγειν as the speaking of life *through* and *because of* Plato. The history of philosophy, by developing a logical system of thinking, "embodying a dialectical movement to and fro," a movement that has nothing whatsoever to do with speaking and discussing, has abandoned any attempt to incorporate substantive knowledge obtained through speaking into its own research (*G* 19:199/137). Dialectical reflection, when it is devoid of the character of substantively speaking about things themselves, "has become wild and lost in emptiness" (*G* 19:199/137). Therefore, in the *Sophist* course Heidegger is using Aristotle to reach down to an understanding of Plato that has been lost by the tradition of logic. Even though Aristotle radicalized Plato's dialectic because he saw that it was under way toward θεωρεῖν, he nevertheless recognized that it involved speaking about and discussing substantive matters.

That Aristotle recognized the practical, dialogical potential of dialectic will prove critical both for his own research and for Heidegger's understanding of Aristotle. He says here, with reference to a more original understanding of dialectic as speaking, that "according to its original sense and according to its original facticity as well, λόγος is not disclosive at all but, to speak in an extreme way, is precisely *concealing*" (*G* 19:197/136). Heidegger continues by explaining that factical λόγος is prattle, idle talk; it "brings about a blindness with regard to what is disclosed." That being said, Heidegger also recognizes that in order to penetrate the facticity of language, in order to cut through idle talk, λόγος itself would have to be left behind. This, again, is the insight of Aristotle. Dialectical discussion presses toward pure νοεῖν. However, "insofar as the consideration remains in λέγειν and as διαλέγεσθαι continues on in thorough discussion, such 'speaking through' can indeed relinquish idle talk but cannot do more than *attempt* to press on to the things themselves" (*G* 19;197/136). Speaking and discussing (διαλέγεσθαι) cannot obtain a clear seeing. As λέγειν, however, διαλέγεσθαι "need not be a mere game but has a proper function insofar as it cuts through the idle talk, checks the prattle and in the speeches lays its finger, as it were, on what is at issue" (*G* 19:197/136). Factical language conceals and distorts, but it does so insofar as it is language. Language, λόγος, means speaking and discussing: It is in the world and, therefore, subject to distortion. Therefore, any understanding of authentic speaking will recognize that concealment and distortion are immanent within speaking. What is necessary is a new conception of truth that acknowledges the concealing, distorting facticity of speaking.

Specifically with regard to deception, Heidegger points out that Aristotle's understanding of λόγος was more original than that of Antisthenes because he attunes his development of λόγος to "a corresponding *doctrine of beings* and their possible determinability" (*G* 19:510/353). Aristotle recognized the essential and inextricable correspondence between the question of Being and the development of λόγος. As a consequence, deception becomes possible through Aristotle, which was not the case in Antisthenes and the Megarians, who thought that λόγος was simply a matter of naming in correspondence with ἕν, the one, where no contradiction and no ψευδής were possible. For them, λόγος was simply the identification of something with itself: what it looks like, its identity, (the tautological) and not what it is (the λέγειν τι καθ' αὐτό) (*G* 19:510/353). Through Aristotle, λέγειν becomes richer; it is not just tautology but actually "discloses the thing addressed for what it is" (*G* 19:510/353). The disclosure of λόγος that corresponds to Being opens λόγος to the possibility of deception because it is no longer a naming of the one but "an addressing of something for what it itself is," the λέγειν τι καθ' αὑτό. This is the same dynamic we saw in Chapter 7 with respect to κρίνειν. The λόγος is not simply tautological but rather "something as something." The λόγος is deceptive because deception emerges in that difference.

Heidegger is working within the Platonic conception of dialectic here, so when he refers to speeches he means the dialectical talking through of a philosophical problem as takes place in Plato's dialogues. Nonetheless, what is at stake in this analysis is the facticity of speaking, and what we see here is that the "original facticity" contained within speaking itself, because it is the ground of deception, commits human beings to their own existence, and this is something that Aristotle recognized. The foundation for the critique of Plato is not simply that the pure νοεῖν of dialectic is not the best way to philosophize, but rather that pure νοεῖν is not possible for human beings.

Λόγος, addressing something in speech, is our most immediate mode of carrying out ἀληθεύειν, whereas νοῦς, pure perception, is as such not possible for man, the ζῷον λόγον ἔχον. For us, νοεῖν is initially and for the most part διανοεῖν, because our dealing with things is dominated by λόγος. (G 19:196/136)

The tendency toward seeing of the dialectic, Plato's inclination toward νοεῖν, is not a realistic possibility for human beings, whose primary way of being is to be thinking with and through others by speaking with them. The task of philosophy is, therefore, not to pass through λόγος to νοεῖν, but rather to accept the original facticity of λόγος and discern truth from within those deceptions and concealments that are immanent within the factical human situation. Platonic dialectic goes awry—in Being and Time, Heidegger says that dialectic "has been a genuine philosophical embarrassment (BT 25/47)—as it presses toward pure νοεῖν without recognizing that the very matters that it is trying to investigate, speaking and the pure νοεῖν that speaking supposedly elicits, are incompatible. I emphasize: For Heidegger pure νοεῖν is not possible for humans, and speaking does not and cannot lead to pure νοεῖν in Plato's sense. Aristotle's sense of seeing in θεωρεῖν and νοεῖν is one that is fully immersed within the factical deceptions immanent within δόξα. Again, Aristotle grounds his ontology in the σώματα and αἰσθετά. Plato's sense of νοεῖν is a thinking about Being as a manifold of beings (the Ideas), a kind of thinking that ostensibly grasps the whole of truth apart from the concealments implicit within human existence, as though that were at all possible.

The Speaking of Platonic Dialectic

It is, however, too facile to say that Heidegger dismisses Platonic dialectic while embracing Aristotelian praxis and the factical situation of human existence. We know that for Heidegger the history of metaphysics actually started with Plato. Also, it is well known that even Aristotle situates σοφία in a higher position than φρόνησις, at the end of the *Nicomachean Ethics,* where he says that the contemplative life is the most excellent. Hence, the pure knowing of σοφία is a more excellent truthing (ἀληθεύειν) than the practical truthing of φρόνησις. There are practical dimensions of Plato, just as there are theoretical dimensions of Aristotle. Heidegger is tilling the soil of Plato's research, as it were, trying to find clues of more original thinking that ground the dialectic. He is here reading the Greeks as a way of developing a practical ontology, and he takes his understanding from both Plato and Aristotle. What he finds is that for both of these pivotal Greek thinkers, λόγος is central to the development of their ontologies. Heidegger recognizes this, and he draws out the practical consequences of the centrality of λόγος.

Looking at Plato's dialogue we can see that the main issue, the definition of the/a sophist, depends on whether or not there is non-being built into the structure of λόγος. The sophist takes refuge in the Parmenidean principle that there is no non-being (μὴ ὄν). If I am talking about something that is not, then that which I am talking about must have some measure of being because of the fact that I am talking about it. If it were nothing, I could not talk about it; because I *can* talk about it, this means that it must in some way be. Of course, the sophist is accused of engaging in deception and trickery (λόγος ψευδής). He is talking about beings in such a way that what he says about them is not the way that they actually are. But if he can hide behind the principle that there is no such thing as non-being, he cannot possibly be doing what he is accused of doing. He cannot be "making" non-being be because there is no non-being. To account for the existence of the sophist, it must be shown that there is a Not (non-being, which will soon be understood as "otherness," ἕτερον) built into the structure of λόγος. We saw this in a preliminary way in Chapter 7 when we looked at Heidegger's initial foray into Aristotle's experience of phenomenon and λόγος as a way of discovering a more original dimension of phenomenology through the deceptions of factical λόγος (the λόγος of factical-historical Dasein as Being in a world). Here we see a similar, factical dimension in Plato's dialectic insofar as λέγειν is inherently deceptive (shot through with negativity).

In this more original understanding of the dialectic, Heidegger first discovers a certain movement (κίνησις) that is intrinsic to Plato's ontology, a movement that makes dialectic possible. If we construe dialectic more originally, then we see that what enables the soul's journey toward first principles, toward the ἀρχαί, is speaking, λέγειν, and this speaking is guided by a basic movement.

The dialectical consideration properly focuses on the ψυχή and specifically on the ψυχή in its basic comportment of λέγειν, and, further, on the λέγειν of the ψυχη as κίνησις, i.e., precisely with regard to how the ἕτερον can be together with it. (G 19:578/400–401)

The soul's capacity for speaking and discussing bespeaks an intrinsic movement. That basic movement is what makes otherness possible, the co-presence of Being and non-being. Since there is a movement intrinsic to dialectic, "That means that the theme is nothing else than human Dasein, life itself, insofar as it expresses itself and addresses the world in which it is" (G 19:579/401). In short, if there is speaking, then there is otherness, "the addressing of something as something," and if there is otherness, then there is movement. Movement makes otherness possible. Human Dasein exists, it is alive, within that movement. Existence, otherness, and movement are intrinsic to speaking; insofar as speaking is always of something, it is fraught with deception, such that existence, otherness, and movement are also fraught with that same deception, the deception of factical speaking.

Heidegger claims that Plato was able to see the world "more originally" than we can, and because of that original seeing, there are basic ontological determinations to be gleaned from his work. The first is that by situating speaking within the center of the dialectic, Plato is addressing the possibility of human existence. The demonstration of the λόγος ψευδής of the sophist has revealed the κοινωνία τῶν γενῶν, the association of the kinds, whereby being and non-being are shown to be co-present within λόγος. Without that κοινωνία, speech would be impossible, that is, it would be impossible to address something as something, either as what it is or as what it is not. Again, this is similar to what he said about κρίνειν in *Introduction to Phenomenological Research* (G 17). Thus the account of the sophist has revealed the possibility for speech, and, therefore, the possibility of human Dasein, existence. Heidegger says, "Only if there is a λέγειν is human existence possible," because without λέγειν there is no philosophy, and "if there is no philosophy, i.e., no λέγειν in the genuine sense, there is also no human existence" (G 19:577–78/400).

If λόγος as λέγειν is the fundamental theme of the dialogue, then not only is human existence itself at stake, but also the interpretation of Being in terms of time, and this is something that we do, indeed, find in Plato, albeit in an inchoate and implicit way. The association of the kinds, the intermingling of movement, presence, being, sameness, and otherness, attests to the primacy of the one kind, movement, within the dialectical consideration, and even more specifically the movement intrinsic to the soul and to speaking. The true goal of the dialectic, to see the Ideas in their true permanence, στάσις, is accorded a temporal dimension. Heidegger says that "in this concept of permanence, of the perpetual, factually, although implicitly, yet in accord with the matter itself, for Plato the *phenomenon of time* emerges, as the phenomenon which determines beings in their Being: the present, παρουσία" (*G* 19:579/401). This is not to say that Plato investigated that temporal dimension with considerable rigor. It says only that the dimension of time was there for Plato, relucent within his understanding of the permanent. Thus, speaking is not so much an expression of that which is permanent as it is an expression of that which is *present*. Speaking is, in this sense, "presentifying disclosure" of the temporally present (*G* 19:579–80/401).

For Love of Being: Plato on Rhetoric and Human Existence

From the previous analysis, we can see that Heidegger is searching through Plato in order to provide a positive ontological analysis of those clues (speaking, movement, temporality) in his philosophy that might suggest a more fundamental way of thinking about Being. On the way, Heidegger submits the dialectic to a factical analysis that reveals possibilities for human existence and the development of a practical ontology through the original facticity of λόγος, that is, speaking with others. To be sure, Plato went too far when he suggests that the διαλέγεσθαι of the dialectic can actually pass through λόγος to pure νοεῖν, the thinking of Being as apart from beings. Again, pure νοεῖν in the Platonic sense is not possible for human beings. Nonetheless, Plato opens up possibilities for thinking about language that made possible Aristotle's investigations into rhetoric.

We have moved even closer toward understanding why Heidegger uses Aristotle to investigate Plato. The preparation of the interpretative ground of ἀληθεύειν is, more fundamentally, an explication of the primacy of λόγος within Aristotle's demonstration of the five modes of truthing. Once we see that λόγος plays such a foundational role, we can better understand Plato, who also recognizes the "predominance of λόγος within Dasein" (*G* 19:307/213).

Using the *Gorgias* and the *Phaedrus*, Heidegger shows that Plato's position with regard to rhetoric was different in both of these texts. In the *Gorgias* Plato's attitude toward rhetoric is quite negative. There, rhetoric is simply a τέχνη, "the inculcation of a definite opinion in the audience" by the orator

(*G* 19:309/215, quoting Plato's *Gorgias* 452e9ff.). As such, this kind of rhetorical τέχνη need have no grounding in the matters themselves; it is speech without "substantive content" (*G* 19:310/215). We see clearly in this dialogue the realm of idle talk. Here rhetoric is simply a tool of persuasion, a skill of convincing others without concern for any real, substantive understanding of what is being talked about. In the *Phaedrus*, however, Plato provides a very positive description of rhetoric. Aside from the fact that this dialogue from Plato's early work displays "an extraordinary level of questioning," which Heidegger characteristically lauds as the genuine origin of philosophical thinking, it also undermines the typical sense of rhetoric as being just a τέχνη. This dialogue is not about public or political oration. The theme, rather, is the way in which two people talk to each other, and "*both together seek the matter at issue*" (*G* 19:315/218). As such, there is a shift in the meaning of rhetoric from publicly orating and speaking about issues of the day to a genuine dialogue, which, in its genuineness, displays a love of speaking, which is then also an "*urge toward Being itself*" (*G* 19:315/219). At stake in the dialogue is human existence, Socrates' existence, and the constellation of relations—love, speech, the soul—all of which revolve around human Dasein and Socrates' love of speaking.

What Heidegger calls Plato's positive characterization of rhetoric is, in fact, Socrates' own love for listening and speaking to other people, that is, "*genuine, substantive speaking*" (*G* 19:317/220). When we recognize that λέγειν is a matter of speaking with others, then we have, according to Heidegger, begun to grasp this term in a more precise way phenomenologically. That speaking is of such a kind that it involves speaking with others as a way of acquiring genuine knowledge about the self. Socrates' love for λόγος was a manifestation of his desire for self-knowledge, that is, knowledge of his own existence. That being the case, Heidegger draws two conclusions. The first is that when we translate the Socratic experience to the more general level of public rhetoric, we see that that rhetoric requires some foundation in truth. Orators and rhetors cannot simply rely upon rhetorical τέχνη if they intend to address human existence. This positive characterization of rhetoric places the demand on that discipline to deal with substantive content. Second, Heidegger demonstrates how Plato's interest in λέγειν, speaking, was, in fact, not motivated simply by rhetoric as a τέχνη but by human existence and the truth that can be attained with regard to human existence. Platonic λέγειν is concerned with αλήθεια, dialectic, and human existence. The latter is construed in a broad sense to indicate Socrates' concern with the existence of others as that is manifest in speaking with them and trying to guide them.

Analyzing the Socratic/Platonic λόγος in the *Phaedrus*, Heidegger's main concern, he says, is to show "the condition of the possibility of genuine self-expression about something to an other or with an other" (*G* 19:322/223). Heidegger insists that in using this Kantian expression he is not talking about "conditions in consciousness," rather he is concerned with communication. Specifically, he is interested in developing a kind of communication based on a positive understanding of human Dasein. As such, the issue here is the communication of existence, which, founded in λέγειν, is subject to misinterpretation and distortion. All modes of speaking, whether trivial or important, private or public, must be grounded in and take direction from "the matter at issue" (*G* 19:325/225). That being the case, both the true bringing something to light, the εἰς φῶς ἄγειν, that which penetrates through deception, *and* deception itself are both grounded in an "an antecedent knowledge of the truth" (*G* 19:328/227). In order to deceive someone, one must first have a grasp of the matter itself as it is, the matter about which one is being deceptive. Therefore, the possibility of not being deceived is precisely a familiarity with the matters at hand. This orientation with substantive knowledge, an understanding of the matters that are being discussed, makes it possible for a person to fend off the "opinions, hearsay, and common beliefs" that dominate the public realm and that constitute the leveling down of idle talk (*G* 19:328/228). According to Heidegger, a thorough familiarity with the matters themselves necessitates, for Plato, "research into truth" (*G* 19:329/228).

With reference to the grounding of rhetoric in the truth, Heidegger explains that for Plato, rhetoric is founded on dialectic. In order for rhetoric to be a genuine conversation that addresses the matters themselves, the speaker or rhetor must try to guide his or her interlocutor toward the truth, indeed, he or she must guide the *soul* of the other person toward the truth, and this requires a prior seeing of that truth. That prior seeing is at the core of Plato's understanding of λόγος. The phenomenon of ἀνάμνησις emerges here as the ground for the possibility of rhetoric. In the subsequent analysis of Plato's rhetoric, this fact must always be kept in mind, namely, that the guiding of another person's soul toward the truth through rhetorical speaking demands that the truth be seen beforehand. The idea must first be seen, and that seeing of the idea "is not at all obvious, not given immediately to man, but instead . . . requires an overcoming of definite resistances residing in the very Being of man himself, precisely insofar as a man is a man" (*G* 19:334/231).

Those resistances that prevent the seeing of the Ideas are the same resistances that characterize human beings in their factical existence. This point is capital: Those resistances cannot be overcome. As we have seen, facticity has an intimate relationship with finitude. The recognition of the deceptions and errors immanent within the original facticity of language is an acceptance of that way of speaking that acknowledges human finitude. This dimension emerges here as "resistances" that prevent the human being from achieving the pure νοεῖν of dialectic. That being said, Heidegger's task was always to ground metaphysics in a more original ontology. We see the working out of that original ontology here insofar as Heidegger is recognizing where we can follow Plato's dialectic and where we cannot. Specifically, we can agree with some things that Plato says about rhetoric in the *Phaedrus*—it is more than just a τέχνη; it involves communication and speaking; it is grounded in human existence—while recognizing the problems as well—that the truth of rhetoric requires a pure seeing of the Ideas (νοεῖν). Therefore, fending off common beliefs will have to come from somewhere other than an antecedent knowledge of the truth.

The Life of Λόγος: Disclosure

Despite the problems with the dialectic and the problems with Plato's understanding of λόγος, there are important ontological determinations that emerge here. Heidegger points out that for Plato, λόγος was a kind of living thing, a ζῷον with an "organic structure" (*G* 19:330/229). Its structural components were συναγωγη and διαίρεσις, the bringing together of a manifold of views into one and the subsequent laying out of that unified view in such a way that its constituent parts are seen,

> in such a way that the joints become visible, namely the connections among the respective origins of the determinations of the things, so that in this dissection of the whole organism, cutting through the connections of its joints, the entire ontological lineage of the being becomes visible. (*G* 19:332–33/230)

Although the processes of συναγωγη and διαίρεσις are grounded in dialectic and νοεῖν, which as such are philosophically untenable, the mechanics of the living organism of λόγος are nonetheless ontologically relevant. To be sure, Heidegger recognized the originality of Plato's understanding of λόγος and its ability to take hold of living phenomena and exhibit them in the historicality of their ontological lineage. Even for Plato, the speaking of λόγος was central to human existence. That centrality is borne out by the capacity of λόγος to exhibit historical structures through speaking. This comes out in the *Sophist* dialogue.

Heidegger is trying to subvert the present condition of the philosophy of language. That subversion is grounded in a more original understanding of Plato's dialectic. Specifically, Heidegger recognizes a dimension of the dialectic that Plato did not, himself, recognize, namely that the dialectic is, fundamentally, a letting-be-seen (ἀποφαίνεσθαι), a revealing (δηλοῦν). Λόγος is capable of taking apart (διαίρεσις) the whole that συναγωγή has brought together as a way of showing the origins of beings in their most proper meanings. This, indeed, is part of the process of dialectic, which pursues the substantive meanings that are present in what is said. In this sense, dialectic is a letting-be-seen of that which presents itself within what is said, and that letting be seen, Heidegger points out, is founded in non-being (μὴ ὄν). Plato shows that non-being is an otherness (ἕτερον) within λόγος. This is how the existence of the sophist is demonstrated. We see here that non-being is present in λόγος as an otherness insofar as there are beings present within words. Beings are the otherness in words; they are the non-being (non-words) of language. Dialectic pursues that otherness of speaking and so is grounded in non-being as otherness insofar as it pursues the presence of beings within λέγειν (G 19:569/394).

What is at stake in this analysis of non-being as otherness? According to Heidegger, μὴ ὄν as ἕτερον is precisely what makes dialectic possible. Dialectic is not just a game of words, and this is the case because it lets beings (ὄντα) be seen and, therefore, it also lets the Being of those beings be seen, which for Plato are the Ideas (εἴδη). Dialectic, Heidegger writes, "exposes *the limits of a being* in its Being and thus first makes visible *the being in its presence*" (G 19:569/394). It lets-be-seen that which is most properly visible in beings, the ideas themselves, by first exposing what is also there in what is said, beings. Thus, there must be more to words than just mere words. There must be a "not" in words, some measure of non-being, which, as otherness, exhibits beings and thus the Being of beings. So, what is at stake in this analysis is, on one level, the relation of words to things. There are beings (ὄντα) present in what is said, in the λεγόμενον. More important, though, the relation of words to the Ideas is also at stake here, for the Ideas, which Plato construes as true Being, are in what is said, too. Ultimately, then, it is Plato's Ideas that are the non-being as otherness, the μὴ ὄν qua ἕτερον, of what is said.

When we pursue that otherness even further, we see the essential connections between speaking and beings. These are important because they show the limitations of Plato's conception of λόγος and Heidegger's appropriation of the basic ontological clues that he finds in Plato, despite that limitation. Heidegger investigates the three structural components of λόγος through Plato at the end of the course. They all are grounded in the revealing of beings that are present within speaking. What we will see is that the co-presence of speaking and beings, of λέγειν and ὄν, reveals the primacy of δηλοῦν. Beings are present within speaking because speaking is fundamentally and originally a revealing, indeed, a revealing of beings. The three components are as follows: (1) the "onomatic" and "delotic," (2) the structure of the λεγόμενον, and (3) the "manner" of the Being of λόγος, with respect to δηλοῦν, revealing. I will now look at these in order to determine how the δηλοῦν operates within Plato's dialectic.

If we look at the present situation of philosophy of language, as it is currently and as it was when Heidegger was delivering this course, then we see that it is and was dominated by the following patterns:

> there are word-sounds which enter into the psyche; to these are joined, by way of association, so-called general representations; and all these together play out in consciousness. Then the question arises as to how these associations within consciousness can have objective validity for the things outside. (*G* 19:598/414)

What has been lost is a deep understanding of the essential connection between λόγος and ὄν. As Heidegger explains, every λόγος is a λόγος τινός, "every addressing is an addressing *of something*" (*G* 19:597/413). The "of" is thematic here and, as such, it is phenomenologically and logically relevant, even if Plato did not recognize its full import. The fact that every speaking is a disclosure of something has been determinative of the history of logic and also determinative for Husserl, who founded his concept of intentionality on the λόγος τινός, but Heidegger delves deeper still into the λόγος τινός. Paying homage to the phenomenological work of the founder of that movement, Heidegger says that it was Husserl who rediscovered the λόγος τινός and that "only on its basis will the structures of λόγος again be intelligible" (*G* 19:598/414). As Heidegger pursues the consequences of the λόγος τινός in Plato, though, he discovers a fourfold structure within the λόγος: (1) the onomatic, which is the intertwining of nouns and verbs (the κοινωνία between ὄνομα and ῥῆμα); (2) the intentional, which is the λόγος τινός, as we just saw (the κοινωνία between λόγος and ὄν); (3) the logical, which extends the consideration of λόγος τινός by showing that every addressing of something is also an addressing "as" (κοινωνία in a structural sense; the something as something); and (4) the delotic, which, grounded in δηλοῦν, identifies what is said (the λεγόμενον) as being either "with itself" or "other than itself," whereby deception is seen to be "in itself, false" (*G* 19:606/419).

The third stage will prove to be pivotal to the demonstration of the possibility of the sophist because, insofar as every λέγειν is a λέγειν τί, this means that λέγειν contains within itself the possibility of exhibiting something as other than it is. Every λέγειν, whether distortive or not, is a disclosing. Therefore, the deceptive exhibiting of something that belongs to the sophist is founded in a prior disclosure. In this way, the disclosing of λόγος always occurs with regard to a certain mode; it discloses "*in such and such a way*," that is, either as distorting or disclosing what is spoken about (*G* 19:603/417). As such, λόγος can possibly be λόγος ψευδής, and the proof for the possibility of the sophist has been made manifest.

There are three observations that need to be made about the fourfold structure of λόγος Heidegger finds in Plato. First, it raises the question as to why and how philosophy of language has missed the phenomenon of the λόγος τινός. Second, it raises the question regarding Heidegger's position with regard to Plato. Last, it calls on us to rethink λόγος in terms of this structure.

Addressing the last issue will shed light on the first two. If, as Heidegger says, philosophy of language is dominated by the question as to whether the associations of representations in our minds can have objective validity with regard to the things outside of our minds, then that is because the proposition or judgment has become the locus of truth. If the predicate of a sentence is in accord with the subject, then that sentence is said to be true. A true sentence tells us something about the world. The sentence is true if it correctly expresses a state of affairs in the world. Under these terms, the task of philosophy is to develop more and more true sentences about the world. Most important, though, it presupposes a divide between language and reality. In his reading of Plato, Heidegger points out that every speaking is already a speaking about something, so that the world is already immanent within what we say. The divide between language and the world, whereby sentences mirror the world, is thus a derivative mode of this more original sense of λόγος as revealing.

According to this fourfold structure of λόγος, the recovery of the λόγος τί places our thinking about language on different footing. Λόγος, for the Greeks, was speaking, and because every speaking was a speaking about something, then there is, in every speaking, something pre-given, and that pre-given something Heidegger calls the "unarticulated unitary being" (*G* 19:599/415). As unarticulated, however, that unitary being is not at all something like pure noise, white noise, which, Heidegger says, is an entirely abstract theoretical concept that requires a very complex mind to understand. Rather, that unarticulated unitary being is something like "the creaking wagon on the street" or even the person with whom you are having a conversation (G 19:599/415). We do not hear pure sounds; we hear meanings. These meanings, he says, are the "about which" of discourse: the creaking wagon, your interlocutor. Speaking (λέγειν) is, thereby, not a matter of predicating something of a subject but is rather a setting into relief (κρίνειν), the addressing of something as something, which Heidegger calls the "of which": the wagon *as* creaking, the interlocutor *as* speaking. In this process of setting an unarticulated whole into relief a determination of that being is made: The creaking wagon "is then grasped in terms of creaking itself" (G 19:600/415). The "as" is a special determination of the "of"; it is intrinsically there with the "of," so that Heidegger can say that the λόγος τινός, the " '*something as something*,' in which a simply pre-given being is properly brought into presence," manifests this "as-which" character (G 19:601/416). In this way, λόγος is able to display what is said, the λεγόμενον, in its basic structure, and this amounts to a rethinking of language.

> The way runs precisely not from the subject, over the copula, to the predicate but, instead, from the pre-given whole to the setting in relief of what we afterwards call the predicate, and thereby for the first time to a genuine *making prominent* of the subject. (G 19:600/416)

Indeed, what we normally call the subject is based on the scientific analyses of grammar; thought more originally, it is the "of which" of discourse. Predication and the determination of a subject are derivative modes of this more original grasping of wholes and setting them into relief.

It is not so difficult to see that this basic structure of λόγος has been hidden within grammatical structures that analyze subjects and objects. Heidegger is searching through Plato here for a more original understanding of the basic structures of speaking. The process whereby unarticulated wholes are set into relief through speaking has become solidified into more scientific grammatical rules that govern propositions and judgments. Such rules would analyze the creaking wagon and then claim that we do not, in fact, hear a creaking wagon in the first place. We hear pure, abstract noises, and so on, and so on, and so begins the modern history of philosophy of language.

Does this mean that grammatical rules should be done away with? By no means. Heidegger is simply retrieving more original structures within language in order to till the soil within which modern linguistic theory is grounded. How modern philosophy of language can adjust to that more original thinking of language, he does not say. There are, however, positive ontological clues within Plato's sense of λόγος. Heidegger is clearly not trying to do away with Plato. To be sure, he finds serious problems with Plato's dialectic and with his theory of the Ideas. Nonetheless, Plato was an original thinker, and by reading and lecturing on this text, Heidegger is trying to say what Plato did not and could not say. As an original thinker, Plato's texts contain rich ontological insights. We find his ontological insights into λόγος in the first stage of the analysis.

In the first stage of λόγος, we recognize the basic features of Socratic λέγειν, which Heidegger had made reference to in his analysis of the *Phaedrus*. Those features are thoroughly developed at the end of the course, where Heidegger again turns to the *Phaedrus*. This is the first and most original determination of λόγος that Plato offers: It involves self-expression (ὄνομα) and speaking about an issue in such a way that a disclosure (δηλοῦν) of that issue is made. These structures, Heidegger says, are "phenomenally one and the same" (*G* 19:583/404). Pursuing this primary dimension of self-expression and disclosure, Heidegger thematizes speaking in its phonetic, audible dimension[3] as well as the structural manifold of words implicit within speaking. His use of the *Phaedrus* and Plato's positive reading of rhetoric in that text are here important. Heidegger emphasizes the concrete givenness of speaking, which, in its very Being, is a "speaking with others *about something*" (*G* 19:584/404). This original dimension of speaking, which incorporates both togetherness with others and the pre-given "about which" of speaking, provides access to a basic ontological feature of λόγος, namely the structural manifolds of words. Within what we say there are these contexts, these structural manifolds, and the words we use reveal themselves ontologically as belonging to those contexts. These contexts are, Heidegger says,

> *the matter at issue, what is properly visible in it, word, word-sound—beings, world, disclosure of beings, discourse, manifestation.* This is nothing else than the *universal context of phenomena within which man, the* ζῷον λόγον ἔχον, *ever exists. This context is ultimately grounded in Being-in, in the antecedent uncoveredness of the world.* (*G* 19:585/405)

Heidegger maintains that this "foundational context" was not one that Plato actually recognized. Nonetheless, the ontological dimension of Being-in and the structural—ontological—context within which words find their origin, meaning, and determination provide a necessary foundation for research into Platonic λόγος. Heidegger says that this context was "still operative" for Plato even though he did not investigate it; as such, this context is the unsaid in his theory of λόγος. We see here the seminal importance of the unsaid insofar as it provides the context within which we can understand a thinker.

The thrust of Plato's dialogue is to show the different κοινωνία operative within λόγος. Here, the structural manifolds that are implicit in the words we use and that are revealed through the phonetic dimension of speaking provide the ground for the intertwining of names, the κοινωνία of ὀνόματα. As a consequence, φαίνεται, "to show itself," is the more original meaning of names, which are now to be construed in terms of those manifolds within which and through which they are disclosed. The original κοινωνία of names and verbs in speaking that we are here investigating is to be sought in the way in which it shows itself through the structural manifold of word-sound-beings-world-disclosure-discourse-manifestation, and that is because λόγος, the first stage of which is the κοινωνία of ὀνόματα, "stands connected to the innermost existence of man" (*G* 19:586/406). Heidegger is making manifest the connection between λόγος as speaking and the structural contexts of words. which, when investigated, shows that the process of revealing, δηλοῦν, defines the very existence of the human being.

In this, the first of the four stages of λόγος that are implicit in Plato's dialogue, Heidegger draws the conclusion that "the original and phenomenal connection between the phenomenon of language and the *Being of man*" requires that we "get rid, at the very outset, of the proposition as the point of departure for our orientation toward language" (*G* 19:594/411). We must recognize the structural manifolds immanent within speech, and we can do that through a "proper hearkening [ὑπακούειν]to the manifold of spoken words," and specifically to the disclosive power of those words (*G* 19:588/407). This is not, by any means, a mere listening to another person. It is an attentive hearkening (in *Being and Time*, Heidegger even says that hearkening is tied to feeling); it is, perhaps, a hearkening with feeling, that is, within a certain disposition, which "properly signifies genuine perception, understanding what is said" (*G* 19:588/407). Hearkening is a disposed, affective listening that is grounded in the understanding.

What hearkening hears is the "Being of words in the unity of discourse," the originary determination of those manifolds of words that can genuinely go together (*G* 19:595/412). That originary determination is δηλοῦν. By hearkening to the spoken words of discourse, the disclosive character of words is made prominent. In this way, Heidegger shifts the locus of philosophy of language from analysis of the proposition to an investigation into the primordial disclosive character of words in discourse. This is to say that speaking is not disclosive simply *because* it puts together nouns and verbs in propositions that are then able to disclose certain truths about reality. Quite the contrary, propositions have the power to disclose because λέγειν (speaking) "in itself is a δηλοῦν [disclosing]" (*G* 19:596/412). Indeed, "The criterion for the Being of words in the unity of discourse is their disclosive character" (*G* 19:595/412). Further, if δηλοῦν is the original meaning of λέγειν and constitutive of the structural manifolds of discourse, then words are not signs; they are, Heidegger says, δηλώματα, "revealing beings" (*G* 19:589/408). Philosophers such as Husserl and structuralists, as well, who found theories of language and meaning on the belief that words are signs are, in Heidegger's view, operating within an understanding of language that "is strictly speaking not in accord with the matter itself" (*G* 19:589/408). For Heidegger, these "revealing beings" are prior to signs because disclosing is prior to speaking. Λέγειν is fundamentally δηλοῦν; with this realization, δηλοῦν can then be recognized as an essential dimension of human existence *because* speaking, as has already been shown, is fundamental to human existence. Heidegger says,

> *The* δηλοῦν *is primary. It is the fundamental phenomenon. . . . The* δηλοῦν, *which harbors the possibility of discourse, is a constitutive determination of Dasein itself, a determination I am wont to designate as Being-in-the-world or Being-in.* (*G* 19:594/411)

Certain advances in Heidegger's thinking with regard to discourse and disclosure emerge through his reading of Plato. Heidegger does claim that Plato's understanding of λόγος was not thought through in an original way. He left uninvestigated the worldly dimension of λόγος and its primordial disclosive character. Heidegger believed, however, that Plato was a profound thinker who saw the world in a more original way than we are able to see it now. By saying that which Plato left unsaid, Heidegger is able to penetrate the ground of Plato's research into λόγος and retrieve the way that Plato's understanding of λόγος is grounded in Being-in-the-world, even if Plato did not recognize this, as such.

In my view, Heidegger was not at all discomforted by Plato's interest in determining the original unity of beings within Being. Heidegger would agree with Plato that the purpose of philosophy is to determine the unity of the meaning of Being. The problem with Plato, for Heidegger, is that his investigations of Being are founded on dialectic, and for Plato dialectic ultimately leads to a seeing of the Ideas as beings and a seeing of those "creative powers" of prudence, movement, life, understanding, and soul as beings. They are beings that are co-present with the Ideas and that give them life.

Those Ideas are, according to Plato, Being; but, they can be viewed and grasped as beings. Heidegger's understanding of the unity of Being is the process whereby truth as ἀλήθεια comes to pass and lets beings be in their Being. Being, for Heidegger, is a unity, but it is not a being, so perhaps it would be more appropriate to say that for Heidegger Being is a kind of unifying process. In *Being and Time*, Dasein achieves authenticity when it retrieves its own Being by first bringing itself into view *as a whole*. It is not the sense of wholeness that Heidegger finds problematic in Plato, but rather the dialectical approach to the wholeness of Being that grasps Being as though it were a being.

Insofar as Plato's conception of λόγος and, specifically, the truth of λόγος and, by extrapolation, the truth of rhetoric and speaking, are founded in dialectic, that conception is fundamentally problematic. But in researching Platonic λόγος, Heidegger does find more original ontological dimensions of λόγος, dimensions that were operative in Plato's philosophy but which Plato himself did not see, such as time, Being-in, Being-in-the-World, the fourfold structure of λόγος, words as "revealing beings," and the primacy of disclosure. For a more thorough explanation of rhetoric, however, Heidegger emphasizes, even in this course, the contributions of Aristotle. We have seen already Heidegger's investigations into Aristotle and rhetoric. It is important to remember, though, that Plato provided a preliminary understanding of rhetoric to Aristotle. By looking at those Platonic considerations as well as the limitations in Plato's understanding, we can recognize both the debt that Aristotle owes to Plato and the advances that Aristotle made over Plato, advances that Heidegger recognizes as critical if an authentic understanding of speaking is going to be realized. Aristotle's conception of rhetoric consists of a radicalization of Plato's dialectic as well as a conception of everyday speaking that is not aimed at Plato's sense of ἀλήθεια. Heidegger writes,

> The fact remains that *Aristotle brought to realization the idea of rhetoric, the idea Plato himself positively elaborated with the help of his dialectic.* Aristotle's success in penetrating through to the proper structure of λόγος makes it possible to institute a genuine investigation into λόγος itself. It likewise makes it possible for the λόγος that is not theoretical, i.e., for speech that is not in service to διαλέγεσθαι, to receive a certain justification within the context of everyday Dasein. The result is that the insight into the justification of everyday interlocution can provide the motive to create a rhetoric. For this everyday speaking (here we have Aristotle's genuine discovery) does not aim at ἀλήθεια yet still has a certain justification, since it pertains to

the sense of everyday Dasein to move within the circuit of appearances. On this basis, then, even the speaking that is not explicitly an
ἀληθεύειν receives its independent justification. Thereby rhetoric
comes by a more positive justification than it does in Plato, who to be
sure provided the guiding lines for the elaboration of the phenomenon. What is important, above all, in Plato's predelineation of the idea
of rhetoric is that he does not stop at anchoring λέγειν in ὁρᾶν but
goes on to maintain that the ψυχή of the auditor also belongs to the
field of such dialectic, i.e., to rhetoric. (*G* 19:338–39/234–35)

There is much to be gained from this paragraph, which not only asserts
the importance of Plato for Aristotle's research, but also confirms the possibility of a kind of everyday being and speaking with one another that,
while not directed toward ἀλήθεια in the Platonic sense, receives, nonetheless, a certain justification. It shows, too, that Aristotle was not concerned
with θεωρεῖν or pure νοεῖν as Plato had conceived them. Aristotle is trying
to develop a nontheoretical language. To return to my primary theme, I am
trying to determine the importance of factical language, itself a nontheoretical language, which nonetheless receives justification insofar as it reveals
human existence (Dasein as Being in the world) and the deceptions immanent therein. This is not to say that speaking or even rhetoric is the original
function of λόγος for Heidegger. From the current chapter, we can see that
that is not the case insofar as δηλοῦν is prior to λέγειν. What we have seen,
however, is that the possibility is opened up for a factical, everyday speaking
that does have a certain justification, especially insofar as factical speaking
makes it possible for us to recognize that λόγος is fundamentally and more
originally δηλοῦν. From Heidegger's reading of Plato, we already recognize
that discourse, insofar as it hearkens to that which is said and understands
what is said in terms of the matters themselves, is constitutive of Dasein's
existence, its Being-in-the-World.

Heidegger will go on to deliver two more lecture courses in 1925 before
writing *Being and Time*: *History of the Concept of Time* (*G* 20) and *Logic: The
Question of Truth* (*G* 21). Neither of these courses focuses on factical life or
on the speaking dimension of Being-in-the-world. There are some provocative ideas about communication in both of them, and I address these in the
Conclusion. But my analysis of the lecture courses ends here because in
Plato's Sophist (*G* 19) the idea of λέγειν has already undergone an important
transformation from speaking to disclosing. This shift, from factical speaking about human existence to the ontological structure of language, is significant. We have seen, though, in these three lecture courses, *Introduction
to Phenomenological Research* (*G* 17), *Basic Concepts of Aristotelian Philosophy*

(*G* 18), and *Plato's Sophist* (*G* 19) how Heidegger maintained an interest in factical speaking throughout his readings of Plato and Aristotle. This research has informed his understanding of the meaning of Being. Indeed, from 1919 all the way up through 1924, Heidegger has been making connections between factical life and the Being of the human being. Although he has replaced the term "factical life" with Dasein as Being-in-the-world, the term Dasein retains, nonetheless, the vitality and richness of those factical meanings that belong to its development, as well as the modes of deception and concealment that are intrinsically part of Being-and-speaking-in-the-world with others. In the Conclusion, I draw upon my own analyses in order to prove that the early Heidegger's project synthesized ontological and existential concerns, presenting a realistic portrayal of human life as suffused with deception, error, and even perversity and yet charged with meaning and open to revelation and insight.

Conclusion

The problems of facticity persist for me with the same intensity as they did
in my Freiburg beginnings, only much more radically now, and still in the
perspectives that were guiding me even in Freiburg.
—**Martin Heidegger, Letter to Karl Löwith, August 20, 1927**

From his earliest lecture courses, as we have seen, Heidegger was interested
in the relationship that the facticity of life has to the meaning of Being.
This connection between human existence and ontology crystallizes in the
notion of Dasein, which, as the *there* of Being, we might also call the Being
of factical human life. As he will say explicitly in *Ontology: The Hermeneutics of Facticity* (G 63) from 1923, *"Dasein (factical life) is Being in a world"*
(G 63:80/62). Throughout all his early philosophical investigations into
science, religion, history, language, and the Greeks, this notion of Dasein,
factical life, as a worlding being persists.

Since the publication of Kisiel's *The Genesis of Heidegger's Being and
Time* and van Buren's *The Young Heidegger*, numerous commentators have
looked at what Heidegger says about factical life. There is, however, a fundamental ambiguity in Heidegger's depiction of it, and this has led to confusion about what, exactly, he means by it. At times, factical life is a dynamic source of vitality, whereas at other times, it is a source of fallenness,
inauthenticity, and ruinance. One of the most important developments in
Heidegger scholarship to address this ambiguity connects destruction to
the problem of factical life and the achievement of authenticity. On this
account, destruction is a method of retrieving genuine meaning from out
of a fallen and inauthentic life. Although it is especially helpful in clarifying
the religious dimension of Heidegger's thought, in particular the relationship between Heidegger's early work and Luther's *destructio*, this view,
nonetheless, presents authenticity as a choice between conformity on the
one hand and resolve on the other, where the goal is to eliminate the ambiguity in factical life. This view suggests, consequently, that Dasein might
be able to remain authentic. With this kind of binary opposition, where

Dasein is either authentic or inauthentic, the notion of Dasein as a worlding being ceases to make sense, for there is, then, no meaningful context of life into which concepts from the past can be imported.

My goal in this conclusion is to contrast the notion of destruction with the notion of worlding in order to show that there is a fundamental "richness" (*G* 17:37/28) and "vitality" (*G* 56/57:90/70) in factical life, to use Heidegger's own words, that must be countenanced together with—and not, even in authenticity, separated out from—its negativity and fallenness. This conclusion is divided into two sections. The first section addresses the notion of destruction explicitly. I identify the fundamental confusion that persists in Heidegger research regarding how he understands the worldly nature of Dasein, and then I argue that to read destruction as a kind of choice or binary opposition between two different ways of life goes against some of Heidegger's deepest impulses as a philosopher. This leads to the second section, on worlding, which looks at facticity in *Being and Time* and attempts to demonstrate the intimate connection between authenticity and inauthenticity within the factical life of Dasein. Together, these modes of Dasein's Being constitute its essential ambiguity and thus present a meaningful and nuanced sense of human life. Authenticity is not simply a matter of destroying or overcoming human fallenness, but, together with fallenness, it is a moment of revelation (καιρός) through insight (φρόνησις) into who we are, that is, into who the human being is as a whole.

The Problem of Destruction

What I have tried to show throughout this book is that the early Heidegger was interested in the Being of life. This helps to now clarify a confusion that runs through our understanding of the notion of Dasein as a worlding being. Consider the following readings of what Heidegger means by "worldly." In his essay on formal indication, Dan Dahlstrom points to an inconsistency in Heidegger's understanding of formally indicative concepts. Formal indications are drawn from factical experience, and thus from life.[1] But when Heidegger describes, in *Being and Time* and elsewhere, the average way of living in the world, he says that the human being is fallen and inauthentic. The "worldly," therefore, offers us only a fallen and, on Dahlstrom's reading, a theoretical and objectified understanding of ourselves. Therefore, formal indications require a reversal, in order to overcome the fallen, theoretical foundation on which they are based. Here, worldly (*weltlich*) means fallen, theoretical, and scientific.

Contrast this reading of "worldly" with what Charles Guignon says about "worldliness" in his article on authenticity. He writes, "*Being and Time* attempts to combat the groundlessness (*Bodenlosigkeit*) of the contemporary world by uncovering enduring values and meanings within the framework of 'worldliness' (*Weltlichkeit*) and human finitude."[2] Here we see that for Heidegger 'worldliness' refers neither to fallenness nor to theory, but rather to the vitality of lived experience reminiscent of the descriptions of factical life in *Toward the Definition of Philosophy* (G 56/57) and *The Phenomenology of Religious Life* (G 60).

Some readings of Heidegger, like Guignon's, make reference to his successful attempt to deconstruct theories back to their ground in the vital experience of factical life. Other readings, like Dahlstrom's, show how authenticity individualizes Dasein, distancing human beings from the fallen or theoretical interpretations of the common understanding found in factical life. Kisiel addresses this problem by pointing to the essential ambiguity of factical life. He writes, "We now see that factic life experience, which is to be the starting point of philosophizing, is also the starting point of that which hinders philosophizing."[3] Kisiel and others recognize this essential ambiguity, which includes both deception as well as moments of insight.

On some recent interpretations of destruction, however, it seems as though Heidegger's understanding of factical life is not a presentation of the ambiguity of life but rather a dichotomy between two different ways of life, one of which might be able to be overcome. For van Buren, Heidegger employs destruction as a way of retrieving the more genuine, historical origins of human existence.[4] But in the same article, he also writes that "Heidegger's position is that in moral action one's 'possibilities' are bound up with one's 'actuality,' one's destiny or heritage, which is enacted interpretively within one's current situation."[5] If Heidegger is saying simply that the history of philosophy needs to be deconstructed (or destructed), so that the philosophical resources within our heritage can surface, and so that individuals might then cultivate their moral possibilities, then a number of philosophical problems arise. First, the present, which is fallen and inauthentic, would not have enough philosophical substance for individuals to "enact interpretively" their authentic moral possibilities within their current situation. One might achieve authenticity, but there would be no meaningful context within which their authentic life could have any real sense, and it would then be unclear what authenticity would mean.

Kisiel's reading of factical life attempts to preserve its ambiguity and indeterminacy. He writes, "Phenomenological destruction is not a senseless devastation but a very precisely guided and systematic deconstruction (*Abbau*). Individual meanings must first be regarded as indeterminate and unclear, just as they emerge in factic life, and must be retained in this indeterminacy."[6] Kisiel may be making a direct reference here to *Phenomenology of*

Intuition and Expression (*G* 59, summer semester 1920), the lecture course in which Heidegger provides his most sustained treatment of the problematic of phenomenological destruction.[7] Heidegger affirms in that course that in phenomenological destruction, "The reduction to the genuine sense-contexts and the articulation of the genuine sense-directions comprised in them is what is final in the phenomenological task" (*G* 59:74/56). Destruction starts "from the living present" (*G* 59:93/74) and from the human being, philosophically considered, as an "object of rich and multiform philosophical consideration" (*G* 59:87/69), that is, from "the human being as something achieving, creating, experiencing life—*life as manifoldness of lived experience*" (*G* 59:88/70).

The second, and related, problem emerges with the sense that authenticity and inauthenticity are a dichotomy or binary opposition, and that inauthenticity might somehow be overcome. Benjamin Crowe presents in great detail the influence of Luther on the early Heidegger's approach to philosophy. He argues, correctly, that the early Heidegger—and not just *Being and Time*—is guided by an attempt to show how human beings can achieve authenticity in their lives. In his conclusions, however, he moves closer to van Buren than to Kisiel by contrasting resolve against conformity and then suggesting that authenticity might be a way to overcome its opposite.[8] He writes, for example, that "the 'how' of our belonging to a tradition is either a matter of conformity and superficiality (inauthenticity) or of clear-sightedness and self-critical resolve (authenticity)."[9] Interpreting history can happen in one of two ways, "either by abdicating self-responsibility to the anonymous public discourse of the 'one' or by facing up to the task of living one's own unique life and making a vocational commitment."[10] Crowe says, further, that Heidegger is advocating "a way of life that is not beholden to the common ways 'one' thinks or acts, but rather is a genuine attempt to confront one's cultural inheritance, freed from the constraining hegemony of the 'idle talk' of the 'today.'"[11] István Fehér makes a similar claim about authenticity when he describes it as a shift from one condition to another. He writes, "It is only after having performed the passage from the inauthentic to the authentic that inauthentic being as such—and together with it, the very distinction itself—becomes first disclosed and accessible,"[12] as though inauthenticity has now been left behind. He says further that "Dasein, effecting the passage from the inauthentic to the authentic, gains awareness of itself for the first time and it does so in terms of existing always already in an inauthentic way."[13] Here, Fehér does acknowledge that Dasein is always already inauthentic, but if that is the case, then there cannot be a "passage" from inauthenticity to authenticity; it cannot not involve moving from one state of being to another.

Even in *Being and Time*, Heidegger says that "Dasein is already both in the truth and in untruth" (*BT,* 222/265). Moreover, in *Phenomenological Interpretations of Aristotle: Initiation into Phenomenological Research* (*G* 61), which discusses factical life's ruinance, he shows just how profoundly the human being lives in deception.[14] That deception can be resisted, but it cannot be overcome, so the difference between authenticity and inauthenticity is not a dichotomy but, rather, the elements of light and darkness that are intrinsic to human life.

Worlding

Looking at texts from the early period, as I have done in this book, we find that Heidegger did not simply view the world as inauthentic. He recognized the deceptions and errors that are built into worldly experience, but he also discerned the "vitality" and "richness" of living in the world. Thus, he is not interested in simply "clearing away" "distortions," "deformations," and "objectifications," as Crowe suggests.[15] His goal, rather, was to grasp the ambiguity and indeterminacy of factical life in order to show how authenticity involves not just destruction and resistance, but also the cultivation of contexts of meaning. Error and deception belong to human life inevitably and unavoidably. Authenticity was, for him, not a matter of overcoming fallenness, but rather of making "phronetic" insights into the meaningfulness of human life despite those distortions and, as we will see, by going through those distortions and not abandoning them.

In a lecture he gave in 1924 titled *Being-There and Being-True according to Aristotle,* Heidegger looks at why human beings live in deception. With reference to Aristotle, he claims that if we define the human being as a rational animal, a ζῷον that has λόγος, which Heidegger understands as a living being that speaks, then we can see quite clearly that the primary source of deception for human beings is λόγος, speaking. Human beings live in deception as they live in language, in speech. Accordingly, the truth of the human being would involve an uncovering of that deception, through true speaking, a correct λόγος. In the *Nicomachean Ethics*, this is exactly what Aristotle says the prudent person does. Prudence, for Aristotle, allows one to discern the mean, and the mean is a correct λόγος.

Heidegger's lecture identifies three modes of concealment. It is worthwhile to note that his reading of language here is based on Aristotle's *Rhetoric*, which, he claims, is "none other than the interpretation of the basic phenomenon of speaking-with-one-another."[16] As such, it provides us with an analysis of the "modes of speaking" present in the natural, everyday language of the Greeks. The first mode of concealment has to do with the way that common opinions hide the truth from us. The second has to do with ignorance or unfamiliarity. This would be a straightforward concealment. The last one is a kind of concealment based on objectification and conformity.[17] Corresponding to these three modes of concealment are three modes of unconcealment: (1) disclosure through common opinion, (2) disclosure of completely concealed domains, and (3) the struggle against common speech.

What is important about all of these is that the unconcealment that Heidegger is describing here *is based on* ignorance, concealment, conformity, and objectification. Unconcealment is not simply a matter of overcoming these modes of fallen speech, but of *passing through them*. We see here the notion of ἀλήθεια developing, an understanding of truth that includes the distortion of concealment. He is reading Aristotle in order to discern a more original understanding of the truth of life conceived as the disclosure or unconcealment of the world. Book 6 of the *Nicomachean Ethics* outlines the five different modes of truth, including φρόνησις. In the *Sophist* course, Heidegger says, "A person can be concerned with things of minor significance; he can be so wrapped up in himself that he does not genuinely see himself." We see here the problem of factical life's ruinance, wherein life avoids itself. But there is hope: Heidegger says here, "Therefore, he is ever in need of the salvation of φρόνησις" (*G* 19:51–52). "Circumspection regarding himself and insight into himself must again and again be wrested away by man in face of the danger of corruption and distortion" (*G* 19:52).

Φρόνησις is an insight into the whole of human life, as Aristotle says in the *Ethics*, which involves, as Heidegger believes, an unconcealment from that which has been concealed, "a constant struggle against a tendency to cover over residing at the heart of Dasein" (*G* 19:56). Phronetic insight, which develops into the structure of conscience in *Being and Time*, works against deception and concealment through insight into who we are. It is not simply the destruction of modes of conformity and objectification, nor does Heidegger believe that those modes of error in human language and in life are meant to be cleared away. Rather, his effort is to *pass through* those modes of concealment in order to achieve truth as unconcealment or revelation; this happens as a phronetic moment of insight into the Being of factical human life.

From as early as the war emergency semester 1919 (*G* 56/57), we have seen that in Heidegger's thinking about the experience of life, he is not suggesting simply that life is inauthentic and needs to become authentic, nor is he saying that lived experience is not genuine experience. On the contrary, from the beginning Heidegger wanted to develop an approach to the vitality of life in its various intensities. This notion of everyday experience as something positive continues. Recall his claim in *Ontology: The Hermeneutics of Facticity* (G 63) that "the 'they' has something definitely positive; it is not just a phenomenon of fallenness, but as such a How of factical Dasein" (G 63:17/14). Overall, in his early work, Heidegger was attempting to connect existential and ontological concerns. His reading of Dilthey, for example, as I discussed in the Introduction, attempted to think about the relationship of history and Being to the whole of life, which is meant both in a temporal sense and in the sense of being a unified context. His interest in Being and his existential interest in factical life reach their terminus in the notion of Dasein. The Greeks were particularly important to his turn toward more ontological concerns, but even there, through close readings of Aristotle's *Ethics* and *Rhetoric* and in his interest in Socratic dialogue, we still see the attempt to synthesize the existential with the ontological.

If that is the case, then it becomes necessary to view what he says about authenticity in the light of what it means for human beings *to be* or, in other words, for human beings to be *there* (Dasein) in the world with others and in speaking relationships with them. Heidegger's understanding of destruction needs to be moderated by what he says about the human being as a worlding being who lives within contexts of meaningful relationships characterized by levels of intensity. There is no denying that factical life is riddled with the darkness of ruinance, fallenness, objectification, conformity, and idle talk, what Crowe rightly calls, with eloquence, "the idols of self-satisfaction and fugitive self-abdication that have accumulated on life like tumors."[18] We might go even further and say that there may very well be a level of perversity at the heart of the human being. But as a worlding being, Dasein cannot simply "clear away" these distortions. The course on factical life, *Phenomenological Interpretations of Aristotle: Initiation into Phenomenological Research* (G 61), demonstrates so convincingly the extent to which human beings suffer ruinance, it is difficult to imagine how Heidegger would ever conceive of a life without distortion. (Certainly, his own life was not free of distortion and conformity.) Nonetheless, he presents a way of grasping human life as riddled with deception but also charged with meaning and open to revelation and insight. Indeed, only by looking at Heidegger's work in this way can we appreciate the force of what William Richardson has said about fallenness, namely that "there is in [Heidegger's] conception of finitude, especially in the notion of fallenness, a ground for human contrariness—even of human perversity—which lets us see how failure can be integrated with authenticity as well as success, like shadows in a Rembrandt painting."[19]

From Heidegger's early interest in phenomenology as a science to his investigations of religion, his development of ontology and hermeneutics, his view of history, and, through close textual readings of Plato and Aristotle, his view on language, we find the competing elements of, on one side, ruinance, fallenness, conformity, and objectivity and, on the other, revelation, insight, the vitality and richness of the world, and the revelatory function of language to open up the world. These elements cannot be separated out from one another, but are, rather, integrated in the rich complexities, distortions, and moments of insight that are part of human life.

We find this same ambiguity and duality in his descriptions of factical human Dasein in *Being and Time*. There, anxiety makes it possible for Dasein to accept that it is finite transcendence. In the disposition of anxiety, Dasein is called by a voice from deep within itself. If Dasein accepts the call, which comes from its own Being, hence from its own no-thingness, then it acknowledges that it is a finite being with limited possibilities. This gesture of resoluteness is liberating because once it accepts that it is who it is, Dasein is then free to take up those possibilities that are properly its own. Heidegger calls this liberating gesture of resoluteness authenticity. Authentic Dasein accepts the finitude of its own transcendence and, thus, the limitation of those possibilities for which it can be free.

With this gesture of resoluteness, it becomes possible for Dasein to retrieve itself. If the unity of Dasein is time and resoluteness is Dasein's acceptance of itself, then resoluteness makes it possible for Dasein to take over its own heritage. This involves Dasein's capacity to reappropriate certain possibilities from its past in order to experience them again in their original vitality. Heidegger calls this retrieval of Dasein's heritage authentic historicality. Dasein is authentically historical when it takes over those limited possibilities that its thrownness presents to it, for which it can be free. It retrieves factical possibilities from its history in order to make them its own.[20]

What is important about Heidegger's use of facticity in *Being and Time* is the way in which it shows the privileged access that Dasein has to Being. Dasein is finite transcendence; this is made possible because Dasein is factical. This is clear from the very beginning of *Being and Time* where Heidegger makes an important distinction between the facticity (*Faktizität*) of Dasein and the factuality (*Tatsächlichkeit*) of Dasein.

> Dasein understands its ownmost Being in the sense of a certain "factual Being-present-at-hand." And yet the "factuality" of the fact [*Tatsache*] of one's own Dasein is at bottom quite different ontologically from the factual occurrence of some kind of mineral, for example. Whenever Dasein is, it is a Fact (*Faktum*); and the factuality of such a Fact is what we shall call Dasein's "*facticity*." . . . The concept of "facticity" implies that an entity "within-the-world" has Being-in-the-

world in such a way that it can understand itself as bound up in its "destiny" with the Being of those entities which it encounters within its own world. (*BT,* 55–56/82)

It is clear from this passage that in the first place facticity designates the dynamic quality of Dasein that makes it distinct from other beings. Factical Dasein is a being, but it is not just any being, which is to say that it is not simply factual, like a mineral or some other thing simply present at hand. Because it is Being-in-the-world, Dasein has the capacity to transcend beings unto Being; in phenomenological terms, it can transcend beings unto the world. In the second place, though, it is also clear from this passage that facticity indicates the finitude of that transcendence insofar as one of the defining features of facticity is that Dasein, as factical, must always comport itself with beings, to the point where its own destiny is intimately tied to the other beings that are in the world with it. Because Dasein is factical, it has inextricably a relation to beings, even as it transcends those beings and encounters, thereby, the Being of beings. Facticity, then, in *Being and Time* names the dual nature of Dasein: its dynamic capacity for transcendence, since it is not just any being but a privileged being that has access to Being, and the limitation of that transcendence by the beings with which and through which that transcendence must take place.

To put this in other terms, facticity names the duality of Dasein in its dynamism and its finitude. If the dynamism of Dasein is its capacity for transcendence, the finitude of Dasein is made manifest by the fact that it is thrown into the world and is, thereby, dependent on other beings.

Dasein's facticity is such that *as long as* it is what it is, Dasein remains in the throw, and is sucked into the turbulence of the "they's" inauthenticity. Thrownness, in which facticity lets itself be seen phenomenally, belongs to Dasein, for which, in its Being, that very Being is an issue. Dasein exists factically. (*BT,* 179/223)

Certainly, facticity and fallenness are related. In *Being and Time* one of the modalities of Dasein's fallenness is manifest in what Heidegger calls the "they" (*das Man*). This phenomenon describes the way that Dasein is inclined to interpret itself only by what other people say; as such, Dasein is not its own. Instead of achieving itself in its own Being, inauthentic Dasein is absorbed in ontic distraction; that is, Dasein's commerce with beings distracts it from its prerogative to transcend beings unto Being. Clearly, this phenomenon is part of Dasein's facticity. The facticity of Dasein is such that Dasein cannot relinquish its thrownness. It cannot simply shed its inauthenticity. As such, authenticity is not a state or condition of Dasein in which it has extricated itself from the "they."[21] For this reason, Dasein's transcendence unto Being is always factical. In other words, Dasein *exists* factically, which means that its transcendence is always mediated by beings: It always takes place in and through beings.

The depth to which beings penetrate Dasein's existence cannot be overemphasized. To be sure, Heidegger's insistence on Dasein's *factical* existence is a confirmation of its profound onticity, that is, its immersion among beings, in spite of its transcendence. This is perhaps most clearly manifest in his description of ontological disposition, which has an important relation to facticity. Disposition, one of the three ways that Dasein is in the world, reveals to Dasein its thrownness, that is, that it is referentially dependent on beings. In this sense, disposition (*Befindlichkeit*) reveals the way in which Dasein simply finds itself (*sich befinden*) in the world. In disclosing Dasein's thrownness, disposition also reveals Dasein's facticity. This is because it shows to Dasein how its way of Being-in-the-world is fundamentally determined by its comportment with beings. Because Dasein is factical, beings reverberate through it, and in a profound way. This is the sense of facticity that disposition discloses and that, Heidegger insists, is something that we never behold (*BT,* 135/174). What we behold is the factual. Since Dasein is not factual but factical, its referential dependence on beings is not beheld; it is, rather, experienced in Dasein's dispositions.

In the various places throughout *Being and Time* where the concept of facticity appears, this sense of it is operative: At the same time that facticity renders possible Dasein's transcendence (since it is not just factual, i.e. some thing present at hand, but dynamic and so able to transcend beings) it also places limitations on that transcendence. This limitation is viewed in both a negative and a positive sense. Negatively, this limitation is a mark of Dasein's finitude: its referential dependence on beings, its fallenness. Positively, though, this limitation releases Dasein *into* those possibilities that it can take over, those that are properly its own. Dasein's facticity is revealed by anxiety: "The entire phenomenon of anxiety shows Dasein as factically existing Being-in-the-world" (*BT,* 191/235). Since anxiety is the disposition wherein it becomes possible for Dasein to accept that it is who it is, then authenticity belongs to that possibility. In other words, by disclosing factical existence, anxiety makes it possible for Dasein to accept its own finite transcendence. This is the case because factical Dasein remains "in the throw" and, as such, is never master of its own origin. This nonmastery of its origin points to a "not" at the very basis of Dasein's Being: "This '*not*' belongs to the existential meaning of 'thrownness'" (*BT,* 284/330). This means that Dasein is *not* its own origin, but rather has been released, he says, "*to* itself" (*BT,* 285/330). Accordingly, Dasein cannot ever become the master of its own origin "from the ground up" (*BT,* 284/330), rather it must take itself over: It must be itself, and nothing more. This involves accepting that it is what it is, a being with the capacity for *finite* transcendence. This acceptance of itself is resoluteness and constitutes Dasein's authenticity. To put this in other terms, this means that Dasein accepts those possibilities that are available to it, and not others. Indeed, by accepting certain possibilities, Dasein does not accept others. Factical Dasein's capacity for transcendence is limited by those possibilities that it has chosen over and against those possibilities that it has not chosen and those which it cannot choose. Although this limitation is the result of the "not" that permeates Dasein's origin, it is precisely this "not" or nullity that is liberating insofar as Dasein accepts some possibilities and not others. Freedom, he says, "*is* only in the choice of one possibility" (*BT,* 285/331).

In a later text by Heidegger, "On the Essence of Ground" (written in 1928) this sense of facticity returns (*G* 9: 63/128–29). There he says that by virtue of Dasein's facticity, that is, by virtue of the fact that Dasein finds itself in the midst of beings, certain possibilities have withdrawn from it. This withdrawal of possibilities is liberating in that in the withdrawal Dasein becomes free for those possibilities that are thereby available to it. In this withdrawal, wherein certain possibilities for Being *come to* Dasein, the finitude of Dasein's freedom becomes manifest: because it is thrown into the world amid other beings, nonmaster of its origin, capable only of exploiting those possibilities that are rendered available by the withdrawal of other possibilities, its freedom for possibilities is radically finite. The facticity of Dasein reveals its fundamentally finite existence, but that limited existence is, nonetheless, rich with possibilities.

To some, it may be disappointing that Heidegger replaces the term "factical life," which retains connotations of vivacity, richness, vitality, and meaningfulness, with the more antiseptic term "Dasein." As I have shown, however, Heidegger was not a life-philosopher, nor was he an existentialist. The early Heidegger's "philosophy of life" included an attentiveness and a sensitivity to the Being of life from the very beginning. Dasein is thus a profoundly complex and rich structure. It indicates neither the human being nor Being itself, but factical human life insofar as it is concerned about its own existence. Factical life and Being crystallize in the idea of Dasein.

What is disappointing is that in the early lecture courses there are so many provocative hints about what it means, factically, to live an authentic life, but *Being and Time* does not explore those possibilities in any great detail. Consider all that he says about the following possibilities: how to live within meaningful contexts and how to experience average, everyday life in all of its various intensities (Chapter 1), how to cultivate a vital religious sensibility (Chapter 2), how to engage in counter-ruinance through radical questioning (Chapters 3–4), how to engage in the countermovement against fallenness through research into *Existenz*, bringing the radical questioning and temporalizing history of the past into a truthful safe-keeping (Chapter 5), how to maintain a vigilant, hermeneutic awareness about one's own way of Being-in-the-world (Chapter 6), how to experience the richness of the world through language (Chapter 7), how to develop an authentic language, authentic being-with-others, and ethical excellence (Chapter 8), and how to engage in substantive, meaningful dialogue about human existence (Chapter 9). Recall his remarkable descriptions of average, everyday life, which showed their philosophical import: the lectern from *G* 56/57, the person waving to him from across the street in *G* 58, the factical spatiality of the table from *G* 63, the average, everyday way in which the ancient Greeks spoke with each other from his course on Aristotle's *Rhetoric* in *G* 18. For that matter, he will even say in *History of the Concept of Time* (*G* 20) from 1925 that

> Speaking with one another about something is not an exchange of experiences back and forth between subjects, but a situation where the being-with-one-another is intimately involved in the subject matter under discussion. And it is only by way of this subject matter, in the particular context of always already Being-in-the-world, that mutual understanding develops. (*G* 20:363/263)

Shortly thereafter, in the same lecture course, he claims that idle talk is primarily a function of the written word and not of the spoken word: "Much more idle talk today comes from what is written" (*G* 20:371/269). In 1925, just before writing *Being and Time*, Heidegger said the following about inauthenticity:

> What is more, the inauthenticity of existence does not refer to less being or an inferior grade of being. Rather, inauthenticity precisely can indicate existence in its full concretion—its many activities, its liveliness, its interestedness, its ability to enjoy—in all of which it concretely lives and moves. For the most part—and this is important—existence comports itself neither in the mode of authenticity nor in that of simply being lost, but instead in a remarkable indifference. That, in turn, is not nothing but something positive—the averageness of existence, which we call "everydayness," and which is especially difficult to understand categorially in its structure and in the meaning of its being. I have said something about this in earlier lecture courses and will not go into it here. (*G* 21:229–30/192)

Unfortunately, in *Being and Time*, average everydayness takes on a decidedly negative character, and idle talk seems very much a function of speaking, hearsay, and rumors that come from what people have heard (and not from what they have read). Heidegger has been criticized for having drawn such a negative picture of average, everyday life and for never having described authentic living and speaking. What I have shown in this book is that in his early lecture courses *he had already provided* many different hints and indications of what such a life might look like. It is disappointing that these were not more fully developed in *Being and Time* or afterward. Perhaps this is why Gadamer once said, "Heidegger tried to develop a philosophy that would help us in our practical lives. He failed."[22]

Nonetheless, there is a profound duality to factical life, and Heidegger has made us sensitive to it. As we have seen, throughout all of Heidegger's writings on facticity, deception and distortion are ineluctable. From the various ways that factical life is ruinant and avoids itself (*Phenomenological Interpretations of Aristotle: Initiation into Phenomenological Research, G* 61), to the deception that is intrinsic to speaking (*Introduction to Phenomenological Research, G* 17), and into the notions of fallenness and inauthenticity in *Being and Time* and elsewhere, Heidegger was profoundly aware of the negativity of human life. It has also become apparent, however, that the factical life of Dasein is such that human beings live within vital, dynamic, and rich contexts of meaning. These we have seen in everything that he says about the experience of life in its intensities, which he called, very early in his career, worlding (*Toward the Definition of Philosophy, G* 56/57). We saw these dynamic contexts, as well, in his descriptions of the layeredness of life and the rhythmic echoing between life and world (*Basic Problems of Phenomenology, G* 58). They are there, too, in the contexts of activity of the early Christians (*The Phenomenology of Religious Life, G* 60). They are there in what he says about discursive practices in the *Rhetoric* course (*Basic Concepts of Aristotelian Philosophy, G* 18), contexts of language in the *Sophist* course (*Plato's Sophist, G* 19), and contexts of meaning in *Being and Time*. It was essential to Heidegger's thinking that the negativity of life and its richness belong together. In a lecture he delivered in 1926, "On the Essence of Truth" (Pentecost Monday, 1926), as he was preparing the manuscript for *Being and Time*, he affirms that error and truth belong together in Dasein.

> Only because Dasein is essentially in the truth and its world is already uncovered for it, while it itself by and large loses itself and forgets itself, only because Dasein is in this way, can it and must it *be in untruth*.

Co-original with truth factically there is also error. Error and untruth are not matters that are left out and, regarded as unsuitable surplus, left to the common sense for discussion. Untruth, error, insanity, illness are co-original with what we are calling Dasein. Only so do we sense the power and uncommon dedication that lie in the excellence of our be-ing, such that we may acknowledge this power and become *free for the matters themselves.*[23]

Indeed, as I have tried to show throughout this book, the richness of factical life and its vitality are achieved only insofar as we open ourselves up to the possibility of distortion and deception. If philosophy is fully immersed within the factical, average, everyday world, then it risks the distortions that belong to that world. This is why truth is always also untruth, why authenticity is trammeled with darkness, and why transcendence is essentially finite. Heidegger presents us with a realistic portrayal of the human person, and a profoundly meaningful one. Despite the distortions and deceptions in human life, it is still possible to have an insight into who we are. Darkness and even perversity, "untruth, error, insanity, illness" can become integrated into an authentic and meaningful human life, as Richardson says, "like the shadows in a Rembrandt painting."

Notes

Introduction

1. Crowe 2006, 6.

2. Theodore Kisiel's *The Genesis of Heidegger's "Being and Time"* (Berkeley: University of California Press, 1993) and John van Buren's *The Young Heidegger: Rumor of the Hidden King* (Bloomington: Indiana University Press, 1994) are excellent studies of Heidegger's early work. Interestingly, and to the benefit of Heidegger scholarship, the books work well together: By taking very different approaches to basically the same material, they avoid being repetitive. Kisiel's approach is three-pronged: biographical, chronological, doxographical. Meticulously and systematically, Kisiel works through almost all of the published and unpublished material that figures into the storied development of *Being and Time*, providing extremely close and detailed readings of the early lecture courses in chronological order. He provides the best account of the maturation of Heidegger's thinking under way toward *Being and Time*. By contrast, van Buren's account of the early Heidegger is not strictly chronological but thematic; also, inspired by Derrida, his interpretations are in many respects more radical. He stresses the anarchic, antimetaphysical strategies in the early Heidegger's formal indications of philosophizing as these indications present nonobjective, historical, and deconstructive possibilities for different ways of thinking. I am heavily indebted to both men for the contributions they have made, having benefited greatly from their work.

3. Sheehan 2001, 189.

4. Sheehan claims it is scandalous that the term "Dasein" remains untranslated in the literature on Heidegger, offering "openness" as an effective translation

(Sheehan 2001, 194). It is important to emphasize, as Sheehan does, that for Heidegger the human being is openness. But "openness" does not capture the extent to which this openness is connected with human being or the sense in which this openness can be identified with the human being. Although Heidegger insists that Dasein is not the same as the human being, Dasein is something to be achieved by and through human beings. The ways in which "Dasein" is currently spoken of, in its untranslated form, does capture that sense.

5. Sheehan 2001, 193.

6. In addition to neo-Kantianism, some commentators have suggested that Heidegger may have appropriated the term from Fichte or Dilthey. For that matter, I should add that according to Gadamer, Heidegger's understanding of facticity is one that originated amid a dispute among Rothe and other Hegelian and post-Hegelian theologians "over faith in the Resurrection" and was then filtered through Dilthey, Bergson, Nietzsche, and Natorp, for whom it meant "the irreducibility of 'life' . . . precisely the thing back of which and behind which one cannot go" (Gadamer 1994b,24).

7. This analysis of the prehistory of the word "facticity" comes from Kisiel 1986–1987, 92–94.

8. In Heidegger's later work this changes: In the *Logos* essay from 1944, he continues to say that λόγος does not mean "reason, rationality, or logic," but he says further that it does not mean "speaking" either. For the later Heidegger, although λόγος does need to be thought as λέγειν, the standard meaning of which is "to speak," the original meaning of λέγειν is, Heidegger says, not "to speak" but rather a primordial collecting and gathering. It is important to be aware of this development even though in the present book I take account of Heidegger's understanding of λόγος only as he presented it before *Being and Time*. In this early period, the critical role of speaking in the understanding of λόγος is described in considerably more detail than in any of the later works. As such, it becomes clear from the early work how the insight into λόγος as speaking figures into the development of Heidegger's understanding of λόγος. As evidence for this, note that even in that later essay the importance of speaking to the understanding of λόγος is manifest, for the meaning of λόγος there involves a deeper understanding of λέγειν and thus a deeper understanding of speaking. In other words, in Heidegger's later work the original meaning of λόγος is reached by rethinking the origin of speaking (λέγειν).

9. See Scharff 1997, 117: "To state my thesis bluntly, I think the new information about the early Heidegger shows that in working out the problem of how to *approach* the Being-question—i.e. in determining how to *be* a phenomenological philosopher—Heidegger receives more help from 'the researches of Dilthey' than from *anyone else*."

10. What distinguishes Heidegger from classical philosophers of life is the method he uses. As Fehér points out, Heidegger agreed with life-philosophy about the object of investigation, namely life, itself, but he did not conclude, as many of them did, that life and the myriad concepts surrounding it are either

irrational or static. According to Fehér, the failure to develop an appropriate method to investigate life either leads to the claim that life is irrational or ends up in the reification of the concept of life. He identifies history and existence along with life as concepts that philosophers of life ultimately claim are irrational. He notes, further, that in Heidegger's analysis of Jaspers, he shows how Jaspers's methodology, with its Bergsonian influences, results in a static notion of existence. In both cases, the problem is not with the topic under investigation, be it life, history, or existence, but with the importation of a method that cannot grasp that topic. See Fehér 1994,88.

11. Many of the early courses reveal a sustained effort to develop a method that is able to grasp and to articulate the topic of factical life in the right way. Heidegger's development of hermeneutics, a milestone in the evolution of his thought, grew out of an attempt to find a method that was appropriate to the investigation of life. In 1920/1921, he will call this method formal indication; in 1923 he will call it ontology, which he takes to be the hermeneutics of facticity; in 1927, this method becomes fundamental ontology. Throughout, his effort is to find a method and a language appropriate to the Being of factical life.

12. Heidegger's first significant treatment of Dilthey appears in *G* 56/57 from 1919.

13. A translation of these lectures can be found in *Supplements: From the Earliest Essays to Being and Time and Beyond*, ed. John van Buren, Albany: State University of New York Press, 2002, 147–76, subsequently cited as *S*.

14. Kisiel and Sheehan 2007, 238–39.

15. Scharff 1997, 117. Scharff also shows how Heidegger's struggle with Dilthey over a ten-year period leading up to *Being and Time* resulted in his elucidation of hermeneutics as Dasein's method for understanding itself and its own factical situation, not from the standpoint of consciousness, but rather from the standpoint of life.

16. This is in contrast to the epistemological perspective that one gets from looking on at life from the standpoint of consciousness. As Scharff points out, Heidegger is setting Dilthey's standpoint of life against the Cartesian—as well as the Husserlian—standpoint of consciousness, in spite of some of the Cartesian elements in Dilthey's own epistemological method. Heidegger was working both with and against Dilthey, who was not aware of the (Cartesian) intellectual milieu within which he was working and the effect that it had on his own understanding of life and history. At the same time that he was trying to grasp the historical reality of human life, Dilthey often viewed life from the perspective of the internal workings of consciousness, as a subject looking on at objects (Scharff 1997, 112, 120). Heidegger was able to recognize that despite the epistemological orientation of Dilthey's time, he was nonetheless able to have in view the whole of life as a pretheoretical and prescientific phenomenon.

17. Though not directly, Scharff seems to imply that Heidegger's notion of taking-notice (*Kenntnisnahme*) from *G* 56/57 derives from Dilthey's notion of *Selbstbesinnung*. Whether that is true or not, Scharff is certainly correct when

he says that what Heidegger saw in this notion is a way to grasp life in its *How*, that is, as possibilities that are lived through, rather than as apprehending what life is.

18. Scharff 1997, 118.

19. It is remarkable that in the Kassel lectures, Heidegger is much more interested in the phenomenon of life than he is in *Being and Time*, where he will state with clarity that philosophy of life has led to a philosophical anthropology that lacks an adequate ontological foundation (*BT,* 47/73). Even in *Being and Time*, however, he will assert that "the philosophy of life" is just like saying "the botany of plants" (*BT,* 46/72). In the same way that botany implies the study of plants, philosophy implies the study of life. This was a point that he had also made much earlier, in *G* 18, from 1924. As it has been since 1919 and as it still is in *Being and Time*, for Heidegger, philosophy is about life. Thus, the Kassel lectures do not take such a remarkably different view of the phenomenon of life from *Being and Time* as it may at first appear. Heidegger recognized in Dilthey an effort to grasp the whole of life, but he also saw that Dilthey, Bergson, Scheler, and other philosophers interested in life were not able to do so. A sense of the whole of life requires an investigation into the Being of life.

20. Working through what Dilthey says about trying to grasp the reality of historical life, Heidegger concludes the Kassel lectures by saying, "We focus our treatment on the history of philosophy on a fundamental problem, one that we already constantly have had in view but have not expressly formulated, namely, the question of the *being of beings*" (*S,* 175).

21. Hans-Helmuth Gander uses the lecture courses on religion to justify his claim that for the early Heidegger, the self is always situational. He connects those courses to the influence of Dilthey on Heidegger and concludes that "for Heidegger the situation as phenomenon of expression articulates the being-character of the self. In the sense of the self of Heidegger's early ontology of facticity, it is neither meaningful nor possible to speak of a being of the I that is independent from that which is given situationally; hence Heidegger addresses this I as the 'situational-I'" (See Gander 2002, 385).

22. See Crowe 2006, 257.

1. Science and the Originality of Life

1. Golfo Maggini calls our attention to the importance of the early Heidegger's analyses of movement, providing convincing interpretations of Heideggerian concepts from the perspective of movement or "motility." She goes so far as to claim that movement may be the essential concept for the early Heidegger, not just in his development of concepts (such as λόγος, αλήθεια, fallenness, care, unrest, ecstatic temporality, and the categories of factical life) but, more broadly, in his shift from the phenomenology of life to ontology or what she calls "a hermeneutic ontology of life" (Maggini 1999, 97). For her, Aristotle is the key figure here, as Heidegger's analyses of Aristotelian "kinesis" can be found in between his interpretations of the phenomenology of life and his development of an ontology of Dasein.

Recognizing the importance of the notion of movement, even as "kinesis" in Aristotle, one ought to note that in his analyses of life, Heidegger's focus is not simply on movement per se but on the moving directions of experience in factical life. This movement is always already charged with factical meaning, which is how Heidegger differentiates himself from the life-philosophers. This meaningful movement into the world is central to his analyses of life and Being. Moreover, although Heidegger certainly finds Aristotle's concept of "kinesis" compatible with his own notion of the "motility" or movement of life, Heidegger's understanding of the meaningful flow of life predates the Aristotle courses that Maggini references. One could argue that it is there from the beginning, as early as 1919. Accordingly, the shift from a phenomenology of life to an ontology of Dasein may be owing less to a focus on movement or "kinesis" in Aristotle and more to a deepening sense of the origin of life, and a reappropriation of that origin, through an exploration of the meaning of Being.

2. For a good basic overview of *G* 58, see Hogemann 1986–87.

3. According to George Kovacs, this course must be seen as being exclusively a meditation on method in philosophy: "In the final analysis, the entire course 'The Idea of Philosophy and the Problem of Worldview,' i.e. the idea of philosophy as primordial, pre-theoretical science, is concerned with the problem of method (*G* 56/57:110)" (Kovacs 1994, 102). The reference to Heidegger here is somewhat misleading, and Kovacs overstates the point. Heidegger claims, rather, that, "this whole lecture course has actually pivoted around the problem of method" (*G* 56/57:110/84). What is important about the overstatement is that, as we see both in this course and in subsequent lectures, for Heidegger, method is inextricably bound to content. Indeed, the method must be determined by the content. If, as I am maintaining throughout this book, the primary object of philosophy for the early Heidegger is life (factical life), then the method of investigation into life must derive from life, as well. At the beginning of this course, Heidegger will say that the object of his investigation is philosophy itself. Accordingly, he writes, "The sense of every genuine scientific method springs from the essence of the object of the science concerned, thus in our case the idea of philosophy. Primordial-scientific method cannot be derived from a non-primordial, derivative science. Such an attempt must lead to blatant nonsense" (*G* 56/57:16/15). This connection between method and object will become critical to Heidegger's development of the hermeneutics of factical life.

4. In his analysis of this course, Kovacs connects this discussion of worldview with what Heidegger will later say about philosophy in his 1964 essay "The End of Philosophy and the Task of Thinking." In both texts, Heidegger's interest is in the nature and task of philosophy, so the connection is, in that regard, an appropriate one. For Heidegger, philosophy should not be an attempt to construct an ultimate worldview. In that a great deal of what calls itself "philosophy" attempts to develop a worldview, Heidegger will suggest in that later text that philosophy, at least in this sense, has, indeed, come to an end, and philosophy, as he understands

it, must involve thinking and not the development of a worldview or picture of reality. But it is better, perhaps, to look at a text that is contemporaneous with this lecture course. See Kovacs 1994, 95.

5. See Kisiel and Sheehan 2007, 110, for the dating of this essay.

6. See Kisiel 1993, 25: "The original something is an original motion, the facticity of our being is an event or happening, the facticity of Time itself."

7. See ibid., 46.

8. See ibid., 9.

9. Jean Greisch's writings on the hermeneutics of facticity address the problem of the life of Dasein or the self in Heidegger. (Greisch has also written a brief yet helpful summary of Heidegger's early period which traces the philosopher's development through phenomenology and the hermeneutics of facticity to fundamental ontology and the project, developed in his dialogue with Kant, of grounding metaphysics. See Greisch 1993, 177–98.) Although his central question, like mine, is the meaning of facticity, he is admittedly less interested in the facticity of the phenomenon of life (he does not mention the facticity of language) than he is in (1) the *hermeneutics* of factical life, (2) the confrontation with neo-Kantianism (especially Rickert) and with Husserl's transcendental idealism, and (3) "the issues involved in Heidegger's critical discussion of Dilthey, Bergson, and Nietzsche's life-philosophy" (Greisch 1998, 5). Furthermore, he takes account of the appropriation of facticity by thinkers such as Landgrebe, Sartre, and Levinas, and the impact of facticity on contemporary debates about the meaning of phenomenology, phenomenology's factical relation to affectivity and the body, the concepts of religion and selfhood, and even deconstruction (Greisch 1998, 6).

Interestingly, one of the primary tasks of Greisch's analysis is to show that Dasein, because it is factical, is marked by an interior affectivity that precedes its involvement with the world. This approach is surprising insofar as some of the recent studies on Heidegger (by Lawrence Hatab and Will McNeill, among others) have endeavored to defend the philosopher against the charge of worldless solipsism, a danger Heidegger recognized himself (*BT*, 233). Greisch is explicitly contending with M. Henry's claim that Heidegger, in his fidelity to Husserlian intentionality, has privileged Dasein's ek-static structure to such a degree that he misses the originary phenomenon of life in its "self-affection" (Greisch 1998, 17, quoting from Henry 1985, 52). In response to Henry, Greisch maintains that Heidegger suggests "at least *in nuce*" that it is possible for us to "try to think the phenomenon of life as such," i.e., "life *which is not yet* invested in the production of a particular life-world and, so to speak, to catch it in the very act of investing" (Greisch 1998, 17). He draws this analysis from *Towards the Definition of Philosophy* (*G* 56/57) (war emergency semester, 1919 and summer semester, 1919)—courses which, incidentally, do not mention the word facticity—where Heidegger makes a distinction between the "pre-worldly something" (the "basic moment of life as such") and the "*world-laden* something" (the "basic moments of particular spheres of experience") (Greisch 1998, 16, quoting from (*G* 56/57:115/88)). Greisch does not elaborate on how, through Heidegger, he would characterize "life as such." If he means to replace the Husserlian transcendental subject with a pre-worldly, yet nonetheless affective *subject*, this position would have to be challenged. If, however, he means to show that preworldly life indicates Dasein's transcendence unto Being, in which case life's affectivity discloses the finitude of that transcendence, then he will have made a valuable connection between these very early courses and *Being and Time*. In the latter case, though, I do not see how Greisch can make Heidegger's position compatible with what Henry calls "a more profound dimension, where life touches itself long before the rise of the world" (Henry 1985, 7, as quoted in Greisch 1998, 9) and this dimension's "interior" affectivity.

10. Rudolph Makkreel emphasizes the impact that the notion of concern had on Heidegger's understanding of philosophy. Quoting from *G* 59 and describing Heidegger's idea of philosophy from that text, Makkreel writes, "Philosophy does not need to work out a world-view, rather it fosters the 'concern for one's own Dasein,' from which the 'tendency toward world-view' first arises. This disturbance in the heart of life, which we gladly suppress, should be renewed, so that we can retain the original motive of philosophy" (Makkreel 1990, 184).

11. See in particular István Fehér's reading of Heidegger's early lecture courses. He makes the point that while claiming that phenomenology was methodologically necessary for grasping the phenomenon of life, Heidegger was nonetheless articulating a very different sense of phenomenology than Husserl, as early as 1919–20. In particular, Heidegger believes that experience is not simply given; it must be won. Moreover, he believes that pure description is as problematic as pure theory. See Fehér 1994, 81–83.

12. See especially Chapter 7, which describes factical speaking as a language which encounters the worldly dimensions of factical life, and Chapter 8, an analysis of Heidegger's reading of Aristotle's *Rhetoric*, in which the senses of conviction and πάθος become especially prominent.

13. We witness this same dynamic in *Phenomenological Interpretations of Aristotle* (*G* 61), where Heidegger says that he is starting with life as it is pre-grasped, which is to say that he is looking at life as it is lived, before being made into an object for study.

14. Heidegger is not explicit in his lecture courses about where he gets the term "life-world." Husserl was using the term *Lebenswelt* prior to 1920, and considering that Heidegger was working closely with Husserl at this time, it is fair to say that Heidegger adopts the term from his mentor. Even if Heidegger gets the term from Husserl, however, it is not at all clear that it meant the same thing for both men. Although Husserl had used the term prior to 1920, he did not fully explicate its meaning until the 1920s, and especially during the years 1925–28. It seems, then, that both philosophers were developing their understanding of the term during Heidegger's early tenure in Freiburg (1919–23) as Husserl's assistant. Consequently, each seems to understand the term differently. Although both are interested in grounding the various sciences in the life-world, for Husserl this meant that the life-world, the world of primordial experience, would provide access to the inner structure of the world, and this would then serve as the foundation for all the

empirical sciences. Husserl was committed to the idea that philosophy is a strict science, that is, a body of objective truths. The life-world was the place from which that universal science could be developed. Although Husserl later construed the life-world as historical and became interested in the problem of temporality, this was not initially the case. The life-world, at first, was for Husserl ahistorical. By contrast, the life-world was for Heidegger from the very beginning a temporal-historical phenomenon. In this regard it seems that Heidegger was influenced as much by Husserlian phenomenology as he was by the *Lebensphilosophen* or life-philosophers. It is generally thought that life-philosophy can be traced back to Nietzsche and Schopenhauer, for whom philosophy was, in part, a reaction to enlightenment rationalism. These and the life-philosophers whom Heidegger seemed to be reading at that time, such as Henri Bergson, Georg Simmel, Oswald Spengler, Ernst Troeltsch, and Wilhelm Dilthey, were interested in the movement of life, its vitality and development, and thus in life's temporal-historical character. They believed that because life was temporal and historical, it was vital, and this vitality could not be grasped by rational concepts. Heidegger, it seems, is strongly influenced by the idea that philosophy needs to be directed toward the vitality of life and thus to its basic historicality. His understanding of the life-world, I believe, strongly reflects this influence, in spite of some of his criticisms of life-philosophy.

15. As such, it is not science that provides access to life but, interestingly, the humanities, of which science is but one specific discipline. The full spectrum of the humanities (art, religion, science, literature) is composed of, Heidegger says, layers of manifestation (*Bekundungsschichten*) of the self-world (*G* 58: 54–55). Of course, this is not to say that factical life is simply a matter of taking all the humanities as a whole. Rather, it means that the richness of factical life is not engaged by science alone. Literature, too, for example, encounters factical life in a way that is entirely different from science. Phenomenology, therefore, grounds all of the sciences and all of the humanities by preparing the original ground experience of factical life from which all of those disciplines receive their determinations.

16. Interestingly, and in support of this claim, Heidegger says in his analysis of self-sufficiency that through an understanding of factical life, self-sufficiency, "experiences thereby a new enlightening" (*G* 58:63).

17. It is clear that Heidegger is working within an experience of the nothingness and emptiness of factical life (experiences that, as we will see, motivate questioning), insofar as nothingness and emptiness render factical life incomplete and temporal, even though he does not use those terms here.

2. Christian Facticity

1. There are a number of excellent examinations of Heidegger's early theological courses. Otto Pöggeler's book on Heidegger (*Martin Heidegger's Path of Thinking*, originally published as *Der Denkweg Martin Heideggers*) came out in the same year (1963) as William Richardson's book, *Heidegger: Through Phenomenology to Thought*. Since Pöggeler had access to some of Heidegger's early lecture courses, his book includes an analysis of Christian facticity. Although his treatment of this

theme is brief, he stresses the nonobjectifiable historicality of factical life and how for Heidegger the early Christians lived temporality. He also traces *Being and Time*'s analysis of the anxiety of Being-in-the-world to Augustine's anxiety about factical existence. Furthermore, Pöggeler points out the importance of Kierkegaard and Luther to Heidegger's understanding of Christian facticity. See also *A Companion to Heidegger's Phenomenology of Religious Life*, ed. S. J. McGrath and Andrzej Wiercinski (Amsterdam: Rodopi, 2010). This wide-ranging volume of essays, which was published as this book was going into production, covers the historical contexts of this course and includes essays on both Heidegger's phenomenological method and on his interpretations of Paul and Augustine.

These influences are developed more fully by Merold Westphal and John van Buren. Westphal demonstrates how Kierkegaard's indirect communication is operative in Heidegger's radicalization of Husserlian intentionality into the formal indication of historical-factical life. Pressing this issue further, Westphal focuses on Heidegger's subsequent radicalization of Kierkegaard in the formalization of factical life, which, he says, extricates all Christian content from Christian facticity (see Westphal 1997). Taking a very different approach, I accentuate that content here.

In his book on Heidegger, and in an article titled "Martin Heidegger, Martin Luther," van Buren stresses Heidegger's appropriation of the young Luther's theology of the cross, "the concrete, historical realities [or "concrete, historical *logos*,"] of 'the cross'" and its critique of the theology of glory and its contemplative enjoyment of the highest beings (van Buren 1994a, 167). He shows how Heidegger extends this Lutheran critique to the analyses of Aristotle. Accordingly, van Buren traces such concepts as destruction, anticipatory running toward death, and the basic categories of life in *G* 61, as well as "fall, care, anxiety, death, flight, and conscience" (170) back to various texts of Luther's. Although van Buren does not focus on facticity, and so leaves room for just such an analysis as I am attempting here, he does conclude that "Heidegger's destruction prepared the way for uncovering and repeating on an ontological level the historicity of factical life in (1) primal Christianity and (2) Aristotle's own practical writings, so as to effect what he called a new 'genuine beginning' for the question about being" (van Buren 1994a, 172), and I certainly agree with this conclusion.

2. Section three of *G* 60, titled *Philosophical Foundations of Medieval Mysticism*, is a compilation of *Notes and Sketches* for a lecture that Heidegger was supposed to deliver in 1918–19. The course was canceled. Though philosophically interesting, these notes do not address the issue of facticity, so I leave them out of the present endeavor.

3. I should note here that the entire course was supposed to be a meditation on methodological considerations. Heidegger says on the first day that he is going to spend so much time with preliminary questions as to make this practice into a virtue (*G* 60:5). Kisiel points out, though, and Gadamer has confirmed, that in the middle of the semester some of the students in the class complained to the dean of Freiburg University that the course was lacking in theological content. Heidegger

immediately broke off his preliminary considerations and delved right into Paul's letter to the Galatians.

4. Although I have not quoted from Kisiel's book *The Genesis of Being and Time* in this paragraph, reading the sections that correspond to this particular part of the lecture course (158–64) were particularly helpful, and I acknowledge my debt of gratitude.

5. In an interesting article on the philosophical relationship between Heidegger and Husserl in the light of this course, Sheehan points to this course on religion as a defining moment in Heidegger's shift away from his mentor during these early years (Sheehan 1986). Although Heidegger was still Husserl's assistant in Freiburg during this period, Sheehan cites correspondence by a Frau Walter that mentions a discussion with Husserl during which Heidegger participated in a "campaign . . . against the pure ego" (Sheehan 1986, 48). Sheehan concludes from this that not only was Heidegger moving away from Husserl at this point, he was vocal in doing so. In the light of this revelation, Sheehan claims that, "since factical life-experience is intrinsically historical" (49), Heidegger radically changes Husserl's sense of phenomenology by making the factical, lived experience of historicality the "theme and method of the new phenomenology" (51). Accordingly, Sheehan says that Heidegger transforms the Husserlian "transcendental correlation . . . of cognitive *noesis* and *noema*" into the correlation between "lived experience" and "modalities of the world (i.e., lived meaning)" (48). As a result, the fundamentally temporal-historical structures of Christian facticity as Heidegger describes them end up sounding very different from what Husserl says the phenomenology of religion needs, namely, "a systematic eidetic typification of the levels of religious data, indeed in their eidetically necessary development" (59, Sheehan quoting at length a March 1919 letter from Husserl to Rudolf Otto).

6. Dahlstrom offers helpful examples to explain the way in which formally indicating concepts work. Heidegger will say that the "am" of "I am," "death," and the "as-structure" can all be construed not simply in a theoretical way, but as formal indications. Taken in a theoretical sense, the "am" would refer to the mere presence or presence-at-hand of a person, an objectified, perhaps Cartesian, I. As a formal indication, or what Dahlstrom calls a formally indicating concept, the "am" indicates or signals the temporal way of being of something, such as what Heidegger calls in *G* 56/57 the historical-I. Similarly, taken in a theoretical sense, "death" is a present-at-hand event, the moment of death. As a formally indicating concept, "death" signals the temporal understanding one has of oneself as always dying, and thus as being-toward-death. Lastly, as a theoretical or scientific process, the "as-structure"identifies the relation found in a theoretical judgment or proposition. As a formal indication, the "as-structure" signals the way in which we interpret things in terms of their hermeneutical possibilities (see Dahlstrom 1994, 784–85). Dahlstrom's reading, which was published before *G* 60 was available, anticipates this lecture course, for he argues that Heidegger's understanding of formal indication, which indicates or signals phenomena without ordering, categorizing, or otherwise establishing a theoretical determination of them, derives from

Heidegger's understanding of Christian faith. As he says, just like in an artistic or musical work, Christian faith must be realized or acted upon, by the performer or, in this case, by the believer. Similarly, concepts that are not theoretical but rather are formal indications must be enacted or fulfilled; they require "that the philosopher carries out or performs some activity himself" (Dahlstrom 1994, 784). For Dahlstrom, however, science is equivalent to theory, so he believes that Heidegger runs into problems when he attempts to develop formal indications whose purpose is to grasp pretheoretical phenomena while also claiming to understand phenomenology and even philosophy itself as primordial science. This is a salient criticism, which, perhaps, reveals Heidegger's own ambivalence about Husserlian phenomenology and the endeavor of phenomenology to be a strict science. We do see, though, from *G* 56/57 that Heidegger's understanding of primordial science was anything but theoretical.

7. Note that this sense of trying to understand a thinker's concepts from within the conceptuality of that thinker's own situation will appear again in the summer semester 1924 course on Aristotle's *Rhetoric* (see Chapter 8). There, Heidegger tries to understand Aristotelian concepts as emerging from Aristotle's own factical-historical situation. Again, the focus there will be on communication, especially speaking and its pivotal importance to Greek facticity.

8. For a good account of the relationship between Heidegger's account of temporality in this course and what he says about temporality in *Being and Time*, as well as an explanation of the importance of eschatology to the notion of temporality in this course, see Nicholson 2010, 219–31.

9. The knowledge the early Christians had did not provide them with any certainty about their faith. Rather, they lived in complete uncertainty, and this was an essential ingredient of their facticity. Thus, the same ambiguity in factical life belongs to Christian facticity. In his essay on authenticity in this course, Dermot Moran seems to suggest that the experience of the early Christians, on Heidegger's account, was exemplary and free of distortion. He writes, "In all these discussions in the early Heidegger, the Christian characterization of the life experience turns out to be exemplary; it offers nothing less than a phenomenological 'formal indication' of the vital temporality of life, free of imposed and distorting philosophical concepts" (see Moran 2010, 372). Moran remarks that in this lecture course, Heidegger spends more time on inauthentic life than he does on authentic life (373). This is because authenticity is a modification of inauthenticity and an insight into it, as Moran points out (370). But this does pose a challenge to his claim that both inauthenticity and authenticity involve choosing a hero. Fallenness is a condition of Dasein in *Being and Time*, not a choice. Dasein may choose to follow the "they" as a "model" or "hero," as Moran suggests (371–72), but even if it does not, Dasein is still subject to everydayness. In the passage Moran references to support his claim, Heidegger writes, "Everydayness is determinative for Dasein even when it has not chosen the 'they' for its hero" (*BT*, 371/422). With respect to authenticity, Moran brings up the important point that for Heidegger, Dasein does choose its heroes. But, again, in the section of *Being*

and Time that Moran refers to support his position, Heidegger claims that the repetition wherein one chooses a hero is a *"moment of vision"* (*BT*, 386/438), and thus a momentary insight. It is not "a deliberate decision to make one's life a kind of repetition of an original authentic life," as Moran suggests (371). In the Conclusion to this book, I explain how Heidegger's notion of authenticity, understood from the perspective of Dasein's factical life, is a kind of insight into the Being of life that is, nonetheless, riddled with distortion and deception. In this course, Heidegger is emphasizing that the knowledge and, with that, the life-experience of the early Christians, which is based on the uncertainties and ambiguities ("turns and refractions") of factical life, could not be "exemplary" or an "ideal." Although Heidegger's method may be free of "imposed" or "distorting philosophical concepts," I do not see how Christian life experience, itself, could be characterized in this way.

10. Besides urgency and torment, another dimension of the context of activity engendered by one's acceptance of the word of God here is joy. This joy comes from the Holy Spirit, who is a gift from God. Indeed, joy is (present) the gift, which comes (future) from having-become (past).

11. Without question, there are themes here that resemble Heidegger's later development of ecstatic temporality in *Being and Time*.

12. In his book *Heidegger's Phenomenology of Religion: Realism and Cultural Criticism*, Crowe discusses conversion in advancing his theory of "ontological realism." His method accentuates the givenness of God in Heidegger's interpretations, the role of grace in Heidegger's descriptions of religious life, and the tacit sense of religious meaning that is embedded in the practices of the early Christians as Heidegger describes them. See Crowe 2008, 80–91. In Crowe's analysis, though, there is an interesting tension. He insists that conversion comes from outside the self, but at times he seems to be saying that it comes from something internal. Since God is given, conversion would seem to come from the external, and yet Crowe also talks about how, for Heidegger, Christ is "in" a person (81) and how people live within religious meaning prethematically (82). Does religious meaning come from something external to us, so that in conversion we get a new life, coming from a mysterious source outside of us? Or is religious meaning immanent within life already? Heidegger focuses on Paul telling his people that they already know when the second coming will happen. I think this shows the extent to which religious meaning is discovered from within factical human life, and this includes one's experience of the various life-worlds. As such, conversion would not come from the internal or from the external, since the factical self is prior to this distinction.

13. In William Richardson's more recent work on Heidegger, he has returned to the problem of facticity. Starting with the early lecture courses, he traces the negativity of facticity and fallenness through the turn to Being itself and the *letheic* component of truth as ἀλήθεια. He explains the important shift in Heidegger's thinking from the facticity of fallenness in early Christian experience to the secular descriptions of factical life's ruinance, which Heidegger culls from

Aristotle's practical philosophy, in order to show how the later descriptions of errancy developed from a theological experience of fallenness into an ontological analysis of the origin of fallenness in the negativity of Being, itself. With this genealogy, Richardson attempts to show how Heidegger's failure to recognize the distortions and deceptions of Nazism can be explained in his own terms by the mystery and errancy that belong to truth in its negativity. This serves two purposes: In the first place, it shows how profoundly errancy belongs to truth, and, thus, to Heidegger's own genius in his uncovering of Being as ἀλήθεια. In this way, Heidegger gives us a way to try to understand the Nazi phenomenon, if not a way to try to understand evil as such and the bearing it has on human life. In the second place, Richardson claims that the mystery and errancy of truth provide Christians with important "conceptual tools" to negotiate the "'post-modern' experience" and the "historicity" of "finite truth" (Richardson 1995, 253). One of these tools, as Heidegger points out, would be φρόνησις, whose task is "to discern deceptive concealment within revealment and deal with it as best errant Dasein could" (251), which for Christians would involve, presumably, a kind of insight into distortion which is based on religious experience.

14. In another line of critique, Westphal calls Heidegger's treatment of Augustine a misreading by saying that Augustine never meant to quell all distress from factical existence, as Heidegger claims. In the following, I focus only on what Heidegger draws from facticity in Augustine and not on his evaluation of how Augustine subsequently overcomes that distress. See Westphal 1997, esp. 258–60. For some very helpful diagrams of Heidegger's religion courses, complete with explanations, see Kisiel 1994.

15. Kisiel and Sheehan 2007, 99–100.

3. Grasping Life as a Topic

1. In 1986, at the Collegium Phaenomenologicum in Perugia, Italy, David Farrell Krell heard Gadamer say, with reference to *G* 61 (Heidegger's most direct treatment of factical life), "I have read this text, but it is very difficult and I do not understand it well yet. And so I shall have to live a few years longer" (Gadamer, quoted by Krell 1992, 147). Since then, Krell has become arguably the most enthusiastic proponent of this text, especially insofar as the disquiet of factical life exhibits what Heidegger says are temporalizing powers (*Zeitigungsmächte*). Krell calls these powers daimonic forces that temporalize life and account for its vitality. They are, he says, the forces of daimon life, and he suggests that they persist, under various guises, throughout the Heideggerian corpus in such themes as transcendence, existence, "temporality, freedom, anxiety, the overpowering, language, and the holy" (Krell 1992, from the preface). Significantly, Krell emphasizes that the daimonic, temporalizing forces of factical life are related to life's ruinant crash through the nothingness. In this light he says that "the nothing of factical life is nihilation" (49), where nihilation = *temporalizing* nothingness, so that life's temporality and its care are dynamized (moved, temporalized) and, accordingly, contaminated by negativity. This, Krell maintains, is why life is

marked by the categories of inclination, destruction of distance, blocking-off, and ease, that is, why life is always dispersed in its cares and is, therefore, always missing itself. Krell's reading of facticity is thorough and accurate; still, it is also somewhat severe insofar as it does not take account of how life can retrieve its own temporality and thus its own history in such a way that it becomes aware of itself in its own historical Being, a point that I emphasize in my analysis of ruinance in the next chapter.

2. Since Heidegger's early lecture courses have become available, a number of philosophers have taken up the issue of facticity and, in particular, this volume from the *Gesamtausgabe* (*G* 61), which explicitly addresses the problem of factical life. See especially the following: Richardson 1995; Caputo 1993, chap. 2, "Heidegger's *Kampf*: The Difficulty of Life and the Hermeneutics of Facticity," and chap. 3, "*Sorge* and *Kardia*: The Hermeneutics of Facticity and the Categories of the Heart"; Krell 1992, chap. 1, " 'You in front of Me, I in front of You' "; Crowe 2006, chap. 3, "Inauthenticity"; and Gadamer 1994b.

3. Heidegger is highly critical of the traditional approaches to life-philosophy. He writes, "The way in which this expression has pushed its way forward is itself unclear, and that is the reason why men of letters and philosophers, who would rather go into raptures than think, have been able to take hold of the matter so lightly. One ought not to see and to criticize the problem situation of *Lebensphilosophie* in the form which it is currently in, namely waste products" (*G* 61:80/61–62). Unfortunately, he does not provide a satisfactory critique of modern or traditional approaches to the field of life philosophy, so that his caustic use of language here gives the impression that he is being unduly critical. Nonetheless, this acrimonious and incomplete critique belies a deeply rooted belief in the need to investigate the basic tendencies within the expression "life" and the consequent need to achieve a renewed, rigorous approach to life in its most basic tendencies; though I may not be able to agree with his term, I can certainly agree with him that the expression "life" had become dispersed into various different meanings through numerous interpretations and reinterpretations.

4. Gadamer 1997, 271–73.

5. Interestingly, the obscurity that results from "life" splitting into numerous meanings, all of which strive for objective validity, gives the impression that the word has a kind of philosophical fruitfulness. This fruitfulness only obscures life's basic meanings and actually prevents a more searching analysis of it. In this sense, "fruitfulness" becomes a basic philosophical determination, so that even though the basic meaning of "life" is purportedly sought after, the full import of the word is not achieved: "One is constantly prevented from disturbing the alleged fruitfulness of the word by the possibilities of the expression itself and inquires about its basic sense and possibilities for explication without due consideration" (*G* 61:82/63). The interpretation proceeds by taking a certain objective distance from life itself, and in that distance we again see that a kind of complacency is secured. This complacency accepts the multifacetedness of the expression as inherently positive philosophical theorizing, which ought not then be disturbed by

questions about its basic meanings. Such basic, radical questioning might deny the word its fruitfulness.

6. We can already see here in 1921–22 that Heidegger has begun to make a break from the transcendental philosophy of his mentor, Edmund Husserl.

7. Note here in passing that the complacency of life-philosophy, which I mentioned earlier, manifested a shallow absence of questioning.

8. Note the similarity between the dynamic that Heidegger is describing here and what he says in §7 of *Being and Time* regarding the inner relationship between phenomenon and *logos*. In the later text he explains that a phenomenon is that which shows itself, while *logos*, which comes from *legein*, means to let be seen. Phenomenology, therefore, is to let be seen that which shows itself and to do so from itself, as it shows itself. In the present text, it is clear that Heidegger is practicing phenomenology in that very sense. The difference between the two endeavors is that in *Phenomenological Interpretations of Aristotle* (G 61), he is describing world and life, letting them show themselves as they are, whereas in *Being and Time* he is describing world and Dasein. The importance of this difference will become clear as I proceed further.

9. From the very beginning of this section, Heidegger explains that if we do not follow the basic tendencies of the expression "life," that is, if we refuse the use of the word its inherent unclarity, then we will never discover, "if this [expression] and its use does not give expression to certain basic tendencies of Dasein" (G 61:82/63).

10. This is no small revelation. Indeed, the effort to determine the relationship between language and the world was the guiding motivation of Wittgenstein's *Tractatus*. Specifically, he meant to demonstrate how it is possible that words and sentences can actually tell us something about the world, in his terms, how language indicates an actual state of affairs.

11. Note that the word *prinzipielle* does not refer to principles. By claiming that the categories interpret life in a *prinzipielle* way, Heidegger is not saying that they explain life in terms of a few general principles. To make the latter claim, Heidegger would have to use the more abstract term *prinzipial*. Rather, he is saying that the categories try to interpret life according to its concrete facticity. *Prinzipielle*, as I understand it, is another way of saying factical.

12. The word "concern" as it is used here is a translation of the German word *Bekümmerung*. As I show in the following analysis, Heidegger uses this term to indicate the way in which life is open to the meaningfulness of the world and open to Being. To translate *Bekümmerung* with "worry," as is often done, suggests that Heidegger is describing a psychological condition of life, like fretting or panicking, a connotation that he does not intend to make. A better translation for *Bekümmerung* as Heidegger means it is "concern."

13. It would be a stretch to say at this point that Heidegger's conception of experiencing the facticity of objects directly presages his later thoughts on letting objects be in their Being. Without going that far, however, it does seem possible at this point to take some risk and suggest that the same motivation in his later

work against the dangers of manipulating objects in order to control them is operative here. There is certainly a sense in this text that the facticity of life can be reached only when proper access is made to the object, and that that proper access involves letting objects be interpreted from themselves. See above the section on *"zuspringen lassen."*

4. Ruinance

1. The word "ruinance" is my translation of the German word *Ruinanz*. This word does not translate easily. In my view, "ruination" would not convey the meaning of *Ruinanz* because there are normal German words that Heidegger could have used to express the meaning of "ruination." *Zerstörung, Verderben*, and *Ruinierung* all mean "ruination," but these are not words he chooses to use. By using *Ruinanz*, which is not a German word, Heidegger seems to want to use an unfamiliar term. My translation attempts to capture that unfamiliarity. Moreover, ruinance is a basic structure of factical life. As such, "ruination" would be the result of ruinance.

2. Note that there are similarities between what Heidegger says about retrieval (*Wiederholung*) in this course and what he says about it in *Being and Time*. To be sure, the concept is more fully developed in the later text, where it comes to mean the recovery of the antecedent comprehension of Being latent within Dasein, and thus the self's capacity to achieve itself in its own Being, as well as the recovery of a philosophical problem in order to determine what makes that problem possible. All of this is made possible by Dasein's historicality. As a temporal-historical being, Dasein can retrieve possibilities from its own heritage that have already been exploited in order to experience them again in their original freshness. In this course, similarly, retrieval involves the way in which temporality and historicality are still there within those modes of life that hide or conceal life's basic movement. Facticity, then, is the condition for the possibility of retrieval because it reveals to life that its own temporal-historical constitution makes possible those very forms of life that conceal temporality. One can see how this dynamic, although still in its initial stages and, therefore, not orchestrated with respect to the Being-problem, develops in *Being and Time* into the self's retrieval of itself in its own Being. In brief: In this course we see the retrieval of temporality and historicality through life's ruinance; in *Being and Time* we see the retrieval of Being through temporality and historicality. The similarities between the two senses of retrieval as well as the author's development from one to the other are clearly manifest.

3. See Carl Friedrich Gethmann: "Philosophie als Vollzug und als Begriff: Heideggers Identitäts-philosophie in der Vorlesung vom Wintersemester 1921/22 und ihr Verhältnis zu Sein und Zeit." This is an important reference for those who are interested in the place of *Being and Time* in the development of Heidegger's thinking from the early lecture courses to the later period. Gethmann refers in this piece to Gadamer and O. Becker, who believed that Heidegger went against his most deeply rooted convictions, convictions which are manifest in the early courses, when in *Being and Time* he constructed a more Husserlian analysis of transcenden-

tal self-interpretation. Accordingly, Gethmann attempts to show that the more variegated and differentiated basic categories of life as they are depicted in this course become unified and systematized in *Being and Time* by the effort to discern the Being of beings in their unity. In turn, Gethmann says that whereas care in 1921/22 is a moment of rhapsody, in *Being and Time* it becomes one important moment within a unified structural system (Gethmann 1986–87, 51). Although the question of whether *Being and Time* is a systematic analysis is as such outside the scope of the present book, I believe that the existential analytic of Dasein in *Being and Time* resists systematization. To say that Dasein is unified in the three ecstases of temporality is not to say that Dasein is a systematic structure.

4. These are my translations of the terms *Reluzenz* and *Praestruktion*. Exceedingly difficult to translate accurately, they do not appear in any German dictionaries, nor are they recognizable by native German speakers.

5. Although the concept of "fallenness" does not come up in this course, it is clear that ruinance develops into fallenness later. This is clear, I believe, insofar as both fallenness and ruinance are related to facticity. In this course, ruinance is the defining feature of factical life: The ruinance of factical life is such that life identifies itself with worldly distractions, that is, with objects in the world. In *Being and Time*, Heidegger will explain that thrownness reveals Dasein's facticity. Because it is thrown into the world with other beings, Dasein is referentially dependent on beings, and this is a mark of its facticity. Insofar as this thrownness is an abiding condition of Dasein, Heidegger calls it fallenness. Hence, fallenness in *Being and Time* describes Dasein's referential dependence on other beings in the same way that ruinance in this course describes life's dependence on worldly distractions, that is, on objects in the world.

6. The German word *Besorgen* is normally rendered as "concern." As stated in the last chapter, I have chosen to use the word "concern" as a translation for *Bekümmerung*. Although Heidegger uses *Bekümmerung* and *Besorgen* in similar ways, to avoid confusion between the two words I do not translate *Besorgen* or the related word *Besorgnis* with "concern." Instead, I render *Besorgen* as "taking-care." This captures the relation that *Besorgen* has to the word *Sorge*, which means "care." Sometimes, though, Heidegger will say that life or Dasein is *besorgt* with the world. Since "taken-care of" does not work in these cases, I use instead the word "preoccupied." This word also captures the important nuance that in its "taking-care of" the world, factical life or Dasein becomes distracted and preoccupied by its commerce with beings. Depending on the context, then, I use *Besorgen* to mean either "to take-care of" or "to be preoccupied with." Accordingly, what factical life or Dasein "takes-care of" and becomes "preoccupied with" are its cares and preoccupations.

7. Kisiel and Sheehan 2007, 108–9. I have not modified this translation to maintain its consistency with how I have been translating some of the key terms in it because it is a letter, and I do not have access to the original German version.

5. The Retrieval of History

1. "Phenomenological Interpretations with Respect to Aristotle: Indication of the Hermeneutical Situation," translated by Michael Baur, *Man and World* 25 (1992): 355–93, originally published as "Phänomenologische Interpretationen zu Aristoteles (Anzeige der hermeneutischen Situation)," edited by Hans-Ulrich Lessing, *Dilthey-Jahrbuch für Philosophie und Geschichte*, 1989, 6:237–69. (hereafter cited as PIA). Throughout this chapter I rely on Baur's translation of this text, although I have made some modifications. Baur translates *Bekümmerung* as "worry" and *Besorgen* as "concern." In keeping with the rest of this book, I have altered Baur's translation so that *Bekümmerung* is rendered as "concern" and *Besorgen* as either "to take-care of" or "to be preoccupied with."

2. For a good overview of this manuscript see Brogan 1994. Brogan's article is particularly helpful in showing some of the major steps that Heidegger made in this piece toward the development of *Being and Time*.

3. In this context, the phrase "to take-care of" means "to be concerned about".

4. There are clearly meaningful relationships among the words for concern (*Bekümmerung*), "to take-care of" and "to be preoccupied with" (*Besorgen*), and care (*Sorge*), and these relationships show that anxiety (*Angst*), the conceptual descendant of concern, reveals the movement of care. *Kümmern* and *Besorgen* have similar meanings: to be concerned about or to take-care of something. *Sorge*, meaning care, is an indication of Dasein's temporality. Anxiety, the disposition that reveals how care is the Being of Dasein, does not remove Dasein from the world in any way. On the contrary, anxiety reveals the movement and temporality that belong to Dasein's Being as a being that is in movement as to its basic dealings with the world. Insofar as philosophical research investigates factical Dasein, it is thereby investigating the movement that makes all questioning possible.

5. In private conversation, Gadamer confirmed this claim by saying that Heidegger had tried to develop a philosophy that would assist in the life of πρᾶξις but that, ultimately, he failed to do so.

6. Walter Brogan also calls our attention to Heidegger's ambiguous treatment of σοφία and the relative primacy he accords to πρᾶξις and φρόνησις. He writes, "It is in πρᾶξις that this phronetic moment of factical life [the καιρός] is revealed in its fullness and brought to fruition" (Brogan 1994, 218).

7. Although his reading here is at odds with most Aristotle scholarship, which claims that Aristotle did conceive of truth as judgment, Heidegger is adamant about his claim: "In determining the sense of 'truth,' one used to appeal to Aristotle as the original progenitor. According to him, 'truth' was supposed to be something 'that occurs in judgment'; more specifically, the 'agreement' of thought with the object. At the same time, one understands this concept of truth as the basis for the so-called 'representation-theory' of knowledge. In Aristotle, there is not a trace either of this concept of truth as 'agreement' or of the common conception of logos as valid judgment or—least of all—of the 'representation-theory' " (PIA, 255–56/378).

8. Although Heidegger is clearly working with two senses of "world" here, this is not to say that he is proposing a two-world theory, for example, in the Platonic sense. There is the world of Dasein's fallenness and the world of Dasein's *Existenz*, but *Existenz* does not alter Dasein's "factical position" at all, so to speak of two senses of world is not meant to suggest any spatial difference. What changes between the two senses of world, he says, is the "How of the movement of life" (PIA, 245/367). Dasein's *Existenz* is such that by way of a countermovement against a natural inclination to flee, "the authentic Being of life temporalizes itself" (PIA, 245/366). Therefore, Dasein flees *into* that sense of world wherein it remains unaware of its own temporality, and it flees *from* the sense of world wherein it acknowledges that temporality.

9. Note that in both this text from 1922 and in *Being and Time* there is an intimate relationship between facticity and existence. There is, however, an important difference between the two texts as to how facticity and existence relate, which points to an important aspect of Heidegger's development of these two concepts. In this earlier text, Heidegger maintains that *Existenz* is one possibility of life's facticity. He writes, "Facticity and Existenz do not mean the same thing, and life's factical Being-character is not determined by Existenz; Existenz is only one possibility which temporalizes itself within the Being of life (which is characterized as factical). But this means that the possible radical problematic concerning the Being of life is centered in facticity" (PIA, 245–46/367). In 1922, then, there is a clear priority given to facticity; *Existenz* is one mode of that facticity. The question of the Being of life is posed with regard to facticity and not to *Existenz*. In *Being and Time*, however, this will change, so that priority is given to Dasein's existence. Indeed, one year prior to *Being and Time*, in the lecture course titled *Logik: Die Frage nach der Wahrheit* (winter semester, 1925–26), Heidegger will identify Dasein with *Existenz* (G 21:402/332). In *Being and Time*, he develops this analysis further so that Dasein, as existence, is finite transcendence unto Being. (For an explanation of finite transcendence, see the Conclusion.) Heidegger will say more than once in *Being and Time* that Dasein exists factically. Facticity belongs to the process of finite transcendence because it restricts that transcendence to Dasein's matter of fact situation in the world. The development, then, from 1922 to 1926 is a shift from the priority of facticity to the priority of existence.

6. Facticity and Ontology

1. In *Demythologizing Heidegger* John Caputo presents a powerful argument against Heidegger's hermeneutics of facticity. The second and third chapters of his book are devoted to this theme. He maintains there that with facticity Heidegger was, actually, "getting it right," so to speak, and so he initially lauds the philosopher's effort to have the concreteness of factical life disrupt philosophical conceptuality. Caputo discerns a disturbing ambiguity, however, in Heidegger's hermeneutics of facticity insofar as it demands that faith and philosophy make life more difficult, more of a struggle (*Kampf*). On the one hand, he shows that with the hermeneutics of facticity Heidegger "wants to let philosophical conceptuality

be disrupted by the concrete experience of life in the New Testament and by an Aristotle conceived in terms of the practical philosophy rather than the metaphysics" (Caputo 1993, 57). In this sense, Heidegger's effort to make life, faith, and philosophizing more difficult by deconstructing "comforting" metaphysical absolutes back down into factical life's "concerned struggle" for "passion and resolve" (61) is "brilliantly conceived" and "an immensely salutary and suggestive move" (57). On the other hand, he points out that this "revolutionary" effort to portray factical life as "difficult" and "hard," a struggle against ease and comfort, suggests militaristic tendencies in Heidegger's thinking. For Caputo, the "concerned struggle" for "passion and resolve" in life, faith, and philosophy, that is, life's "battle" against "dispassionate objectivity" (50), can be read, in retrospect, as the seeds of Heidegger's subsequent avowal of Nazism: seeds that emerge, in 1930, into a very political *Kampf*-philosophy. Indeed, Caputo calls Heidegger's hermeneutics of facticity "pre-political," (55–56) so that what is, in 1921, revolutionary philosophy becomes, in the 1930s, revolutionary politics.

Caputo suggests, therefore, a "repeating" (57) of factical life that takes account of the "ethics of mercy" (57), as one finds in the New Testament. Such a rereading, he argues, acknowledges the debt that philosophy owes to Heidegger for having redirected abstract principles back to life's facticity but then also recognizes that which Heidegger's understanding of factical life missed, namely, "the cry for justice, the appeal that issues from flesh and pain, from afflicted flesh" (57). Caputo maintains, then, that Heidegger's hermeneutics of facticity was not factical enough, for it did not take account of "the infirm and the afflicted" (63). For this reason, he concludes that there was nothing in facticity to prevent it from turning into "a great myth of Being's struggle" (59), which ignores and even disdains New Testament ethics and its care for the downtrodden.

2. As I have maintained throughout this book, factical life can be objectified (bracketed), but when that happens, its temporal-historical constitution gets covered over. Furthermore, I mentioned in the last chapter that there are factical structures within every field of research. As such, those fields are, for the most part, already bracketed. For Heidegger, researchers must retrieve factical structures by removing brackets. This submits the concepts with which they work to their own factical-historical originality.

3. Interestingly, Heidegger describes hermeneutics quite differently here than he does in *Being and Time*. To be sure, there are some similarities. In both texts, hermeneutics attempts to discern the structure of Being in Dasein: In *Ontology: The Hermeneutics of Facticity* (G 63), he calls this the Being-character of Dasein; in *Being and Time* he says that by way of ἑρμηνεύειν, "the authentic meaning of Being, and also those basic structures of Being which Dasein itself possesses, are *made known* to Dasein's understanding of Being" (*BT*, 37/62). In this lecture course, however, hermeneutics is Dasein's way of understanding itself insofar as it tracks down and uncovers its own self-alienation. This is different from hermeneutics as he describes it in *Being and Time*, where he says that it is the interpretation of a λόγος (*BT*, 37/61–62). Interpretation here means laying-out (*Auslegung*);

λόγος comes from λέγειν, which means ἀποφαίνεσθαι, that which shows itself as itself. Hermeneutics, then, in *Being and Time* is the interpretation, the laying-out, of Dasein as it shows itself. It is, in other words, Dasein's laying of itself out in its own Being.

7. Factical Speaking

1. Heidegger edited this section of the lecture course with a footnote, which reads, "better summer semester 24," his analysis of Aristotle's *Rhetoric* (Chapter 8).

2. It also suggests that the claim from Heidegger's later thinking that language speaks through the human being (a claim that Gadamer also adheres to) is here in place, albeit in an incipient and inchoate way. Although it would be premature to interpret this passage in terms of the later Heidegger, I can say that Heidegger's investigations here into λόγος are striving toward an ontological dimension to which the human being is submitted and through which life is lived.

3. Uncanniness (*Unheimlichkeit*) is the experience of not being at home. This term reappears in *Being and Time*, where Heidegger explains that anxiety reveals to Dasein that it is not at home among beings. Facticity belongs to this experience insofar as anxiety discloses Dasein in its thrownness and thus in its facticity, that is, Dasein is not the master of its own origin, and it is referentially dependent on other beings. Insofar as Dasein is not at home in its dependence on other beings, it comes to recognize that its commerce with beings is not its true home, and so it is called upon to recognize that its true home is not any particular being. Its true home is not a being or thing, it is no-thing, or nothing, or Being, since Being is precisely not a being or thing. In this lecture course from 1923–24, uncanniness is used in a similar way. The experience of uncanniness reveals to Dasein its no-thingness. Importantly, Heidegger claims here that since science comports itself exclusively with beings and not with the question of nothingness, it closes off the possibility for uncanniness. Uncanniness, he says, can only be experienced through everydayness.

8. Rhetoric

1. P. Christopher Smith has written an excellent article on this lecture course titled "The Uses and Abuses of Aristotle's Rhetoric in Heidegger's Fundamental Ontology: The Lecture Course, Summer 1924" (Smith 1995). Kisiel presents an interesting and very insightful analysis of this course in his essay "Situating Rhetorical Politics in Heidegger's Protopractical Ontology, 1923–1925: The French Occupy the Ruhr," which focuses on political life and political rhetoric in the light of the political situation in Germany in 1924, the year this lecture was delivered (Kisiel 2000). I restrict my analysis to the text itself. Also, I deal with the material somewhat differently from the way both Smith and Kisiel treat it insofar as I address the possibility of developing a kind of authentic factical speaking on Heidegger's terms. Smith acknowledges that Heidegger deconstructs scientific demonstration and theoretical dialectic down into the sphere of factical-rhetorical speaking but concludes that he ultimately adopts a

visual, theoretical paradigm that prevents a genuine dialogue with others. Although Kisiel does not discuss "authentic" speaking as such in his article, he confirmed in private conversation that such an attempt can be made through this remarkable lecture course. For a good basic introduction to this course, see Kisiel 1993, 286–301.

In his introduction to *Heidegger and Rhetoric*, a book he co-edited with Ansgar Kemman, Daniel M. Gross situates Heidegger's work in this course into the philosophical history of rhetoric as well as into debates about politics and humanism. In this interesting collection, every essay except for one is chiefly devoted to this lecture course from 1924. As a whole, these essays show how Heidegger's interest in rhetorical speech in this lecture course reflects an attempt to develop discursive practices grounded in everyday modes of speaking, which are then able to address issues pertaining to ethical and political life. But every essay except for one sees a discontinuity between the 1924 course and what *Being and Time* says about language and everydayness. Gross, himself, is sensitive to the subtle shifts of emphasis that take place between this lecture course and *Being and Time*, especially with respect to the place of everydayness and to the resoluteness of Dasein, but he draws too strong a connection between Heidegger's turn away from proto-communitarian rhetoric in this course and toward totalitarian politics. I do not think we can say that Heidegger's association with National Socialism is connected to his having moved "decisively out of the emotional public sphere" in *Being and Time* (Gross 2005, 40). On the contrary, he moved decisively into the "emotional public sphere," with tragic results. Indirectly, Kisiel challenges Gross's reading of *Being and Time* in his essay from the same book, which is an elaboration of the essay mentioned above. Kisiel writes, "But what many readers (Bourdieu, Marcuse, Arendt) of the political-rhetorical ontology of *Being and Time* have not noticed is that Heidegger also formally outlines a path out of the leveling impersonal anonymity of the masses whereby a 'being-with-one-another in the same world . . . in *communication* and in *struggle* (Kampf)' [*BT,* 384/436 Kisiel's emphasis of these two rhetorical dimensions] finds its way to an authentic grouping by actualizing the historical uniqueness and self-identity of its community" (Kisiel 2005, 142). Looking at this lecture course in the context of what Heidegger has been saying in his lecture courses since 1919 about factical life and since 1923 about factical language, as I am doing in this book, we see that even in his early work on language and rhetoric, he was attentive to the deceptions and distortions built into the facticity of speaking, along with the possibility for cultivating authentic language and an authentic life. In *Being and Time* we find the same ambiguity in life and language as we find in this course. There may be a shift in emphasis, but there is not a discontinuity between the two texts.

2. The extent to which Heidegger is a philologist is explored by Mark Michalski in his essay "Hermeneutic Phenomenology as Philology." He affirms that Heidegger understands philology as a science of human existence (Michalski 2005, 74) and that Heidegger's study of concepts is a way of exploring the contexts of everyday Greek discourse (70).

3. Moving closer to the more well known breakthroughs into the meaning of language that Heidegger made in *Being and Time* and afterward, we will see that language undergoes a more radical transformation so that the authentic meaning of language is not speech but rather the more original sense of letting beings come to words through ontological naming, that is, naming beings in their Being by letting them come to language as what they are in and through names and words.

4. The connection between hermeneutics and dialogue has been taken up by Hans-Georg Gadamer, unquestionably one of the staunchest proponents of Heidegger's thought. As one of Heidegger's students during the mid-1920s, he had a unique and, as it turns out, lasting exposure to Heidegger's beginnings. It is telling that the first lecture course of Heidegger's that he attended was "Ontology: The Hermeneutics of Facticity" (1923) and that now the philosophical movement with which Gadamer's name is most closely associated is hermeneutics. Gadamer has advanced beyond Heidegger and made hermeneutics his own unique way of thinking, but it is equally undeniable that he has passed through doors that Heidegger opened. Particularly important is the dialogical aspect of Gadamerian hermeneutics. With Heidegger's understanding of Being as ἀλήθεια, coupled with the Platonic model of dialectical discussion, Gadamer has developed a theory of understanding that is grounded in dialogue and that endeavors to uncover hidden prejudices that are built into our language. The latter, to be sure, is an appropriation of Heidegger. For Gadamer, the simultaneity of revealment and concealment that belongs to the truth of Being as ἀλήθεια proves that there are distortions in the language we use: hidden prejudices and predispositions that inform what we say and how we understand the world. Gadamer writes, "The recognition that all understanding inevitably involves some prejudice gives the hermeneutical problem its real thrust" (Gadamer 1994c, 270). Through discussion (*Dialog, Gespräch*), however, we have the capacity to uncover these prejudices. This will happen only when we open ourselves to the other person with whom we are speaking. Gadamer writes, "Dialogical communication is in principle impossible when one of the partners in the dialogue does not really open himself [*sich wirklich freilassen*] to the discussion" (Gadamer 1997, 56). This applies equally well to the reading of a text, what in *Truth and Method*, Gadamer calls being "sensitive to the text's alterity" (Gadamer 1994c, 269). In both cases, Gadamerian dialogue captures the three ecstases of temporality. As a discussion moves forward, trying to come to terms with a particular problem, it also moves backward, as each interlocutor (or the reader) attempts to uncover hidden prejudices and predispositions within himself or herself. All of this takes place in the present insofar as a particular situation (a text or a philosophical problem) is being discussed. Since, according to the structure of ἀλήθεια, there is always the concealment ingredient to that which is revealed in the conversation, the process of uncovering prejudices through dialogue is never-ending: in Heideggerian terms we are always on the way (*Unterwegs*) to language; in Platonic terms, this explains why every dialogue ends in an ἀπορία and thus the need for further thought.

It is worth mentioning that the distortion ingredient to the negativity of ἀλήθεια becomes particularly evident here. Both Gadamer and Heidegger stress that human beings are historically constituted and that this is manifest in the prejudices and predispositions hidden in the language we use; what we say is determined by these historically constituted yet unexpressed hidden motives. In this sense, Gadamer says, in conjunction with what Heidegger means by ἀλήθεια, that "what is not said first puts what is said into words which can reach us" (Gadamer 1997, 26). As much as these unsaid prejudices play a role in how our understanding of the world gets projected and articulated, they also place limitations and distortions on that projection and articulation, as when a particular prejudice, unbeknown to you yet operative in your understanding, informs how you grasp something and what you say about it. The consequences of such hidden prejudices can be disastrous. This is one sense of factical errancy grounded in the truth of Being as ἀλήθεια. The process of trying to uncover those prejudices is certainly an important and worthwhile activity. Indeed, this is what facticity makes possible, that is, looking not just at "the facts" but at the motivations (prejudices and predispositions) that enter in to how we understand and interpret those facts. *However*, as Hannah Arendt has pointed out, the modus operandi of every fascist regime has been to turn every matter of fact into a question of motive. If she is right, then as much as facticity opens human beings to their historically constituted situations, and thus to their hidden prejudices, it also opens them to the distortions of fascist terror. The negativity of ἀλήθεια, the simultaneity of revealment and distortion, is at work here.

Paying specific attention to facticity, Gadamer has said that *G* 61, *Phenomenological Interpretations of Aristotle: Initiation into Phenomenological Research*, the lecture course in which Heidegger addresses factical life with the most rigor, "is one of the most important preparatory paths in Heidegger's experience of thinking" (Gadamer 1994b, 20). This is the case, he claims, because of important similarities between the hermeneutics of facticity and the existential analytic of Dasein in *Being and Time*. With explicit reference to Richardson's distinction between Heidegger I and Heidegger II, Gadamer confirms the hypothesis that Heidegger followed one path. Moreover, he claims that facticity was a critical first step along that path—and, therefore, a critical first step in working out the Being-question—insofar as it involves the retrieval of origins from within theoretical objectivity. Significantly, speaking belongs to this process of retrieval: "Facticity, which lays itself out, which interprets itself, does not bring interpretive concepts to bear on itself, rather it is a kind of conceptual speaking that wants to hold onto its origin and, thus, onto its own life's breath, once it is translated into the form of a theoretical statement" (Gadamer 1994b, 25). This is an important passage. It confirms that from the beginning facticity meant for Heidegger probing into origins in search of an original conceptual speaking. Although Gadamer does not pursue the dimension of speaking here, he certainly believes that facticity involves the retrieval of originary speaking from the theoretical statement, that is, from the λόγος ἀποφαντικός. A key thesis of this book is that in Heidegger's analyses of the Greeks, by deconstructing theoretical λόγος back down into the factical life-world from which it originally springs, that is, from the sphere of historically constituted human beings who are in the world speaking with one another, he makes a kind of authentic speaking possible. Insofar as facticity is a retrieval of origin and that origin, as we know, is Being as ἀλήθεια, then this authentic, original, conceptual, factical speaking is an articulation of life's retrieval of Being as ἀλήθεια.

5. Michel Haar provides an extremely interesting analysis of the facticity of the human body in chapter 3 of his book *The Song of the Earth: Heidegger and the Grounds of the History of Being* (Haar 1993b, 34–38). He shows there that the body belongs to Dasein's thrownness into the world. Thrown affectivity is the body's factical openness to the world, that is, the historically constituted situation of the body in the world, with all the cultural interpretations that that involves. Accordingly, Dasein's attunement or *Stimmung* also affects its intraworldly (cultural, historical) body. In this sense, the factical attunement of Dasein's worldly body broadens bodily stimuli to a qualitative interpretation of what those stimuli mean in the light of the factical situations in which they occur.

6. Heidegger identifies five dimensions of σῶματα upon which ontology is founded in Aristotle:

> ὑποκείμενον, which are those things which are present-at-hand (*Vorhanden*), already there, such as "animals, plants, humans, mountains, sun" (*G* 18:30/22)
>
> αἴτιον ἐνυπάρχον, the cause of that which is there from the beginning, which accompanies what is present-at-hand. One example of this is the soul. Heidegger explains that the soul is an indication of the Being-character of a being that is present-at-hand. As such, it determines the Being of a living being, so that that being is not simply present-at-hand. More than that, it is *there*, and here the *there* of a being is an indication of its factical livedness: It can "see, do, move itself" (*G* 18:30/23). So, the two "moments" of this οὐσία, since the soul is an οὐσία, are κρίνειν and κινεῖν: "the 'drawing out' against something else, orienting oneself in a world" and the "moving oneself therein" (*G* 18:31/23). Already we can see that the soul embodies the basic features of the facticity of speaking. The primary function of λόγος is κρίνειν and the basic feature of life is κίνησις. Since rhetoric involves guiding the soul of the other, it, rhetoric, correlates to that factical speaking, the moving/setting-into-relief, which constitute the two basic moments of the soul.
>
> μόριον ἐνυπάρχον, a piece or portion of that which is there from the beginning, for example the surface of a body. The surface of a body is not the whole body, only a part. Nonetheless, that surface is a determination of the Being of that being in that it determines the "that-there" of the being, which places a limitation on the being. Thus, the μόριον ἐνυπάρχον "'describes' the being, insofar as it is present-at-hand as a 'that there,' so that this 'that there' is grasped, determined, visible in its Being-ness" (*G* 18:31/23). Heidegger points out that the that-there of a being was particularly important

to the Greeks as a determination of the Being of a being because of the fact that limitation (*Grenzhaftigkeit*) was, for them, such a fundamental dimension of the *there* of a being.

τὸ τί ἦν εἶναι, the What-Being (*Was-Sein*) of a being, which is an indication of the provenance of a being, what it was or, more precisely, "what it already was, where it comes from in its Being, with regard to its *origin*, coming-from into the there-being [*Daseiendes*]" (*G* 18:32/23). In this sense, the τὸ τί ἦν εἶναι is an indication of the particularity (*Jeweiligkeit*, τὰ καθ᾽ ἕκαστα) of a being, the way in which it is *there* in such a way that it comes to its *there* from an origin. Heidegger admits that this particularity is not at all evident in the everydayness of life; it is passed over; it disappears within the everyday: "Only by some kind of event of a peculiar sort can something with which I interact daily suddenly become present to me. Particularity is not in the first place and directly given. One must take distance in order to see everydayness in its Dasein, to have it present" (*G* 18:32/24).

That peculiar event that takes distance and, in doing so, makes everydayness present is an event that recognizes the origin of a being, its provenance. This is an important point, because even though a certain distance is taken in that event (which, here and in *Being and Time*, Heidegger will call anxiety), insofar as the provenance of a being is made present in its *there*, this taking-distance is anything but the intuiting of essences. Rather, it makes present the history (*Geschichte*) of a being, where it comes from. Heidegger says, "I see a there-being [*Daseiendes*] authentically in its Being, when I see it in its *history*" (*G* 18:35/26). This history is the authentic Being-dimension that obtrudes in beings when they are viewed with regard to their particularity through that event that makes them present in their everydayness.

This τὸ τί ἦν εἶναι is a determination of the "was" of a being, which Heidegger says is the "Dasein of a being" in terms of its origin (*G* 18:35/26). Significantly, speaking comes from that origin; it comes from history: "When the human being is determined as ζῷον λόγον ἔχον, then speaking *comes from* its ζῷον-, 'living-thing'—Being, this is its γένος" (*G* 18:35/26). The "was" of the human being is its living-ness—a human being is as having been; if the human being is defined as a being that has speech (ζῷον λόγον ἔχον), then speaking emerges from life construed as origin, as γένος. To say life is to say origin or, more originally, Being; in that speaking comes from life, it comes from the originary dimension of Being.

εἶδος, the way a being looks. This is, Heidegger says, the basic way in which a being is lived. To live in a house is to live in the εἶδος of the house, the way it looks.

With these five determinations of bodies, σώματα, or beings, Heidegger has, through Aristotle, achieved a basic orientation for the meaning of the *there* of a being: (1) it is present-at-hand; (2) it is *there* as Being-in-the-world; it exists; it has a soul and lives and speaks factically; (3) it is fundamentally limited; (4) it has an origin and can be viewed in the way it comes to presence; (5) it has a certain look to it. As I continue to pursue the meaning of factical language, keep these determinations in mind because such a language will address the *there* of beings in their Being. Language is factical insofar as it addresses *beings* in their Being. It is basically an ontic consideration. However, as we have seen, οὐσία is an indication of the ontological difference. Hence, authentic speaking will be a modification of factical speaking in that it will give voice to the Being-character immanent within beings.

7. It should not be thought that φωνή, sounds, which are the ways that animals encounter the world as either pleasant or distressing, are beneath human beings. The encountering dimensions of animals through φωνή are there within the ways of encountering for human beings. Indeed, they belong to the Being, οὐσία, of human beings. For one, the sounds of animals are indications of the pleasant or distressing (temptations and warnings, for example), which reveal an original togetherness. Their φωνή reveal that they are already in a world with other animals. This, says Heidegger, provides the necessary background for investigating λόγος because sound is a dimension of λόγος that reveals the original and essential togetherness of humans. The φωνή of animals, in that they are indications of the pleasant and the distressing, can reveal the authentic possibility of the Being of an animal, which is the disposition of ἡδυ, the pleasant. The pleasant is a disposition (*Befindlichkeit*) that belongs essentially to the Being of an animal, and it is there when the animal is what it is according to its Being.

For this reason, the human dimension of pleasure, ἡδονή, will be a modification of the pleasant, which is the disposition that indicates the authentic possibility of Being for animals (G18 53/38). Also, φωνή, the sounds of animals, because they reveal Being-with-others as the Being of animals, provide an important acoustical context for understanding the λόγος of human beings. Sound is an essential dimension of human λόγος because it speaks to the original disposedness of human beings to living together in a world. Heidegger is opening λόγος to the rhetorical dimensions of disposition and togetherness. That requires a retrieval of the φωνή that are acutely significant to animals. Heidegger is not reducing human λόγος to the φωνή of animals, rather he is opening λόγος to the disposedness and the togetherness that are co-determinations of human λόγος which can get covered over.

8. One example of this is Plato, who maintained that movement is itself an Idea in which individual beings participate. As such, movement does not belong intrinsically to a being; it belongs to Being. Other categories of indeterminateness that were used to explain movement were otherness, inequality, and non-being (*G* 18:318–20/215–17). Even the latter is unsatisfactory because if non-being is just a determination of Being and not of the Being of a being, then everything, per se (all Being), is in movement while particular beings are not in movement. If you say that beings move because movement is Being (even as non-being), then the

beings themselves are not limited. The sun and stars will *always* move across the sky. They move, but they are not limited, which means that they do not really move, Being moves them. To recognize the movement that belongs to the Being of a being is to take account of the being in its intrinsic movement and thus in its limitedness.

9. Note here that Heidegger has found in Aristotle the same dynamic that he found in Paul: the experience of the immanence of nothingness. See Chapter 2.

10. The experiences that Aristotle attributes to the soul are actually experiences of the body, the πάθη, which are undergone physically. Heidegger points out the connection between πάθη and σῶμα to show that bodiliness must be taken into consideration if one is going to "secure the full Being of the human being" (*G* 18:199/134). To that end, he explains that thinking (νοῦς) is related to and dependent on body (σῶμα) because νοῦς is characterized by memory and imagination, and is, therefore, the experience of remembering or imagining something that the body underwent, a passion or πάθος.

More important, Heidegger discusses the πάθη of fear and anxiety here and explains that they, too, have a relation to bodiliness. To be sure, the clear distinction between fear and anxiety in *Being and Time* is not as evident in this course. The point that he makes, though, is that sometimes we fear something that is not there. Fear is a πάθος that sometimes comes over us even when there is nothing there to fear (this is anxiety). This means that fear and anxiety must be intrinsic possibilities of the Being of the human being. As such, they are πάθη that are grounded in the body itself, in bodiliness, because Dasein is Being-in-the-world. He writes, "In the phenomenon of πάθος, body is co-constitutive, namely as something that carries in itself the possibility of Being in a world" (*G* 18:204/137). Fear and anxiety are possibilities of the Being of the human being as a living and embodied being that is in the world. This is important for my purposes because Heidegger says that there is a λόγος that is thereby also addressed in the living, embodied experience of fear as anxiety.

11. Gadamer claims that Heidegger's assertion here about uncanniness as the origin of speaking is "said in slight mockery" (Gadamer 2005, 58). Following up on his remarks, however, Gadamer is clearly criticizing the idea that speaking is somehow motivated by fear. But uncanniness is different from fear, and Heidegger's point here is about the ontological origin of speaking. Gadamer is right that fear is a not a genuine motivation for true discourse, but I do not see Heidegger trying to make that point in this lecture course.

12. Although Heidegger does not ever attempt to work out the specifics of an authentic rhetorical speaking, that task is taken up by Michael J. Hyde in his essay "A Matter of the Heart." Hyde reads this lecture course in order to do his own measure of violence to Heidegger's admittedly violent reading of Aristotle. He connects the call of conscience with epideictic rhetoric. Hyde's focus, like Smith's, is on the enthymeme and the various ways in which the everyday modes of discourse that we find in rhetorical speech enrich "the emotional fabric of a person's existence" (Hyde 2005, 89). But Hyde's analysis is ethical in a way that

Heidegger's is not. Heidegger is attempting to probe the ontological ground of ethics in the ἦθος of human existence, connecting human existence with ontological concerns about the meaning of Being itself. Hyde is more interested in how rhetorical speech about human existence might develop into a moral language and even into "systems of morality" (Hyde 2005, 91). As such, he laments the later Heidegger's turn away from "the truth and goodness of rhetoric" (99). Heidegger's focus was never on the truth and goodness of rhetoric; he was too sensitive to the Being of rhetoric (the Being of language), which can be used both for good and for ill. Throughout this book, I am attempting to show that language opens up the human being not only to responsible thought and action but also to deception and error. In the Conclusion, I demonstrate how Heidegger provides ways of thinking about error and perversity as integral dimensions of authentic human existence, which Hyde would, I believe, not abide.

13. Although Gadamer has appropriated Heidegger's insight into Being as ἀλήθεια and developed, with additional help from Plato, a philosophy of hermeneutic discussion from it, P. Christopher Smith, a student of Gadamer's, has investigated with the utmost rigor whether Heidegger himself ever truly succeeded in retrieving the existential possibility for audible voice and the rhetorical speech of people living in the world. Looking specifically at Heidegger's analyses of Aristotle, especially the Aristotle Introduction of 1922 and the 1924 course on Aristotle's *Rhetoric*, Smith is interested in how well Heidegger is able to read the metaphysical Aristotle of σοφία and the λόγος ἀποφαντικός back down into the practical Aristotle of φρόνησις and rhetoric. Accordingly, he has made extremely valuable contributions to Heidegger scholarship by carrying out the necessary concrete, textual work of showing how Heidegger deconstructs Aristotle's *Physics* and *Metaphysics* down into the *Ethics*. Smith concludes that although Heidegger succeeds in deconstructing much of Aristotle's metaphysical overlay and, thus, succeeds in retrieving the ground of the practical human situation, that is, factical life, Heidegger still falls prey to a visual, theoretical paradigm, indeed the same one to which Aristotle fell prey. As such, Smith says that the project of a hermeneutics of facticity is fraught with tensions and contradictions. (Smith 1995, 317).

These conflicts become particularly important when Heidegger writes about rhetoric. On the one hand, Smith explains that in the rhetoric course, Heidegger is able to show that scientific demonstration is an abstraction from theoretical dialectic, which is itself a derivative form of rhetoric's practical means of persuasion (Smith 1995, 316). By grounding science and dialectic in rhetoric, Heidegger effectively brings λόγος and πάθος back together, thus assigning to the πάθη, feelings and emotions, a philosophical importance that the history of philosophy since Aristotle's *Rhetoric* has denied them. For example, Heidegger shows that enthymemes are more than just truncated syllogisms, for they are aimed at "the practical will," that is, how we feel; in this vein Smith points out that the term "enthymeme" comes from "*enthumeisthai*, or 'taking something to heart [*thumos*]'" (Smith 1995, 322). In all of this, theoretical certainty is replaced by persuasion, conviction, and decision as these are mediated through speech. Overall, Smith believes that Heidegger, through Aristotle, restores philosophical importance to the oral-acoustical/pathetical realm of rhetorical speech, thus establishing the concrete and practical world of people living and speaking together, communicating with each other, and taking care of things as the proper ground for all philosophical inquiry. On the other hand, Smith also points out that in the 1924 course, *Being and Time*, and elsewhere there are indications of the visual paradigm taking over the acoustical dimension of speech: The motif of light, the voiceless call of conscience, and the analysis of idle talk in *Being and Time* all attest to this. In the end, Smith believes that Heidegger has "foreclosed on the possibility of hearing the rhetorical . . . voiced word spoken to us by another outside of us" (Smith 1995, 331). This is brought on by a "fascination" with the theoretical and a general disdain for the fallen idle talk of the they (*das Man*) (318–19).

14. Nancy S. Streuver puts the point even more strongly: "Politics, according to SS 1924, in confronting and undertaking these tasks of discursive negotiation constitutes the authentic life. Rhetoric gives us the means for and analysis of authenticity" (Streuver 2005, 124).

15. Throughout this lecture course, Heidegger talks about ethics. This is not surprising considering that he spends a considerable amount of time analyzing Aristotle's *Nicomachean Ethics*. Note, though, that he rarely employs the German word *Ethik*. In almost every case, when he talks about ethics he uses the Greek expression, ἀρετὴ ἠθική meaning ethical excellence. When Heidegger speaks about *Ethik*, he is referring to normativity, which has to do with ethical principles. By referring to the Greek ἀρετὴ ἠθική, rather than the German *Ethik*, Heidegger keeps his discussion of "ethics" closer to the original meaning of "ethics" as ἦθος. In this lecture course, he wants to show how ἀρετὴ ἠθική, ethical excellence is grounded in ἦθος, an ontological structure that indicates how one carries oneself in the world with others. Thus, ἦθος refers neither to a set of norms or principles, nor to how people ought to act according to norms and principles. However, his discussion of ἦθος and ἀρετὴ ἠθική does have a moral valence in that it refers to how people can act in order to become who they are, that is, how one can achieve oneself, one's own end.

16. As Heidegger says, "In this bringing to language of the συμφέρον, of the world, as it is concretely there, is then the world authentically first brought into its there. The Now and Here of the Being of the human being becomes explicit in a particular kind of contemplation; through this contemplation the human being is, to use modern language, in the concrete situation, in the καιρόσ. The Being of the human being is in this λόγος; λέγειν as λογίζεσθαι is a having-there of the world, so that I am in it in a certain way that is now and here" (*G* 18:59/42).

17. Streuver makes a sharp, yet confusing distinction between *Alltäglichkeit* and everydayness, confusing because everydayness is the translation of *Alltäglichkeit*. Referencing the work of William Blattner (*Heidegger's Temporal Idealism* [Cambridge: Cambridge University Press, 1999]), Streuver writes, "If Blattner is correct that Alltäglichkeit is later eroded by the philosophical program of *Being*

and Time, and slides into everydayness, ordinariness, and inauthenticity, in the 1924 lectures the extraordinary emphasis on Hellenic political rhetoric as originary matrix is at the same time an emphasis on Alltäglichkeit as timeful, or the solvent of eternity, the mode of eroding the timeless" (Streuver 2005, 126). Although Heidegger's descriptions of everydayness are more negative in *Being and Time*, his understanding of it in that text is not so different that it warrants a different term. Authentic life draws on average everydayness both in Heidegger's early lecture courses and in *Being and Time*.

9. Sophistry

1. See in particular Gonzalez 1997. Gonzalez says that since Plato made no distinction between φρόνησις and σοφία, philosophy was for him always immersed in human activity, always limited and unfulfilled, and therefore never a pure and absolute seeing of the things themselves. It was Aristotle who first made the distinction between φρόνησις and σοφία. Hence, according to Gonzalez, it was Aristotle who turned the highest form of philosophy into the nonrelational pure seeing of θεωρία. Accordingly, Gonzalez interprets this passage as saying that Heidegger, siding with Aristotle, is critical of Plato's dialectic because it was merely under way to θεωρεῖν without ever reaching it. He sees Heidegger and Aristotle together looking down on Platonic dialectic from the vantage of philosophical θεωρία (Aristotle's "first philosophy") and its capacity for a pure seeing of the things themselves. It seems clear from this passage, however, that Heidegger is not evaluating Platonic dialectic from the point of Aristotle's "first philosophy" but rather from Aristotle's *Rhetoric*. Hence, the problem that Heidegger identifies here is not that Platonic dialectic was merely under way; the problem has to do with what it was under way toward, namely, θεωρεῖν. Whether Heidegger's understanding of dialectic is fair to Plato or not is immaterial in this situation to the fact that he believed that Plato's dialectic culminated in θεωρεῖν, a pure seeing of the Ideas, which meant to extricate itself from human existence— and, thus, from λόγος and rhetoric—at which point it would cease to be still under way. Recall that in the *Republic*, the philosopher, who has *seen* the Ideas, goes back down into the cave, into the city, only under extreme duress and against his own nature. Heidegger ascribes to this interpretation of Plato's dialectic. He writes unambiguously, "Above all we must exclude—this should be clear on the basis of the foregoing—every extrinsic technical interpretation of dialectic. *The essential element in it is the* ὁρᾶν," pure seeing (*G* 19:349/242). This is why he believes that Aristotle's *Rhetoric, not* his "first philosophy," provides a foundation for speaking that is more concrete, more concerned with human existence, than Plato's dialectic and what Heidegger believed to be its culmination in a seeing of the Ideas.

In this light, I argue that Heidegger uses the *Rhetoric*, that is, λόγος as rhetorical speaking, the "λέγειν within life," to deconstruct *both* Platonic dialectic (and its "pure seeing") *and* Aristotle's "first philosophy" (and *its* "pure seeing") back down into the world of human existence. Later in this chapter I show how Heidegger demonstrates that Platonic λόγος (unbeknown to Plato) is immersed in what Heidegger understands as Being-in-the-world, human existence. In the last chapter we saw how important the *Rhetoric* is to Heidegger's understanding of Aristotle. Even in this course, though, one hears the importance of λόγος and λέγειν to Heidegger's deconstruction of Aristotelian seeing. At the very end of his analysis of Aristotle, indeed, in the final paragraph of that analysis, just before he moves to the main part of the lecture course, "Plato's Research into Being: Interpretation of the *Sophist*," Heidegger says this to his students about Aristotle: "As we have seen, Aristotle strives, precisely with his idea of σοφία, to go beyond λόγος to a νοεῖν that is free of λέγειν. *But closer inspection shows* that even his determination of the ultimate ἀρχη, the ἀδιαίρετον, is acquired only within an orientation toward λόγος" (*G* 19:224/155, my emphasis). In fairness to both Plato and Aristotle, Heidegger recognizes that they both considered θεωρία, pure seeing, to be the highest and most excellent form of philosophy. This tendency belonged to Greek philosophy as such and its understanding of Being as pure presence. Through a positive deconstruction of both senses of seeing, Heidegger traces them back to λόγος, human existence as Being-in-the-world, and human speaking in an effort to develop a practical ontology and thus the Being, not of pure presence, but of factical human life. On this topic see also Brogan 1997, 11, where he writes, "In Heidegger's view, one indication of the fact that Aristotle's philosophy is the culmination of Platonic and Greek thought is his ability to offer a positive and detailed articulation of the legitimate domain of rhetoric."

2. A quick look forward bears this out. In *Being and Time*, Heidegger reaffirms that the "ontological clue" handed down to us from the Greeks needs to be reinterpreted in terms of λόγος in order for a more radical understanding of Being to be reached. He writes, "As the ontological clue gets progressively worked out—namely, in the 'hermeneutic' of the λόγος—it becomes increasingly possible to grasp the problem of Being in a more radical fashion" (*BT* 25/47).

3. "*The* λέγειν *in every discourse is present first of all in its being uttered, in its being spoken out loud, in its phonetic character.* This sound presents itself, and encounters me, *within the being, that is there in the world.* The word is spoken, it is outside, on the streets, just as a wagon creaks on the pavement. Creaking and speaking thus present themselves openly; they are conspicuous" (*G* 19 583/404).

Conclusion

1. Dahlstrom affirms here that "they are themselves derived from the way of life that informs the normal use of language" (Dahlstrom 1994, 785).

2. Guignon 1984, 321–22.

3. Kisiel 1993, 156.

4. Van Buren writes, "Heidegger proposed an ontological destruction or deconstruction of the history of philosophy, so as to expose its unacknowledged origins in concrete historical life, in terms of which philosophy could be repeated or retrieved in a new beginning" (van Buren 1992, 171).

5. Van Buren 1992, p. 177.

6. Kisiel 1993, p. 126.

7. Heidegger writes in this lecture course that that the phenomenological destruction is based on "fundamental experience" and on the meanings that are embedded in our preconception. It is not simply the return to a prior way of thinking or experiencing but a cultivation of our current preconceptions: "Phenomenological destruction—as a fundamental part of phenomenological philosophizing—is therefore not without direction; it does not fortuitously take up meanings of words in order to explain them by means of other taken up meanings. It is not mere shattering but a 'directed' deconstruction [*Abbau*]. It leads into the situation of the pursuit of the pre-delineations, of the enactment [*Vollzug*] of the preconception and thereby of the fundamental experience. From that it is evident that all phenomenological-critical destruction is *bound to preconception*—and therefore not ultimately primordial and ultimately decisive, but presupposes philosophical fundamental experiences" (*G* 59:35/25).

8. Given the way that Heidegger talks about authenticity and inauthenticity in *Being and Time*, it is not surprising that one might reach the conclusion that he is presenting a choice between two different ways of life. Further, viewing Heidegger from the perspective of Luther, as van Buren and Crowe both do, one might see in Heidegger's destruction a religious dismantling of one's sinful life and a subsequent rebirth into a new life.

9. Crowe 2006, 257.

10. Ibid., 255.

11. Ibid., 263.

12. Fehér 2010, 49.

13. Ibid., 57.

14. In doing so, Heidegger draws upon Aristotle's claim in the *Nicomachean Ethics* that in trying to be virtuous, "it is easy to miss the mark, difficult to hit it" (*NE* 2.1106b28).

15. Crowe 2006, 241–42.

16. This lecture can be found in Kisiel and Sheehan 2007, 214–37. The quotation is on page 222.

17. It is, Heidegger writes, "something that was already originally discovered once and at one time had been a proper possession of someone who had original knowledge of it, submerges once more and thus becomes something that 'everyone' understands, 'everyone' repeats and says to others until it becomes 'valid.' What was brought forth once in an originary and creative manner now becomes uprooted. It loses its ground." See Kisiel and Sheehan 2007, 225. An example of this, for Heidegger, would be the meaning of λογός itself. Λογός is always understood to mean reason, rationality, or logic. But that is because it has lost its ground. The original meaning of λογός, what it meant to the Greeks, has been lost. To them it meant speaking. It meant Being in the world with others and speaking with them.

18. Crowe 2006, 256.

19. Richardson 1977, 136. When William Richardson's book, *Heidegger. Through Phenomenology to Thought* was published, in 1963, the English-speaking

world was presented, for the first time, with a comprehensive study of Heidegger's work. Richardson pursues the meaning of foundational thinking through almost the entire Heideggerian corpus available at that time. He determines that for Heidegger foundational thinking or thought is a meditation on Being as the process of truth, whereby truth (ἀλήθεια) means the positive-negative lighting process that takes place within beings. The human being, as ek-sistent, is uniquely open to this process, standing out into the truth of Being; hence, the human being is the there of Being among beings, or Dasein. In Heidegger's later writings, where he identifies Being with Logos, the process of truth as ἀλήθεια comes to pass through the correspondence between Dasein and Being as Logos. This correspondence is thought or poetizing and marks the coming-to-pass of Being (Logos) as "Truth . . . Ground . . . Utterance" (Richardson 1974, 501).

In Richardson's conclusion, he maintains that the important relation between Being and language was evident in Heidegger's writings from the very beginning, albeit in an obscure and inchoate fashion. This and the fact that from early on Heidegger was engaged in the process of historical retrieval suggest to Richardson that Heidegger followed a single path, which, though it led through phenomenology to the thinking of Being, maintained an important unity. The original unity of this path Richardson calls the Ur-Heidegger, "the living center of Heidegger's experience" (Richardson 1974, 628). Because of the unity of this experience, Richardson claims that the early Heidegger's (Heidegger I's) phenomenological analysis of Dasein's finite transcendence unto Being is one with the later Heidegger's (Heidegger II's) analysis of Being itself as an active force that presents itself to and withdraws from, conceals itself from, ek-sistent Dasein. The two experiences are one insofar as Heidegger II is a retrieval of Heidegger I, a retrieval of that which remained latent, unsaid, within Heidegger I but which, nonetheless, made Heidegger I possible. In this sense, Heidegger II is more original than Heidegger I. Importantly, the turn itself from I to II was brought about when Heidegger focused his attention on the negativity of truth as such, whereby he came to "appreciate the full import of what it means for concealment somehow to precede non-concealment in the coming-to-pass of a-letheia" (624) Therefore, the Ur-Heidegger, which is more original than both I and II, is sheer negativity, the lethe of a-letheia, about which nothing can be said except that it is "Wealth, Treasure, a hidden Fullness" (640).

20. The texts available to Richardson that addressed the concept of facticity were *Being and Time* and *The Essence of Ground*, both of which contain important references to facticity, even though, clearly, facticity no longer carries the same weight in these works as it did in the early lecture courses. In both texts, facticity involves Dasein's situation in the world as a historical being. Richardson emphasizes that because of Dasein's factical historicality, it is a task that is still to be achieved. This means that Dasein's Being is an issue for it. As such, facticity connotes Dasein's "existence, with all the dynamic propulsion toward Being that this implies" (Richardson 1974, 62n). Moreover, this means that Dasein is historical, that is, that it already is and will continue to be in such a way that it has a past (its origin) and a future (its destiny). Though both of these remain obscure, in-

deed, *because* they remain obscure, Dasein can achieve itself in its origin and, thereby, accept its destiny. This takes place in and through the present, Dasein's factical situation as Being in a world, wherein Dasein projects possibilities for itself. Importantly, Dasein's facticity "contracts this project to the matter of fact situation" (167). Since facticity is Dasein's history, its having been, then it is *history* that contracts Dasein's possibilities. The withdrawal of Dasein's possibilities comes from the past: History places limits on factical human Dasein. Hence, by Richardson's analysis, facticity opens Dasein to its own history as to its own Being in such a way that Being submits Dasein to the profound limitedness of its historically constituted situation.

21. With reference to Levinas, Jacques Taminiaux believes that Heidegger's fascination with the theoretical causes him to blank out the practical realm of human otherness and to conclude, moreover, that the theoretical is itself the apex of πρᾶξις. This invites, he says, a critical reevaluation of fundamental ontology. Focusing on Aristotle's distinction between φρόνησις (along with its mode of disclosure, πρᾶξις) and τέχνη (along with its mode of disclosure, ποιήσις), Taminiaux provides an excellent account of how Heidegger's appropriation of these concepts into fundamental ontology governs the existential analytic of *Being and Time* (Taminiaux 1991, 111–43, and Taminiaux 1992, 188–207). In particular, ποιήσις-τέχνη becomes production-practical circumspection while πρᾶξις-φρόνησις becomes resoluteness-moment of insight (Taminiaux 1992, 194–95). Taminiaux points out, though, that whereas Aristotelian πρᾶξις "individuates someone at the heart of plurality" (Taminiaux 1992, 195), Heidegger's ontological reappropriation of πρᾶξις as resoluteness is "radically private" (195) and, therefore, opposed to any form of pluralism. In this way, fundamental ontology as Heidegger conceives it reflects a Platonic bias: Like Plato, Heidegger submits the "difference of opinion" and "uncertainty" of πρᾶξις (201) to the theoretical realm of solitary thinking in an effort to obliterate all ambiguity from the public sphere. For both Plato and Heidegger, then, theory becomes "*the highest realization of true* πρᾶξις" (202). In his conclusions, Taminiaux thoroughly explicates all of the ramifications this has concerning Heidegger's involvement with National Socialism. He explains that the πρᾶξις of the *polis*, that is, plural debate and the sharing of speech and acts, is destroyed when it is ontologized first into isolated Dasein and then into the equally isolated Dasein of the State and its "unanimous passion for the Being of beings" (202).

Interestingly, although Francisco Gonzalez draws similar conclusions about Heidegger's ontologization of πρᾶξις, he attributes that ontologization not to Plato but rather to Aristotle for having distinguished σοφία from φρόνησις in the first place (Gonzalez 1997, 16–60). In making this distinction, Gonzalez claims, Aristotle made it possible for σοφία to become something separate from φρόνησις. Accordingly, Aristotle turned contemplation into solitary, nonrelational meditation on true being. By taking over this distinction from Aristotle, Heidegger, too, turns theory into something meditative, solipsistic, and nonrelational. According to Gonzalez, since Plato made no such distinction, theoretical knowledge was for him always immersed in human activity; σοφία could not be disengaged from human πρᾶξις, and so it could not become solitary and nonrelational. This is in marked distinction from Taminiaux, who says that it is precisely the Aristotelian distinction between the two that prevents them from melding together; for Taminiaux this melding together happens in both Plato and Heidegger, so that for each of them σοφία turns into the highest and most excellent form of πρᾶξις.

Responses to these positions have come from many sides, and the issue of Heidegger's ontologization of πρᾶξις is now a matter of some controversy. The stakes are especially high insofar as this issue speaks directly to Heidegger's political debacle and the viability of his philosophy in the light of that debacle. Of note by way of response is the work of Walter Brogan, Franco Volpi, Jean Grondin, William McNeill, Theodore Kisiel, and John van Buren. As a whole, their responses do not so much deny that Heidegger "ontologizes" practical concepts as much as they merely accentuate the practical elements of these ontological structures and, thereby, attempt to develop what Kisiel calls Heidegger's practical ontology, that is, ontological structures that accommodate the temporal flux, ambiguity, and change that belong to the world of concrete human πρᾶξις. For them, Heidegger's philosophy is an ontology of practical life.

Brogan compares what Aristotle says about the moral weakness of an irresolute person to Heidegger's descriptions of "the they." He correspondingly believes that authentic conscience in *Being and Time* is similar to Aristotelian φρόνησις in that both involve the kind of self-understanding (and, accordingly, a recognition of who we are not, that is, of other people), preparedness, resoluteness in making choices, and capacity to acknowledge limits that people need both in political life and in their friendships with others (Brogan 1990, 137–46). Volpi, for his part, provides extremely detailed and concrete analyses of Heidegger's appropriation and ontologization of concepts drawn from Aristotle's practical philosophy. In doing so, he insists that despite the differences between Heidegger and Aristotle that this ontologizing engenders, Heidegger again and again "goes back to the Aristotelian understanding of the moral being of human being" (Volpi 1994, 205. See this article as well as the longer version of it in Volpi 1996, 27–66). This does not make fundamental ontology intrinsically ethical, but it does provide, according to Volpi, a practical horizon against which and in the light of which *Being and Time's* ontological structures need to be read.

Grondin responds directly to the Levinasian critique that fundamental ontology is so totalizing that it subsumes every form of alterity into the sameness of Being and, consequently, totally excludes the possibility of an ethics. He says that ontology was for Heidegger from the beginning an ethical enterprise, which, though it came to Heidegger through Kierkegaard, resembled the young Hegelians' effort to confront self-alienation insofar as it sought to retrieve Dasein from fallenness through a vigilant awareness of Dasein's own Being as Being-in-the-world. This translates, he says, into a critique of ideologies, "a fundamental critique of the levelling effect of prevailing dogmatisms that restrict the possibilities of human freedom and self-awareness," through the hermeneutic task of questioning foundations (Grondin 1994, 352–53). Two interesting comments that Grondin makes in this article are also worth mentioning. On the absence of an ethics in Heidegger's thought he says, "If Heidegger did not develop any specific 'ethics,' it is only because his entire project, founded as it is on the self-preoccupation of Dasein, which is also 'there' collectively, was ethical from the ground up" (355). He also says that the revival of practical philosophy by Gadamer, Strauss, Arendt, Jonas, Patocka, and Tugendhat, even where it conflicts with what Heidegger had originally intended, "has to be traced back to Heidegger, more specifically to the rediscovery of the human being as an essentially caring and ethical being that was made by his hermeneutics of facticity" (355). Indeed, because of the hermeneutics of facticity, Dasein's own Being is a task for which it must take responsibility: This includes taking responsibility for its decisions and for its dialogical existence in a community. (Remarkably, Grondin makes an admittedly controversial move when he suggests that Heidegger's foray into politics in 1933 can be attributed to a principle of responsibility that he felt compelled to heed and that followed directly from his fundamentally ethical philosophical enterprise [356–57]).

Looking at both the *Sophist* course and *Being and Time*, McNeill makes a similar argument by stressing the importance of temporality to the experience of Dasein's authenticity in the *Augenblick* (see especially McNeill 1998). He suggests that the authentic existence of Dasein as presented in *Being and Time* occurs as a fully temporalized unfolding. Conscience, he says, refers to "the full unfolding and accomplishment of *praxis* itself, where this unfolding is to be understood as the coming into full, concrete presence of a finite action" (6). As such, authenticity is a kind of *originary* action that precedes the theory/*praxis* distinction (3). Accordingly, the different themes that characterize authenticity, such as transparency, open resolve, conscience, and especially the *Augenblick*, itself, as well as the Aristotelian concepts that figure into Heidegger's understanding of authenticity such as φρόνησις, αληθεύειν, εὐβουλία, and λόγος need to be understood in terms of authentic Dasein's ecstatic temporal unfolding *into* "the realm of worldly possibility accessible to others" (15). Authenticity is Dasein's resolute openness: as its own (resolute) it leaps ahead "into worldly freedom (i.e., into the openness of the world)" (16).

Kisiel refers to Heidegger's ontologization of *praxis* as practical ontology: an effort "to transform the ontology of constant presence inherited from the Greeks into a radical ontology of history and the temporal human world" (Kisiel 2005, 138). As when McNeill calls authenticity an originary *praxis*, Kisiel says that Heidegger's "temporal ontology" is protopractical, that is, prior to the distinction between theoretical and practical, even if it is, in a sense, more practical insofar as it refers to the Being of temporal human life. Accordingly, Kisiel says that although authenticity is self-referential, this is only the case insofar as one "then accommodates one's own self-referential action to the actions of others by becoming the conscience for others" (139). One does not try to dominate other people, extracting their responsibility from them; rather, one tries to liberate them for their own situations and the finite possibilities of those situations for which they can be responsible. In this framework, rhetoric is an authentic speaking, which, as a kind of "phronetic" power of situational insight mediated through speaking, conveys to others how they can become free for their own situations and thus responsible for (responsive to) the rhetor's particular issue or problem as it relates to them (144–46).

Taking a somewhat different approach, van Buren focuses on the early Heidegger's effort to fuse together different humanist traditions (Aristotle, Kierkegaard, Husserl). Accordingly, he discerns an ethical resonance in Heidegger's appropriation of Aristotle's practical philosophy insofar as the ontologization of practical Aristotelian concepts was part of his project to ground these traditions and other practical humanist disciplines in a phenomenological ontology that then could present human beings with a basic outline for how they can live their lives. Such an ontology, he says, could "provide ethics, politics, and theology only with formal indications of the general characteristics of human existence" and insofar as these disciplines are themselves meant to give only "a rough outline of the practical sphere in question that has to be interpretively concretized in the historical situation of one's own existence" (see van Buren 1992, 178), van Buren concludes that phenomenological ontology can be said to provide important yet basic formal indications for Πραξις, even if these indications then stand in need of concrete, historical actualization. He justifies this claim by pointing to those who have pursued these indications and creatively reinscribed them: He cites Arendt and Gadamer for having taken up Heidegger's suggestive formal indications for new ways of thinking about ethical and political theory (178), and on a broader scale he includes hermeneutics, narrative theory, critical theory, poststructuralism, and American neopragmatism as examples of disciplines that can be counted as "creative effective histories (in Gadamer's sense) of the young Heidegger's fusion of horizons" (181) into a practical ontology.

22. This was said to me during a private conversation in Gadamer's office at the University of Heidelberg in the fall of 1997.

23. This lecture can be found in Kisiel and Sheehan 2007, 275–88. See page 288 for this quotation.

Glossary of Greek Terms and Expressions

ἀγαθόν   (*agathon*) good
ἀγορεύειν   (*agoreuein*) speaking in the marketplace
ἀδιαίρετον   (*adiaireton*) indivisible
αἵρεσις   (*hairesis*) grasping
αἴσθησις   (*aisthēsis*) perception
αἰσθετά   (*aistheta*) perceived things
αἴτιον ἐνυπάρχον   (*aition enuparchon*) the cause of that which is there
                          from the beginning
ἀκούειν   (*akouein*) to hear
αλήθεια   (*alētheia*) truth, unconcealedness
αλήθεια πρακτική   (*alētheia praktikē*) unconcealedness pertaining
                          to action
ἀληθεύειν   (*alētheuein*) to disclose, truthing
ἀληθευτικός   (*alētheutikos*) the one who speaks the truth
ἀνάμνησις   (*anamnēsis*) recollection
ἀνθρώπινον ἀγαθόν   (*anthrōpinon agathon*) the good of the human being
ἀόριστον   (*aoriston*) undetermined
ἀπορία   (*aporia*) blocked way
ἀποφαίνεσθαι   (*apophainesthai*) to let be seen
ἀπόφασις   (*apophasis*) denial
ἀποφαντικός   (*apophantikos*) letting-be-seen
ἀρετή   (*aretē*) excellence
ἀρετή ἠθικη   (*aretē ethikē*) ethical excellence
ἀρχή, ἀρχαί   (*archē, archai*) source, first principle(s)
γενεσις   (*genesis*) origin

γένος	(*genos*) stem, kind
δηλοῦν	(*dēloun*) to disclose, reveal
δηλώματα	(*dēlōmata*) revealing beings
διαίρεσις	(*diaresis*) taking-apart
διαλέγεσθαι	(*dialegesthai*) discussing
διανοεῖν	(*dianoein*) to think through
διχῶς	(*dichōs*) doubling
δίωξις	(*diōzis*) pursuit
δόξα	(*doxa*) opinion
δυνάμει ὄν	(*dunamei on*) being potentially
δύναμις	(*dunamis*) potentiality
ἕξις	(*hexis*) disposition
ἕξις προαιρετικὴ μετὰ λόγου	(*hexis proairetikē meta logou*) anticipatory disposition that takes place in language
εἶδος, εἴδη	(*eidos, eidē*) the way a being looks
εἰς φῶς ἄγειν	(*eis phōs agein*) bringing something to light
ἐλπίς	(*elpis*) hope
ἐλπὶς σωτηρίας	(*elpis sōtērias*) hope for rescue
ἕν (hen) one, unity	
ἓν δηλῶν	(*hen dēloun*) the unity of revealing
ἐνέργεια	(*energeia*) presence
ἐντελέχεια	(*entelecheia*) full presence
ἔργον	(*ergon*) finished work
ἑρμηνεύειν	(*hermēneuein*) to understand, comprehend
ἕτερον	(*heteron*) other
εὐβουλία	(*eubolia*) good counsel
εὐδαιμονία	(*eudaimonia*) happiness
εὐζωία	(*euzōia*) to live well
ζωή	(*zōē*) life
ζῷον	(*zōon*) living being
ζωή πρακτική τις τοῦ λόγον ἔχοντος	(*zōē praktikē tis tou logon echontos*) a practical life, of such a being that has language
ζῷον λόγον ἔχον	(*zōon logon echon*) a living being that speaks
ἡδονη	(*hēdonē*) pleasure
ἡδύ	(*hēdu*) the pleasant
ἦθος	(*ēthos*) comportment
θεωρεῖν	(*theōrein*) to see, behold
θεωρία	(*theōria*) pure seeing
καθ᾽ αὐτο	(*kath auto*) for itself
καιρός	(*kairos*) decisive moment
κατάφασις	(*kataphasis*) affirmation
κατηγορεῖν	(*katēgorein*) to speak, predicate
κινεῖν	(*kinein*) to move
κίνησις	(*kinēsis*) movement

κίνησις κατὰ τόπον	(*kinēsis kata topon*) to move with respect to place
κοινωνία	(*koinōnia*) association, intertwining
κοινωνία τῶν γενῶν	(*koinōnia tōn genōn*) association of kinds
κρίνειν	(*krinein*) to set into relief, to draw something out against something else, to decide
λέγειν	(*legein*) to speak
λέγειν τι	(*legein ti*) an addressing of something
λέγειν τι καθ᾽ αὑτο	(*legein ti kath auto*) an addressing of something for what it itself is
λέγεσθαι	(*legesthai*) speaking
λεγόμενον	(*legomenon*) the spoken
λογίζεσθαι	(*logizesthai*) discussing
λόγον θεου	(*logon theou*) the word of God
λόγος, λόγοι	(*logos, logoi*) speech, word, discourse, discussion, sentence
λόγος ἀποφαντικός	(*logos apophantikos*) an addressing of something, proposition, assertion, judgment
λόγος δέ ἐστι φωνὴ σημαντική	(*logos de esti phōnē sēmantikē*) Language is articulated Being, which means something, it is voice
λόγος οὐσίας	(*logos ousias*) speaking of Being
λόγος τί	(*logos ti*) an addressing of something
λόγος τινός	(*logos tinos*) an addressing of something
λόγος ψευδής	(*logos pseudēs*) false or deceptive speech, the presentation of something as other than it is
λύπη	(*lupē*) pain
λυπηρόν	(*lupēron*) the distressing
μὴ ὄν	(*mē on*) non-being
μόριον ἐνυπάρχον	(*morion enuparchon*) a piece or portion of that which is there from the beginning
νοεῖν	(*noein*) to understand, discern
νόησις	(*noēsis*) understanding, discernment
νοῦς	(*nous*) understanding, discernment
οἴεσθαι	(*oiesthai*) loss of hope
ὅλον	(*holon*) whole
ὁμιλία	(*homilia*) communion, being-together
ὄν, ὄντα	(*on, onta*) being, beings
ὄν ὡς αληθές	(*on hōs alēthes*) the being in the How of its Being-uncovered
ὄνομα, ὀνόματα	(*onoma, onomata*) name(s), self-expression
ὁρᾶν	(*horan*) to see
ὁρισμός	(*horismos*) definition
οὐσία	(*ousia*) Being
πάθη	(*pathē*) affects
πάθος	(*pathos*) affect, something undergone

παρουσία	(parousia) presence, the second coming of Christ
πέρας	(peras) limit
ποιήσις	(poiēsis) production
πόλις	(polis) city-state
πρακτική	(praktikē) pertaining to action
πρακτόν	(prakton) something to be done
πρᾶξις	(praxis) action, taking-care
πράγματα	(pragmata) practical objects
προαίρεσις	(proairesis) anticipation, choice in advance
πρός	(pros) directedness-toward
ῥῆμα	(rhēma) name
σοφία	(sophia) wisdom
στάσις	(stasis) rest, permanence
στέρησις	(sterēsis) absence, lack
συζῆν	(souzēn) to live with
συναγωγη	(sunagōgē) a bringing together
συμφέρον	(sumpheron) the useful
σχολή	(scholē) time-possessing
σῶμα, σῶματα	(sōma, sōmata) body, bodies
ταραχή	(tarachē) disquiet
τὰ καθ᾽ ἕκαστα	(ta kath hekasta) the particularity of a being
τέλειον	(teleion) something complete, beyond-which-nothing
τέλος	(telos) limit, beyond-which-nothing
τέλος δι᾽ αὑτο	(telos di auto) an end for the sake of itself
τέχνη	(technē) art, skill, know-how
τὸ τί ἦν εἶναι	(to ti ēn einai) the What-Being of a being
ὑπακούειν	(hupakouein) to hearken
ὑποκείμενον	(hupokeimenon) what remains there underneath, that which is present at hand
φαινόμενον	(phainomenon) that which shows itself
φαίνεται	(phainetai) to bring to light, make appear, show
φαίνω	(phainō) to bring something into the daylight
φόβος	(phobos) fear
φρόνησις	(phronēsis) prudence
φυγή	(phugē) fleeing
φωνή	(phōnē) voice, sound
ψευδής	(pseudēs) deceptive, distortive, false
ψεῦδος	(pseudos) deception, remaining concealed, Being-covered
ψυχή	(psuchē) the soul
ὡς ἄνθρωπος ψευδής	(hōs anthrōpos pseudēs) false human being
ὡς πρᾶγμα ψεῦδος	(hōs pragma pseudos) false thing
ὡς φύσεώς τινος, ὡς φύσις τις	(hōs phuseōs tinos, hōs phusis tis) something already present by means of itself

Bibliography

Agamben, Giorgio. 1996. "The Passion of Facticity: Heidegger and the Problem of Love." In *The Ancients and the Moderns,* edited by Reginald Lilly, 211–29. Bloomington: Indiana University Press.

Aristotle. 1941. *The Basic Works of Aristotle.* Edited by Richard McKeon. New York: Random House.

Bernasconi, Robert. 1985. *The Question of Language in Heidegger's History of Being.* Atlantic Highlands, N.J.: Humanities Press.

———. 1989. "Heidegger's Destruction of Phronesis." *Southern Journal of Philosophy* 28: 127–53. Supplement.

———. 1993. *Heidegger in Question: The Art of Existing.* Atlantic Highlands, N.J.: Humanities Press International.

Bernet, Rudolf. 1994. "Phenomenological Reduction and the Double Life of the Subject." Translated by François Renaud. In *Reading Heidegger from the Start: Essays in His Earliest Thought,* ed. Theodore Kisiel and John van Buren, 245–67. Albany: State University of New York Press.

Biemel, Walter. 1977. "Husserl's Encyclopedia Britannica Article and Heidegger's Remarks Thereon." In *Husserl: Expositions and Appraisals,* edited by Frederick Elliston and Peter McCormick, 286–303. Foreword by Paul Ricoeur. Notre Dame, Ind.: University of Notre Dame Press.

Brogan, Walter. 1990. "Heidegger and Aristotle: Dasein and the Question of Practical Life." In *Crises in Continental Philosophy,* edited by Arleen B. Dallery and Charles E. Scott with P. Holley Roberts, 137–46. Albany: State University of New York Press.

———. 1994. "The Place of Aristotle in the Development of Heidegger's Phenomenology." In *Reading Heidegger from the Start: Essays in His Earliest Thought,* edited by Theodore Kisiel and John van Buren, 213–27. Albany: State University of New York Press.

———. 1997. "Plato's Dialectical Soul: Heidegger on Plato's Ambiguous Relationship to Rhetoric." *Research in Phenomenology* 27:3–15.

Caputo, John. 1986. "Husserl, Heidegger and the Question of a 'Hermeneutic' Phenomenology." In *A Companion to Martin Heidegger's "Being and Time,"* edited by Joseph Kockelmans, 104–26. Washington, D.C.: Center for Advanced Research in Phenomenology and University Press of America.

———. 1993. *Demythologizing Heidegger*. Bloomington: Indiana University Press.

———. 1995. "Dark Hearts: Heidegger, Richardson, and Evil." In *From Phenomenology to Thought, Errancy, and Desire*, edited by Babette Babich, 267–75. Dordrecht: Kluwer.

Coriando, Paola-Ludovica. 1998. "Die 'formale Anzeige' und das Ereignis: Vorbereitende Überlegungen zum Eigencharakter seinsgeschichtlicher Begrifflichkeit mit einem Ausblick auf den Unterschied von Denken und Dichten." *Heidegger Studies* 14:27–43.

Crowe, Benjamin. 2006. *Heidegger's Religious Origins*. Bloomington: Indiana University Press.

———. 2008. *Heidegger's Phenomenology of Religion: Realism and Cultural Criticism*. Bloomington: Indiana University Press.

Crowell, Steven Galt. 1990. "Husserl, Heidegger, and Transcendental Philosophy: Another Look at the Encyclopedia Britannica Article." *Philosophy and Phenomenological Research* 1 (3): 501–18.

Dahlstrom, Daniel O. 1994. "Heidegger's Method: Philosophical Concepts as Formal Indications." *Review of Metaphysics* 47 (4): .775–95.

Dodd, James. 1998. "Attitude—Facticity—Philosophy." In *Alterity and Facticity: New Perspectives on Husserl*, edited by Natalie Depraz and Dan Zahavi, 57–85. Dordrecht: Kluwer.

Dostal, Robert J. 1993. "Time and Phenomenology in Husserl and Heidegger." In *The Cambridge Companion to Heidegger*, edited by Charles Guignon, 141–69. Cambridge: Cambridge University Press.

Fehér, István M. 1994. "Phenomenology, Hermeneutics, *Lebensphilosophie*: Heidegger's Confrontation with Husserl, Dilthey, and Jaspers." In *Reading Heidegger from the Start: Essays in His Earliest Thought*, edited by Theodore Kisiel and John van Buren, 73–89. Albany: State University of New York Press.

———. 2010. "Religion, Theology, and Philosophy on the Way to Being and Time: Heidegger, Dilthey, and Early Christianity." In *A Companion to Heidegger's Phenomenology of Religious Life*, edited by S. J. McGrath and Andrzej Wiercinski, 35–65. Amsterdam: Rodopi.

Figal, Günter. 1992. *Heidegger: Zur Einführung*. Hamburg: Junius.

Gadamer, Hans-Georg. 1976. *Philosophical Hermeneutics*. Translated and edited by David E. Linge. Berkeley: University of California Press.

————. 1986–87. "Erinnerungen an Heideggers Anfänge." In *Dilthey Jahrbuch für Philosophie und Geschichte der Geisteswissenschaften*, edited by Frithjof Rodi, 4:13–26.

————. 1994a. *Heidegger's Ways*. Translated by John W. Stanley. Albany: State University of New York Press. Originally published as *Heideggers Wege: Studien zum Spätwerk* (Tübingen: J. C. B. Mohr [Paul Siebeck], 1983).

————. 1994b. "Martin Heidegger's One Path." Translated by P. Christopher Smith. In *Reading Heidegger from the Start: Essays in His Earliest Thought*, edited by Theodore Kisiel and John van Buren, 19–34. Albany: State University of New York Press.

————. 1994c. *Truth and Method*. Translated by Joel Weinsheimer and Donald G. Marshall. New York: Continuum. Originally published as *Wahrheit und Methode* (Tübingen: J. C. B. Mohr [Paul Siebeck], 1960). Translation based on 5th German ed. *Gesammelte Werke*, vol. 1. Tübingen: J. C. B. Mohr (Paul Siebeck), 1986.

————. 1997. *Gadamer Lesebuch*. Edited by Jean Grondin. Tübingen: J. C. B. Mohr (Paul Siebeck).

————. 2005. "Heidegger as Rhetor: Hans-Georg Gadamer Interviewed by Ansgar Kemman." Translated by Lawrence Kennedy Schmidt. In *Heidegger and Rhetoric*, edited by Daniel M. Gross and Ansgar Kemman, 47–64. Albany: State University of New York Press.

Gander, Hans-Helmuth. 2002. "Religious Life, Facticity, and the Question of the Self: The Early Heidegger's Hermeneutics of Religious Texts." In *Between the Human and the Divine: Philosophical and Theological Hermeneutics*, 378–86. Toronto: Hermeneutic Press.

Gethmann, Carl Friedrich. 1986–87. "Philosophie als Vollzug und als Begriff. Heideggers Identitäts-philosophie des Lebens in der Vorlesung vom Wintersemester 1921/22 und ihr Verhältnis zu Sein und Zeit." In *Dilthey Jahrbuch für Philosophie und Geschichte der Geisteswissenschaften*, edited by Frithjof Rodi, 4:27–53.

Gonzalez, Francisco. 1997. "On the Way to *Sophia*: Heidegger on Plato's Dialectic, Ethics, and *Sophist*." *Research in Phenomenology* 27:16–60.

Greisch, Jean. 1993. *Hermeneutik und Metaphysik: Eine Problemgeschichte*. See especially chapter 9, "Von der Hermeneutik der Faktizität zur Metaphysik des Daseins (Martin Heidegger)." Munich: Wilhelm Fink Verlag.

————. 1998. "The Tree of Life and the Tree of Knowledge: Current Implications of Heidegger's Hermeneutics of Factical Life." Paper delivered at the 32nd Annual Heidegger Conference, Villanova University, April 17–19.

Grondin, Jean. 1990. "Die Hermeneutik der Faktizität als ontologische Destruktion und Ideologiekritik: Zur Aktualität der Hermeneutik Heideggers." In *Zur philosophischen Aktualität Heideggers: Symposium der Alexander von Humboldt-Stiftung vom 24.–28. April 1989 in Bonn-Bad Godesberg*, vol. 2: *Im Gespräch der Zeit*, edited by Dietrich Papenfuss and Otto Pöggeler, 163–78. Frankfurt am Main: Vittorio Klostermann.

————. 1994. "The Ethical and Young Hegelian Motives in Heidegger's Herme-neutics of Facticity." In *Reading Heidegger from the Start: Essays in His Earliest Thought*, edited by Theodore Kisiel and John van Buren, 345–57. Albany: State University of New York Press.

Gross, Daniel M. 2005. "Introduction: Being-Moved: The Pathos of Heidegger's Rhetorical Ontology." In *Heidegger and Rhetoric*, edited by Daniel M. Gross and Ansgar Kemman, 1–45. Albany: State University of New York Press.

Guignon, Charles B. 1984. "Heidegger's 'Authenticity' Revisited." *Review of Metaphysics* 38 (2): 321–39.

Haar, Michel. 1993a. "The Enigma of Everydayness." In *Reading Heidegger: Commemorations*, edited by John Sallis, 20–28. Bloomington: Indiana University Press.

————. 1993b. *The Song of the Earth: Heidegger and the Grounds of the History of Being*. Translated by Reginald Lilly. Foreword by John Sallis. Bloomington: Indiana University Press. Originally published as *Le Chant de la terre: Heidegger et les assises de l'Histoire de l'Etre* (Paris: Editions de l'Herne, 1987).

Heidegger, Martin. "Brief an William J. Richardson" (April 1962). In *Heidegger. Through Phenomenology to Thought*, 3rd ed., viii–xxiii. The Hague: Martinus Nijhoff, 1974. Translated by Father William J. Richardson, S.J, as "Letter to William J. Richardson," also in *Heidegger: Through Phenomenology to Thought*.

————. *Einführung in die phänomenologische Forschung* (winter semester, 1923–24). Edited by Friedrich-Wilhelm von Herrmann (1994). Vol. 17 of *Gesamtausgabe*. Translated by Daniel O. Dahlstrom as *Introduction to Phenomenological Research* (Bloomington: Indiana University Press, 2005). Abbreviated as *G* 17 in the text.

————. *Gesamtausgabe*. Frankfurt am Main: Klostermann, 1976–.

————. *Grundbegriffe der aristotelischen Philosophie*. Edited by Mark Michalski. Vol. 18 of *Gesamtausgabe*. Translated by Robert D. Metcalf and Mark B. Tanzer as *Basic Concepts of Aristotelian Philosophy* (Bloomington: Indiana University Press, 2009). Abbreviated as *G* 18 in the text.

————. *Grundprobleme der Phänomenologie* (winter semester, 1919–1920), Edited by Hans-Helmuth Gander. Vol. 58 of *Gesamtausgabe*, 1992. Abbreviated as *G* 58 in the text.

————. *Logik: Die Frage nach der Wahrheit* (winter semester, 1925). Edited by Walter Biemel. Vol. 21 of *Gesamtausgabe*. Translated by Thomas Sheehan as *Logic: The Question of Truth* (Bloomington: Indiana University Press, 2010). Abbreviated as *G* 21 in the text.

————. *Ontologie (Hermeneutik der Faktizität)*. Vol. 63 of *Gesamtausgabe*. Translated by John van Buren as *Ontology: The Hermeneutics of Facticity* (Bloomington: Indiana University Press, 1999). Abbreviated as *G* 63 in the text.

————. *Phänomenologie der Anschauung und des Ausdrucks: Theorie der philosophischen Begriffsbildung* (summer semester, 1920). Edited by Claudius Strube, (1993). Vol. 59 of *Gesamtausgabe*. Translated by Tracy Colony as *Phenomenol-*

ogy of Intuition and Expression: Theory of Philosophical Concept Formation (London: Continuum, 2010). Abbreviated as *G* 59 in the text.

———. *Phänomenologie des religiosen Lebens.* 1. *Einleitung in die Phänomenologie der Religion* (winter semester, 1920–1921). Edited by Matthias Jung and Thomas Regehly. 2. *Augustinus und der Neuplatonismus* (summer semester, 1921). Edited by Claudius Strube. 3. *Die philosophischen Grundlagen der mittelalterlichen Mystik* (1918/1919). Edited by Claudius Strube (1995). Vol. 60 of *Gesamtausgabe.* Translated by Matthias Fritsch and Jennifer Anna Gosetti-Ferencei as *The Phenomenology of Religious Life* (Bloomington: Indiana University Press, 2004). Abbreviated as *G* 60 in the text.

———. *Phänomenologische Interpretationen zu Aristoteles: Einführung in die phänomenologische Forschung* (winter semester, 1921–1922). Edited by Walter Bröcker and Kate Bröcker-Oltmanns (1985, 1994). Vol. 61 of *Gesamtausgabe.* Translated by Richard Rojcewicz as *Phenomenological Interpretations of Aristotle: Initiation into Phenomenological Research* (Bloomington: Indiana University Press, 2001). Abbreviated as *G* 61 in the text.

———. "Phänomenologische Interpretationen zu Aristoteles (Anzeige der hermeneutischen Situation)" (composed September–mid-October, 1922). Edited by Hans-Ulrich Lessing, in *Dilthey Jahrbuch für Philosophie und Geschichte der Geisteswissenschaften* (Göttingen: Vandehoeck and Ruprecht, 1989), 6:237–69. Translated by Michael Baur as "Phenomenological Interpretations with Respect to Aristotle: Indication of the Hermeneutic Situation,",*Man and World*, 25 (1992): 355–93. Abbreviated as PIA in the text.

———. *Platon: Sophistes* (winter semester, 1924–1925). Edited by Ingeborg Schüßler (1992). Volme 19 of *Gesamtausgabe.* Translated by Richard Rojcewicz and Andre Schuwer as *Plato's Sophist* (Bloomington: Indiana University Press, 1997). Abbreviated as *G* 19 in the text.

———. *Prolegomena zur Geschichte des Zeitbegriffs* (summer semester, 1925). Edited by Petra Jaeger. Volume 20 of *Gesamtausgabe.* Translated by Theodore Kisiel as *History of the Concept of Time* (Bloomington: Indiana University Press, 1985).

———. *Sein und Zeit.* (Tübingen: Max Niemeyer Verlag, 1927, 1953, 1993.) Translated by John Macquarrie and Edward Robinson as *Being and Time* (New York: Harper and Row, 1962). Abbreviated as *BT* in the text.

———. *Supplements: From the Earliest Essays to Being and Time and Beyond.* Edited by John van Buren. Albany: State University of New York Press, 2002. Abbreviated as *S* in the text.

———. *Wegmarken* (1919–58). Edited by Friedrich-Wilhelm von Herrmann (1967). Vol. 9 of *Gesamtausgabe.* Translated by William McNeill as *Pathmarks* (Cambridge: Cambridge University Press, 1998). Abbreviated as *G* 9 in the text.

———. *Zur Bestimmung der Philosophie,* 1: *Die Idee der Philosophie und das Weltanschauungsproblem* (Kriegsnotsemester 1919) 2: *Phänomenologie und transzendentale Wertphilosophie* (summer semester, 1919). Edited Bernd Heimbüchel (1987).

Vol. 56/57 of *Gesamtausgabe*. Translated by Ted Sadler as *Towards the Definition of Philosophy* (London: Continuum, 2002). Abbreviated as *G* 56/57 in the text.

Held, Klaus. 1992. "The Finitude of the World: Phenomenology in Transition from Husserl to Heidegger." In *Ethics and Danger: Essays on Heidegger and Continental Thought*, edited by Arleen B. Dallery and Charles E. Scott with P. Holley Roberts, 187–98. Albany: State University of New York Press.

Henry, Michel. 1985. *Généalogie de la psychoanalyse: Le commencement perdu.* Paris, P.U.F.

Hogemann, Friedrich. 1986–87. "Heideggers Konzeption der Phänomenologie in den Vorlesungen aus dem Wintersemester 1919/20 und dem Sommersemester 1920." In *Dilthey Jahrbuch für Philosophie und Geschichte der Geisteswissenschaften*, edited by Frithjof Rodi, 4:54–71.

Husserl, Edmund. 1971. " 'Phenomenology,' Edmund Husserl's Article for the *Encyclopedia Britannica* (1927)." Revised translation by Richard E. Palmer. *Journal of the British Society for Phenomenology* 2:77–90.

Hyde, Michael J. 2005. "A Matter of the Heart: Epideictic Rhetoric and Heidegger's Call of Conscience." In *Heidegger and Rhetoric*, edited by Daniel M. Gross and Ansgar Kemman, 81–104. Albany: State University of New York Press.

Jamme, Christophe. 1986–87. "Heideggers Begründung der Hermeneutik." In *Dilthey Jahrbuch für Philosophie und Geschichte der Geisteswissenschaften*, edited by Frithjof Rodi, 4:72–90.

Kisiel, Theodore. 1986–87. "Das Entstehen des Begriffsfeldes 'Faktizität' im Frühwerk Heideggers." In *Dilthey Jahrbuch für Philosophie und Geschichte der Geisteswissenschaften*, edited by Frithjof Rodi, 4:91–120.

———. 1992a. "The Genesis of *Being and Time*." *Man and World* 25:21–37.

———. 1992b. "Heidegger's Apology: Biography as Philosophy and Ideology." In *The Heidegger Case: On Philosophy and Politics*, edited by Tom Rockmore and Joseph Margolis, 11–51. Philadelphia: Temple University Press.

———. 1993. *The Genesis of Heidegger's "Being and Time."* Berkeley: University of California Press.

———. 1994. "Heidegger on Becoming a Christian: A Conceptual Picture Show." In *Reading Heidegger from the Start: Essays in His Earliest Thought*, edited by Theodore Kisiel and John van Buren, 175–92. Albany: State University of New York Press.

———. 1995a. "*Existenz* in Incubation underway toward *Being and Time*." In *From Phenomenology to Thought, Errancy, and Desire*, edited by Babette Babich, 89–114. Dordrecht: Kluwer.

———. 1995b. "Why Students of Heidegger Will Have to Read Emil Lask." *Man and World* 28:197–240.

———. 2000. "Situating Rhetorical Politics in Heidegger's Protopractical Ontology 1923–1925: The French Occupy the Ruhr." *International Journal of Philosophical Studies* 8 (2): 185–208.

———. 2005. "Rhetorical Protopolitics in Heidegger and Arendt." In *Heidegger and Rhetoric*, edited by Daniel M. Gross and Ansgar Kemman, 131–60. Albany: State University of New York Press.

Kisiel, Theodore, and Thomas Sheehan, eds. 2007. *Becoming Heidegger: On the Trail of His Early Occasional Writings, 1910–1927.* Evanston, Ill.: Northwestern University Press.

Kovacs, George. 1994. "Philosophy as Primordial Science in Heidegger's Courses of 1919." In *Reading Heidegger from the Start: Essays in His Earliest Thought*, edited by Theodore Kisiel and John van Buren, 91–107. Albany: State University of New York Press.

Krell, David. 1992. *Daimon Life: Heidegger and Life Philosophy.* Bloomington: Indiana University Press.

———. 1994. "The 'Factical Life' of Dasein: From the Early Freiburg Courses to *Being and Time*." In *Reading Heidegger from the Start: Essays in His Earliest Thought*, edited by Theodore Kisiel and John van Buren, 361–79. Albany: State University of New York Press.

Lehmann, Karl. 1966. "Christliche Geschichtserfahrung und ontologische Frage beim jungen Heidegger." *Philosophisches Jahrbuch* (Freiburg) 74 (1): 126–53.

Maggini, Golfo. 1999. "Movement and the Facticity of Life: On Heidegger's Early Interpretation of Aristotle." *Philosophical Inquiry* 21 (2) 93–108.

Makkreel, Rudolf Adam. 1990. "Heideggers ursprüngliche Auslegung der Faktizität des Lebens: Diahermeneutik als Aufbau und Abbau der geschichtlichen Welt." In *Zur philosophischen Aktualität Heideggers: Symposium der Alexander von Humboldt-Stiftung vom 24.–28. April 1989 in Bonn-Bad Godesberg*, vol. 2: *Im Gespräch der Zeit*, edited by Dietrich Papenfuss and Otto Pöggeler, 179–88. Frankfurt am Main: Vittorio Klostermann.

McKeon, Richard. 1987. *Rhetoric: Essays in Invention and Discovery.* Edited by Mark Backman. Woodbridge, Conn.: Ox Bow Press.

McNeill, Will. 1994. "The First Principle of Hermeneutics." In *Reading Heidegger from the Start: Essays in His Earliest Thought*, edited by Theodore Kisiel and John van Buren, 393–408. Albany: State University of New York Press.

———. 1998. "The Time of the Augenblick." Paper delivered at the 32nd Annual Heidegger Conference, Villanova University, April 17–19.

———. 1999. *The Glance of the Eye: Heidegger, Aristotle, and the Ends of Theory.* Albany: State University of New York Press.

Michalski, Mark. 2005. "Hermeneutic Phenomenology as Philology." Translated by Jamey Findling. In *Heidegger and Rhetoric*, edited by Daniel M. Gross and Ansgar Kemman, 65–80. Albany: State University of New York Press.

Moran, Dermot. 2010. "Choosing a Hero: Heidegger's Conception of Authentic Life in Relation to Early Christianity." In *A Companion to Heidegger's Phenomenology of Religious Life*, edited by S. J. McGrath and Andrzej Wiercinski, 349–75. Amsterdam: Rodopi.

Nichols, Mary P. 1987. "Aristotle's Defense of Rhetoric." *Journal of Politics* 49 (3): 657–77.

Nicholson, Graeme. 2010. "The End of Time: Temporality in Paul's Letters to the Thessalonians." In *A Companion to Heidegger's Phenomenology of Religious Life*, edited by S. J. McGrath and Andrzej Wiercinski, 219–31. Amsterdam: Rodopi.

Olafson, Frederick A. 1998. *Heidegger and the Ground of Ethics: A Study of Mitsein*. Cambridge: Cambridge University Press.

Ott, Hugo. 1993. *Martin Heidegger: A Political Life*. Translated by A. Blunden. New York: Basic Books.

Owensby, Jacob. 1989. "Some Roots of *Being and Time* in Life-Philosophy." A review of *Dilthey-Jahrbuch für Philosophie und Geschichte der Geisteswissenschaften*, edited by Frithjof Rodi, vol. 4, 1986–87. Göttingen: Vandenhoeck and Ruprecht, 1987. *Research in Phenomenology* 19 (1): 311–15.

Petkovsek, Robert. 1998. *Heidegger-Index (1919–1927)*. Ljubljana: Universitas Labacensis, Facultas Theologica.

Pöggeler, Otto. 1986–87. "Heideggers Begegnung mit Dilthey." In *Dilthey Jahrbuch für Philosophie und Geschichte der Geisteswissenschaften*, edited by Frithjof Rodi, 4:121–60.

———. 1987. *Martin Heidegger's Path of Thinking*. Translated by Daniel Magurshak and Sigmund Barber. Atlantic Highlands, N.J.: Humanities Press.

Richardson, William J., S.J. 1974. *Heidegger: Through Phenomenology to Thought*. Preface by Martin Heidegger. 3rd ed. The Hague: Martinus Nijhoff.

———. 1977. "Personal Human Development." In *Human Life: Problems of Birth, of Living, and of Dying*, edited by William C. Bier, S.J. New York: Fordham University Press.

———. 1983. "Psychoanalysis and the Being-question." In *Interpreting Lacan*, edited by Joseph H. Smith, M.D., and William Kerrigan, 139–59. New Haven, Conn.: Yale University Press.

———. 1992. "Heidegger's Truth and Politics." In *Ethics and Danger: Essays on Heidegger and Continental Thought*, edited by Arleen B. Dallery and Charles E. Scott with P. Holley Roberts, 11–24. Albany: State University of New York Press.

———. 1995. "Heidegger's Fall." In *From Phenomenology to Thought, Errancy, and Desire*, edited by Babette Babich, 277–300. Dordrecht: Kluwer.

Rodi, Frithjof. 1986–87. "Die Bedeutung Diltheys für die Konzeption von *Sein und Zeit*: Zum Umfeld von Heideggers Kasseler Vorträgen (1925)." In *Dilthey Jahrbuch für Philosophie und Geschichte der Geisteswissenschaften*, edited by Frithjof Rodi, 4:161–77.

Rojcewicz, Richard. 1997. "Platonic Love: Dasein's Urge toward Being." *Research in Phenomenology* 27 (1): 103–20.

Rorty, Amélie Oksenberg, ed. 1996. *Essays on Aristotle's "Rhetoric."* Berkeley: University of California Press.

Sallis, John. 1990. *Echoes: After Heidegger*. Bloomington: Indiana University Press.

Scharff, Robert C. 1997. "Heidegger's 'Appropriation' of Dilthey before *Being and Time*." *Journal of the History of Philosophy* 35 (1): 105–28.

Schürmann, Reiner. 1987. *Heidegger on Being and Acting: From Principles to Anarchy*. Translated by Christine-Marie Gros. Bloomington: Indiana University Press.

Sheehan, Thomas. 1981a. "Heidegger's Early Years: Fragment for a Philosophical Biography." In *Heidegger: The Man and the Thinker*, edited by Thomas J. Sheehan, 3–19, Chicago: Precedent.

———. 1981b. "Introduction: Heidegger and the Project of Fulfillment." In *Heidegger: The Man and the Thinker*, edited by Thomas J. Sheehan, vii–xx. Chicago: Precedent.

———. 1981c. "On Movement and the Destruction of Ontology." *Monist* 64 (4): 534–42.

———. 1983. "On the Way to Ereignis: Heidegger's Interpretation of *Physis*." In *Continental Philosophy in America*, edited by Hugh Silverman, John Sallis, and Thomas Seebohm, 131–64. Pittsburgh: Duquesne University Press.

———. 1986. "Heidegger's 'Introduction to the Phenomenology of Religion.'" In *A Companion to Martin Heidegger's "Being and Time,"* edited by Joseph Kockelmans, 40–62. Washington, D.C.: Center for Advanced Research in Phenomenology and University Press of America.

———. 1988. "Heidegger and the Nazis." *New York Review of Books* 35 (10): 38–47.

———. 1993. "Reading a Life." In *The Cambridge Companion to Heidegger*, edited by Charles Guignon, 70–96. Cambridge: Cambridge University Press.

———. 2001. "A Paradigm Shift in Heidegger Research." *Continental Philosophy Review* 34:183–202.

Smith, P. Christopher. 1998. *The Hermeneutics of Original Argument: Demonstration, Dialectic, Rhetoric*. Evanston, Ill.: Northwestern University Press.

———. 1995. "The Uses and Abuses of Aristotle's Rhetoric in Heidegger's Fundamental Ontology: The Lecture Course, Summer, 1924." In *From Phenomenology to Thought, Errancy, and Desire*, edited by Babette Babich, 315–33. Dordrecht: Kluwer. Another version of this article can be found in Smith's book, *The Hermeneutics of Original Argument: Demonstration, Dialectic, Rhetoric* (Evanston, Ill.: Northwestern University Press, 1998).

Sokolowski, Robert. 1974. *Husserlian Meditations*. Evanston, Ill.: Northwestern University Press.

Spiegelberg, Herbert. 1981. "On the Misfortunes of Edmund Husserl's *Encyclopedia Britannica* Article 'Phenomenology.'" In *Husserl: Shorter Works*, edited by Frederick Elliston and Peter McCormick, 18–20. Notre Dame, Ind: University of Notre Dame Press.

Streuver, Nancy S. 2005. "Alltäglichkeit, Timefulness, in the Heideggerian Program." In *Heidegger and Rhetoric*, edited by Daniel M. Gross and Ansgar Kemman, 105–30. Albany: State University of New York Press.

Taminiaux, Jacques. 1985. "Heidegger and Husserl's Logical Investigations: In Remembrance of Heidegger's Last Seminar (Zähringen, 1973)." In *Dialectic and Difference*, 91–114. New York: Palgrave Macmillan.

———. 1987. "Phenomenology and the Problem of Action." In *Critical and Dialectical Phenomenology*, edited by Donn Welton and Hugh J. Silverman, 90–102. Albany: State University of New York Press.

———. 1988. "The Interpretation of Greek Philosophy in Heidegger's Fundamental Ontology." *Journal of the British Society for Phenomenology* 19 (1): 3–14.

———. 1991. *Heidegger and the Project of Fundamental Ontology*. Translated by Michael Gendre. Albany: State University of New York Press.

———. 1992. "Heidegger and *Praxis.*" In *The Heidegger Case: On Philosophy and Politics*, edited by Tom Rockmore and Joseph Margolis, 188–207. Philadelphia: Temple University Press.

———. 1994. "Philosophy of Existence I: Heidegger." In *Twentieth Century Continental Philosophy*, edited by Richard M. Kearney. New York: Routledge.

Thiele, Leslie Paul. 1995. *Timely Meditations: Martin Heidegger and Postmodern Politics*. Princeton, N.J.: Princeton University Press.

Volpi, Franco. 1994. "'Being and Time': A 'Translation' of the *Nicomachean Ethics?*" Translated by John Protevi. In *Reading Heidegger from the Start: Essays in His Earliest Thought*, edited by Theodore Kisiel and John van Buren, 195–211. Albany: State University of New York Press.

———. 1996. "Dasein as *Praxis*: The Heideggerian Assimilation and the Radicalization of the Practical Philosophy of Aristotle." Translated by Christopher Macann. In *Critical Heidegger*, edited by Christopher Macann, 27–66. New York: Routledge.

Van Buren, John. 1992. "The Young Heidegger, Aristotle, Ethics." In *Ethics and Danger: Essays on Heidegger and Continental Thought*, edited by Arleen B. Dallery and Charles E. Scott with P. Holley Roberts, 169–85. Albany: State University of New York Press.

———. 1994a. "Martin Heidegger, Martin Luther." In *Reading Heidegger from the Start: Essays in His Earliest Thought*, edited by Theodore Kisiel and John van Buren, 159–74. Albany: State University of New York Press.

———. 1994b. *The Young Heidegger: Rumor of a Hidden King*. Bloomington: Indiana University Press.

Westphal, Merold. 1997. "Heidegger's *'Theologische' Jugendschriften.*" A review of *Phänomenologie des Religiosen Lebens*, vol. 60 of *Gesamtausgabe* (Frankfurt am Main: Vittorio Klostermann Verlag, 1995). *Research in Phenomenology* 27 (1): 247–61.

Index

Note: Greek words are alphabetized according to their English transliteration. Notes that carry over multiple pages are listed by only the page number on which the notes start (e.g., 247n4, not 247–249n4).

ambiguity: Christianity, 235n9; hermeneutics of facticity, 243n1; in life and language, 64–67, 74–75, 167–168, 245n1; retention of, 64, 67; ruinance, 83; worldly nature of Dasein, 211–213, 215, 217–218
ἀνάμνησις (*anamnēsis*), defined, 263
Angst, 242n4
annihilation, 172–174
ἀνθρώπινον ἀγαθόν (*anthrōpinon agathon*), 181, 183; defined, 263
anticipation, 50, 58
Antigone, 38
Antisthenes, 193
anxiety, 164, 172–173, 218, 242n4, 245n3; Dasein, 176, 220–221; and fear, 252n10
Arendt, Hannah, 23, 247n4, 259n21
ἀόριστον (*aoriston*), 170, defined, 263
ἀπορία (*aporia*), 247n4; defined, 263
ἀποφαίνεσθαι (*apophainesthai*), 165–166, 192, 201, 244n3; defined, 263
ἀπόφασις (*apophasis*), defined, 263
ἀποφαντικός (*apophantikos*), defined, 263
appropriation, 6–7, 30, 56, 71, 111–113, 148–149, 154
ἀρχή/ἀρχαί (*archē/archai*), 191, 192, 195–196, 255n1; defined, 263
ἀρετή (*aretē*), 184; defined, 263
ἀρετὴ ἠθικη (*aretē thikē*), 180–181, 254n15; defined, 263
Aristotle, absence, 174; appropriated by tradition, 107; categories, 176–177; commonality of experience, 105; deception, 148; deconstruction of, 253–254n13; *De Anima*, 148, 153, 154, 155–156; *De Interpretatione*, 147; dialectic, 190–191; as entry point for Plato, 197; *Ethics*, 216; falsity, 157; first philosophy, 255n1; immanence of nothingness, 252n9; influence of, 15, 186; interpretation of, 8, 14–15, 136, 232n1, 235n7; kinesis, 228n1; λόγος, 142, 192; λόγος ἀποφαντικός, 153, 192; Luther, 56, 59; metaphysical overlay, 253–254n13; *Nicomachean Ethics*, 89–90, 177–178, 195, 215–216, 254n15, 257n14; nonrelational philosophy, 259n21; ontological research, 168–169; phenomenology, 141; rhetoric, 17–18, 208–209; *Rhetoric*, 17, 143, 162–185, 191, 215, 253n13, 255n1; σώματα, 168–169, 192, 249n6; truth, 109, 110, 242n7; truthing, 109, 189, 195, 197; on vice and virtue, 6, 257n14
asceticism, 42
"as-structure," 234n6
attunement (*Stimmung*), 249n5
audibility, 147, 169–170, 251n7
Augenblick, 53, 176, 183–184, 259n21
Augustine, 15, 104, 232n1, 237n14
Augustine and Neo-Platonism (lecture course), 46, 47, 56–59
Auslegung (laying-out), 244n3
authenticity, 115–116, 211–212, 235n9, 245n1; Crowe on, 214; Fehér on, 214; and language, 247n3
authentic conscience, 259n21
authentic life, 18–19, 213, 221–222; 245n1; Being-with-others, 177–179; everydayness, 254–255n17; rhetoric, 254n14; and transcendence, 218
authentic speaking, 163, 169–177
averageness, 131, 133, 135, 166–167, 178–179, 222. *See also* everydayness
awaiting, 52, 56
awareness: of Being, 58, 222, 259n21; Dasein, 124–125, 214, 259n21; self-awareness, 12–13, 121

bankruptcy of philosophy, 66
Basic Concepts of Aristotelian Philosophy (lecture course), 136, 162–185
Basic Problems of Phenomenology (lecture course), 14, 24, 32, 34, 45, 223
Becker, O., 240n3
becoming, 51, 52, 57–58, 143, 170–171, 173–175; Dasein, 124, 126
Bedrängnis (torment), 53
Befindlichkeit (disposition), 220, 251n7
Begebenheit (occurrence), 5
being, modes of, 12; and non-being, 187

Being: as ἀλήθεια, 247n4; care,
105–106, 242n4, confrontation with
Dasein, 18; defining, 1; existence of,
68; historical, 58; issue for life, 57;
as limit, 17; language, 257–258n19;
movement, 251n8; Now and Here
of, 254n16; Plato's view, 189–190;
primary topic for Heidegger, 2–3,
4; pre-having, 125–127, 130–131;
process of truth, 257–258n19;
retrieval, 240n2; translation of, 19;
there-character, 174; unity, 152
Being and Time (Heidegger), Dasein in, 4;
dialectic, 194; genesis of, 225n2;
hermeneutics in, 244n3; priority of
existence, 243n9; retrieval in, 240n2
Being-as-having-become, 51–52
Being-in-the-πόλις, 163
Being in the world, 81, 211, 218–220,
255n1; Dasein, 131, 144, 160–161;
δηλοῦν, 207; factically, 130–132; good,
181; Greeks, 147, 165, 191; language,
165; λόγος, 175–176; *Ontology: The
Hermeneutics of Facticity*, 120, 141–142;
orienting self, 171, 183–184
Being of being, 182, 184, 189, 228n20,
259n21
Being of that being (οὐσία), 168–169,
249n6
Being of the I, 27, 68
*Being-There and Being-True according to
Aristotle* (lecture), 215
Being-with-oneself, 94, 175
Being-with-others, 94, 175, 177–179,
182
Bekümmerung (concern), 33, 105, 239n12;
objective historical reality, 48;
relationship with *Besorgen*, 241n6,
242n1, 242n4
Bekundungsschichten (layers of
manifestation), 41, 232n15
Bergson, Henri, 39, 226n6, 228n19,
230n9, 231n14
Besorgen (to take-care of, to be
preoccupied with), 96–97, 106,
133–134, 179–180, 241n6, 242n1,
242n4
Between, the, 80–81

Beunruhigung (disturbing character), 48, 54
beyond-which-nothing, 181–182
binary opposition, 211–212, 214
bindingness, 63
birth, 12
Blattner, William, 254–255n17
blocking off (*Abriegelung*), 89, 93
body, 39, 168, 230n9, 249n5, 249n6,
252n10
brackets, 30, 72, 122–123, 133, 244n2
Brentano, Franz, 122
bringing to light, 134–136, 199
Brogan, Walter, 242n6, 255n1, 259n21

Caputo, John: *Demythologizing Heidegger*,
243n1
care, 57, 78–79, 81, 241n6, 242n4;
curiosity, 130; directionality, 84, 86;
history, 113; openness, 143;
overburdened, 96–97; preoccupation,
134–135; retrieval of, 95
carelessness, 90, 133
care-worlds, 84, 86, 92, 240n3
Cartesian I, 73–74, 234n6
Cartesian standpoints, 12, 70, 85, 89,
227n16
categories: Aristotle, 176–177, 190; of
caring movement, 87–90, 93, 95;
grammatical, 75; indeterminateness,
170, 251n8; of life, 70–71, 76–81,
84–86, 99, 228n1, 232n1, 237n1,
240n3; objects, 145–146; *prinzipielle*,
239n11
Christianity: ambiguity, 235n9;
conversion, 51–52, 236n12;
facticity, 24; formal indication,
234n6; insecurity, 46; "More of
observing," 108–109; roots in
Aristotelian concepts, 103; self-world,
41–42; temporality and, 14, 232n1,
234n5
Christian knowledge, 51, 52, 53, 56
Christian theo*logian*, 58–59
cogito, 44, 56, 69, 72, 85, 133
common sense, 127
communication, 50–51, 124, 178, 209,
245n1, 247n4; Dasein, 199; hearing,
177–178; rhetoric, 200

λόγος ἀποφαντικός, 151;
philosophy, 187; ψεῦδος, 110, 156;
sophists, 195; speaking, 154–156, 167;
world, 148, 158–159
decisions: Christians, 53, 235n9; Dasein,
171–173, 259n21; life, 90; possibility,
81–82; rhetoric and, 18, 164,
171–173
deconstruction: of the historical, 111–112;
and origins, 130, 256n4;
preconceptions, 257n7; pre-having,
130–131; retrieval, xvi; scientific
approach to speaking, 141–160;
σοφία, 107–111; systematic, 213
definition, 164–165, 168–169
De Interpretatione (Aristotle), 147
δηλοῦν (dēloun), 152,165–166, 201, 202,
205, 206; defined, 264; λέγειν, 207
δηλώματα (dēlōmata), 207; defined, 264
delotic, 202
Demythologizing Heidegger (Caputo),
243n1
denial, 153–154
Derrida, Jacques, 225n2
Descartes, René, 16, 56, 227n16;
ahistoricality, 58; avoiding deception,
89; "I am," 64, 69–70, 74, 141;
phenomenology, 141
description, problematic, 231n11
destiny (Schicksal), 131, 213, 219, 258n20
destruction, 211, 212–215, 216, 217,
257n7; distance, 87–88, 91, 92, 237n1;
ruinance, 83, 84, 97–98
determinability, 193
devivification of life, 25, 30, 34, 36, 41,
44, 45, 99
dialectic, 255n1; Being-in-the-world of, 8;
Dasein, 196; grounded in rhetoric,
253n13; positive contributions of,
192–193
διαλέγεσθαι (dialegesthai), 191, 192–193,
197, 208–209; defined, 264
dialogue and hermeneutics, 247n4
διανοεῖν (dianoein), 194, defined, 264
διαίρεσις (diaresis), 200–201; defined,
264
διχῶς (dichōs), 9–10, 174, 176; defined,
264

dichotomy, 171–172, 211–212, 214,
217–218. See also duality
die Sache selbst, 2–3, 4, 39
δίωξις (diōzis), 172; defined, 264
Dilthey, Wilhelm, 226n6, 228n20,
230n9; approach to history, 47;
influence on Heidegger, 11–13, 217,
226n9, 227n16, 227n17, 228n21,
231n14
disclosure, 10, 18, 152, 158, 165–166,
205, 216; λέγειν, 203. See also
revealing
discourse, 204–205, 206–207, 246n2,
252n12
disposition (Befindlichkeit), 183–184, 220,
251n7
disquiet, 56, 79–81, 171–172, 237n1
distance (Abstand), 87–89, 92–93
distortion, 10–11, 247n4
distractions, 87, 88, 91–92, 114, 116,
241n5
disturbing character (Beunruhigung), 48,
66
doctrine of beings, 193
doubling (διχῶς), 9–10, 174, 176
δόξα (doxa), 17, 194, defined, 264
duality, 99, 217–218, 219, 223; of life's
temporality, 93, See also duality
δυνάμει ὄν (dunamei on), 145, 190;
defined, 264
δύναμις (dunamis), 9–10, 173, 190;
defined, 264

ego, 44, 68, 69, 72, 85, 89, 133, 154,
234n5
εἶδος/εἴδη (eidos/eidē), 201, 249n6;
defined, 264
Einfühlung (understanding), 50
εἰς φῶς ἄγειν (eis phōs agein), defined,
264
ἐλπίς (elpis), 171–172; defined, 264
ἐλπὶς σωτηρίας (elpis sōtērias), defined,
264
emotional public sphere, 245n1
emptiness, 94–95, 143–144, 232n17
encountering, 78–79, 109, 133, 134, 147,
169, 177, 251n7
endangerment (Gefährdung), 57

"The End of Philosophy and the Task of Thinking" (essay), 229n4
ἐνέργεια (*energeia*), 173–175, 190; defined, 264
enlightening (relucence), 90–94
ἐντελέχεια (*entelecheia*), 173–175; defined, 264
enthymeme, 252n12; 253n13
Entscheidung (decision), 53
Ereignis (event), 5, 30, 249n6
ἔργον (*ergon*), 183; defined, 264
errancy and truth, 223–224; 236n13
error and perversity, 176, 252n12
eschatology, 55, 59, 235n8
ethics, 179–184; ontological ground of, 252n12, 254n15, 259n21
Ethics (Aristotle), 216
ethics of mercy, 243n1
Ethik, 254n15
ἦθος (*ēthos*), 179–184; 252–253n12; defined, 264; difference from *Ethik*, 254n15
εὐβουλία (*eubolia*), 110, defined, 264
εὐδαιμονία (*eudaimonia*), 183; defined, 264
εὐζωία (*euzōia*), 181; defined, 264
event (*Ereignis*), 5, 30, 249n6
everydayness, 32, 39, 45, 235n9, 254n17; αἴσθησις, 169; anxiety, 172–173; Being, 133; cares, 57; concreteness of, 120–121; existence, 159; fixity, 135–136; language, 118–119, 162–163, 166–167; negative view of, 222–223; openness, 135; pleasure, 175; positivity, 39–40, 132, 136, 163, 216–217; speaking, 208–209; temporality, 131, 134
"everyone," 257n17. *See also* they
excellence, 163–164, 176, 178, 180, 183–185, 222, 254n15
existentialism, denial of, 23
Existenz, 58–59, 68, 125, 243n8, 243n9; fallenness vs., 104, 115–116; talking, 147
experience: actualized, 57; ground of experience, 36; meaningful, 37–39; moving directions of, 228n1; not

given, 231n11; partitioning of, 5–6; perception, 35; sensation, 35
explication (*Explikation*), 50

factical ambiguity, 64, 65–66
factical life: ambiguity, 211–212; categories, 87–90, 99; deception, 18; defining, 38, 78; devivification, 44; distress, 54; early form of Dasein, 8; engagement, 232n15; epochs, 106; historicity, 232n1, 234n5; How, 56; meaningfulness, 18; methodology, 227n11; movement and, 228n1; multiplicity, 37; not object, 124; nothingness of, 9, 54; origin, 33–34, 38–39, 41, 43–44, 77; original sources, 15, 247n4; ought, 28; φρόνησις, 107–111; ruinance as defining feature, 241n5; self-concern, 33; σοφία, 107–111; temporality, 43, 59, 94–96; vitality, 63, 95–96; world, 73–74
factical spatiality, 134
factical speaking, 16, 38, 142, 156–158
facticity, being-in-a-world, 130–132, 141–142, Christian religiosity, 24, 46–59, 235n9; countermovement, 95; and Dasein, 4–5, 15–16, 81–82, 159, 258–259n20; defining, 2, 123; determinant of ruinance, 98; *Existenz* vs., 116; factical life vs., 24; fallenness, 236n13; ground of science, 25; hermeneutics vs., 125; historical-temporal nature, 77, 111; history of word, 5, 226n6; human body, 249n5; language, 156–158, 188, 193; living philosophy, 67–68; λόγος, 194; and models, 112–113; meaning of, 27; movement, 91, 93, 98; ontology and, 120–137; relation to existence, 33, 243n9; renewal of, 46; and retrieval, 6, 111; Richardson, 258n20; speaking, 156–158; temporality, 126–127; *there*, 120
factuality, 5, 218–219, 220
faith, 55–56; and lack of certainty, 235n9; living context, 55; and struggle, 243n1
falsity, 20, 149–150, 153–156, 156–158

ἓν δηλῶν (*hen dēloun*), defined, 264
Henry, M., 230n9
Here and Now, 179
ἑρμηνεύειν (*hermēneuein*), 124, 244n3;
  defined, 264
hermeneutical possibilities, 234n6
"Hermeneutic Phenomenology as
  Philology" (Michalski), 246n2
hermeneutics, 227n11, 230n9; argument
  against, 243n1; defined, 124–125;
  facticity vs., 125; Gadamerian, 247n4;
  λόγος, 255n1; and method-object
  connection, 229n3
hermeneutics of facticity, 120–137, 243n1,
  247n4, 253n13, 259n21; ontology,
  227n11, 230n9; task of, 103, 126,
  retrieval, 112, 117
heroes, 235n9
ἕτερον (*heteron*), 195, 196, 201; defined,
  264
ἕξις (*hexis*), 183; defined, 264
ἕξις προαιρετικὴ μετὰ λόγου (*hexis
  proairetikē meta logou*), 184; defined,
  264
historical, deconstruction of, 112–113
historical-I, 26, 27, 30, 234n6
historical life, 12, 227n16, 228n20;
  and Christianity, 232n1; Dasein,
  258–259n20; and retrieval, 240n2
historical motivations, 6, 247n4
Historisches Wörterbuch der Philosophie
  (Ritter), 5
history, 249n6; appropriation of, 6, 113;
  concrete reappropriation of, 111–113;
  formal indication, 48–49; How of
  having death, 115; objectification of,
  47–48; onset of, 42; retrieval of, 8, 105
History of the Concept of Time (lecture
  course), 222
ὅλον (*holon*), 190; defined, 265
home, 245n3
ὁμιλία (*homilia*), defined, 265
hope, 171–173
ὁρᾶν (*horan*), 178, 209, 255n1; defined,
  265
ὁρισμός (*horismos*), 165, defined, 265
ὡς ἄνθρωπος ψευδής (*hōs anthrōpos
  pseudēs*), 157, defined, 266

ὡς φύσεώς τινος/ὡς φύσις τις (*hōs
  phuseōs tinos/hōs phusis tis*), 189;
  defined, 266
ὡς πρᾶγμα ψεῦδος (*hōs pragma pseudos*),
  157, defined, 266
How, 51, 52–53, 56, 227n17; of Being,
  123–124, 133, 167; of care, 130;
  curiosity, 130; of Dasein, 110–111,
  123–124, 132, 149, 180, 217;
  directionality of, 77; disquiet, 79;
  encounters, 145; everydayness, 179;
  having death, 104, 113, 115–116; of
  human beings, 68, 69, 72–73; of
  inquiry, 122; of life, 63, 166, 181;
  νοῦς, 183; past, 104; φρόνησις,
  109–110; they, 120, 179
human being: concrete existence of, 188;
  deception, 158; definition, 165; How,
  68, 69; language as dimension, 76;
  οὐσία, 165; temporality, 72
humanist traditions, 259n21
humanities vs. science, 232n15
human knowledge, 191
ὑπακούειν (*hupakouein*), 206, defined,
  266
ὑποκείμενον (*hupokeimenon*), 249n6;
  defined, 266
Husserl, Edmund, 2, 16, 45; Heidegger's
  shift away from, 234n5; intentionality,
  122, 202, 232n1; *Lebenswelt*, 231n14;
  phenomenology, 141, 231n11;
  transcendental idealism, 230n9
Hyde, Michael J., 252–253n12
hyperbole, 88, 92

I: Being of the I, 27, 68; Cartesian, 73–74,
  234n6; historical-I, 26, 27, 30, 234n6;
  isolation, 135; not central, 68; not
  objective, 44; not self-world, 85–86;
  object, 133; situational-I, 228n21;
  theoretical I, 29
"I am," 6, 27, 58, 64, 69–70, 234n6
*Idea of Philosophy and the Problem of
  Worldview* (lecture course), 25–26,
  229n3, 229n4
Ideas, 47, 186, 194, 205, 255n1; Being,
  189, 190, 207–208; resistances,
  199–200; seeing, 188, 191, 197, 201

idle talk, 133, 163, 166, 193, 198–199, 214, 217, 222–223, 253n13
impersonal sentences, 28–29. *See also* grammar
inauthenticity, 18, 211–212, 214–215, 222, 235n9; inability to shed, 219–220
inclination (*Neigung*), 84, 87, 91–92, 93, 98, 99, 115, 237n5
incompleteness, 43–44, 54, 96
indeterminacy, 70–71, 128, 170, 213–214, 215, 251n8
indifference, 222
insecurity, 46, 55–56, 67
intensification: of care, 143; of life-worlds, 25, 34; of ruinance, 96–97; of self, 31–32, 41–44, 57–58
intentionality, 122, 202, 230n9, 232n1
interpretation, 244n3
interpretive violence, 184
Introduction to Phenomenological Research (lecture course), 16, 136, 141–161
Introduction to the Phenomenology of Religion (lecture course), 14, 24, 49
ist da (is there), 13, 36–37

Jaspers, Karl, 5, 27, 43–44, 226n10
Jeweiligkeit, 126, 134, 179. *See also* particularity
Jonas, Hans, 23
joy, 236n10
judgment, 16–17, 109, 150–151, 152, 159, 203, 242n7

καιρός (*kairos*), 84, 96, 98, 164, 176, 179, 254n16; Dasein, 183–184; defined, 264; mean, 183–184
Kampf (struggle), 243n1, 245n1
Kant, Immanuel, 28, 67, 230n9
Karl Jaspers's Psychology of Worldviews (Heidegger), 5, 27
κατάφασις (*kataphasis*), defined, 264
κατηγορεῖν (*kategorein*), 117; defined, 264
καθ' αὐτο (*kath auto*), 165, 189; defined, 264
Kemman, Ansgar, *Heidegger and Rhetoric*, 245n1

Kenntnisnahme (taking notice), 14, 33, 37–38, 227n17
Kierkegaard, Søren, 232n1
κινεῖν (*kinein*), 249n6; defined, 264
κίνησις (*kinēsis*), 174, 190, 195–196, 228n1; defined, 264
κίνησις κατὰ τόπον (*kinēsis kata topon*), 155–156, defined, 265
Kisiel, Theodore, 259n21; on ambiguity, 213; on Being, 3; *Genesis of Heidegger's "Being and Time,"* 225n2, 234n4; "Situating Rhetorical Politics in Heidegger's Protopractical Ontology, 1923–1925: The French Occupy the Ruhr," 245n1
know-how, 180
knowledge: absolute, 67, 70, 128, 146; Christian, 51, 52, 53, 56; vs. conviction, 37–38; fixed, 148–149; human, 191; objective, 127–129, 130–132, 134, 135; practical, 180; self, 198; vs. understanding, 124
κοινωνία (*koinōnia*), 202, 206; defined, 265
κοινωνία τῶν γενῶν (*koinōnia tōn genōn*), 196; defined, 265
Kovacs, George, on *The Idea of Philosophy* course, 229n3, 229n4
κρίνειν (*krinein*), 154, 155–156, 171–172, 194, 249n6; defined, 265
Krug, W. T., *Allgemeines Handwörterbuch der philosophischen Wissenschaften*, 5

lack, 78, 146
Landgrebe, Ludwig, 230n9
language, actual state of affairs, 239n10; authentic meaning of, 247n3; Being, 143, 257n19; Being-in-the-world, 165; becoming, 143; disclosive power, 137; encounters, 146; everydayness, 166–167, 245n1; factical speaking, 16, 156–158, 188, 193; grammar, 14, 73, 75, 143, 146–147, 204; Greeks and, 8–9, 142–145, 146–147; objects, 144–145; perception 154; philosophy of, 202; reality and, 203; speaking

λόγος δέ ἐστι φωνὴ σημαντική (*logos de esti phōnē sēmantikē*), 147; defined, 265
λόγος οὐσίας (*logos ousias*), 165–167; defined, 265
λόγος ψευδής (*logos pseudēs*), 157, 187, 195–196, 203; defined, 265
λόγον θεοῦ, 52
λόγος τί (*logos ti*), defined, 265
λόγος τινός (*logos tinos*), 202, 203; defined, 265
Löwith, Karl, letters to, 58–59, 211
λύπη (*lupē*), 171, 174–175, defined, 265
λυπηρόν (*lupēron*), 169, defined, 265
Luther, Martin, 15, 232n1, 257n8; dislike of Aristotle, 56, 59; influence on Heidegger, 214

Maggini, Golfo, 228n1
making things easy (*das Leichte*), 89–90, 114, 116
Makkreel, Rudolph, 231n10
manifestation, layers of (*Bekundungsschichten*), 41, 232n15
"Martin Heidegger, Martin Luther" (van Buren), 232n1
Martin Heidegger's Path of Thinking (Pöggeler), 232n1
masks, xvi, 32, 80–81, 89, 93, 98, 127, 130, 187
material success, 88
mathematics: exactitude lacking, 44, 50; phenomenology, 122; rules, 35
"Matter of the Heart" (Hyde), 252n12
McGrath, S. J., *A Companion to Heidegger's Phenomenology of Religious Life,* 232n1
McNeill, William, 259n21
meaning, fixed, 143
meaningfulness, 18–19, 25, 37–38, 44; and *Bekümmerung,* 239n12; care, 57, 78–79; distance, 87–88; encountering others, 135; experience of self, 41; factical experience, 134; grounded in movement, 76, 79; preoccupation, 133; self-world, 85–86; world, 78–79
μὴ ὄν (*mē on*), 187, 195, 201; defined, 265

methodology: critical-teleological method, 26, 28; determined by content, 229n3; *Introduction to the Phenomenology of Religion,* 49; *Phenomenology of Religious Life,* 233n3; suiting to topic, 226n10, 227n11
Michalski, Mark, "Hermeneutic Phenomenology as Philology," 246n2
militaristic thinking, 243n1
Misch, Georg, letter to, 99
models, 112–113; mathematics, 122; problem-awakening model, 105–106
molestia (hardship), 47, 57
moment of vision, 235n9
morality, systems of, 252n12
Moran, Dermot, 235n9
"More of observing," 108
μόριον ἐνυπάρχον (*morion enuparchon*), 249n6; defined, 265
motility, 228n1
motivations, 247n4; for speaking, 252n11
movement, 170–171, 228n1, 231n14, 242n4; Aristotle, 190; caring movement, 105–107; Dasein, 171; facticity, 91; from self, 114; ontology, 195–196; Plato on, 190, 251n8; presence, 167–168; temporality of life, 93; world-relatedness, 76, 79

National Socialism (Nazism), 236n13, 243n1, 245n1, 259n21
Natorp, Paul, 35, 40, 226n6
nature, 121–122
Nazism (National Socialism), 236n13, 243n1, 245n1, 259n21
negation, 116–117
Neigung (inclination), 87, 91–92
neo-Kantianism, 5, 35, 230n9; experience, 43; shadow of, 38–39
Neoplatonism, 15
New Testament, ethics of mercy, 243n1
das Nichts (nothingness), 9
Nicomachean Ethics (Aristotle), 89–90, 177–178, 195, 215–216, 254n15, 257n14
Nietzsche, Friedrich, 226n6, 230n9
nihilation, 237n1

πάθη (*pathē*): 171, 173, 175; defined, 265; experiences of, 252n10; fear and anxiety, 252n10

πάθος (*pathos*), 171; defined, 265; and fear, 252n10

Paul, experience of early Christian religiosity, 24; factical-historical situation, 136–137; influence on Luther, 15; letters of, 14, 52–54, 233n1; meaning of damnation, 54–55; non-systematic approach, 50; religious meaning, 236n12; self-world, 50

peace and security, 54

Pensées (Pascal), 79

πέρας (*peras*), 179–180; defined, 266

perception, 35, 154, 155

personality, 126–127

Phaedrus (Plato), 197–199, 205

φαίνεται (*phainetai*), defined, 266

φαίνω (*phainō*), 145, defined, 266

φαινόμενον (*phainomenon*), 141, 145, 160, defined, 266

phenomenological destruction, 111–112, 213–214, 257n7

Phenomenological Interpretations of Aristotle: Initiation into Phenomenological Research (lecture), 9, 14, 29, 231n13, 237n1; complacency, 42; counter-ruinance, 143–144; deception, 215; grammar, 147; retrieval in, 240n2; rigor, 247n4; ruinance, 217

"Phenomenological Interpretations with Respect to Aristotle: Indication of the Hermeneutical Situation," 15

phenomenology: analysis as science, 25, 34, 44; clarification of, 141–161; concretization of life, 40; defining, 148, 239n8; Husserlian, 122, 234n6; mathematical exactitude, 122; necessary, 231n11; objects, 122; origin, 35–36

Phenomenology of Intuition and Expression (lecture course), 24, 213–214

Phenomenology of Religious Life (lecture course), 14, 24, 143; methodological considerations, 233n3

phenomenon of life, 23–24, 26

philology, 162, 246n2

Philosophical Foundations of Medieval Mysticism (lecture course), 233n2

philosophical research, object of, 106–107

"Philosophie als Vollzug und als Begriff: Heideggers Identitäts-philosophie in der Vorlesung vom Wintersemester 1921/22 und ihr Verhältnis zu Sein und Zeit" (Gethmann), 240n3

philosophy of life, xxiii, 64, 221, 228n19

philosophy: bankruptcy of, 66; human activity, 255n1; λέγειν, 196; of language, 202; origin of, 187; as primordial science, 25, 26, 27–28; separation from worldview, 27, 229n4; as strict science, 231n14; and struggle, 243n1; way to live life, 63

φόβος (*phobos*), 172, 174; defined, 266

φωνή (*phōnē*), 147, 169–170, 251n7; defined, 266

φρόνησις (*phronēsis*), 11, 13, 109, 216, 236n13, 242n6; ἀλήθεια, 109; authentic conscience, 259n21; defined, 266; Plato, 190; rhetoric, 253n13; vs. σοφία, 104, 255n1, 259n21; τέχνη, 259n21; truthing, 195

φυγή (*phugē*), 171, defined, 266

placement, 145–146, 161

Plato, absence, 174; approach to history, 47; *Gorgias,* 197–198; interpretation of, 8, 18, 253n13; λόγος, 207; on movement, 251n8; *Phaedrus,* 197–199, 205; philosophy and human activity, 255n1; *Sophist,* 186–210; theory, 259n21

Platonic dialectic, inadequacy of, 190

Plato's Sophist (lecture course), 137, 186–210

pleasant, 169, 251n7

pleasure, 171–172, 174–175, 251n7

Pöggeler, Otto, 232n1

ποίησις (*poiēsis*), 259n21; defined, 266

πόλις (*polis*), 163, 164, 178, 185; defined, 266

politics, 178, 180–181, 243n1, 245n1, 254n14, 259n21

possibility, 146, 163, 170, hearing, 178; τέλος, 183; they, 179

σοφία (*sophia*), ambiguous treatment of, 242n6; deconstruction of, 107–111; defined, 266; metaphysical, 253n13; vs. φρόνησις, 104, 255n1, 259n21; pure beholding, 107–108; truthing, 195
Sophist (Plato), 18, 186–210
sophistry, 17, 163, 186–210
Sorge (care), 96–97, 106, 134–135, 241n6
soul, 196, 197, 199, 249n6
sound, 251n7; as presence, 256n3
συζῆν (*souzēn*), 175, defined, 266
speaking, 8–9, 16, 226n8; authentic, 163, 169–177; Being of, 141; Being-with-others, 177–179, 222; beings, 201–202; deception, 16–17, 154–156, 160–161; everyday modes, 245n1; facticity, 156–158; grammar, 14, 73, 75, 143, 146–147, 204; hearing, 177–178; idle talk, 133, 163, 166, 193, 198–199, 214, 217, 222–223, 253n13; life, 192; λόγος, 4–5, 16, 144; judgment, 152; movement, 195–196; νοεῖν, 194; not authentic meaning of language, 247n3; origin of, 164; on origins, 164–165; ontological source, 252n11; otherness, 196, 201; passion, 17–18; Platonic dialectic, 188, 201, 255n1; relationships, 136; retrieval, 141–142, 144, 162–163; revelation of world, 17; structures of, 203–205; unsaid, 117; with others, 198. *See also* λέγειν (*legein*)
Spengler, Oswald, 47, 128, 231n14
springing-to, 71, 72, 77
standpoints, 129, 132
στάσις (*stasis*), 197; defined, 266
στέρησις (*sterēsis*), 9–10, 145, 174–176; defined, 266
Stimmung (attunement), 249n5
Streuver, Nancy S., 254n14, 254n17
structuring process (prestructuring), 90–94
struggle (*Kampf*), 243n1, 245n1
subject (of sentence), 204. *See also* grammar
subjectivism vs. retrieval, 7
συμφέρον (*sumpheron*), 254n16; defined, 266

συναγωγη (*sunagōgē*), 200–201, defined, 266
surrounding-world, 37, 40, 84–86, 93–94, 107
systemization, 240n3

τὰ καθ᾽ ἕκαστα (*ta kath hekasta*), 249n6; defined, 266
taking-care, 96–97, 106, 179–181, 241n6, 242n1, 242n3
taking-notice (*Kenntnisnahme*), 14, 33, 37–38, 227n17
Taminiaux, Jacques, 259n21
tapestry of life, 46
"The Tapestry of Life" (George), 37
ταραχή (*tarachē*), 171–172; defined, 266
Tatsache, 5
Tatsächlichkeit (factuality), 218–219
teaching-learning, 170–171
τέχνη (*technē*), 197–200, 259n21; defined, 266
τέλειον (*teleion*), 173, 181–183; defined, 266
τέλος (*telos*), 179–180, 182; defined, 266
τέλος δι᾽ αὑτο (*telos di auto*), 181; defined, 266
temporal-historical phenomena, 6, 14, 231n14; Christian facticity, 47, 234n5; covered over, 244n2; emergence from care, 97; retrieval, 240n2; structure of life, 45
temporality: acknowledgement of, 71; authenticity, 259n21; based on faith, 14; care-relations, 86, 143; and change, 259n21; curiosity, 129; of Dasein, 131; and eschatology, 235n8; factical life, 43, 49, 59; facticity, 126–127; fallenness, 113–114; fear, 172; How of having death, 115; human being, 72; life's haziness, 65–66; objective knowledge, 129; Paul, 51–52; ruinance, 94–99; στάσις, 197; three ecstases, 247n4; unification in, 240n3
"that-there" of being, 169, 249n6
theology, 58–59
theology of the cross, 232n1

θεωρεῖν (theōrein), 174, 178, 255n1; defined, 264; dialectic, 191–193; σοφία as, 107

theoretical I, 29

θεωρία (theōria), 255n1; defined, 264

theory, problematic, 231n11; ignoring practical, 259n21

there, 89, 120, 217, 249n6; Dasein, 123, 182; κίνησις, 174; limits, 179; meaningfulness, 135; οὐσία, 167; taking care, 181; world, 133, 169–170

Thessalonians, 52–53

they (das Man), 51, 217, 219–220, 253–254n13, 259n21; everydayness, 179; knowledge, 131–132; positivity, 120, 132–133

they-self, 114

thing itself (die Sache selbst), 2–3, 4, 39

thought, 257–258n19; mathematical laws of, 35

thrownness, 168, 218, 219–221, 241n5, 245n3, 249n5

time, destruction of, 97; Plato, 197

timeful vs. timeless, 254–255n17

Today, 120, 121, 126, 127; as object, 128

togetherness, 205, 251n7. See also Being-with-others, with-world

tools, words as, 143–144

torment (Bedrängnis), 53, 55, 97

τὸ τί ἦν εἶναι (to ti ēn einai), 249n6; defined, 266

Toward the Definition of Philosophy (lecture course), 44–45, 230n9

toward-which (Wozu), 170

Tractatus (Wittgenstein), 239n10

transcendental idealism, 230n9

transcendental self-interpretation, 240n3

translation, note on, 19–20

trivialities, 37, 38, 45

Troeltsch, Ernst, 231n14

true sentences, 203. See also grammar

truth, 20, 215, 216, 257n19; affirmation, 153–154; Aristotelian usage, 109, 110, 242n7; concealment, 109–110; and errancy, 223–224, 236n13; factical speaking, 193; lethic component, 236n13; λόγος, 208; λόγος

ἀποφαντικός, 149–150; rhetoric, 199. See also ἀλήθεια (alētheia)

Truth and Method (Gadamer), 247n4

truthful safe-keeping, 104, 105, 109, 110, 111, 115, 116. See also φρόνησις (phronēsis)

truthing, 109, 189, 195, 197

two-world theory, 243n8

unarticulated unitary being, 203–204

uncanniness (Unheimlichkeit), 159–160, 164, 172–173, 176, 245n3, 252n11

unchangeability, 133

unconcealment, 110, 216

uncoveredness, 169–170, 174–176

understanding (Einfühlung), 50, 124, 132, 155–156, 190

Unheimlichkeit (uncanniness), 159–160, 245n3, 252n11

unity: of Being, 207–208; of Dasein, 218; of λόγος (logos), 16–17, 151–156

universal (Allgemein), 48

Unruhe (disquiet), 171–172

unsaid, 117, 205–206

Untergang des Abendlandes (Spengler), 128

Unterwegs (on the way), 247n4

untruth, 10, 215, 223–224

urgency, 53, 55–56, 59, 168

Ur-Heidegger, 257n19

Urwirklichkeit (primal reality), 33

"Uses and Abuses of Aristotle's Rhetoric in Heidegger's Fundamental Ontology: The Lecture Course, Summer 1924" (Smith), 245n1

values, historically contingent, 47

value-taking, 28–29

van Buren, John, 259n21; on Being, 3; on destruction, 213; on deconstructionism, 256n4; on Heidegger and Luther, 232n1; The Young Heidegger: Rumor of the Hidden King, 225n2

verbs, 72–75, 146–147, 153, 154, 202, 206, 207. See also grammar

Veründigung (proclamation, word), 55

vice, Aristotle on, 6, 90, 257n14

Perspectives in Continental Philosophy
John D. Caputo, series editor

Karl Jaspers, *The Question of German Guilt*. Introduction by Joseph W. Koterski, S.J.

Jean-Luc Marion, *The Idol and Distance: Five Studies*. Translated with an introduction by Thomas A. Carlson.

Jeffrey Dudiak, *The Intrigue of Ethics: A Reading of the Idea of Discourse in the Thought of Emmanuel Levinas*.

Robyn Horner, *Rethinking God as Gift: Marion, Derrida, and the Limits of Phenomenology*.

Mark Dooley, *The Politics of Exodus: Søren Keirkegaard's Ethics of Responsibility*.

Merold Westphal, *Overcoming Onto-Theology: Toward a Postmodern Christian Faith*.

Edith Wyschogrod, Jean-Joseph Goux, and Eric Boynton, eds., *The Enigma of Gift and Sacrifice*.

Stanislas Breton, *The Word and the Cross*. Translated with an introduction by Jacquelyn Porter.

Jean-Luc Marion, *Prolegomena to Charity*. Translated by Stephen E. Lewis.

Peter H. Spader, *Scheler's Ethical Personalism: Its Logic, Development, and Promise*.

Jean-Louis Chrétien, *The Unforgettable and the Unhoped For*. Translated by Jeffrey Bloechl.

Don Cupitt, *Is Nothing Sacred? The Non-Realist Philosophy of Religion: Selected Essays*.

Jean-Luc Marion, *In Excess: Studies of Saturated Phenomena*. Translated by Robyn Horner and Vincent Berraud.

Phillip Goodchild, *Rethinking Philosophy of Religion: Approaches from Continental Philosophy*.

William J. Richardson, S.J., *Heidegger: Through Phenomenology to Thought*.

Jeffrey Andrew Barash, *Martin Heidegger and the Problem of Historical Meaning*.

Jean-Louis Chrétien, *Hand to Hand: Listening to the Work of Art*. Translated by Stephen E. Lewis.

Jean-Louis Chrétien, *The Call and the Response*. Translated with an introduction by Anne Davenport.

D. C. Schindler, *Han Urs von Balthasar and the Dramatic Structure of Truth: A Philosophical Investigation*.

Julian Wolfreys, ed., *Thinking Difference: Critics in Conversation*.

Allen Scult, *Being Jewish/Reading Heidegger: An Ontological Encounter*.

Richard Kearney, *Debates in Continental Philosophy: Conversations with Contemporary Thinkers*.

Jennifer Anna Gosetti-Ferencei, *Heidegger, Hölderlin, and the Subject of Poetic Language: Towards a New Poetics of Dasein*.

Jolita Pons, *Stealing a Gift: Kirkegaard's Pseudonyms and the Bible*.

Jean-Yves Lacoste, *Experience and the Absolute: Disputed Questions on the Humanity of Man*. Translated by Mark Raftery-Skehan.

Charles P. Bigger, *Between* Chora *and the Good: Metaphor's Metaphysical Neighborhood.*

Dominique Janicaud, *Phenomenology "Wide Open": After the French Debate.* Translated by Charles N. Cabral.

Ian Leask and Eoin Cassidy, eds., *Givenness and God: Questions of Jean-Luc Marion.*

Jacques Derrida, *Sovereignties in Question: The Poetics of Paul Celan.* Edited by Thomas Dutoit and Outi Pasanen.

William Desmond, *Is There a Sabbath for Thought? Between Religion and Philosophy.*

Bruce Ellis Benson and Norman Wirzba, eds., *The Phenomoenology of Prayer.*

S. Clark Buckner and Matthew Statler, eds., *Styles of Piety: Practicing Philosophy after the Death of God.*

Kevin Hart and Barbara Wall, eds., *The Experience of God: A Postmodern Response.*

John Panteleimon Manoussakis, *After God: Richard Kearney and the Religious Turn in Continental Philosophy.*

John Martis, *Philippe Lacoue-Labarthe: Representation and the Loss of the Subject.*

Jean-Luc Nancy, *The Ground of the Image.*

Edith Wyschogrod, *Crossover Queries: Dwelling with Negatives, Embodying Philosophy's Others.*

Gerald Bruns, *On the Anarchy of Poetry and Philosophy: A Guide for the Unruly.*

Brian Treanor, *Aspects of Alterity: Levinas, Marcel, and the Contemporary Debate.*

Simon Morgan Wortham, *Counter-Institutions: Jacques Derrida and the Question of the University.*

Leonard Lawlor, *The Implications of Immanence: Toward a New Concept of Life.*

Clayton Crockett, *Interstices of the Sublime: Theology and Psychoanalytic Theory.*

Bettina Bergo, Joseph Cohen, and Raphael Zagury-Orly, eds., *Judeities: Questions for Jacques Derrida.* Translated by Bettina Bergo and Michael B. Smith.

Jean-Luc Marion, *On the Ego and on God: Further Cartesian Questions.* Translated by Christina M. Gschwandtner.

Jean-Luc Nancy, *Philosophical Chronicles.* Translated by Franson Manjali.

Jean-Luc Nancy, *Dis-Enclosure: The Deconstruction of Christianity.* Translated by Bettina Bergo, Gabriel Malenfant, and Michael B. Smith.

Andrea Hurst, *Derrida Vis-à-vis Lacan: Interweaving Deconstruction and Psychoanalysis.*

Jean-Luc Nancy, *Noli me tangere: On the Raising of the Body.* Translated by Sarah Clift, Pascale-Anne Brault, and Michael Naas.

Jacques Derrida, *The Animal That Therefore I Am.* Edited by Marie-Louise Mallet, translated by David Wills.

Jean-Luc Marion, *The Visible and the Revealed.* Translated by Christina M. Gschwandtner and others.

Michel Henry, *Material Phenomenology.* Translated by Scott Davidson.

Jean-Luc Nancy, *Corpus.* Translated by Richard A. Rand.

Joshua Kates, *Fielding Derrida.*

Michael Naas, *Derrida From Now On.*

Shannon Sullivan and Dennis J. Schmidt, eds., *Difficulties of Ethical Life.*

Catherine Malabou, *What Should We Do with Our Brain?* Translated by Sebastian Rand, Introduction by Marc Jeannerod.

Claude Romano, *Event and World.* Translated by Shane Mackinlay.

Vanessa Lemm, *Nietzsche's Animal Philosophy: Culture, Politics, and the Animality of the Human Being.*

B. Keith Putt, ed., *Gazing Through a Prism Darkly: Reflections on Merold Westphal's Hermeneutical Epistemology.*

Eric Boynton and Martin Kavka, eds., *Saintly Influence: Edith Wyschogrod and the Possibilities of Philosophy of Religion.*

Shane Mackinlay, *Interpreting Excess: Jean-Luc Marion, Saturated Phenomena, and Hermeneutics.*

Kevin Hart and Michael A. Signer, eds., *The Exorbitant: Emmanuel Levinas Between Jews and Christians.*

Bruce Ellis Benson and Norman Wirzba, eds., *Words of Life: New Theological Turns in French Phenomenology.*

William Robert, *Trials: Of Antigone and Jesus.*

Brian Treanor and Henry Isaac Venema, eds., *A Passion for the Possible: Thinking with Paul Ricoeur.*

Kas Saghafi, *Apparitions—Of Derrida's Other.*

Nick Mansfield, *The God Who Deconstructs Himself: Sovereignty and Subjectivity Between Freud, Bataille, and Derrida.*

Don Ihde, *Heidegger's Technologies: Postphenomenological Perspectives.*

Françoise Dastur, *Questioning Phenomenology.* Translated by Robert Vallier.

Suzi Adams, *Castoriadis's Ontology: Being and Creation.*

Richard Kearney and Kascha Semonovitch, eds., *Phenomenologies of the Stranger: Between Hostility and Hospitality.*

Michael Naas, *Miracle and Machine: Jacques Derrida and the Two Sources of Religion, Science, and the Media.*

Alena Alexandrova, Ignaas Devisch, Laurens ten Kate, and Aukje van Rooden, *Re-treating Religion: Deconstructing Christianity with Jean-Luc Nancy.* Preamble by Jean-Luc Nancy.

Emmanuel Falque, *The Metamorphosis of Finitude: An Essay on Birth and Resurrection.* Translated by George Hughes.

Scott M. Campbell, *The Early Heidegger's Philosophy of Life: Facticity, Being, and Language.*

Françoise Dastur, *How Are We to Confront Death? An Introduction to Philosophy.*

Christina M. Gschwandtner, *Postmodern Apologetics? Arguments for God in Contemporary Philosophy.*

Ben Morgan, *On Becoming God: Late Medieval Mysticism and the Modern Western Self.*